Gender Equality and Diversity in Indonesia

The **Australian National University (ANU) Indonesia Project** is a leading international centre of research and graduate training on the economy and society of Indonesia. Since its inception in 1965 by Professor H.W. Arndt, the Project has been at the forefront of Indonesian studies in Australia and internationally. The ANU Indonesia Project is part of the Arndt-Corden Department of Economics in the Crawford School of Public Policy, College of Asia and the Pacific, ANU.

Through producing and disseminating high-quality research, including publishing the respected *Bulletin of Indonesian Economic Studies*, and hosting public dialogues, institutional capacity building and institutional networking, the ANU Indonesia Project aims to support the establishment of critical research-based public policies in Indonesia, particularly in the areas of (i) trade and development; (ii) agriculture, resources and the environment; (iii) politics, media and governance and (iv) social policy, gender equality, social inclusion and human capital. Furthermore, our activities aim to ensure the next generation of Indonesian researchers are nurtured and fostered.

The Indonesia Update has been conducted annually since 1983. It is organised by the ANU Indonesia Project, and receives support from the Australian Government Department of Foreign Affairs and Trade, the ANU Department of Political and Social Change, and the ANU Indonesia Institute.

The **ISEAS – Yusof Ishak Institute** (formerly Institute of Southeast Asian Studies) is an autonomous organisation established in 1968. It is a regional centre dedicated to the study of sociopolitical, security, and economic trends and developments in Southeast Asia and its wider geostrategic and economic environment. The Institute's research programs are grouped under Regional Economic Studies (RES), Regional Strategic and Political Studies (RSPS), and Regional Social and Cultural Studies (RSCS). The Institute is also home to the ASEAN Studies Centre (ASC), the Singapore APEC Study Centre, and the Temasek History Research Centre (THRC).

ISEAS Publishing, an established academic press, has issued more than 2,000 books and journals. It is the largest scholarly publisher of research about Southeast Asia from within the region. ISEAS Publishing works with many other academic and trade publishers and distributors to disseminate important research and analyses from and about Southeast Asia to the rest of the world.

Indonesia Update Series

Gender Equality and Diversity in Indonesia

Identifying Progress and Challenges

EDITED BY

ANGIE BEXLEY · SARAH XUE DONG · DIAHHADI SETYONALURI

First published in Singapore in 2023 by
ISEAS Publishing
30 Heng Mui Keng Terrace
Singapore 119614

E-mail: publish@iseas.edu.sg
Website: http://bookshop.iseas.edu.sg

All rights reserved. No part of this publication may be reproduced, translated, stored in a retrieval system, or transmitted in any form or by any means, electronic, mechanical, photocopying, recording or otherwise, without the prior permission of the ISEAS – Yusof Ishak Institute.

© 2023 ISEAS – Yusof Ishak Institute, Singapore

The responsibility for facts and opinions in this publication rests exclusively with the authors and their interpretations do not necessarily reflect the views or the policy of the Institute or its supporters.

ISEAS Library Cataloguing-in-Publication Data

Names: Bexley, Angie, editor. | Dong, Sarah Xue, editor. | Setyonaluri, Diahhadi, editor.
Title: Gender equality and diversity in Indonesia : identifying progress and challenges / edited by Angie Bexley, Sarah Xue Dong and Diahhadi Setyonaluri.
Description: Singapore : ISEAS – Yusof Ishak Institute, 2023. | Series: Indonesia Update Series | Includes bibliographical references and index.
Identifiers: ISBN 9789815104547 (softcover) | ISBN 9789815104554 (hardcover) | ISBN 9789815104561 (ebook PDF) | ISBN 9789815104745 (epub)
Subjects: LCSH: Cultural pluralism—Indonesia. | Gender identity—Indonesia. | Indonesia—Social conditions.
Classification: DS644.4 I41 2022

Cover image: *Women's March* by Fitri DK. Woodcut print on paper 60 cm × 80 cm, 2018.

Edited, typeset and indexed by Tracy Harwood, Canberra
Printed in Singapore by Mainland Press Pte Ltd

Contents

Tables	vii
Figures	viii
Contributors	x
Acknowledgements	xii
Glossary	xiv

1 Introduction   1
   Angie Bexley, Sarah Xue Dong and Diahhadi Setyonaluri

PART 1 GENDER IDEOLOGIES: PUBLIC AND PRIVATE REALMS

2 Dismantling the old gender order: A work in progress   9
   Kathryn Robinson

3 Gendering Islamic and Islamist movements in contemporary
   Indonesia: KUPI gender-just *ulama* and *hijrah* movements   34
   Eva F. Nisa

4 Transgender citizenship and public gender in Indonesia   53
   Benjamin Hegarty

5 Gender diversity in parliament, cabinet and ambassadorial
   appointments: A work in progress?   70
   Ella S. Prihatini

PART 2 ECONOMIC EQUALITY: OPPORTUNITIES AND LIMITATIONS

6 Human capital development and gender equality in Indonesia   93
   Sri Mulyani Indrawati

vi *Gender Equality and Diversity in Indonesia*

7 New opportunities and old constraints: Gender equality in the post-Suharto era from an economic perspective 122
   Sarah Xue Dong and Nurina Merdikawati

8 Women and digitisation: Promises and challenges of internet use in the Indonesian labour market 145
   Niken Kusumawardhani

9 Deconstructing care work in Indonesia 169
   Atnike Nova Sigiro

PART 3 SOCIAL POLICY REFORMS AND AGENDAS: CHALLENGES TO POLICY IMPLEMENTATION

10 In anticipation of perennial contestation: Progress and challenges to national laws and by-laws concerning sexual violence and sexuality in the *reformasi* era 185
    Andy Yentriyani

11 Indonesia's social protection landscape: Women, exclusion and deservingness in social assistance 205
    Vania Budianto

12 Leaving no girls behind: Inclusive ways to address child marriage in Indonesia 222
    Santi Kusumaningrum, Ni Luh Putu Maitra Agastya and Andrea Andjaringtyas Adhi

PART 4 GENDER EXPRESSION, REPRESENTATION AND PRACTICE

13 *Perempuan mengkaji seni*: Gender, activism and Indonesian visual arts 245
    Wulan Dirgantoro

14 Feminist intervention in cultural activism 263
    Intan Paramaditha

15 Male caregiver protagonists on the silver screen: A middle-class biased shift of ideal masculinity 280
    Evi Eliyanah

Index 301

Tables

2.1	Women's representation in national parliament and quota legislation	13
5.1	Share of female ministers by president, 1998–2022	78
5.2	Distribution of female ministers by president, 1998–2022	79
5.3	Distribution of ambassadorial appointments by president, 1998–2022	81
6.1	Indonesia's policies in human capital since the 1960s	97
6.2	Average PISA scores for reading, maths and science, OECD and ASEAN countries, 2018	109
8.1	Profile of female gig workers, 2019 (%)	154
8.2	Distribution of female online merchants and female workers (%)	155
8.3	Reasons cited by women for not having a mobile phone (%)	160
8.4	Women's internet use by age and education (%)	161
8.5	Internet use at work among women workers, 2021 (%)	162
9.1	Women's income contribution in the family in Indonesia (%)	170
9.2	Population aged 15 years and over (male and female) by the type of main activity in urban and rural Indonesia	173
9.3	Female population aged 15 years and over by the type of main activity in urban and rural Indonesia	173
11.1	History of Indonesia's main social assistance programs	207
12.1	Child marriage prevalence in Indonesia, 2012–2021	224
12.2	Court decisions based on applicant characteristics and situations	226
12.3	Results of the total sample of court decisions	227
12.4	Age among applicants in child marriage cases, by sex	228
12.5	Education of applicants among child marriage cases, by sex	228
12.6	Applicants' employment status, by sex	229
12.7	Applicants' employment type among child marriage cases	229
12.8	Reasons for dispensation application among child marriage cases	232
12.9	Reasons for dispensation approval (by the judge) among child marriage cases	233
12.10	Court decisions among child marriages by pregnancy cases	235

Figures

5.1	Indonesia's position in the Global Gender Gap Index, 2022	71
5.2	Women's share in Asian parliaments, June 2021 (%)	76
5.3	Percentage of female ambassadors appointed by country, 1947–2022	82
6.1	Indonesia's growth trajectory towards 2045 (GDP per capita, US$)	94
6.2	Women's secondary school enrolment rate, 2010–2021 (%)	101
6.3	Gender Development Index and Gender Empowerment Measure	104
6.4	Indicators reflecting the improvement of human capital quality in Indonesia	105
6.5	Educational attainment: Gross and net enrolment rates (%)	106
6.6	Proportion of employment by gender and education 2022 (%)	106
6.7	Poverty rate and Gini ratio	107
6.8	Indonesia's PISA score, 2000–2018	109
6.9	Women's representation in parliament and the professional workforce (%)	112
6.10	Stunting prevalence, Indonesia and ASEAN countries (%)	113
6.11	Indonesia's GDP growth compared to other emerging markets, 2006–2022 (%)	115
6.12	Indonesia's inflation compared to other emerging markets, 2006–2022 (%)	116
6.13	Government debt, 2006–2022 (% of GDP)	118
6.14	Government fiscal deficit, 2006–2022 (% of GDP)	118
7.1	Women who have three children or more by age, cohort and education level (%)	128
7.2	Educational attainment in urban areas by year of birth (aged 25+), 1950–1995 (%)	129
7.3	Educational attainment in rural areas by year of birth (aged 25+), 1950–1995 (%)	130

7.4	Female labour force participation by age (aged 20–65) and cohort, urban and rural areas (%)	131
7.5	Female labour force participation in wage work and self-employed work by age (aged 20–65) and cohort, urban and rural areas (%)	132
7.6	Employment rate of working-age population (aged 15–65) by sector, 2000–2021 (%)	133
7.7	Log of average real wages by sector, 2000–2021	135
7.8	Gender wage ratio by sector, 2000–2021	135
7.9	Women married by age (aged 15–49) and cohort, urban and rural areas (%)	136
7.10	Women with at least 1 child by age (aged 15–49) and cohort, urban and rural areas (%)	137
8.1	Proportion of villages with BTS towers (%)	147
8.2	Deployment of BTS towers by Telkomsel (thousands)	148
8.3	Proportion of villages with access to the 4G network (%)	149
8.4	Internet access by decile of per capita consumption (%)	149
8.5	Indonesia's annual gross merchandise value (US$ billion)	150
8.6	Female labour force participation by age group, 2003–2021 (%)	152
8.7	Gender gap in internet access (%)	158
8.8	Women's access to the internet by age, education and area of residence (%)	159
8.9	Digital skills of the labour force	161
8.10	Proportion of men and women performing paid and domestic work, 2021 (%)	164
9.1	Comparison between minimum monthly wages and domestic workers' salaries in selected provinces, 2022 (rupiah)	177
10.1	Number of sexual violence cases reported to Komnas Perempuan and to community service organisation–based service providers, 2017–2021	187
11.1	Family Hope Program (PKH) coverage, 2007–2020	210

Contributors

Andrea Andjaringtyas Adhi, Lead for Social Inclusion and Protection, Center on Child Protection PUSKAPA Universitas Indonesia

Ni Luh Putu Maitra Agastya, Senior Researcher, Center on Child Protection PUSKAPA Universitas Indonesia; and Social Welfare Department, FISIP, Universitas Indonesia

Angie Bexley, Head of Technical and Partnerships, KONEKSI, Indonesia

Vania Budianto, PhD candidate, Crawford School of Public Policy, College of Asia and the Pacific, Australian National University, Canberra

Wulan Dirgantoro, Lecturer in Contemporary Art, School of Culture and Communication, Faculty of Arts, University of Melbourne

Sarah Xue Dong, Fellow, Crawford School of Public Policy, Australian National University, Canberra

Evi Eliyanah, Associate Professor in Gender Studies, Universitas Negeri Malang, Indonesia

Benjamin Hegarty, Senior Research Associate, Kirby Institute, UNSW Sydney; Honorary Fellow, Asia Institute, University of Melbourne

HE Sri Mulyani Indrawati, Minister of Finance of the Republic of Indonesia

Santi Kusumaningrum, Director, Center on Child Protection PUSKAPA Universitas Indonesia; and Criminology Department, FISIP, Universitas Indonesia

Niken Kusumawardhani, Senior Researcher, The SMERU Research Institute, Jakarta

Nurina Merdikawati, Postdoctoral Research Fellow, Abdul Latif Jameel Poverty Action Lab (J-PAL) Southeast Asia, Indonesia

Eva F. Nisa, ARC DECRA Fellow and Senior Lecturer of Anthropology, School of Culture, History and Language, College of Asia and the Pacific, Australian National University, Canberra

Intan Paramaditha, Senior Lecturer, Department of Media, Communications, Creative Arts, Languages and Literature, Macquarie University, Sydney

Ella S. Prihatini, Senior Lecturer, International Relations Department, President University, Indonesia

Kathryn Robinson, Professor Emerita in Anthropology, College of Asia and the Pacific, Australian National University, Canberra

Diahhadi Setyonaluri, Head of Gender in Economic and Social Inclusion Research Group, Institute for Economic and Social Research (LPEM), Faculty of Economics and Business, Universitas Indonesia

Atnike Nova Sigiro, Chairperson, National Human Rights Commission of the Republic of Indonesia (Komnas HAM); Senior Lecturer, Paramadina Graduate School, Universitas Paramadina, Indonesia

Andy Yentriyani, Chairperson, Indonesian National Commission on Violence against Women (Komisi Nasional anti Kekerasan terhadap Perempuan, Komnas Perempuan)

Acknowledgements

The chapters in this volume were produced from papers written by contributors to the 39th annual Indonesia Update conference held at the Australian National University (ANU), 16–17 September 2022. This was the first conference to focus specifically on gender in 20 years. Emerita Professor Kathryn Robinson was one of the two editors for the volume in 2002 and we were so pleased that we could mark this date and honour Professor Robinson's contributions to the field of gender studies in Indonesia by having Kathy as the keynote. We extend our deepest appreciation to the authors who have all developed the approaches and offered new frameworks and insights into gender over the past 20 years in Indonesia. We were delighted that Minister of Finance Sri Mulyani Indrawati gave the closing remarks.

The Indonesia Update is made possible due to the work of many women, and we pay our respects to each of them, in particular, the Indonesian Project's Kate McLinton, Lydia Napitupulu, Nesita Anggraini and Alex Gotts, who organised this conference seamlessly with the help of volunteers. Our culture night featured Yogyakarta-based artists Fitri DK and Bulan Fi Sabilliah and the Borobudur Dance Troupe led by Ifa Barry.

The Indonesia Update is jointly hosted by the ANU Indonesia Project and the Department of Political and Social Change (PSC) and we thank Head of the ANU Indonesia Project, Blane D. Lewis, and Head of PSC, Edward Aspinall. We would also like to express our deep gratitude to the ANU College of Asia and the Pacific and particularly our Dean, Helen Sullivan, for subsidising this year's conference and to her unwavering support for gender equality.

We acknowledge the support from the Australian Government Department of Foreign Affairs and Trade for this year's conference and continued support for the Indonesia Project. We extend our thanks to the Embassy of the Republic of Indonesia, and Ambassador HE Siswo Pramono for supporting the Balinese gamelan by Gede Eka Riadi.

Finally, we would like to express our gratitude to Tracy Harwood, who copyedited the volume, and the team at ISEAS for producing the Indonesia Update book.

This book is dedicated to the memory and work of Santi Kusumaningrum, who passed away as this book was being finalised. Santi's contribution to scholarship and praxis on issues of gender and young people will continue to positively impact Indonesia's public policy agenda.

Angie Bexley, Sarah Xue Dong and Diahhadi Setyonaluri
Canberra, September 2023

Glossary

adat	custom or tradition; customary law, traditional law
AILA	Aliansi Cinta Keluarga Indonesia (Family Love Alliance Indonesia)
Aliansi Laki-laki Baru	New Men's Alliance
ASEAN	Association of Southeast Asian Nations
ASEAN-5	Indonesia, Malaysia, the Philippines, Singapore and Thailand
banci	a term used widely to refer to gender and sexual nonconformity, and an offensive term of address for transgender women in particular
Bangga Kencana Program	Pembangunan Keluarga, Kependudukan dan Keluarga Berencana (Family Development, Citizenship and Family Planning)
banjar	'neighbourhood'; the lowest level of local government in Bali
Bantuan Produktif	Productive Assistance (for micro, small and medium enterprises)
bapakism	men's breadwinning, leadership in family and society, and heteronormativity as the official and dominant ideal of masculinity
Bappenas	Badan Perencanaan Pembangunan Nasional (National Development Planning Agency)
BidikMisi	Bantuan Biaya Pendidikan Bagi Mahasiswa Miskin Berprestasi (Education Cost Support for Poor and Excellent University Students)
BIMAS	Bimbingan Massal (former nationwide rice intensification program, including subsidised loans)
bissu	a spiritual practitioner or shaman
BKKBN	Badan Koordinasi Keluarga Berencana Nasional (National Family Planning Coordinating Board, up to 2009)

Glossary xv

BKKBN	Badan Kependudukan dan Keluarga Berencana Nasional (National Population and Family Planning Agency, from 2009)
BKN	Badan Kepegawaian Negara (National Civil Service Agency)
BKPM	Badan Koordinasi Penanaman Modal (Investment Coordinating Board)
BLT	Bantuan Langsung Tunai (direct cash assistance)
BLT Dana Desa	Bantuan Langsung Tunai Dana Desa (Village Funds Direct Cash Assistance; created for COVID-19 response)
BOS	Bantuan Operasional Sekolah (Schools Operational Assistance)
BPS	Badan Pusat Statistik (Statistics Indonesia), the central statistics agency
BTS	base transceiver station
cadar	face veil
CCT	conditional cash transfer
CGS	Center of Gender Studies
COVID-19	coronavirus disease (COVID-19), an infectious disease caused by the SARS-CoV-2 virus
Dana Desa	Village Funds
da'wa	proselytising
Dharma Wanita	an organisation for civil servants' wives
DPD	Dewan Perwakilan Daerah (Regional Representative Council)
DPR	Dewan Perwakilan Rakyat (People's Representative Council), also known as the House of Representatives or parliament
Fahmina	non-government organisation founded in 1999 focusing on the study of the contextualisation of Islamic classical texts and gender
fakir miskin	the destitute, or poorest of the poor
familism	an ideology that prioritises family
fatwa	religious ruling; pronouncement by a recognised Islamic religious authority
FDS	family development session
FLFP	female labour force participation
GDP	gross domestic product
Gerwani	Gerakan Wanita Indonesia (Indonesian Women's Movement); a large organised political women's movement, 1963–1967

xvi *Gender Equality and Diversity in Indonesia*

GMV	gross merchandise value
Gus Dur	born Abdurrahman Wahid Dur; a Muslim intellectual, religious leader and politician; fourth president of Indonesia (1999–2001)
hadith	the narration of the words, deeds or approvals of the Prophet Muhammad
haji	pilgrim
haram	forbidden, unclean (to Muslims)
hijrah	literally 'emigration'; refers to the religious transformation to be a better Muslim
hikmah	lessons
HTI	Hizbut Tahrir Indonesia (Indonesian Liberation Party)
ibu	mother
ibu rumah tangga	housewife
ICT	information and communication technology
IFC	International Finance Corporation
INMAS	Intensifikasi Massal (former 'Mass Intensification' agricultural program)
Inpres	Presidential Instruction, a program of special grants from the central government
INSISTS	Institute for the Study of Islamic Thought and Civilization
Jokowi	(President) Joko Widodo (2014–present)
Kalyanamitra	feminist non-government organisation
Kartu Keluarga	Family Card
Kartu Prakerja	Pre-employment Card
Kartu Sembako	Staple Food Card (from *sembilan bahan pokok*, nine basic commodities, originally rice, sugar, cooking oil, meat, eggs, milk, corn, kerosene and salt); fomerly known as BPNT
kawin tangkap	the kidnapping of women for marriage
kebaya	Javanese blouse
Keluarga Berencana	Family Planning program
kerja	work
kesusilaan umum	public morality
ketertiban umum	public order
kiai	religious scholar
Koalisi Seni	Arts Coalition

Glossary xvii

Komnas Perempuan	Komisi Nasional anti Kekerasan Terhadap Perempuan (National Commission on Violence against Women)
KPU	Komisi Pemilihan Umum (General Elections Commission)
KTP	Kartu Tanda Penduduk (national identity card)
KUPI	Kongres Ulama Perempuan Indonesia (Indonesian Congress of Women Religious Scholars)
LGBTQI	lesbian, gay, bisexual, transgender, queer and intersex
LPDP	Lembaga Pengelola Dana Pendidikan (Educational Fund Management Institution)
Mahkamah Konstitusi	Constitutional Court, established in 2001
masyarakat umum	the general public
Mekaar	Membina Ekonomi Keluarga Sejahtera (Empowering Household Economy)
merariq	abduction of girls for arranged marriage
Merdeka Belajar Program	'Free Learning' Program
MP	member of parliament
MPR	Majelis Permusyawaratan Rakyat (upper house of parliament)
MSME	micro, small and medium enterprise
mubalig	preacher
Muhammadiyah	modernist Islamic organisation founded in 1912
MUI	Majelis Ulama Indonesia (Indonesian Council of Islamic Scholars)
Nahdlatul Ulama	traditionalist Islamic organisation founded in 1926
NasDem	Partai Nasional Demokrat (National Democratic Party)
New Order	political regime under President Suharto, 1966–1998
NGO	non-government organisation
nikah	marriage contract
nusantara	archipelago
nyai	female leader of a *pesantren*
OECD	Organisation for Economic Co-operation and Development
PDI-P	Partai Demokrasi Indonesia-Perjuangan (Indonesian Democratic Party of Struggle)
peci	cap (head covering)
pembangunan	development

xviii *Gender Equality and Diversity in Indonesia*

PEN	Program Pemulihan Ekonomi Nasional (National Economic Recovery Program)
Penerima Bantuan Iuran	government national health insurance subsidy program for the poor and vulnerable
Perempuan Pengkaji Seni	'women who study art'
Peretas	Perempuan Lintas Batas (Women across Borders)
Perkawanan Perempuan Menulis	Women Writers Collective
perkumpulan	group or association
pesantren	Islamic boarding school
PIP	Program Indonesia Pintar (Smart Indonesia Program)
PISA	Programme for International Student Assessment
PKB	Partai Kebangkitan Bangsa (National Awakening Party)
PKH	Program Keluarga Harapan (Family Hope Program)
PKK	Pembinaan Kesejahteraan Keluarga (Family Welfare Association, an organisation to increase women's domestic skills)
PKS	Partai Keadilan Sejahtera (Prosperous Justice Party)
Podes	Survei Potensi Desa (Village Potential Survey; a village census conducted three times every decade, covering more than 70,000 villages in Indonesia. It collects detailed information on village-level characteristics such as size, infrastructure, geographic location and crime statistics.)
posyandu	*pos pelayanan terpadu* (community-based integrated health care post)
PPP	Partai Persatuan Pembangunan (United Development Party)
Program Keluarga Berencana	Family Planning Program
Puan Seni	Association of Women Art Workers
puskesmas	*pusat kesehatan masyarakat* (community health centre)
Qur'an	sacred scripture of Islam
Rahima	non-government organisation founded in 2000 focusing on Islam, gender and women's rights
Ramadan	ninth month of the Islamic calendar during which fasting is required
Raskin	Beras untuk Keluarga Miskin (Rice for the Poor)
reformasi	'reform'; name for the post-Suharto period (since 1998)

Repnas	Relawan Pengusaha Muda Nasional (Volunteer National Young Entrepreneurs)
Rifka Annisa	feminist non-government organisation
Rp	rupiah
RPJMN	Rencana Pembangunan Jangka Menengah Nasional (National Medium Term Development Plan)
RUU	*rancangan undang-undang* (draft law, bill)
Sakernas	Survei Angkatan Kerja Nasional (National Labour Force Survey)
sastrawangi	'fragrant literature'
Satpol PP	Satuan Polisi Pamong Praja (civil service police unit)
sekolah	school
Sekolah Pemikiran Perempuan	School of Women's Thought
Sekolah Penggerak	School Mover Program
Survei Industri	annual census of large and medium manufacturing plants in Indonesia
Suara Ibu Peduli	The Voice of Concerned Mothers
Suharto	former president (1968–1998)
suku	ethnic group
Susenas	Survei Sosio-Ekonomi Nasional (National Socioeconomic Survey)
tawhīd	the Oneness of God
TFR	total fertility rate
TNP2K	Tim Nasional Percepatan Penanggulangan Kemiskinan (National Team for the Acceleration of Poverty Reduction)
transpuan	a transgender woman
ulama	Muslim scholar
Umi	Ultra Micro Credit program
Unified Database	Basis Data Terpadu; now DTKS (Data Terpadu Kesejahteraan Sosial, Integrated Database for Social Welfare)
wadam	a transfeminine person
wali	guardian
waria	a transfeminine person
wasatiyya	middle-path or centrist Islam that espouses and advocates tolerance and humanitarian perspectives
Yayasan Jurnal Perempuan	Women's Journal
zakat	a Muslim tax for charity
zina	premarital sex

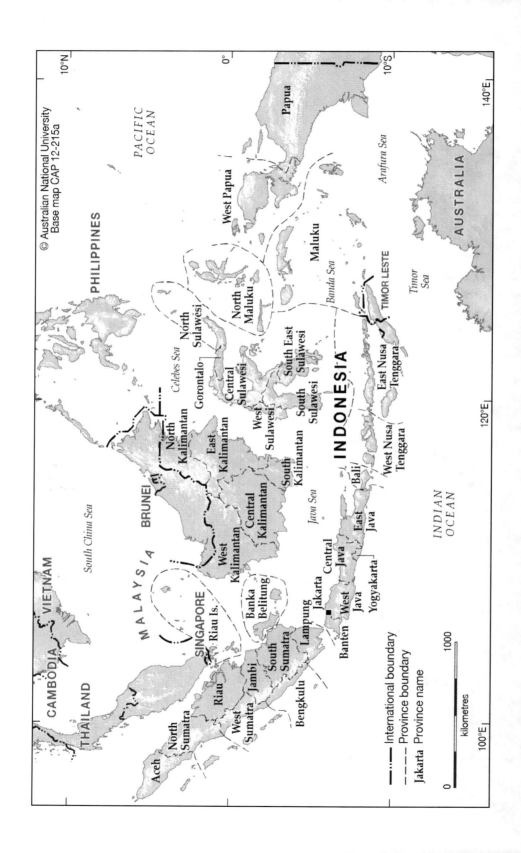

1   Introduction

Angie Bexley, Sarah Xue Dong and
Diahhadi Setyonaluri

Gender ideologies, representation and contestation

The *reformasi* era of the past twenty years has ushered in many changes that have simultaneously progressed and challenged gender equality. At the end of the Suharto era, gender equality was a major political demand that underpinned democratic reform. Many legislative changes were made, and with these changes the dismantling of the 'gender order' that the New Order established began to be disrupted. However, with every legislative change came also contrary moves that sought to challenge progress towards gender equality. The political ideology of the New Order seems difficult to dismantle completely and has found new expressions and contestations.

The 'gender order' that underpinned the political ideology of Suharto's New Order had heteronormative, binary and static understandings at its core. This period saw 'male' and 'female' defined more clearly according to a specific set of appearances, social roles and spatial distinctions that privileged the family or *kekeluargaan* as the foundation on which development—*pembangunan*—took place. Motherhood for example, was the basis of citizenship for women and assumed subordinate to men in what Julia Suryakusuma (2011) termed 'state ibuism'. Repressive and restrictive representations of women and circumscribed female roles in public life underpinned the political system. Its binary counterpart, *bapakism*, heralded the construction of fathers of the nation, as well as the household. These binary constructs were underpinned by *kodrat* (biologically specific nature), assumed to be God-given and sanctioned by Islam.

Kathryn Robinson (2008, and this volume) developed an approach that identified ways in which this gender order mapped on to specific areas of power during the New Order. Drawing on social theory of gender from R.W. Connell, Robinson's analysis reflected that 'gender relations are present in all types of institutions. They may not be the most important structure in a particular case, but they are certainly a major structure of most' (Connell 1987: 120). Gender relations can be understood as foci for the exercise of social, political and economic power in society; as a multidimensional structure operating in a complex network of institutions. As Kathy Robinson updates in her contribution to this volume, these institutions include, for example, marriage, political representation, laws on domestic violence and sexual violence, and employment settings. Changes to these institutions and processes over the past twenty years have provided room for gender equality gains to be made.

The gender order and norms in the public and domestic sphere also continue to be shaped by the currents of Islam. Eva Nisa illustrates two competing articulations of gender by the online engagement of the gender-just network initiated by gender-just *ulama* of the 2017 Indonesian Congress of Women Religious Scholars (Kongres Ulama Perempuan Indonesia, KUPI) as a response to the resurgence of piety in contemporary Indonesia, referred to as *hijrah* (religious renewal) activity among young Muslims within various Islamic movements, including Islamist groups who articulate gender orders in everyday activism. While they are active in the media landscape, the loudest voices in the field belong to conservative voices. Nisa concludes that despite an increasing online presence of gender-just *ulama* and their opponents, digital activism remains gendered and does not weaken the influence of patriarchal norms.

The work of the New Order's gender order in prescribing was never complete or whole. As Benjamin Hegarty notes in his contribution on public gender, the ways that masculinity and femininity have been regulated is both a matter of public concern as well as a way to define the boundaries of full belonging to the nation. Public gender has also been a way to contest these boundaries. The spaces that Indonesia's transgender population have occupied and claimed are symbolic of the ways in which they were able to contest the limits of belonging; however, these claims were always contingent. The ways in which LGBTQI communities in Indonesia continue to be marginalised and used as scapegoats to progressive legislative changes, for example, are clear ways in which public gender continues to inform boundaries of national belonging.

Legislative changes have allowed women into parliament. As Ella Prihatini charts, the number of Indonesian women legislators is higher than the average for Asia. However, foreign ministry and ambassadorial

Chapter 1 *Introduction* 3

positions lag behind. The gendered patterns of ministerial constitutions apply to Indonesia, as elsewhere, with more women holding 'feminised' portfolios such as health and education.

Economic aspects of gender equality

The changing economic conditions of Indonesia in the past two decades have significantly affected economic aspects of gender equality, while traditional gender ideologies and norms still play an important role in shaping economic outcomes for men and women.

In her chapter, Sri Mulyani Indrawati points out the important connection between human capital development and gender equality in Indonesia. Improving human capital is one of the highest priorities of the current Indonesian government, and Sri Mulyani argues that improving gender equality and utilising women's talents are crucial in achieving overall improvement and use of human capital in Indonesia. She also analyses how policy endeavours in the past twenty years that were designed to improve human capital, in the areas of education, health and social protection, are connected to gender equality advancement in Indonesia.

Sarah Dong and Nurina Merdikawati map the changing trajectory of various economic indicators of gender equality in Indonesia in the past twenty years. They show that increases in education level and decreases in the number of children, coupled with an increase in labour market opportunities for women driven by an increasing middle-class and changing consumptions patterns, have resulted in more women working in the formal sector and in highly paid professional jobs. Nevertheless, there are still signs that traditional gender norms limit women's ability to take advantage of these new labour market opportunities, especially after they marry and have children. The authors also find that the youngest cohort of women in Indonesia are getting married and having children earlier than their immediate previous cohorts, most likely driven by recent more conservative attitudes towards dating and marriage.

Looking at more specific aspects of economic gender equality, Niken Kusumawardhani uses novel data and evidence to analyse the opportunities and challenges digitisation brings to the advancement of gender equality. She argues that while digitisation has the potential to bring more economic opportunities to women, both in terms of the number of jobs and the flexibility of jobs, there is still a large gender gap in access to the internet and in digital skills. Furthermore, the flexibility of working arrangements brought by internet use could add to women's burden, as they are expected to do housework while working.

Atnike Sigiro looks at an important but poorly understood aspect of economic gender equality: care work. Without systematic data collection on care work in Indonesia, she uses various data sources to trace evidence on how much care work Indonesian women carry out and how they are rewarded. She estimates that 41 million individuals in Indonesia do unpaid care work as their main activity, and 97 per cent of them are women. The scale and intensity of unpaid care work done by women in Indonesia is tremendous and the gender inequality in this realm is also huge. Atnike also looks at the remuneration of paid care work, mainly in the form of domestic workers, who are mostly women, and finds that most of these workers earn below the minimum wage and have no formal labour protection. All this evidence suggests a dramatic change of the treatment of care work both in terms of policy framework, and research and data collection, is needed.

Social policy reforms and agendas

The changing political landscape and democratisation process that began in 1999 gave rise to new opportunities to promote women's rights. The government responded to calls from the women's movement and established the National Commission on Violence against Women (Komnas Perempuan) to address gender-based violence. In 2004, the government passed the Law on the Elimination of Domestic Violence, which criminalised domestic violence, and in 2007 gender mainstreaming was strongly stated as an agenda item in long-term development planning, which was aimed at promoting gender equality in all aspects of development. Despite the formulation of these policies, challenges to their implementation still exist. One of the most significant challenges is that persistent stereotypes and norms continue to perpetuate, and have been rearticulated in parallel with repressive customs and religious laws such as the infamous Pornography Law, issued in 2008. Andy Yentriyani in her chapter takes us through the long power struggle in the trajectory of policies and by-laws regulating sexual violence and sexuality in Indonesia. She argues that *reformasi* creates 'deficits' as indicated in contradictions and setbacks in the agenda of better fulfilment of women's rights.

While the political agenda seemed preoccupied with trying to regulate women's bodies/privacy, lawmakers have made efforts to bring gender equality into broader social policies that affect women's welfare. Social protection systems have slowly improved post–New Order. Programs have been created that specifically target women as beneficiaries. However, as Vania Budianto highlights, most social assistance programs have positioned women as an instrument in achieving social development

Chapter 1 Introduction 5

objectives, and are less concerned with achieving gender equality goals. Such targeting perpetuates conservative socially acceptable gender roles. The prioritising of social assistance programs for those considered 'deserving' meant that only mothers were constructed as targets. This approach means that women's vulnerability over her life cycle is often overlooked, and also leads to insufficient recognition of female heads of households and elderly women.

Some progress has been made in improving the welfare of women and girls. The amendment of Law 1/1974 on Marriage was the hallmark achievement of the women's movement in combating child marriage. The new law increases the minimum age of marriage from 16 to 19 years old for all women and men. However, the pathways in reducing child marriage face challenges from gender norms and socioeconomic disadvantage. Santi Kusumaningrum, Ni Luh Putu Agastya and Andrea Adhi describe court decisions about marriage dispensation as a way the state actually facilitates child marriages, often exercised under the thin veil of children's agency. The chapter also invites deeper thinking in mitigating child marriage and its consequences, by investing in prevention of child marriages performed secretly and using marriage formal registration as a way to protect children from the risk of child marriage.

New feminist movements

Women in the arts have challenged traditional gender roles prescribed by the New Order regime by reclaiming their agency as creators and decision-makers in literary, music, film, performance and visual art scenes. Wulan Dirgantoro discusses how creative practices by individual artists and art collectives, by women and non-binary artists, have demonstrated innovation, resilience and hope in the face of democratic decline in Indonesia. Intan Paramaditha in her contribution traces the currents of two prominent trajectories of feminist thought, liberal feminism and Islamic feminism, which have shaped the discussions around women, gender and feminism, and these influences have continued to thrive in the subsequent decades. In more recent times, new articulations of feminism are also being drawn. In response to the free market focus on *kerja* (work), the Jokowi administration focuses on women leaders in digital economy and creative entrepreneurship. In response to this focus on the individual breaking the glass ceiling, a promising new movement is forging connections with collectives across the *nusantara* (archipelago) to reshape the value of artistic endeavour towards Java-centric decoloniality. A critical part of this decoloniality work has been

6   *Angie Bexley, Sarah Xue Dong and Diahhadi Setyonaluri*

not only in the production of visual arts but also in its reception, which has often been framed through the lens of gender politics.

Indonesian gender politics after the onset of *reformasi* is also seen on the 'silver screen'. In her chapter, Evi Eliyanah describes filmmakers' efforts to challenge the hegemony of *bapakism* by presenting a 'new man' masculinity that displays a compromise between the male-breadwinning role and sharing care and domestic work. Despite its bias towards middle-class men, the silver screen in Indonesia has attempted to critique the hegemonic ideal and promote an alternative ideal masculinity.

The 2002 gender-focused Indonesia Update edited volume brought together a group of women leading the forefront of struggles at the time of the democratic transition. They pushed issues of gender and politics to the forefront of the public agenda, and there have been many changes to representation, policy and debates since. Still, gender ideologies of the past are being revamped and finding new articulations. Twenty years later, in 2022, a younger generation with renewed energy and focused attention are driving change towards equality and gender diversity.

References

Connell, R.W. 1987. *Gender and Power.* Cambridge: Polity Press.

Robinson, Kathryn. 2008. *Gender, Islam and Democracy in Indonesia.* Routledge. doi.org/10.4324/9780203891759

Suryakusuma, Julia I. 2011. *State Ibuism: The Social Construction of Womanhood in New Order Indonesia.* Komunitas Bambu.

PART 1

Gender ideologies:
Public and private realms

2 Dismantling the old gender order: A work in progress

Kathryn Robinson

Indonesia's path to democracy—the aspiration of the popular movements that led to the toppling of the authoritarian New Order 24 years ago—encompassed ideals of electoral democracy, social justice and equity, summed up in the catchcry of that euphoric moment: *pemberdayaan* (empowerment) (Manning and van Diermen 2000). This aspiration encompassed women's rights and gender equity (Robinson and Bessell 2002).[1]

Women's activism was critical to the genesis of that revolutionary moment. Difficulties faced by households in meeting the needs of everyday life consequent on the 1997 Asian financial crisis sparked street protests against Suharto's government, the first being Suara Ibu Peduli Demo Susu (Voices of Concerned Mothers Milk Demonstration), held at Jakarta's iconic HI (Hotel Indonesia) roundabout in February 1998 (Oey-Gardiner 2002: 110). The reactive political theatre deployed by the failing regime included orchestrated rapes of Chinese women in Jakarta as part of a 'shadow play' scapegoating Indonesia's Chinese for the economic chaos (ibid.); this had the unintended consequence of bringing violence against women—hitherto a rumbling complaint from women's rights activists—into public view.

Interim president Habibie (1998–1999) directed the legislative changes that ushered in the central pillars of the move away from authoritarian rule: direct elections of legislatures and of the president (Hosen 2007);

---

1 The minister for women appointed by the first elected president post-*reformasi* insisted on changing the name of the ministry to the Ministry of Women's Empowerment.

10   *Kathryn Robinson*

towards decentralising political authority to newly empowered district governments. Habibie decreed the formation of the National Commission on Violence against Women, Komnas Perempuan (Oey-Gardiner 2002: 111; Robinson 2009: 155; Yentriyani, this volume). These political and legal institutions, and a new institution established in 2001—the Constitutional Court, Mahkamah Konstitusi—have been crucial sites for contestations over gendered power in democratising Indonesia.

Gendered power—the sites of struggle

Sex/gender differences are strongly marked in all aspects of society (economics, politics, culture) and there is a tendency to frame issues of gender equity or social participation in terms of 'status' or 'position', using single indicators such as the number of women in parliament as opposed to the number of men. But of course, 'status' is inherently a synthesis of several factors or dimensions. 'Gender relations are imbricated in the exercise of power in all social arenas' (Robinson 2014: 107),[2] and connected to power in 'gender regimes' understood as the overall patterning of gender relations in an institution, for example, school, nation state or clan (ibid.: 117).

Gendered power was at the heart of the authoritarian style of the New Order. The policies that Suryakusuma (2012) termed 'state ibuism' were a pillar of a state ideology in which the naturalised authority of the *bapak* president as the head of the nation mirrored the 'natural' authority of the male household head, a model enshrined in the 1974 marriage law (more of this below). The 'citizen mother' (Robinson 1994) was defined through wifeliness and motherhood of her two carefully spaced children.[3] The New Order ideological creation of the figure of the *ibu* (mother) whose social role and citizenship are defined in the family and household is frequently invoked as encompassing the 'traditional roles' of women in Indonesia. 'Gendered ideology which links women to domestic life and households formally "headed" by a man can legitimate male domination of public institutions and support assertions that female leadership is "against nature"' (Robinson 2014: 119) in, for example, debates about whether a woman can be a president (Robinson 2004). The gendered ideology of the New Order played a critical role in creating and sustaining these definitions and roles, enforced and reproduced through its social policies.

---

2   Current approaches emphasise 'gender relations' rather than the 1970s concern to 'bring women in' (Robinson 2014: 109).
3   Women were the *penerus bangsa* ('caretakers of the nation'), responsible for continuing (reproducing) the nation through generations.

Chapter 2 Dismantling the old gender order: A work in progress 11

The formerly dominant state ideology is proving to have residual strength defining women's social, political and economic roles, and the cultural construction of womanhood, highlighted in several of the contributions to this volume (see, for example, chapters by Sigiro, Budianto, Kusumaningrum et al. and Eliyanah).

'Women's exclusion from public life, far from being "traditional", is in many parts of the archipelago an innovation on traditional norms and practices' (Robinson 2018: 310).

The many cultural-linguistic groups (*suku bangsa*) that comprise the Indonesian nation express wide variations in gender orders and gender regimes in customary relations between men and women in everyday life: domestic authority, economic power, cultural values and more, plus a range of juridical relations within the household, governed by norms of kinship, marriage and descent (Robinson 2009).

New Order familist ideology reached right into the household, as the 1974 marriage law defined men as household heads, a patriarchal dividend to men inhabiting non-hegemonic forms of masculinity otherwise shut out of power. They were 'kings' in their domestic domains, and this aspect of law cannot be separated from the failure of the state to protect women from violence in the home.

State power was behind the enforcement of these ideals concerning gender roles: women were compulsorily enrolled in corporatist movements (Family Welfare Association, PKK; the civil servants' wives organisation, Dharma Wanita) that emphasised motherhood and wifely duties. In this space, women were named as 'Ibu X' (Mrs X—X being the husband's name) even in instances where the custom of their community used, for example, teknonymous terms, 'Mother of Y'. Another key area where women were attached to the state was the official Family Planning Program where (only married) women seeking contraception were required to have the permission of husbands. Unpacking the gendered politics of the New Order has thus entailed a lot more than enabling of women in positions of formal political power. State ideology naturalised the role of the male as household head and simultaneously rendered unnatural the possibility of women having a role in formal politics (see, for example, Aspinall et al. 2021: 9–10).

Male prerogative was thoroughly shored up under the New Order, part of the 'patriarchal dividend' that flowed to men in general from the capture of the state by a militarised male hegemonic elite. Gender equity in social life demands that men must relinquish power to accept movement towards a new kind of gender order. This is invariably a fight: power is never given up lightly.

12 *Kathryn Robinson*

Women's 'seat at the table'—formal political representation

The results of the first democratic parliamentary elections in 1999 were disappointing for women, as they accounted for only 8.8% of seats in the national parliament (Dewan Perwakilan Rakyat, DPR), hardly a change from the last semi-elected parliament of the Suharto era where women had held about 12% of seats (Robinson 2009: 159).

Women activists responded with demands for gender quotas to be implemented as a key element of electoral democracy, adopting a United Nations quota of 30% women in legislative and other public bodies.[4] Law 12/2003 on General Elections encouraged parties to 'consider' that women comprise at least 30% of candidates on party candidate lists for the multi-member electorates for national, provincial and district parliaments. But results in the 2004 elections were disappointing: only a slight rise to 11.8% women of members elected to the DPR. There were no sanctions for noncompliance: many parties had no female candidates, and women candidates were too often placed in unwinnable positions at the bottom of party lists (*urutan sepatu*, shoe order) (Robinson 2018: 310).

The disappointing result led to a coalition of non-government organisations drafting a clause that was included in Law 10/2008 on General Elections, requiring that parties have at least 30% women in candidate lists for multi-party electorates of parliaments at national, provincial and district levels, and that at least one of the top three (the potentially winnable seats in this electoral system) must be a woman. Six out of 38 parties contesting the election failed to meet the quota and only three placed women in one of the top three positions, but in the end 34.7% of candidates for DPR and 17.6% of elected representatives were women.

The significance that democracy and gender equity activists gave to amplifying women's voices in politics is indicated by ongoing demands for revisions to laws regulating the 30% quota, as weakness in its implementation has been identified. A Constitutional Court ruling in 2008 found the constitution required that, in the open list system, votes for candidates in the multi-member electorates needed to go to the candidate, not the party, as had been the case in prior elections. Many women had been successful in attracting voter support, but because parties failed to put them at the top of their lists the men placed at the top of the lists benefited from their success in attracting votes. This change had unintended consequences for women candidates in the 2009 elections:

---

4 Indonesia has enthusiastically participated in global forums such as United Nations bodies and embraced global movements for changes, perhaps facilitated by the importance of aid from bilateral and multilateral bodies.

Chapter 2 Dismantling the old gender order: A work in progress 13

candidates began campaigning as individuals, and men on average had more to spend, perhaps as they were more open to money politics.

The 2014 campaign saw some enforcement of the quotas—and the proportion of women candidates rose to 37.3%, but they won only 17.4% of seats in the DPR.

By 2019, the electoral changes ushered in by several iterations of quota regulation (Table 2.1) resulted in the proportion of women candidates reaching 40%, and women gaining 120 of 575 seats (20.9%) (Wardani and Subekti 2021). Currently, the proportion of women members in the DPR is 21.4%, still far short of the aspirational 30% but just above the 21.2% average for Asia.

Table 2.1 Women's representation in national parliament and quota legislation

Year	Success in DPR (%)	Changes
2004	11.8	Voluntary 30% quota on party lists
2008	17.6	Required 30% female candidates and in at least 1 of the top 3 positions. Challenged in the Constitutional Court
2014	17.4	Greater scrutiny of compliance by the General Elections Commission; more women candidates
2019	21.4	Above 21.2% average for Asia

Factors identified as obstacles to women achieving a greater share of seats include the male-dominated structures of political parties: they provide the 'nursery' for candidates and control the nomination process. Another factor is women's lesser ability to raise funds for campaigns (Aspinall et al. 2021; White and Aspinall 2019).

We can draw some conclusions from other electoral contests. The Indonesian parliament is bicameral and election to the upper house, the DPD (Dewan Perwakilan Daerah, Regional Representative Council), is by proportional representation, based on single non-transferable votes in multi-member electorates. DPD elections are not subject to a gender quota. Women accounted for 26.5% of seats in 2009, rising to 30% (41/136) currently. This supports a conclusion reached by Siregar (2010) that parties are the main impediment to women achieving legislative seats. Women's success in the DPD has been attributed to the relative lack of involvement of political parties in nomination and campaigning. Candidates are judged on an individual basis, on political and community work (Robinson 2018: 311). I heard from women candidates in the field that some from established parties were overlooked for nomination by party machines,

14   *Kathryn Robinson*

and 'jumped ship' to newer parties who welcomed experienced political actors to fill their gender quotas.

Commentators refer to ideologies that assert women's primary domestic responsibilities as barriers to successful candidacy, but Dewi's (2015) study of three female candidates in Java argues that these politicians self-consciously presented themselves as pious married women who deferred to their husbands as the basis of their claim to suitability to assume political power. A 'good woman' is a good candidate for public office.

Direct elections for district and provincial legislatures, held since 2004, have also been subject to the laws on gender quotas, but have been even slower than national parliament to achieve changes. In 2009 women won an average of 16% of seats in 33 provincial parliaments and 9% at district and municipal levels. The proportion of women elected to provincial parliaments declined to 14.6% in 2014, but there was a small increase in district and municipal levels to 14.2%. Success of quotas in increasing representation has an important demonstration effect: 'Since [the inception of] direct elections for positions of government and the head of districts more women are getting those positions too' (Robinson cited in Chalmers 2014). There is great diversity in regional legislatures, however: many regional bodies have no women and in some small parliaments all legislators are women (Robinson 2018: 312).

The other major political shift under Habibie's interim presidency, decentralisation of political authority to the district level, has heightened political contestation at subnational levels and this has stirred up political discourse asserting 'customary institutions' as a means to electoral success (Davidson and Henley 2007). In some cases, this rhetoric has disadvantaged women in their contest for a seat at the table. For example, in Bali (Rhoads 2012) women are denied a vote in village government (*banjar*) and this flows on to no women in district and provincial legislatures (Robinson 2018: 312).

There is evidence that support for female candidates is more likely to come from women voters. As women make up 52% of the population, this is not insignificant (Aspinall et al. 2021).

The Inter-Parliamentary Union, a major global advocate for parliamentary democracy and equitable representation, concludes that 'quotas are one of the most critical success factors in increasing women's representation' (IPU 2022: 2). As well as promoting rule changes that help women candidates, quotas have also done ideological work, acting as 'a kind of lightning rod—and encourag[ing] a kind of political discourse—for women to organise around issues of political representation' (Robinson cited in Chalmers 2014).

Does women's representation matter? Does it signal a change in the gender order or gender regime?

Why does gender equity in representation matter? 'Gender order' refers to 'a historically constructed pattern of power relations between men and women and definitions of femininity and masculinity' (Connell 1987: 98–99). Male monopoly of state power expresses hegemonic masculinity and 'expends energy in controlling [the gender order]' (ibid.: 128). Women's exclusion from the exercise of power in public institutions is an active gender process. Increasing women's representation in elected governing institutions is a significant form of attack on a gender order in which hegemonic masculinity is in control. Claiming women's right to representation is a form of defiance and a mode of attack.

Political scientists differentiate between 'formal/descriptive' and 'substantive' representation: does the make-up of elected bodies reflect that of the population (formal or descriptive), or is it substantive in that individuals or groups represent and argue for positions in the interest of the publics they feel they represent? Female politicians can provide substantive representation for women or for other groups or sectors in their electorates and the community at large. But many Indonesian women politicians act as substantive representatives of women in that they use their political power to advance what are deemed to be women's interests, and to champion gender equity policies in their legislative activity.

An official gender quota expresses a public discourse, supported by the state, that women as a group have shared interests that can be addressed in part through women's representation. It is formal recognition that women representatives can take the lead on issues deemed to be of interest to female citizens, or that concern women's rights, and that such issues are a marked domain of political debate.

In the complex multi-party Indonesian parliaments, women politicians have amplified their substantive voice by forming cross-party women's caucuses, formal bodies within the parliaments. Potential legislation brought before the DPR is considered in one of the multi-party specialist committees and this also allows women substantive representation.

The discussion of quotas and women's representation reflects a feminist politics that posits that women as a group have collective and common interests vis-a-vis men as a group. Gender equity and women's rights as political goals are not only measured by numbers in positions of power. However, women have membership of and identification with many collectivities and their interests as 'women' may not always be shared, or more important to them than other senses of duty or belonging. Nonetheless, women in an elected body, and especially when organised

16   *Kathryn Robinson*

in a women's caucus that cross cuts interests of party and perhaps region, promotes a form of seriality (Young 1994) where they can (and have) come together to support policy changes promoted by women's rights activists outside the parliament.

Executive

Despite the important symbol of Megawati Sukarnoputri as Indonesia's first female president in 2001, women are still under-represented in executive government. She was elected under the 'old rules' by the members of the Upper House (Majelis Permusyawaratan Rakyat, MPR). Direct election, beginning in 2004 (Law 32/2004), encompasses executive as well as legislative roles: the president, governors and the heads of districts, all previously elected by legislators. There has been a small rise in the number of women elected to these executive positions (Robinson 2018: 312), but a 2010 regulation limiting incumbency to two terms has had an unexpected effect on female candidates (Tidey 2018). In 2015 at least 16 candidates for regional executive positions had kinship or affinal connections to the previous incumbent—as wife, daughter and daughter-in-law. Analysis of women legislators after the 2019 elections shows a similar phenomenon of political cronyism supporting women candidates, that especially in major parties there is a growing trend for women candidates to have family connections to former legislators (Wardani and Subekti 2021).

There has been a rise in the number of women cabinet ministers post-Suharto. The first directly elected president, Susilo Bambang Yudhoyono (2004–2014), had four women ministers in his first cabinet and six in the second. His appointments were innovative in that he appointed women portfolios like finance and trade, not just the 'social' portfolios female ministers tended to hold in New Order cabinets.

In the case of his successor, President Joko Widodo (2014–2019, 2019–), the aura of optimism around his ascent to power congealed around the number and calibre of women in his first cabinet. Women were very active in his 'grassroots' campaign, through social media and volunteer groups and 'there is an argument to say it was women who got him home' (Tapsell cited in Chalmers 2014). Jokowi included eight women in his 2014 cabinet, 24% of the total, and above the world average of 17% at the time, including Sri Mulyani Indrawati as finance minister, Retno Marsudi in foreign affairs and Siti Nurbaya Bakar as minister of environment and forestry. But his pick of 'high school dropout' businesswomen and pilot, Susi Pudjiastuti, as fisheries minister was a surprise and came in for criticism that she lacked suitable qualifications or experience (Nazeer 2014). She proved

Chapter 2 Dismantling the old gender order: A work in progress 17

remarkably tough and effective in the job, however. When I spoke with young women in Kupang, East Nusa Tenggara, (the home of her airline business) in 2017 about what national cultural heroine Kartini meant to them they agreed enthusiastically that 'Ibu Susi' was the modern day 'Kartini' who they admired (see below). Jokowi's second cabinet (2019–) included only 5 women out of 34 ministers, but he reappointed the female ministers for finance, foreign affairs, and environment and forestry (see Prihatini, this volume).[5]

Women in other public positions

Indonesian women and girls have benefited from expanded opportunities for education. But 'Indonesia's remarkable strides in women's education and the historic involvement of women in the economy have not readily translated into women's participation in other areas of public life' (Robinson 2018: 313).

Despite policies of 'gender mainstreaming' that date back to the New Order, women are still poorly represented in the upper echelons of the civil service—and mostly concentrated in lower levels in the service areas of health and education (*Jakarta Post* 2020). The UNDP (2021) reported that, in 2021, only two of ten high-level officials in the public service leadership were women. According to the National Civil Service Agency (Badan Kepegawaian Negara, BKN), in 2019 women held only 18% of senior positions with decision-making roles, such as deputy ministers or deputy cabinet secretaries, in Indonesia's civil service.

Women and work

While New Order ideology of patriarchal familism constrained women and their opportunities, other Suharto-era policies had contrary consequences. Public education expanded after 1975 and by the early 1980s almost all Indonesian children were enrolled in primary school.

In 2010 female students accounted for 47.6% of students in higher education (UNDP 2010: 21). Education increases labour force participation (Robinson 2018: 310)—around 50% of Indonesian women participate in the workforce compared to 75% of men (Manning and Pratomo 2018), 'higher than in India or Malaysia, very close to the Philippines but below Thailand, China and way below Vietnam' (ibid.).

Rural women have provided the international labour migrants who, since the 1980s, have made a strong contribution to Indonesia's gross

---

5   The continued demands from women voters for consideration of women for executive positions is exemplified in the report by Harish (2022).

domestic product through remittances. Indonesia was a late entrant into global labour markets, and by the time enabling legislative and administrative arrangements were in place in the late 1970s, Indonesia had missed out on the opportunities for male construction jobs in the Middle East. Practical consequences include changes in the division of labour in regard to household tasks/social reproduction when women travel overseas, and the left-behind husbands take on domestic chores.

It is not easy to chart the overall impact of the experience of women but new responsibilities have been taken on by single male-headed households. Lücking (2020) reports that returned migrants from the Middle East who worked as domestic servants are critical of gender relations in Arab households. This leads to a negative view of the gendered practices of contemporary Islamist movements (see Nisa, this volume) that, the migrants say, want women to behave 'like the Arabs'.

While participation rates of women in post-primary and tertiary education have gone up, women—particularly in urban areas—have expanded opportunities for employment. The same is not true in rural areas. One of the underlying reasons for high rates of child marriage is surely the lack of opportunities for young women to transition to adulthood through the paths of completing education and finding employment (Bennett 2016; see also Kusumaningrum, this volume).

This reshaping of the gender orders of the archipelago instantiated male prerogative in many areas of life where customary relations had given women power—such as headship of family groups relying in seniority, not sex (Robinson 2009). Women are still more likely to be working in agriculture than men. Land rights and access to productive resources for rural livelihoods is a 'hot' issue now. Throughout the archipelago local communities/*suku* have a range of customary rights in respect of different types of land. Customary principles of land use and ownership encompass women's rights—as individual rights; inheritance or other kinds of gifting from parents; use rights as members of landowning groups; and women's rights in common property after divorce, recognised by Indonesia's religious courts. The Indonesian government is embarking on a process of certifying or formalising land rights and the modern systems of land titling tend to annihilate women's customary rights through assigning titles to household heads, assumed to be male. Currently, only 25% of titles issued through the national agency are to women, evidence of an unreflected assumption (to be generous) or an inscription of patriarchal values arising from state ideology and practices. This exemplifies how formal state processes override gender-based rights that have been built into customary practices (White 2020: 58).

Chapter 2 Dismantling the old gender order: A work in progress 19

Women are heavily represented among international labour migrants, and in a recent workshop on agrarian relations in Indonesia, Affif (2022) noted that women labour migrants can amass capital and in rural areas she has observed they use it to buy land.

Women and industrial employment

Despite New Order ideology about women's primary role as housewives and mothers, that era saw an expansion of women's industrial employment in the new global market factories that opened in the 1980s, especially in Java. The light manufacturing clothing textiles and electronics that the government enabled to invest in Indonesia preferentially sought female employees (Robinson 2009: 96–101).

In the case of my own ethnographic research in Sorowako, a nickel mine and processing facility in South Sulawesi, when I began fieldwork in 1977 formal employment for women was limited to jobs as nurses, secretaries and housekeepers in the company mess (Robinson 1983). The elite women, the managers' wives, lived in a suburban enclave for both Indonesian and expatriate families. Expat wives could purchase 'minimokes', light vehicles a step up from a golf buggy, to drive around the company town. As *lokalisasi* (localisation) of management proceeded, and expats were gradually phased out (beginning around 1980), the minimokes were bought by the Indonesian elite women. This was the first time I saw women driving in Indonesia, something that is now commonplace. In Sorowako, women now drive the giant trucks that shift the ore in the mine sites.

This anecdote exemplifies the ways in which global influences impact women's social and economic participation. Even in a pre-internet era I have noted the way that protest groups have been able to use government endorsement of United Nations agendas (such as the Convention on the Elimination of All Forms of Discrimination against Women, CEDAW) in mobilising (Robinson 2009: 137–42). In the case of mining, the 1990s witnessed a feminisation of mining on a global scale. Indonesian employment law formally banned women from mining until 2003. The company that initially mined Sorowako, International Nickel of Canada, experienced demands from women that they increase opportunities for women's formal employment in mining, from working in mine sites through to processing. In the past decade increasing numbers of female operators have been driving the giant trucks used in the mining site, and women are increasingly employed in professional roles ranging from engineers and technicians to skilled medical personnel. These changes

20   *Kathryn Robinson*

in global mining affect foreign-owned sites across the archipelago (see, for example, Lahiri-Dutt and Robinson 2008).

The first labour law of the Indonesian republic included recognition of women's rights as workers and their reproductive roles in provisions for maternity leave but also menstruation leave and breast-feeding breaks. The law was enacted by female labour minister S.K. Trimurti, a champion of women's rights. In the *reformasi* period there has been consolidation of Indonesian labour law (Law 13/2003 on Manpower) and these rights have been retained, including 13 weeks maternity leave funded by employers. It contains provisions for women workers, including protections for women working night shifts.

A *Jakarta Post* article (Azwar 2021) reported differing opinions among women workers about the value and significance of menstrual leave, reflecting the issues that Lahiri-Dutt and Robinson (2008) found in the different perspectives of women in a mine site in Kalimantan. The emerging group of female heavy equipment operators saw menstrual leave as an important entitlement due to the difficulties they faced in driving on the pit on the days they were menstruating. Female office workers were happy to bargain the right away for extra pay in the enterprise agreement as menstruation did not impact their work performance or comfort at work: 'Their different points of view arose from different ways that female bodies were drawn into production' (Robinson 2014: 120). I did not find such a controversy in the Sorowako mine, but women workers appreciated the provisions for women's reproductive bodies—in their late pregnancy the women operators are moved to the computerised control room that directs the complex patterns of the trucks on site.

But Cameron (2002) and Contreras Suárez and Cameron (2020) conclude that the ongoing growth in Indonesia's economy has not resulted in women achieving a higher proportion of formal sector jobs (and women still earn less on average than men: the social construction of masculinity is linked to a division of labour that returns more economic benefits to men). Dong and Merdikawati, this volume, unpack the social, economic and demographic factors that impede women's entry into employment.

What is happening in the household? Marriage regulation and regulation of women's sexuality

Gender is 'the active social process that brings reproductive bodies into history' (Connell 2012: 1675). Households are key sites not only for biological but also social reproduction.

'Biological difference is the raw material of cultural elaboration and social arrangements' that defines gender relations and gender roles

Chapter 2 Dismantling the old gender order: A work in progress 21

(Robinson 2014: 121).[6] The costs of social reproduction fall on households, and much of it is unpaid domestic work, mainly by women but also men (such as 'house husbands' in East Nusa Tenggara, see below).

Households are the everyday site of the reproduction of gender relations. Issues of women's rights around sexuality and reproduction have been subjects of political debate and women's political demands since the colonial era: organised women's groups focused on women's rights in relation to regulation of marriage (Robinson 2006). The 1974 marriage law set a minimum age at marriage and outlawed forced marriage. Male prerogatives of unconditional divorce and polygyny (*poligami*) were constrained by the law and brought under the control of religious courts,[7] which were then brought into the state court system in 1991 (by the Islamic Law Compilation, Kompilasi Hukum Islam). On the surface the law gave women rights and protection against forced marriage, polygyny, unilateral divorce and child marriage; but as noted above it inscribed men as household heads.

It is ironic that the legal instantiation of male household heads was contained in the 1974 marriage law, which was on the surface a response to longstanding demands from women activists for a secular marriage law to change the colonial-era law that left regulation of Muslim marriage to Islamic institutions (Robinson 2006). The enshrinement of the role of men as household heads can be considered a patriarchal dividend to men inhabiting non-hegemonic masculinity and this is under threat by women's demands to change the male prerogative enshrined in the marriage law.

But marriage regulation has proven to be unfinished business. Soon after *reformasi*, activist women began raising the issue of a new revision of the marriage law with particular attention to banning polygyny and ending legal child marriage by raising the age of marriage for girls from 16 to 18 to harmonise with the international Convention on the Rights of the Child, to which Indonesia is a signatory. There were also demands to remove the clause establishing men as household heads.

Just as some women seized the chance offered by the new political order to revisit laws restricting their rights, some men also saw the chance to reclaim masculine power that had been eclipsed under the New Order (Robinson 2023). Beginning with the public celebration of the 'Polygamy

---

6 The reproductive arena refers to cultural and social processes relating to 'bodies and what bodies do' (Connell 2000: 27).

7 A presidential instruction further eclipsed rights of male civil servants to *poligami*, requiring them to seek approval from their bosses as well as from the religious court.

22   *Kathryn Robinson*

Awards' (Robinson 2009: 177–78), which publicly celebrated once-hidden arrangements, proponents of male prerogative in marriage soon took their challenge to the newly established Constitutional Court. A male complainant argued for restoration of unfettered rights to polygyny, as constraints in the marriage law transgressed their religious freedom. The appeal was unsuccessful.

The Constitutional Court has become an important site for political contestation and the marriage law 'is among the pieces of legislation most frequently challenged in the Constitutional Court. At least 10 cases arguing that provisions of the Marriage Law are unconstitutional have been brought before the court since it was established in 2003' (Susanti 2022). Women activists joined an appeal concerning child marriage to the court. In this case, the court accepted arguments supporting child marriage derived from *fikih* (Islamic jurisprudence), an innovation in terms of public contestation (Robinson 2023). But in December 2018 the Constitutional Court found that it was discriminatory to have a lower age at marriage for women than men (Reuters staff 2019).

Consequently, in September 2019 the marriage law was amended to lift the minimum age at marriage for women from 16 to 19, making it the same as for men. In February 2020, the Indonesian government launched its National Strategy on the Prevention of Child Marriage addressing the factors contributing to the marriage of children and adolescents (see, for example, Sumner 2022).

The demand for legislation outlawing domestic abuse finally succeeded in the passage of Law 23/2004 on the Elimination of Domestic Violence.

The rape of women in the 1998 crisis surrounding the fall of Suharto was directly implicated in the creation of Komnas Perempuan by the reforming interim president, Habibie. Advocacy by women's rights groups including Komnas Perempuan resulted in the passage of a law on sexual violence in April 2022 (see Yentriyani, this volume), with far-reaching provisions on rape in marriage, on training for police and court officials, and rights to restitution and compensation. The Islamist Prosperous Justice Party was unable to have outlawing sex outside marriage included in the law (Pawestri and Mann 2022) and, as anticipated, this provision has been included in a recent controversial revision of the Criminal Code, which has yet to be implemented (Butt 2022; Lindsey 2022).

Outside the metropole
Decentralisation, gender regimes and family planning

Reformasi-era decentralisation of political authority to districts has been both good and bad for women. Bush (2008) and Noerdin (2002)

Chapter 2 Dismantling the old gender order: A work in progress 23

documented the rise of local regulations based purportedly on sharia law (*perda syariah*, or 'gender discriminatory' regulations), which mainly targeted women. This fever seems to have died down. However, another kind of problem has emerged for women's rights. When the national government passes laws that support women's rights and gender equity, for example outlawing domestic violence, activists report that the courts in the regions are not always up to date. They argue there is a need for similar regulations to be enacted at the local level and judges need to be 'socialised' in the new laws for them to come into effect.

Decentralisation has proven to be a challenge to Indonesia's very successful Family Planning Program (Program Keluarga Berencana), begun in the New Order period with the aim of slowing Indonesia's population growth, with its slogan *dua cukup* (two is enough). It was run from Jakarta by the National Family Planning Coordination Board (BKKBN), which had formal representation in the regions; it reached the whole archipelago and developed novel ways of distributing contraceptives. Women having the ability to control their fertility and the number and timing of their children is fundamental to gender equity.

The reserve powers of the national government post-decentralisation did not encompass this program: distribution of contraception and the management of reproductive health services fell to the districts (Hull and Mosley 2009). There was much commentary and speculation that the program would not survive this change. There was also alarm at the pro-natalist discourse of Islamic hardline groups like Hizbut Tahrir Indonesia, established in 1982 but which came into the public stage in the religious freedom of *reformasi*, publicly proclaiming the virtue of large families (see, for example, quotes in Scherpen 2016).

Districts accommodated the national government requirement for them to provide fertility services in different ways: sometimes attached to women's empowerment agencies, sometimes to health or to the civil registry. But the total fertility rate has continued to decline.[8] Women and men in Indonesia are embracing the small family ideal, continuing to regulate their fertility.[9]

Distribution of contraceptives is now through private providers, most usually village midwives, and this does have an impact on the methods offered: they favour injectables and implants as these require return visits (hence regular fees). But as under the centralised system, the private

---

8   The fertility rate for Indonesia in 2022 was 2.24 births per woman, a 0.88% decline from 2021 (www.macrotrends.net/countries/IDN/indonesia/fertility-rate).

9   The Value of Children debate focused on the relation between the economic niches available for children in rural economies, and family size.

24   *Kathryn Robinson*

providers make contraceptives available only to married women. As longer schooling and entry into the workforce delays marriage, there is an unmet need by sexually active young adults for contraception, and this cannot be separated from the debates around child marriage, a current 'hot' issue. The reproductive health law allows abortion only in restricted instances (such as cases of rape, or threat to the health of the mother) (*Jakarta Post* 2022), so it is not available to young unmarried women or as a 'last resort' in the case of failed contraception.[10]

Rural women and girls

It is not possible to present a simple picture of the developing gender relations/gender orders across the archipelago. But rural areas fall behind on many national indicators, including health and income. Rural women make up a disproportionate part of high maternal mortality statistics, and poor access to health services must be a factor.

Child marriage has been flagged as a significant campaign issue for gender rights activists (such as the Congress of Women Religious Scholars, Kongres Ulama Perempuan Indonesia, KUPI) and it is a problem that is more pronounced in rural areas. We know from ethnographic studies that young women in many rural areas face challenges in attending school and post-secondary education, and in getting jobs—hence marriage remains the principal option for them to move out of their natal home, to transition to adulthood (Bennett 2016).

But in other ways rural women are 'hitting wins'. The democratised village governments provide a place where women can influence decisions about their local communities (Gogali 2022). The piety movement has spawned the growth of *majelis taklim* (religious study) groups in local communities and these vary greatly in their character and purpose, but they are sometimes used by activist women to develop leadership skills in village women that they can then exercise in local elections and government.

Many of Indonesia's international labour migrants are from poor rural areas where work overseas gives the opportunities to amass capital, to buy land and other assets (Affif 2022). It also potentially transforms them into cosmopolitan global citizens who enjoy their new-found status back home. Lücking's (2020) book on international migrants from Java and Madura compares pilgrims and domestic servants. The domestic servants have

---

10 There has been an argument in global development that focusing on girls' education is a better way to bring down fertility rates, cheaper than distributing contraceptives.

up-close encounters with employers in the Middle East and East Asia and they express strong opinions about what they learn. East Asians are 'more like us' as 'we are Asians', and 'K pop fandom' (the passion for contemporary Korean pop music) is a symbol of that identity. Despite being Muslim, they report much that is alien, even hypocritical, about their Muslim employers in Saudi Arabia and this gives them a platform to critique and reject calls for Arabisation of Indonesian Muslims by Islamist groups.

New forms of competing gender ideologies including from new currents of Islam

Masculinity can be understood as a way of accumulating and monopolising power; hence gender relations are a significant arena of political conflict. While the ideology of the New Order concerning gender roles is proving hard to dislodge, there are also new challenges for women and transgender individuals seeking equity, from contemporary waves of Islamist ideologies in the political sphere and the associated organisations and movements (see Hegarty, this volume). The (purportedly) sharia-derived district regulations controlling women's movement and clothing noted above exemplify this trend for the new institutions of *reformasi* to be sites of gender politics.

Political rhetoric and contestation based in Islam have emerged as significant arenas of contention post–New Order. Islamic parties were important in the freewheeling political contestation of the new republic but tamed by the New Order. There were contradictions in the New Order regulation of domestic and gender roles. As noted above, the expansion of education regardless of sex, and the economic policies of the New Order, resulted in openings for women in national and indeed global labour markets. There were contradictions to the family as the 'seat' of the familial authoritarian ideology in government economic policies. The marriage law that guaranteed men the patriarchal dividend as 'king in their households' limited rights under Islamic law to polygyny (*poligami*), unconditional divorce and authority over daughters. Of course some men fight back over the loss of power including the constraining of prerogatives in Islamic family law.

Islamist rhetoric has provided the field for new contestations about male authority, based in ideas about men's authority in the household. Demands for the reinstatement of the right to polygyny emerged, taking the form of appeals to the Constitutional Court to remove restrictions on polygyny on the grounds that it restricted religious freedom (Butt 2010), an argument the court rejected. The court was also the venue for a challenge to the minimum age at marriage, and it determined that the difference in minimum age stipulated in the law for male and female citizens was discriminatory and therefore unconstitutional. It ordered the government amend the law, and this was achieved in 2019. Child marriage as a practice and polygyny remain areas of political contestation, relying on both religious and secular reasoning (Robinson 2023).

The fight against this attempt to expand male prerogative using Islamist rhetoric has been taken up not only by secular activists but also importantly by Muslim gender rights activists, including those with roots in or connections to the major Islamic mass movements Nahdlatul Ulama (NU) and Muhammadiyah. Women associated with NU held the Congress of Women Religious Scholars (KUPI), the first of its kind in the world, in 2017. It was held in an NU-affiliated *pesantren* (religious school) in Cirebon and addressed inter alia by the minister for religious affairs (who was from NU). Speakers at the congress made claims for women's religious authority not only in the present, but for historical precedents. The outcomes of deliberations were delivered as a fatwa, in itself a claim for women's religious authority (Robinson 2017).

Several international Muslim women activists were invited to address the international plenary, including Saudi activist Hatoon al-Fasi whose talk focused on the 'I am my own *wali* [guardian]' campaign by Saudi women: claiming their rights to move about in society without male guardians, and the right to drive, a focus of this. A telling moment occurred when an Indonesian woman in the audience asked in puzzlement about the importance of getting out from under *wali*—she understood the term only in the context of the Islamic *nikah* or marriage contract. KUPI is ongoing as a movement for gender equity won through Islamic struggle and a second international congress was held in November 2022 (see Nisa, this volume).

In the contemporary political scene, Islam is providing political symbolism and rhetoric. Idrus (2014) wrote a satirical column for *Fajar* newspaper in Makassar about women political candidates of necessity expressing their identity as pious Muslim women by always having head covering in their campaign posters, but she points out that Islamic iconography is deployed by both male and female politicians in Muslim-majority electorates, the men necessarily indicating Muslim identity with black *peci* (caps) or even white caps signifying *haji* status. Islam as a language for political contestation may be gendered, and has gendered consequences, however. In formal politics, the female NU politician Khofifah Indar Parawansa, who addressed the 2002 Indonesia Update when she was minister for women's empowerment (Parawansa 2002), was opposed as a candidate for governor of East Java by conservative NU *kiai* (religious scholars) on the grounds that as region head she would be required to lead prayer, and this was *haram* (forbidden) for a woman, according to Islam. In the last presidential elections, radical Islamist supporters of Joko Widodo's rival, Prabowo Subianto, used gendered rhetoric and women associated with those groups organised as 'mothers' in Subianto's support, opposed by groups similarly invoking maternalist rhetoric to support Jokowi: redolent of the politicised 'ibuism' of the Suharto era (Dewi 2020).

Conclusion

Twenty years ago, the Indonesia Update reported on challenges to the gender order that were beginning across public and private spheres of life (Robinson and Bessell 2002), and these have continued over the past twenty years, though not always in a linear fashion. Twenty years ago, the quota for women's representation had not been enacted. Now, women are slowly making inroads into public life, especially in elected political institutions. While women's representation in Indonesia's parliaments are short of the United Nations' 30% goal, gains have been made and Indonesia ranks well in the region. The entry of women into other areas of public life has not been so impressive, with few gains on the situation described in the 2001 Update (Oey-Gardiner 2002). Several speakers at the 2022 Update spoke of the continuing negative influence of New Order familist ideology in government policy and action, and also in public life. The continued legal status of male household heads means government policies still erode women's rights. However, activists have been effective in using new sites of power (elected parliaments, decentralised government, Komnas Perempuan and the Constitutional Court as well as the internet and social media platforms) to achieve gender equity outcomes, such as the law on domestic violence, the sexual crime law and the moves against child marriage. Recently, the revised Criminal Code aims to criminalise sex outside marriage, for example, but this will undoubtedly be challenged before it is implemented (Lindsey 2022).

While new forms of patriarchal ideology and action have emerged in Islamist movements, Islamic women's organisations have effectively used feminist rhetoric based in Islam to press gender equity goals. The movement KUPI is a strong manifestation of this.

In terms of women's reproductive health, contraceptive supply to married women continues to be effective, but sexually active unmarried people are left out, and this is not highlighted in the public debates around child marriage. The total fertility rate remains in decline, indicating that fertility control and the small family is now the new normal, despite the opposition of radical Islamic groups to family planning and the decentralisation of

28   *Kathryn Robinson*

family planning services.[11] Though falling, total fertility rate remains high in comparison with other ASEAN countries, and Indonesia's maternal mortality continues to be high relative to her neighbours.

Indonesia has a high prevalence of child marriage according to UNICEF (2020), and a reduction in the rate of child marriage is one of the gender equity goals that Indonesia has adopted under the United Nations Sustainable Development Goals. Indonesia's embrace of UN-derived global agendas has long been a significant hook for women's policy and women's activists.

Women's participation rates in education remain high but this is not translating into increased workforce participation, and there is still a gender pay gap, despite Indonesia adopting equity principles in the workplace. But Indonesian women are busy in the informal sector, in small businesses including e-commerce. There is concern that the 2020 omnibus law on job creation (Cipta Kerja), which had far-reaching provisions regarding economic activity, threatens women's rights in the informal sector, however.

In the freer society post-Suharto, intergenerational differences among women become clear. There are new focuses on women's health including chronic diseases, and concerns about childcare for working women as intergenerational childcare disappears (due to factors such as migration and intergenerational working women) (see Sigiro, this volume). The growing cohort of older women predicted by Hugo (2002) at the 2002 Update is now a reality and causing concern (Oey-Gardiner 2021) as the population ages and customary family care is no longer assumed.

Young women take up a range of opportunities and identities. They embrace ambition, playfulness and education, and are strong on grassroots activism. They are achieving new and previously unimagined roles in a country that is rapidly changing, economically, socially and culturally. Popular culture and social media increasingly provide space for young women to express themselves and their complex identities that go beyond their sex, or *suku* (see for example Nisa, Dirgantoro, Paramaditha and Eliyanah, this volume).

The colonial-era writer Kartini has been a principal symbol of women's advancement in Indonesia, celebrated in a national holiday. Her story and iconography have been mined by different generations of political

---

11 Family planning has been a popular focus for many development programs over the years, including approaches to the whole life cycle of the girl, utilising village heads as intermediaries between women and health service to transport women to health facilities, and formally recruiting men to be responsible for bringing their wives to birthing facilities.

actors, beginning in the colonial period. I had discussions about what the celebration of Kartini means to Indonesia's youth with groups of young people in Kupang, Surabaya and Makassar in 2017 and found that they mainly engaged with Kartini through social media, posting on platforms like Instagram on Hari Kartini (Kartini Day), often posing with their mothers or women they admired or—most interesting to me—recording a novel achievement. Young women who had climbed Mount Bawakaraeng (South Sulawesi) donned their white kebayas at the summit and posted images of themselves achieving something new that for them is the spirit of Kartini. Indonesian women are active in defining their place in the Indonesian nation, as they have done in the past.

References

Affif, Suraya. 2022. 'Rural migration'. In 'Hari Tani Nasional: A forum on the future of rural Indonesia'. Panel discussion hosted by ANU Crawford School of Public Policy, 23 August. www.newmandala.org/watch-hari-tani-nasional-a-forum-on-the-future-of-rural-indonesia/

Aspinall, Edward, Sally White and Amalinda Savirani. 2021. 'Women's political representation in Indonesia: Who wins and how?' *Journal of Current Southeast Asian Affairs* 40(1): 3–27. doi.org/10.1177/1868103421989720

Azwar, Amahl S. 2021. 'Go with the flow: Indonesian women divided over menstrual leave'. *Jakarta Post*, 12 March. www.thejakartapost.com/life/2021/03/11/go-with-the-flow-indonesian-women-divided-over-menstrual-leave.html

Bennett, Linda Rae. 2016. 'Young Sasak mothers—*"tidak manja lagi"*: Transitioning from single daughter to young married mother in Lombok, eastern Indonesia'. In *Youth Identities and Social Transformations in Modern Indonesia*, edited by Kathryn Robinson, 236–61. Brill.

Bush, Robin. 2008. 'Regional sharia regulations in Indonesia: Anomaly or symptom?' In *Expressing Islam: Religious Life and Politics in Indonesia*, edited by Greg Fealy and Sally White, 174–91. ISEAS Publishing. doi.org/10.1355/9789812308528-014

Butt, Simon. 2010. 'Islam, the state and the Constitutional Court in Indonesia'. *Washington International Law Journal* 19(2): 279–301.

Butt, Simon. 2022. 'The new Criminal Code: Killing off living law?' *Indonesia at Melbourne*, 15 December. https://indonesiaatmelbourne.unimelb.edu.au/the-new-criminal-code-killing-off-living-law/

Cameron, Lisa. 2002. 'Women and the labour market during and after the crisis'. In *Women in Indonesia: Gender, Equity and Development*, edited by Kathryn Robinson and Sharon Bessell, 144–57. Institute of Southeast Asian Studies. doi.org/10.1355/9789812305152-019

Chalmers, Max. 2014. 'Women in cabinet: A tale of two systems'. *New Matilda*, 30 October. https://newmatilda.com/2014/10/30/women-cabinet-tale-two-systems/

Connell, R.W. 1987. *Gender and Power*. Polity Press.

Connell, R.W. 2000. *The Men and the Boys*. University of California Press.

Connell, Raewyn. 2012. 'Gender, health and theory: Conceptualizing the issue, in local and world perspective'. *Social Science & Medicine* 74(11): 1675–83. doi.org/10.1016/j.socscimed.2011.06.006

Contreras Suárez, Diana and Lisa Cameron. 2020. 'Why Indonesia's wealth isn't translating into jobs for women'. *The Conversation*, 10 March. https://theconversation.com/why-indonesias-wealth-isnt-translating-into-jobs-for-women-132770

Davidson, Jamie S. and David Henley, eds. 2007. *The Revival of Tradition in Indonesian Politics: The Deployment of Adat from Colonialism to Indigenism*. Routledge.

Dewi, Kurniawati Hastuti. 2015. *Indonesian Women and Local Politics: Islam, Gender and Networks in Post-Suharto Indonesia*. NUS Press. doi.org/10.2307/j.ctv1nth4c

Dewi, Kurniawati Hastuti. 2020. 'Motherhood identity in the 2019 Indonesian presidential elections: Populism and political division in the national women's movement'. *Contemporary Southeast Asia* 42(2): 224–50. doi.org/10.1355/cs42-2d

Gogali, Lian. 2022. 'Village governance'. In 'Hari Tani Nasional: A forum on the future of rural Indonesia'. Panel discussion hosted by ANU Crawford School of Public Policy, 23 August. www.newmandala.org/watch-hari-tani-nasional-a-forum-on-the-future-of-rural-indonesia/

Harish, Fikri. 2022. 'As VP pick, Khofifah has "sway" over NU, East Java voters'. *Jakarta Post*, 13 December. www.thejakartapost.com/indonesia/2022/12/13/as-vp-pick-khofifah-has-sway-over-nu-east-java-voters.html

Hosen, Nadirsyah. 2007. *Shari'a and Constitutional Reform in Indonesia*. ISEAS Publishing. doi.org/10.1355/9789812305701

Hugo, Graeme. 2002. 'Women's international labour migration'. In *Women in Indonesia: Gender, Equity and Development*, edited by Kathryn Robinson and Sharon Bessell, 158–78. Institute of Southeast Asian Studies. doi.org/10.1355/9789812305152-020

Hull, Terence H. and Henry Mosley. 2009. *Revitalization of Family Planning in Indonesia*. Government of Indonesia and United Nations Population Fund. www.academia.edu/14142340/Revitalization_of_Family_Planning_in_Indonesia

Idrus, Nurul Ilmi. 2014. *Suaraku Expresiku* [My voice, my expression]. Emic Institute.

IPU (Inter-Parliamentary Union). 2022. 'New IPU report: More women in parliament and more countries with gender parity'. Press release, 3 March. www.ipu.org/news/press-releases/2022-03/new-ipu-report-more-women-in-parliament-and-more-countries-with-gender-parity

Jakarta Post. 2020. 'Gender inequality persists in first year of Jokowi–Ma'ruf administration: Komnas Perempuan'. *Jakarta Post*, 22 October. www.thejakartapost.com/news/2020/10/22/gender-inequality-persists-in-first-year-of-jokowi-maruf-administration-komnas-perempuan.html

Jakarta Post. 2022. 'Making abortion legal'. *Jakarta Post* editorial, 29 June. www.thejakartapost.com/opinion/2022/06/28/making-abortion-legal.html

Lahiri-Dutt, Kuntala and Kathryn Robinson. 2008. '"Period problems" at the coalface'. *Feminist Review* 89(1): 102–21. doi.org/10.1057/fr.2008.5

Lindsey, Tim. 2022. 'Indonesia's new Criminal Code isn't just about sex outside marriage. It endangers press and religious freedom'. *The Conversation*, 8 December. https://theconversation.com/indonesias-new-criminal-code-isnt-just-about-sex-outside-marriage-it-endangers-press-and-religious-freedom-196121

Lücking, Mirjam. 2020. *Indonesians and Their Arab World: Guided Mobility among Labor Migrants and Mecca Pilgrims*. Cornell University Press. www.jstor.org/stable/10.7591/j.ctvx1hv5r

Manning, Chris and Peter van Diermen, eds. 2000. *Indonesia in Transition: Social Aspects of Reformasi and Crisis*. Institute of Southeast Asian Studies.

Manning, Chris and Devanto Shasta Pratomo. 2018. 'Labor supply and attachment to the workforce'. In *Indonesia: Enhancing Productivity through Quality Jobs*, edited by Edimon Ginting, Christopher Manning and Kiyoshi Taniguchi, 29–67. Asian Development Bank. dx.doi.org/10.22617/TCS189213-2

Nazeer, Zubaidah 2014. 'Jokowi praised for record number of women in cabinet'. *Straits Times*, 31 October. www.straitstimes.com/asia/se-asia/jokowi-praised-for-record-number-of-women-in-cabinet

Noerdin, Edriana. 2002. 'Customary institutions, syariah law and the marginalisation of Indonesian women'. In *Women in Indonesia: Gender, Equity and Development*, edited by Kathryn Robinson and Sharon Bessell, 179–86. Institute of Southeast Asian Studies. doi.org/10.1355/9789812305152-021

Oey-Gardiner, Mayling. 2002. 'And the winner is ... Indonesian women in public life'. In *Women in Indonesia: Gender, Equity and Development*, edited by Kathryn Robinson and Sharon Bessell, 100–12. Institute of Southeast Asian Studies. doi.org/10.1355/9789812305152-016

Oey-Gardiner Mayling. 2021. 'WHO CARES? Challenges of women aging in contemporary Indonesia'. In *Older Women and Well-Being: A Global Perspective*, edited by Mala Kapur Shankardass, 167–201. Springer. doi.org/10.1007/978-981-16-4605-8_10

Parawansa, Khofifah Indar. 2002. 'Institution building: An effort to improve Indonesian women's role and status'. In *Women in Indonesia: Gender, Equity and Development*, edited by Kathryn Robinson and Sharon Bessell, 68–77. Institute of Southeast Asian Studies. doi.org/10.1355/9789812305152-012

Pawestri, Tunggal and Tim Mann. 2022. 'Indonesia finally has a law to protect victims of sexual violence. But the struggle is not over yet'. *Indonesia at Melbourne*, 20 April. https://indonesiaatmelbourne.unimelb.edu.au/indonesia-finally-has-a-law-to-protect-victims-of-sexual-violence-but-the-struggle-is-not-over-yet/

Reuters staff. 2019. 'Indonesia raises minimum age for brides to end child marriage'. Reuters, 17 September. www.reuters.com/article/us-indonesia-women-marriage-idUSKBN1W212M

Rhoads, Elizabeth. 2012. 'Women's political participation in Indonesia: Decentralisation, money politics and collective memory in Bali'. *Journal of Current Southeast Asian Affairs* 31(2): 35–56. doi.org/10.1177/186810341203100202

Robinson, Kathryn. 1983. 'Women and work in an Indonesian mining town'. In *Women's Work and Women's Roles: Economics and Everyday Life in Indonesia, Malaysia and Singapore*, edited by Lenore Manderson, 111–28. Monograph No. 32. ANU Development Studies Centre.

Robinson, Kathryn. 1994. 'Indonesian national identity and the citizen mother'. *Communal/Plural* 3: 65–82.

32 *Kathryn Robinson*

Robinson, Kathryn. 2004. 'Islam, gender, and politics in Indonesia'. In *Islamic Perspectives on the New Millennium,* edited by Virginia Hooker and Amin Saikal, 183–98. Institute of Southeast Asian Studies. doi.org/10.1355/9789812305367-013

Robinson, Kathryn. 2006. 'Muslim women's political struggle for marriage law reform in contemporary Indonesia'. In *Mixed Blessings: Laws, Religions, and Women's Rights in the Asia-Pacific Region,* edited by Amanda Whiting and Carolyn Evans, 183–210. Brill. doi.org/10.1163/9789047409656_010

Robinson, Kathryn. 2009. *Gender, Islam and Democracy in Indonesia.* Routledge. doi.org/10.4324/9780203891759

Robinson, Kathryn. 2014. 'What does a gender relations approach bring to Southeast Asian Studies?' In *Methodology and Research Practice in Southeast Asian Studies,* edited by Mikko Huotari, Jürgen Rüland and Judith Schlehe, 107–27. Palgrave Macmillan. doi.org/10.1057/9781137397546_6

Robinson, Kathryn. 2017. 'Female ulama voice a vision for Indonesia's future'. *New Mandala,* 30 May. www.newmandala.org/female-ulama-voice-vision-indonesias-future/

Robinson, Kathryn. 2018. 'Gender culture and politics in post–New Order Indonesia'. In *Routledge Handbook of Contemporary Indonesia,* edited by Robert W. Hefner, 309–21. Routledge. doi.org/10.4324/9781315628837-25

Robinson, Kathryn. 2023. 'Regulation of Muslim marriage in Indonesia: Political challenges across the public/private divide'. In *In Tandem—Pathways towards a Postcolonial Anthropology | Im Tandem – Wege zu einer Postkolonialen Ethnologie,* edited by Mirjam Lücking, Anna Meiser and Ingo Rohrer, 189–208. Springer VS. doi.org/10.1007/978-3-658-38673-3_1

Robinson, Kathryn and Sharon Bessell, eds. 2002. *Women in Indonesia: Gender, Equity and Development.* Institute of Southeast Asian Studies. doi.org/10.1355/9789812305152

Scherpen, Bastiaan. 2016. 'Islam and family planning in Indonesia: Force for good or obstacle to change?' *Jakarta Globe,* 12 April. https://jakartaglobe.id/news/islam-family-planning-indonesia-force-good-obstacle-change/

Siregar, Wahidah Zein. 2010. *Gaining Representation in Parliament: A Study of the Struggle of Indonesian Women to Increase Their Numbers in Parliaments in the 2004 Elections.* Lambert Academic Publishing.

Sumner, Cate. 2022. 'Courting change for Indonesia's invisible brides'. *The Interpreter,* 21 February. www.lowyinstitute.org/the-interpreter/courting-change-indonesia-s-invisible-brides

Suryakusuma, Julia. 2012. 'Is state ibuism still relevant?' *Inside Indonesia,* 1 July. www.insideindonesia.org/is-state-ibuism-still-relevant

Susanti, Laras. 2022. 'Another marriage law controversy: Is reform overdue?' *Indonesia at Melbourne,* 29 March. https://indonesiaatmelbourne.unimelb.edu.au/another-marriage-law-controversy-is-reform-overdue/

Tidey, Sylvia. 2018. 'A tale of two mayors: Configurations of care and corruption in eastern Indonesian direct district head elections'. *Current Anthropology* 59: S117–27. doi.org/10.1086/696072

UNDP (United Nations Development Programme). 2010. *Women's Participation in Politics and Government in Indonesia: A Policy Paper.* UNDP Indonesia.

Chapter 2 Dismantling the old gender order: A work in progress   33

UNDP (United Nations Development Programme). 2021. 'A top female civil servant on a mission to build inclusive e-governance'. UNDP Indonesia, 2 December. www.undp.org/indonesia/news/top-female-civil-servant-mission-build-inclusive-e-governance

UNICEF. 2020. 'Child marriage in Indonesia: Latest statistics of child marriage in Indonesia'. www.unicef.org/indonesia/reports/child-marriage-in-indonesia

Wardani, Sri Budi Eko and Valina Singa Subekti. 2021. 'Political dynasties and women candidates in Indonesia's 2019 election'. *Journal of Current Southeast Asian Affairs* 40(1): 28–49. doi.org/10.1177/1868103421991144

White, Ben. 2020. *Agriculture and the Generation Problem.* Practical Action Publishing. doi.org/10.3362/9781780447421

White, Sally and Edward Aspinall. 2019. 'Why does a good woman lose? Barriers to women's political representation in Indonesia'. *New Mandala Research Brief,* December. www.newmandala.org/wp-content/uploads/2019/12/White-Aspinall-Why-Does-a-Good-Woman-Lose.pdf

Young, Iris Marion. 1994. 'Gender as seriality: Thinking about women as a social collective'. *Signs: Journal of Women in Culture and Society* 19(3): 713–38. doi.org/10.1086/494918

3 Gendering Islamic and Islamist movements in contemporary Indonesia: KUPI gender-just *ulama* and *hijrah* movements

Eva F. Nisa

In Indonesia, the world's largest Muslim country, it is not difficult to find voices expressing the agenda of feminism, Muslim women's identity and gender activism. They engage with their religion to articulate their understandings of gender orders using diverse Islamic and Islamist orientations. On one hand, we can see women's movements taking 'modernist' and 'moderate' orientations. On the other hand, some purportedly women's or even gender movements can be seen taking Islamist orientations, focusing on efforts to return to the foundational texts of Islam and critiquing those opposing them.

Indonesia is renowned for its moderate Islam, emphasising *wasatiyya*—middle-path or centrist Islam—that advocates tolerance and humanitarian perspectives, showcasing a progressive vision of Islam. Moderate and progressive Muslims believe that gender justice is part of this vision (Nisa 2019). The middle-path rhetoric, however, has also been used by conservatives and Islamists who claim that their understandings and practices of Islam are also the manifestation of *wasatiyya* Islam. This then leaves us to question, what does 'moderate Islam' or 'moderate Muslim' mean? *Wasatiyya* Islam is vital to the discussion of gender orders and norms in Indonesia: gender-just perspectives advocated by Muslim gender activists are born from the voices of moderate modernist Muslims from different Muslim-majority countries (Schlehe and Nisa 2016: 7).

Chapter 3 Gendering Islamic and Islamist movements in contemporary Indonesia 35

Moderation brought by modernist-cum-reformist thinkers has been influential in Indonesia. This includes Egyptians Rifā'ah Rāfi' al-Tahtāwī (1801–1873), an Azhari modernist of nineteenth-century Egypt who was known as an advocate of women's economic empowerment; his disciple Muḥammad 'Abduh (1849–1905), known as the founder of modernism and for his call for the abolition of polygamy (Nisa 2021: 157); and 'Abduh's disciple, Qāsim Amīn (1863–1908), celebrated as the most important male writer to contemporary free and modernised women (Nisa 2022). In addition to the modernists in Egypt, the Ottoman Tanzimat (1839–1876) was crucial to overcoming gender inequalities in education by establishing the first secondary school for girls in 1858. Following this, later generations of male progressive thinkers have also contributed to the discussion of gender equality in Islam and Muslim women's empowerment, especially Fazlur Rahman (1919–1988), Mohammad Arkoun (1928–2010), Nasr Hamid Abu Zayd (1943–2010), Muhammad Shahrour (1938–2019), Mohammad Mojtahed Shabestari (b. 1936), Abdulkarim Soroush (b. 1945), Abdullahi Ahmed An-Na'im (b. 1946), and Khaled Abou el-Fadl (b. 1963) (Nisa 2021: 157).

Contestation between Islamist and progressive Muslim thinkers on gender-related issues can be found in many Muslim-majority countries. In Iran, for example, Islamist Mortaza Mothahari's writings on women with his Islamist understanding of gender inequality became popular and were uncontested in Iran for a decade, along with the victory of the Islamists early in the Iranian Revolution (1978–1979).[1] This is different from modernist Iranian thinker and sociologist Ali Shari'ati's writings, which reflect his egalitarian reformist understanding of the position of women. This includes his criticism of both the traditional Islamic role and modern Westernised role of women, which unfortunately did not receive significant support and 'faded into obscurity' (Mir-Hosseini 1996: 291). Indonesian modernist-cum-reformists fighting for gender equality and women's empowerment have also been inspired by the progressive figures (Saenong 2021: 131).

Conflict about gender-related issues can also be seen in other countries, such as Egypt and Turkey, where male moderate modernist Muslims are important figures in the early struggle for gender-just thoughts and initiatives (Mir-Hosseini 1996: 296). Dispute over gender-related issues is also present in Indonesia and includes the voices of male *ulama* (Muslim scholars) of the *pesantren* (Islamic boarding school) tradition, which is

---

1 The Iranian Revolution refers to a popular uprising to overthrow the Western-oriented Muhammad Reza Shah Pahlavi regime and establish an Islamic republic. The revolution was led and dominated by Muslim clerics.

36   *Eva F. Nisa*

known for its solid patrilineal culture that engages with religious texts. Former president Abdurrahman Wahid (known as Gus Dur) is a strong example of this. In 2015, a biography titled *Gus Dur di Mata Perempuan* (Gus Dur in the Eyes of Women) highlighted his contribution to gender justice and women's empowerment (Nadjib 2015). All the contributors are women who share their observations about Gus Dur's emancipatory feminist actions, attitudes, thoughts and deeds. Gus Dur's emancipatory position was aligned with his broader position on democracy and humanism. Scholar-cum-feminist Musdah Mulia emphasised that Gus Dur continued the steps taken by his family in fighting for women's emancipation (Mulia 2013: 49). This includes the actions of his grandfather, KH Bisri Syansuri, who established a female *pesantren* in Denanyar, East Java, towards the end of the 1920s. Gus Dur's father, KH Wahid Hasyim (1914–1953), allowed women to enrol in the Faculty of Islamic Law (Syari'ah) when he served as the minister of religious affairs. This policy, which was revolutionary at the time, led to the possibility of women holding the position of judge in a religious court—a position reserved for men in classical Islamic law (Mulia 2013: 49). Wahid Hasyim's view encapsulates the moderate expression of Islam in the country. The opposition to women serving as judges is due to the assumption by its opponents that women are delicate and emotional and are therefore unable to deliver justice (Nurlaelawati and Salim 2017). Along with these moderate Muslims, Hussein Muhammad, Faqihuddin Abdul Kodir and the current Grand Imam of Istiqlal, Nasaruddin Umar, are among male Muslim feminists whose insights have inspired many contemporary gender-just activists and Muslim feminists in this study (Robinson 2009: 185).

This chapter focuses on the intersections between the resurgence of piety in contemporary Indonesia alongside the birth of the new gender-just network initiated by gender-just *ulama* of the 2017 Congress of Women Religious Scholars (Kongres Ulama Perempuan Indonesia, KUPI). It captures the gender-just practices and voices of current key players, who have been inspired by moderate modernist Muslims within the country and beyond. With the rise of religious conservatism, especially since the late Suharto years and the fall of the authoritarian New Order regime in 1998, Indonesia is witnessing the advance of new kinds of activism, including *hijrah* (religious renewal) activity among young Muslims within Islamic movements, including Islamist groups. Drawing on my ethnographic fieldwork among gender-just *ulama* (male and female) and young conservative Muslims in Indonesia in 2019 and 2022, I unpack their activism—including everyday activism using social media—in articulating gender orders, including setting out their aspirational norms. How are gender equality and Islam discussed and contested

Chapter 3 Gendering Islamic and Islamist movements in contemporary Indonesia 37

in contemporary Indonesia? Indeed, Indonesia has strong, well-rooted Islamic feminist movements associated with the moderate Islam of mass organisations Nahdlatul Ulama and Muhammadiyah.

The social media landscape enables diversity of voices and mainstream attention. This chapter focuses on digital activism using Instagram, one of the most popular platforms used by those involved in the discussion of Islam and gender equality. Various perspectives on gender orders are being reconfigured through networking sites by multiple actors. Facing a rise of piety evident from the emergence of *hijrah* movements and conservative female digital creatives, KUPI Muslim feminists labelled as the representatives of moderate voices of Islam have become more proactive in countering the conservative voices on gender inequality and social injustice.

While they are active in the media landscape, the loudest voices in the field belong to conservative voices. Despite an increasing online presence of gender-just *ulama* and their opponents, digital activism remains gendered and does not weaken the influence of patriarchal norms. The contestation between conservative and moderate progressive proponents of gender norms can be regarded as a reproduction of the different interpretations concerning the relation of patriarchy to Islam. Azizah al-Hibri (1982: 207) argues that in the discussion of gender and women there are two distinguishable parties: 'those who believe that Islam as it is today is fair and just to women, and those who believe that Islam *as it is practised today* is utterly patriarchal, but that *true* Islam is not'. These two main groups are present in the case studies of this chapter.

This chapter is divided into three parts: the first focuses on discourses in the battle for gender justice; the second explores the new wave of *hijrah* movements; and the third looks at the impact of social media and digital activism and discourses on gender, as articulated on various social media platforms, in particular two Instagram accounts—@muslimahfeminis and @thisisgender.

Muslim women and the battle for gender justice

The struggle for gender justice in Indonesia faces the common problem for Islamic feminists and gender activists, namely, the use of the terms 'gender', 'feminism', and 'feminists'. Gender-just Muslim activists have been careful in using these terms because they carry connotations of Western and colonial exported beliefs and values. Indeed, colonial powers positioned women in Islam as part of the rhetoric to justify the project of modernisation and the agenda of 'civilising' the 'uncivilised', or as part of the rationale for dominating them (Ahmed 1984, re Egypt; Mir-Hosseini 2006, re Iran).

38   *Eva F. Nisa*

When I conducted research on conservative women of various Salafi[2] groups, an informant shared her thoughts on Islamic feminists, stating 'they are liberal [for her a pejorative term] Muslims. Their understandings of Islam are dangerous. They are Western agents. You know they receive money for their NGOs from the West. *Mereka budak Barat* [they are the "slaves" of the West]'.[3] This is a common view. Therefore, many Islamic feminists and gender-just activists try not to use these terms. For example, Nyai Afwah, a 49-year-old *nyai* (female leader of a *pesantren*) with 1,500 students in Kempek Cirebon, West Java, shared her concerns regarding her gender-just related *da'wa* (proselytising) in a traditional *pesantren* or among the villagers residing near the *pesantren*. She does not use the terms 'feminism' and 'gender'. She replaces these 'Western' terms with Arabic terms: *'adāla* (justice), *musāwa* (equality) and *mubādala* (reciprocity and mutual understanding). She believes that 'these terms are softer in the ears of people within the *pesantren* and village milieus' (Nisa and Saenong 2022). Nyai Afwah's strategies worked soundly. The Arabic terms sound less disruptive in her gender-just *da'wa*.

This problem is not unique to Indonesia and can be found in other Muslim-majority contexts (Badran 2005: 15; Basarudin 2016: 59, re Malaysia). Some scholars have rejected the use of the term 'Islamic feminism'. This includes Asma Barlas, who has been critical about being labelled a feminist due to its ethnocentric undertones (2008: 21–22). From another point of view, Haideh Moghissi has been critical of this term, arguing, 'how could a religion which is based on gender hierarchy be adopted as the framework for struggle for gender democracy and women's equality with men?' (1999: 126). In Indonesia, however, many gender-just activists nowadays are not concerned by the label 'Islamic feminism'. The introduction of this term to the Indonesian gender politics discourse is relatively new, and some scholar-cum-gender activists do not distinguish between Islamic and Muslim feminism. Those who differentiate between the two argue that Muslim feminism refers to the Muslim identity of feminists within the movement, while Islamic feminism specifically refers to a movement consisting of feminists who try to re-read religious texts with gender-just perspectives (further discussed below). Some gender-just activists and Indonesian Islamic feminists have become more courageous in claiming that they are feminists. They are also active in countering

---

2 The Salafi movement is a purist movement that strives to 'purify' Islam through an emphasis on returning to Islam's pristine form as practised by the Prophet Muhammad and his companions or *al-salaf al-ṣāliḥ* (the pious predecessors).

3 Interview with Nazila (pseudonym), East Jakarta, 11 January 2019.

Chapter 3 Gendering Islamic and Islamist movements in contemporary Indonesia 39

those who oppose their position. For example, a post by @mubadalah.id states: 'Feminism is indeed from the West, so what?'.

The increasing presence of male and female gender-just activists and scholars focusing on re-reading Islamic texts can be seen in Indonesia. Many of these activists and scholars are of a *pesantren* background. They can be regarded as the products of modernity and globalisation. The country has witnessed the expansion of well-educated moderate middle-class Muslims thanks to economic growth. The growth of the Muslim middle class in the 1970s and 1980s occurred simultaneously with the impact of the Islamic revival on the urban poor and urban middle class (Hefner 2003). This happened in many Muslim-majority countries where segments of well-educated male and female university students became part of Islamic revivalist movements. They were critical of Western styles of modernisation, including the Western version of gender discourses (Nisa 2022: 166, 168; see Stivens 1998: 113 re Malaysia). Facing complex life conditions, these conservatives, including Islamist women, position returning to religion (Islam) as their comforting 'home'. The success of Ayatollah Khomeini's revolution in Iran, which attacked the Western way of life, or 'westoxification', as the source of sociocultural problems faced by Muslims and emphasised the return to Islam as an 'alternative path to modernity', for example, awakened conservative Muslims from various Muslim groups to glorify and introduce their versions of Islamic ways of life (Stivens 1998: 91). Therefore, moderate, progressive and conservative Muslims are essential segments of middle-class Indonesians with competing agendas, including gender-related agendas. Middle-class gender-just activists of *pesantren* backgrounds call for gender equality, while conservative Muslims call for gender complementarity, a position that was also adopted by women ministry bureaucrats under the Suharto regime and is aligned with the New Order (1966–1998) ideology of *kodrat* (translated by them as biologically determined difference) (Robinson 2009: 10; see also Nisa 2019: 447).

Whose *hijrah*?

This section focuses on moderate progressive voices and practices of gender justice within the KUPI network and gender complementarity voices and practices of *hijrah* movements. The two positions can be equated to the two groups identified by al-Hibri (1982) in her study of the relation between Islam and patriarchy. According to al-Hibri, the first group argues that today's Islam is fair and just to women, as can be seen from the views of conservatives in this study. The second group is critical of patriarchal understandings, which it argues are not true

40   *Eva F. Nisa*

Islam. According to al-Hibri, 'this latter group upholds the position that Islam is not only different from Patriarchy, but that through an historical process of cooptation, Patriarchy was able to devour Islam and quickly make it its own after the death of Prophet Muhammad' (1982: 207). The position of this last group is precisely the position upheld by moderate, progressive Islamic and Muslim feminists and KUPI gender-just *ulama* and their networks.

The KUPI gender-just *ulama* and their networks are the current frontrunners for gender equality within the Islamic domain. I have identified KUPI as a historic phase in the struggle against gender inequality in Indonesia. The first KUPI initiative or congress was a collaboration of the three main non-government organisations (NGOs) that consist of progressive young intellectuals of Nahdlatul Ulama backgrounds, the largest moderate Muslim organisation in Indonesia: Rahima, Fahmina and Alimat (Nisa 2019: 437; see also Nisa and Saenong 2022). It was held from 25 to 27 April 2017 at the Kebon Jambu al-Islamy Islamic Boarding School, Cirebon. In the second congress, held from 23 to 26 November 2022 at Universitas Islam Negeri (State Islamic University) Walisongo and Pondok Pesantren Hasyim Asy'ari, AMAN Indonesia and Gusdurian joined Rahima, Fahmina and Alimat as the organisers. Both congresses were attended by more than 1,500 people comprising intellectuals, Muslim and Islamic feminists, women's activists, human rights activists and social movement activists (see also Nisa 2019: 435). In addition, the second congress was attended by gender-just *ulama* and women's activists from 31 countries.

Hijrah (literally, emigration) means transforming into a better Muslim: the current phenomenon of *hijrah* has been especially popularised since 2016 when public figures such as male and female actors and singers increasingly joined Islamist and other conservative movements (Nisa 2022). Several conservative groups are the champions of gender complementarity. The constituents and proponents of *hijrah* movements are part of this current. In this context, the *hijrah* movement is not monolithic: however, various conservative and Islamist movements, especially their young cohorts, have used the term extensively to signify they have experienced changes in the way they understand and practise religion by adopting what they believe is a true understanding of Islam. This is evident from their more 'Islamic' appearance serving as the symbol of their *hijrah*. This can be seen, for example, in women wearing a longer veil or even a *cadar* (face veil) and men wearing non-*isbal* (trousers below the ankle) (Nisa 2022: 5). During some of the *hijrah* events, a free service to alter men's pants to make them above ankle length, or *isbal*, is provided

Chapter 3 Gendering Islamic and Islamist movements in contemporary Indonesia 41

by *hijrah* activists. And for those who have tattoos, a free tattoo removal program is offered, with the tagline: 'I remove my tattoo, I begin my *hijrah*'.

The zeal of these young, well-educated, middle-class Muslims towards *hijrah* movements to return to their religion mirrors the zeal of the earlier generation of young, well-educated conservative Muslims in the 1980s. Suzanne Brenner (1996) nicely captured how young, well-educated, middle-class women became more pious than their parents and believed that religion was the means to avert the moral decline brought by Western modernisation. Women of the Tarbiyah and its political party vehicle Prosperous Justice Party (PKS)[4] are examples of this group.

The swift growth of *hijrah* movements, new types of religious authority, and young conservative interpreters or preachers and their followers (Nisa and Saenong 2022; Saenong 2020) have led many moderate Muslim organisations to revise their *da'wa* path to also involve young tech-savvy Muslims with strong Islamic educational backgrounds to support their agenda to school Indonesians on Islamic gender-just perspectives. Rahima, an NGO founded in 2000 focusing on Islam, gender and women's rights, for example, recently initiated recruitment of *pengkaderan ulama muda* (young Muslim cleric cadres), to perform *da'wa* especially among young Muslims. During Ramadan 2022, when I met Pera Sopariyanti, the chairperson of Rahima, she was excited to share this initiative. She said:

> Yes, we understand that we are behind in producing new young, tech-savvy religious authorities with moderate and progressive understandings of Islam. We need them to counter those of conservative *hijrah* movements and provide alternative moderate views of Islam and gender-just perspectives.[5]

The tech-savvy aspect is important in the selection criteria mentioning 'active on social media'. This signifies that Rahima and other KUPI networks are aware there is a gap in their online campaign and *da'wa*.

Gender-just KUPI networks, like Rahima through @swararahima, also counter conservative groups' potential monopoly of the term *hijrah* by the introduction of *hijrah untuk kemanusiaan perempuan* (*hijrah* for the humanity of women). In its post on 27 July 2021, Rahima explained:

> Several things often mark one's *hijrah*, such as changing clothes, attending a specific Islamic study gathering, no longer making friends with those who do not have the same understandings [of Islam] or looking down on those who are considered to have not conducted '*hijrah*'. The Prophet's

---

4 Partai Keadilan Sejahtera (Prosperous Justice Party) is an Islamist party established in 1998. It was initially called Partai Keadilan or the Justice Party.

5 Interview with Pera Sopariyanti, Jagakarsa, 25 April 2022.

hijrah, in fact, brought together previously hostile groups. The Prophet's *hijrah* was not used to differentiate one another because everything was left to Allah alone [God judges]. (garnered 101 likes, viewed 8 September 2022, 8:58 pm)

Fahmina, an NGO founded in 1999 in Cirebon focusing on the study of the contextualisation of Islamic classical texts and gender, through its Instagram account @mubadalah posted *'Hijrah Yuk'* (Let's *Hijrah*) stating, 'How do we view women who are menstruating? If you still think that women who are menstruating are dirty, they must be exiled, then this is for sure that you haven't *hijrah'* (garnered 1,621 likes, 10 September 2022, 9:16 pm).

Fahmina and Rahima and their networks highlight a new understanding of *hijrah* in relation to gender norms. *Hijrah* in this context means 'to emigrate them [women] from adversity and oppression, including the inequality and injustice often experienced by women and other vulnerable groups' (Rahima, 27 July 2021).

Contemporary discourses on gender equality and gender complementarity

One striking difference in the discussion of gender norms and orders between the KUPI gender-just and *hijrah* movements is how they identify their enemy. KUPI gender-just *ulama* have focused mostly on criticising patriarchy, especially patriarchal understandings of Islam, and patriarchal interpretations of the Qur'an and the Hadith (the narration of the words, deeds or approvals of the Prophet Muhammad), which have long become the source of gender inequality and women's oppression. KUPI *ulama* emphasise gender-just re-readings of Islamic texts to highlight that these texts, especially the Qur'an and the Hadith, contain solid teachings of gender equality (Ahmed 1992). Thus in Indonesia, KUPI gender-just *ulama* can be regarded as the representatives of the Islamic feminism current, to borrow Margot Badran's (2005) term. These Indonesian Islamic feminists focus their work on how to deconstruct patriarchal readings of Islamic teachings to advocate for gender equality. They are not anti-Western feminist ideas when they believe that the ideas are in line with Islamic teachings. This, however, does not mean they glorify all Western imported ideas. Muslim feminists and Islamic feminists are very critical of Western capitalism when it exploits human beings, especially women, as evident from the feminisation of poverty, which is against Islamic teachings.

Conservative Muslims focusing on gender complementarity position Western ideas and values, including gender equality, as their 'enemy'. Samuel Huntington's 'Clash of civilizations' (1993) is actively produced by the proponents of this current. They want to produce pious 'modern' believers of their version of Islam by emphasising gender differences. An example is women of the Islamist political party PKS (Rinaldo 2013). In his study of post-Islamism, which emerged in the early 1990s, Asef Bayat (2013) mentioned a related concept called 'post-Islamist feminism'. Heavily influenced by the Muslim Brotherhood, PKS is considered a representative of post-Islamist moderation in Indonesia (Hasan 2013). According to Bayat, post-Islamist feminism emphasises 'gender equality in all domains', and post-Islamist feminists (in Iran) 'utilized Islamic discourse to push for gender equality within the constraints of the Islamic Republic' (2013: 46). In the case of post-Islamist feminists in Iran, they are not anti-secular feminism. They have even benefited from, and cited the work of, Western feminists like 'Virginia Woolf, Gilman, de Beauvoir and Faludi' (ibid.). In the case of post-Islamist PKS, however, post-Islamist feminism cannot be seen. Ken Miichi also highlighted that PKS's position on gender relations issues remains 'unchanged' and that PKS maintains its 'uncompromising conservative and Islamist position' (2020: 590). Women of the party and their female supporters and constituents have showcased their increased sociopolitical roles (Rinaldo 2013). However, policing women's bodies and women's morality is always the primary concern of the PKS. It is not gender equality the party is fighting for, as in the case of post-Islamist feminists in Iran. PKS women are indeed against gender equality, as for them it is an imported Western concept. Instead, they focus on the notions of 'complementarity', 'cooperation' and 'partnership' between men and women, or the typical complementarity Islamist view of gender equity, not equality (Nisa 2019: 445). The younger generation of *hijrah* movements within various Islamist movements hold the same position as the PKS. They focus on women's moral concerns and Islamic morality to fight against Western influence.

The next section focuses on the digital activism of both currents through which we can see more clearly the positions of both gender-just KUPI progressive Islamic feminists and conservative *hijrah* supporters. These modern Muslim gender activists from various Islamic currents are testimony of the strengthening role of religion in the public sphere. This type of Muslim public also serves as a critique of how modernisation can lead to the confinement of religion to the private sphere.

Hijrah Yuk (Let's *Hijrah*)?!

The battle over gender-related issues across social media is part of a broader battle between moderate and hypertextualist Muslims. Productive discussions on the position of women in Islam appear in various media

44   *Eva F. Nisa*

formats. Before the birth of social media platforms, the translation of books by progressive modernist Muslims and Islamists from other Muslim countries on women's issues was important. This includes the translations of works by Riffat Hassan, Fazlur Rahman, Fatima Mernissi, Nawal el-Saadawi, Amina Wadud, Asghar Ali Engineer, Khaled Abou el-Fadl, and Asma Barlas (Robinson 2008: 112). Their views significantly coloured and shaped the discourses on gender, women and Islam in Indonesia. The NGO Rahima publishes *Swara Rahima* (Voice of Rahima), which features women's issues from Islamic feminist perspectives. *Swara Rahima* accommodates women's aspirations for equality. The content presented by *Swara Rahima* is similar to *Zanan*, a women's magazine launched in 1992 in Iran, which provides in-depth discussion on gender equality. Both magazines feature the re-reading of Islamic texts, including Islamic law, and deconstruct misogynistic and problematic interpretations by providing alternative gender-just readings.

Internet and social media platforms make gender-related issues and campaigns available online. The young members of *hijrah* movements are particularly active in campaigning for gender complementarity, and on morality issues targeting women's bodies and mobilities. The presence of conservative religio-celebrities and the growth of young conservative *mubalig/mubaligah* (male/female preachers) who suddenly become popular, such as those on YouTube, from 2012 onwards, has supplied the proponents of *hijrah* movements with patriarchal understandings of Islam. Their speeches on the position of women in Islam emphasise what they believe as natural differences between men and women, and highlight the reproduction of well-rooted imbalanced or unequal New Order gender orders.

I now focus on two Instagram accounts, @muslimahfeminis (and its networks) and @thisisgender, representing the contestation between gender equality and gender complementarity stances.

@thisisgender

Created by the Center of Gender Studies (CGS) in 2017, @thisisgender is a vocal social media platform of a conservative group closely connected with INSISTS (the Institute for the Study of Islamic Thought and Civilization). INSISTS is a small but vocal Islamist think-tank created by graduates of Malaysia's Institute for Islamic Thought and Civilization. INSISTS, with its leading figures of graduates from the International Islamic University, including Hamid Fahmy Zarkasyi and Adian Husaini, is known for its campaign against religious pluralism and for anti-Western views (van Bruinessen 2013: 45). Similar to its big brother INSISTS, which uses

Chapter 3 Gendering Islamic and Islamist movements in contemporary Indonesia   45

intellectual effort to express conservative thoughts, CGS also aims to respond intellectually to discourses supported by feminists (as mentioned in its post on 16 January 2019).[6]

There are many Instagram accounts under this current, including @indonesiatanpafeminisme (Indonesia without feminism), @ailaindonesia, @salimah.id and many others within their networks, including conservative *ulama*, INSISTS intellectuals, PKS figures, politicians, *hijrah* public figures and new pop preachers or Instagram preacher-cum-influencers that they follow, such as @husainiadian (Adian Husaini), @felixsiauw, @adihidayatofficial, @hanan_attaki, @bachtiarnasir, @salimafillah, @oemar_mita, @muh.zaitun.rasmin, @syekh.alijaber, @drzakir.naik, @aniesbaswedan, @hnwahid (Hidayat Nur Wahid), @aheryawan (Ahmad Heryawan), @cahyadi_takariawan, @fahiraidris, @ajobendri (Bendri Jaisyurrahman), @muhammadfauziladhim, @okisetianadewi, @teukuwisnu, @shireensungkar and @febriantialmeera. As can be seen here, @thisisgender builds networks with conservative *ulama* from various backgrounds, not only Tarbiyah-PKS *ulama*, but also those from Hizbut Tahrir Indonesia (HTI) and various Salafi movements.

@thisisgender focuses on criticising feminism and Western values by quoting the views from INSISTS' main figures, including Dr Hamid Fahmy Zarkasyi:

> Feminism is a movement of lust for anger ... when it was imported into this country, it had the face of a women's empowerment movement. It's good, but the values, principles, ideas, & concepts are still originated from the West. Defended [by its supporters] with full faith, and justified by religious verses. (23 March 2018, garnering 414 likes, viewed 9 September 2022, 1:42 pm)

Supporters actively reproduce Huntington's 'Clash of civilizations' by emphasising the dichotomy between the East (ethical and modest Indonesia) and the West (evil Western culture).

INSISTS is not the only conservative group that has this understanding of gender norms. Women within other conservative groups, such as Salafi groups, Tablighi Jama'at and the currently banned HTI, share similar beliefs. For example, well-known figure within HTI, Felix Siauw, published the novel *Wanita Berkarir Surga* (Women Who Have Careers to Go to Heaven) (2017), which focuses heavily on criticising feminism. With the presence of digital *da'wa*, it becomes easier for young proponents of *hijrah* movements to look for sources to support what they believe is the 'true' understanding of Islam. One characteristic in the discussion of

---

6   CGS has published its work on www.thisisgender.com since 2012.

gender among proponents of *hijrah* movements is the way they glorify the *hikmah* (lessons) from gender inequality by arguing that it is in harmony with the law of nature. They dismiss equal rights for men and women as a Western concept and alien to the Islamic world view. These tech-savvy, well-educated young people are not against women's education, their political rights and economic activities outside their homes. However, again, the noblest role for women is to manage the household and become a mother. Thus, total equality between men and women is erroneous, according to @thisisgender and its networks.

@muslimahfeminis

@muslimahfeminis is part of the KUPI network. It was born one year after @thisisgender, on 17 December 2018. @muslimahfeminis focuses on the notion of *tawhīd* (the Oneness of God) and the humanistic aspect of Islam to support its anti-patriarchal understandings and practices of Islam. It also aims to counter the anti-feminist position of @thisisgender and like-minded accounts. Emphasising that feminism is in line with Islam, @muslimahfeminis posted:

> If feminism means the liberation of women from inhumane acts, isn't Islam very feminist? (23 February 2019, garnering 1,088 likes, viewed 9 September 2022, 2:02 pm)

@muslimahfeminis is brave in directing its captions towards the groups it wants to criticise. For example, this post incorporated hashtags including #thisisgender, #shift, #yukngaji, #beranihijrah and #yukhijrah. The hashtags are identical to the names of conservative Instagram accounts that oppose feminism. The caption for this post is also strong:

> Your faith is very weak when you hear the term feminism? Don't come here, sisters and brothers. This is an account for people with strong faith as we stand up for victims of violence. Thank you.

@muslimahfeminis also reminds those who oppose their struggle for gender-just orders. It posted:

> Sister, do you believe that God is just?
>
> Brother, do you believe that the Prophet brought the mission of justice?
>
> If there is injustice in the name of Allah and the Prophet, what do you think Sister??? ... So ... If there is injustice in the name of the Qur'an and Hadith, it is definitely not from Allah and the Prophet. But from 'human interpretation' which is influenced by culture that discriminates and weakens women. (20 January 2020, garnering 630 likes, viewed 9 September 2022, 5:51 pm)

Chapter 3 Gendering Islamic and Islamist movements in contemporary Indonesia 47

Aligned with this is the saying of the Prophet Muhammad:

> He who honors women is honorable, he who insults them is lowly and mean. (quoted in al-Hibri 1982: 213)

Before the Prophet died, one of his last sayings was:

> I urge you to treat women kindly. They are a trust in your hands. Fear God in His trust. (quoted in al-Hibri 1982: 213)

On *tawhīd* and its relation to gender equality, @muslimahfeminis posted:

> Anti-Patriarchal Tawheed
> Women are not servants of men
> Because both of them are servants only of Allah.
> (22 December 2018, garnering 673 likes, viewed 9 September 2022, 1:59 pm)

Aligned with this is a post by @fahminainstitute—another Fahmina circle Instagram account besides @mubadalah. It posted views on feminism and *tawhīd* of Islam expert and feminist Muslim, Lies Marcoes:

> Feminism is an awareness of rejecting other forms of divinity besides God.
> (2 April 2019, garnering 151 likes, viewed 9 September 2022, 3:09 pm)

@muslimahfeminis also posted:

> Allahu as-Samad
> [To] Allah everything is passed on
> Not on men!
> Because they are female partners who are equal as fellow human beings.
> (22 February 2020, garnering 627 likes, viewed 9 September 2022, 2:12 pm)

Earlier, @thisisgender posted

> Women need to be glorified, not equalised.

With the caption

> Equality is not the solution.
> (29 November 2017, garnering 249 likes, viewed 9 September 2022, 2:19 pm)

The emphasis on *tawhīd* to accentuate gender equality is not new. It has previously been highlighted by many intellectual-cum-gender activists including Fatima Mernissi, Azizah al-Hibri, Musdah Mulia, Amina Wadud and Asma Barlas. Mulia emphasises that the real meaning of *tawhīd* is an important aspect of the principle of gender equality in Islam:

> the conviction that only Allah is God and that nothing or no one equals Allah necessarily means that all humans are equal before Allah, both as

48   *Eva F. Nisa*

His servants and as His *khalīfa* [representatives on earth]. *Tawhīd* imposes the same obligation on men and women, to worship Allah and no other. (Mulia 2007: 56)

Wadud is especially known for her tawhidic paradigm in promoting gender equality. Similar to Mulia, *tawhīd* and *khalīfa* are key terms for Wadud's understandings of gender equality (2008: 437). Her argument quoted below resonates with the campaigns of Islamic and Muslim feminists in Indonesia. Wadud argues:

Since God is the highest conceptual aspect of all, then no person can be greater than another person, especially for mere reasons of gender, race, class, nationality, etc. The tawhidic paradigm then acts as a basic theoretical principle for removing gender asymmetry, which is a kind of satanic logic or shirk, positing priority or superiority to men. Instead, women and men must occupy a relationship of horizontal reciprocity, maintaining the highest place for God in His/Her/Its uniqueness. (Wadud 2008: 437)

Barlas, in her hermeneutic approach to the Qur'an to counter its literalist and patriarchal understandings, also emphasises the importance of *tawhīd*. She highlights that the concept of *tawhīd* emphasises the 'indivisibility of God's Sovereignty to challenge the theory which assumes male as an extension of God's rule' (Barlas 2002: 14) or what al-Hibri (1982: 218) mentions as 'male's divinely ordained and inherent superiority'. Fatima Mernissi, Azizah al-Hibri, Musdah Mulia, Amina Wadud and Asma Barlas are female Muslim scholars whose thoughts have influenced the development of Islamic and Muslim feminists in Indonesia.

Conclusion

Analysing the contestation and social media battles on gender, we can identify the contrasting narratives used by gender-just *ulama* networks and conservative *hijrah* groups. Various strands of conservative *hijrah* groups advocate 'us' versus 'them' in their strong opposition to gender equality. They uphold the essentialist belief in an innate difference between 'evil West' concepts and 'true' Muslim teachings, and argue the latter supports male prerogative. Conservative Muslims continuously focus on gender complementarity and emphasise feminism as their 'enemy'. Huntington's 'Clash of civilizations' is actively produced and reproduced by proponents of this current.

It is noteworthy that some of the *hijrah* conservatives' everyday understandings of gender-related and women's rights issues, including women's rights to education, economic independence and sociopolitical activities, are in accord with those of the majority of the Indonesian

Chapter 3 Gendering Islamic and Islamist movements in contemporary Indonesia 49

public. At the same time, they emphasise that all these women's rights should not lead them to neglect women's main domestic duties. Here lies the reproduction of Indonesia's patriarchal understandings of women's *kodrat*, which signifies role division within the household, ascribing women's motherly domestic role as their primary duty. They underline that differences in rights and duty should be understood within the realm of complementarity. They believe this does not mean injustice. On the contrary, they believe this signifies justice because it is in accord with human nature or female's natural essence. In this context, too, their complementarity rhetoric gets purchased by many Indonesians because this kind of understanding has been rooted in a potent patriarchal culture in Indonesia, and can also be seen within the patriarchal gender ideology promoted by the New Order's 'state ibuism' (motherism).

On the other hand, KUPI gender-just *ulama* strive to introduce their progressive gender equality understandings—based on the spirit of *maṣlaḥa* (wellbeing), *raḥma* (mercy), *mubādala* (reciprocity and mutual understanding), *ʿadāla* (justice) and *musāwa* (equality)—mentioned in Islamic texts, in particular in the Qur'an and Hadith. Deconstructing the well-entrenched patriarchal culture and patriarchal understandings of Islam in Indonesia, which are often used by the conservatives to justify and solidify their position, is not an easy task for them. Therefore, different avenues—online and offline initiatives—need to be covered to educate many more Indonesians to have more progressive gender-just understandings of Islamic teachings to resist patriarchal hegemonies and systems in the country.

This chapter demonstrates that the conservative voices are louder than the moderate progressive voices. This is evident from the number of their media platforms and their active online *daʿwa* presence exceeding those of the moderate, progressive Muslims. The question is, why are they louder? This phenomenon aligns with the nature of conservative (and extremist) voices and the psychology of their political and digital activism, signifying that the voices of conservatives, ultra conservatives and extremists are the loudest and continuously demand centre stage. This is linked closely to the fact that we are facing a resurgence of piety, evident from the mushrooming of *hijrah* movements and the conservative turn within the country.

Moderate and progressive Muslims in Indonesia started their media encounters later than conservative groups. The moderate and progressive Muslims began conducting their *daʿwa* via social media after seeing the success of conservative *ulama*. Although progressive and moderate voices started to conduct digital activism later than conservative voices, after the birth of KUPI in 2017 and the increasing online presence of

50 *Eva F. Nisa*

KUPI gender-just *ulama* with strong Islamic studies backgrounds, we can see that digital activism on gender, Islam and women has become more vibrant.

This chapter shows that KUPI-based Islamic feminist accounts are doing better than the Islamist conservative voices on engaging in intellectual debates pertaining to the position of women in Islam. However, if we want to involve more online campaigns and *da'wa* on women in Islam, unfortunately this victory of KUPI-based Islamic feminist accounts does not mean a lot. Overall, conservative voices are still winning across digital media.

Through their current more active online presence, however, we can see that gender-just *ulama* and Muslim feminists have become more confident in their ability to counter conservative voices. If this initiative continues, Indonesian moderate and progressive Muslims can be optimistic about winning the battle of spreading gender-just understandings of Islam— especially if their online efforts can be converted to winning the offline *hijrah* stages of conservative young people.

Acknowledgements

This research was funded by the Henry Luce Foundation grant, the Global Politics of 'Moderate Islam', led by Dr James Hoesterey and Dr Yasmin Moll. I am grateful to the ANU Indonesia Project, Professor Blane Lewis and the three convenors of the 2022 Indonesia Update, Dr Angie Bexley, Dr Sarah Dong and Dr Diahhadi Setyonaluri. I also thank Professor Kathryn Robinson for her valuable and constructive comments.

References

Ahmed, Leila. 1984. 'Early feminist movements in the Middle East: Turkey and Egypt'. In *Muslim Women*, edited by Freda Hussain, 111–23. St Martin's Press. doi.org/10.4324/9781003074519-8

Ahmed, Leila. 1992. *Women and Gender in Islam: Historical Roots of a Modern Debate*. Yale University Press.

Badran, Margot. 2005. 'Between secular and Islamic feminism/s: Reflections on the Middle East and beyond'. *Journal of Middle East Women's Studies* 1(1): 6–28. doi.org/10.2979/MEW.2005.1.1.6

Barlas, Asma. 2002. *Believing Women in Islam: Unreading Patriarchal Interpretations of the Qur'an*. University of Texas Press.

Barlas, Asma. 2008. 'Engaging Islamic feminism: Provincializing feminism as a master narrative'. In *Islamic Feminism: Current Perspectives*, edited by Anitta Kynsilehto, 15–24. University of Tampere.

Basarudin, Azza. 2016. *Humanizing the Sacred: Sisters in Islam and the Struggle for Gender Justice in Malaysia*. University of Washington Press.

Chapter 3 Gendering Islamic and Islamist movements in contemporary Indonesia 51

Bayat, Asef. 2013. 'The making of post-Islamist Iran'. In *Post-Islamism: The Changing Faces of Political Islam*, edited by Asef Bayat, 35–70. Oxford University Press. doi.org/10.1093/acprof:oso/9780199766062.003.0002

Brenner, Suzanne. 1996. 'Reconstructing self and society: Javanese Muslim women and "the veil"'. *American Ethnologist* 23(4): 673–97. doi.org/10.1525/ae.1996.23.4.02a00010

Hasan, Noorhaidi. 2013. 'Post-Islamist politics in Indonesia'. In *Post-Islamism: The Changing Faces of Political Islam*, edited by Asef Bayat, 157–82. Oxford University Press. doi.org/10.1093/acprof:oso/9780199766062.003.0006

Hefner, Robert W. 2003. 'Islamizing capitalism: On the founding of Indonesia's first Islamic bank'. In *Shari'a and Politics in Modern Indonesia*, edited by Arskal Salim and Azyumardi Azra, 148–67. Institute of Southeast Asian Studies. doi.org/10.1355/9789812305206-011

al-Hibri, Azizah. 1982. 'A study of Islamic herstory: Or how did we ever get into this mess?' *Women's Studies International Forum* 5(2): 207–19. doi.org/10.1016/0277-5395(82)90028-0

Huntington, Samuel. 1993. 'The clash of civilizations?' *Foreign Affairs* 72(3): 22–49. doi.org/10.2307/20045621

Miichi, Ken. 2020. 'Post-Islamism revisited: The response of Indonesia's Prosperous Justice Party (PKS) to gender-related issues'. *Muslim World* 110(4): 589–604. doi.org/10.1111/muwo.12367

Mir-Hosseini, Ziba. 1996. 'Stretching the limits: A feminist reading of the Shari'a in post-Khomeini Iran'. In *Feminism and Islam: Legal and Literary Perspectives*, edited by Mai Yamani, 285–319. New York University Press.

Mir-Hosseini, Ziba. 2006. 'Muslim women's quest for equality: Between Islamic law and feminism'. *Critical Inquiry* 32(4): 629–45. doi.org/10.1086/508085

Moghissi, Haideh. 1999. *Feminism and Islamic Fundamentalism: The Limits of Postmodern Analysis*. Zed Books.

Mulia, Musdah Siti. 2007. 'Tauhid: A source of inspiration for gender justice'. In *Dawrah Fiqh Concerning Women*, edited by KH Husein Muhammad, Faqihuddin Abdul Kodir, Lies Marcoes Natsir and Marzuki Wahid, 39–59. Fahmina Institute.

Mulia, Musdah Siti. 2013. 'Hukum Islam dan dinamika feminisme dalam organisasi Nahdhatul Ulama' [Islamic law and the dynamics of feminism in Nahdhatul Ulama]. *Al-ahkam* 23(1): 37–56. doi.org/10.21580/ahkam.2013.23.1.72

Nadjib, Ala'i, ed. 2015. *Gus Dur di Mata Perempuan* [Gus Dur in the eyes of women]. Gading Press.

Nisa, Eva F. 2019. 'Muslim women in contemporary Indonesia: Online conflicting narratives behind the Women Ulama Congress'. *Asian Studies Review* 43(3): 434–54. doi.org/10.1080/10357823.2019.1632796

Nisa, Eva F. 2021. 'Women and Islamic movements'. In *Handbook of Islamic Sects and Movements*, edited by Muhammad Afzal Upal and Carole M. Cusack, 151–75. Brill. doi.org/10.1163/9789004435544_010

Nisa, Eva F. 2022. *Face-Veiled Women in Contemporary Indonesia*. Routledge. doi.org/10.4324/9781003246442

Nisa, Eva F. and Farid F. Saenong. 2022. 'Relegitimizing religious authority: Indonesian gender-just "Ulamā" amid COVID-19'. *Religions* 13(6): 485. doi.org/10.3390/rel13060485

Nurlaelawati, Euis and Arskal Salim. 2017. 'Female judges at Indonesian religious courtrooms: Opportunities and challenges to gender equality'. In *Women Judges in the Muslim World: A Comparative Study of Discourse and Practice*, edited by Nadia Sonneveld and Monika Lindbekk, 101–22. Brill. doi.org/10.1163/9789004342200_005

Rinaldo, Rachel. 2013. *Mobilizing Piety: Islam and Feminism in Indonesia*. Oxford University Press. doi.org/10.1093/acprof:oso/9780199948109.001.0001

Robinson, Kathryn. 2008. 'Islamic cosmopolitics, human rights and anti-violence strategies in Indonesia'. In *Anthropology and the New Cosmopolitanism: Rooted, Feminist and Vernacular Perspectives*, edited by Pnina Werbner, 111–33. Berg. doi.org/10.4324/9781003084617-8

Robinson, Kathryn. 2009. *Gender, Islam and Democracy in Indonesia*. Routledge. doi.org/10.4324/9780203891759

Saenong, Faried F. 2020. 'Decoding online Islam: New religious authorities and social-media encounters'. *Alternative Spirituality and Religion Review* 11: 161–78. doi.org/10.5840/asrr202192874

Saenong, Faried F. 2021. 'Nahdlatul Ulama (NU): A grassroots movement advocating moderate Islam'. In *Handbook of Islamic Sects and Movements*, edited by Muhammad Afzal Upal and Carole M. Cusack, 129–50. Brill. doi.org/10.1163/9789004435544_009

Schlehe, Judith and Eva F. Nisa. 2016. *The Meanings of Moderate Islam in Indonesia: Alignments and Dealignments of Azharites*. Occasional Paper No. 31. Southeast Asian Studies, University of Freiburg.

Stivens, Maila. 1998. 'Sex, gender and the making of the new Malay middle classes'. In *Gender and Power in Affluent Asia*, edited by Krishna Sen and Maila Stivens, 87–126. Routledge.

Van Bruinessen, Martin. 2013. 'Overview of Muslim organizations, associations and movements in Indonesia'. In *Contemporary Developments in Indonesian Islam: Explaining the 'Conservative Turn'*, edited by Martin van Bruinessen, 21–59. ISEAS Publishing. doi.org/10.1355/9789814414579-006

Wadud, Amina. 2008. 'Foreword: Engaging Tawhid in Islam and feminisms'. *International Feminist Journal of Politics* 10(4): 435–38. doi.org/10.1080/14616740802393858

4 Transgender citizenship and public gender in Indonesia

Benjamin Hegarty

Debates about the place of transgender, gay and lesbian people are a prominent feature of Indonesian political life in the *reformasi* period. Over the past ten years, same-sex sexuality and gender nonconformity have come to be articulated more explicitly as incompatible with national values.[1] Although initially not the primary targets of the politically motivated violence aimed at gay men following the end of the New Order in 1998 (see Boellstorff 2004), transgender Indonesians have increasingly faced exclusion on the national stage (Wijaya 2019). This is something of a shift, particularly for one transgender population known as *warias*, who have been a visible and widely acknowledged part of Indonesian society since the late 1960s.[2] While the acceptance of *warias* cannot be overstated,

---

1 Since 2016, in Indonesian media and politics, 'LGBT' emerged as a prominent site of struggle in determining the boundaries of national identity. Contrary to framings of Indonesian national identity as exclusively heterosexual, Indonesian queer studies scholars have of course identified how gay, lesbian and transgender identities are 'inextricably linked to claims of national belonging, and are deployed to forge a sense of community and political allegiance among Indonesian sexual minorities to resist heteronormativity' (Wijaya 2019: 135).

2 *Waria* is a term that combines the first syllable of the Indonesian word for 'woman' (*wanita*) and the last syllable of the word for 'man' (*pria*). It replaced an existing portmanteau term, *wadam*, created in 1968 by combining the names of the figures Adam and Eve (Hawa), common to accounts of human origin in the Old Testament and the Qur'an. In the late 2010s, a new term, *transpuan* (a portmanteau combining transgender and *perempuan*), began to be used alongside *waria* Hegarty (2022a). While both terms are to some degree interchangeable, I use *waria* in this chapter because it is the category that has remained prominent in efforts to impose order over public gender both during and after the New Order.

during the New Order they were able to obtain recognition in proximity to international norms of feminine beauty, as reflected in their established reputation as skilled salon workers and performers. While not every *waria* is a beauty expert, of course, these fields of work emerged as historically important for claiming acceptance on the national stage. The politically motivated efforts to tie *warias* to a putatively foreign 'LGBT' imaginary during the *reformasi* period marked a disconcerting shift. Nevertheless, for *warias*, being seen and valued by others remains an important avenue for achieving official forms of recognition.

Much of the discussion about growing hostility towards LGBT Indonesians has approached these transformations as a problem related to shifting currents of sexual morality at the national level. Often, analyses centre the role played by the consolidation and extension of Islamic norms and morality relative to national identity (Wijaya and Davies 2019: 160). This is certainly one part of the picture. Yet what this focus on morality conceals is the fact that *warias* have long been addressed in terms of the regulation of public order at the scale of the city and district. Indeed, the initial impetus for the creation and recognition of the term *waria*, as I describe at length elsewhere (Hegarty 2021), was the desire among city officials in Jakarta to solve the problem of gender nonconformity on city streets. *Warias* have long chafed against state projects that deploy gender as a component of public order, and have had to negotiate this patchwork of regulations accordingly. For this reason, *warias'* capacity to draw on public gender as a resource to lay claims to recognition—while piecemeal—provides important clues for understanding the tensions and fragility of citizenship in Indonesia today.

In this chapter, I outline the historical role of the regulation of public gender in shaping the boundaries of full citizenship in Indonesia. In referring to public gender, I emphasise the association between appearance and bodily comportment (such as clothing, make-up and hairstyle) associated with masculinity and femininity, and its performance and reception in public space. After describing the shifting meanings of public gender during the New Order (1965–1998), I reflect on the implications of this history for the narrowing of who can participate in public life in the *reformasi* period. Rather than disappearing, the regulation of public gender—and associated forms of comportment usually glossed as linked to shifting moral currents—has intensified since 1998, culminating in the passage into law of the revised Criminal Code in December 2022. Why is it that during *reformasi* in Indonesia, public gender is a key site where concrete efforts (in the form of control over the body in space) determine the boundaries of citizenship? How has the regulation of public gender through access to space, terms well understood by *warias*, shifted in the

Chapter 4 Transgender citizenship and public gender in Indonesia 55

context of decentralisation, in which district- and city-level governments have greater authority? What does a focus on transgender citizenship reveal about patterns of continuity and change between the New Order and the *reformasi* period?

An extant analytical focus on gender and sexuality within the domain of morality has meant that most accounts situate the effects of these transformations on *warias* and other citizens as distinct from the domain of politics. Contrary to this view, I argue that rather than linked to morality alone, public gender must be viewed as part and parcel of political and economic processes. The shifting position of *warias* from the New Order through to *reformasi* is important precisely because it reveals how they have been figures through whom the public regulation of gender has been articulated in concrete ways. Nevertheless, the visibility achieved by *warias* provided one way for them to claim the recognition associated with citizenship, even if this recognition rested in part on a consolidation of their position as a public nuisance on city streets. A focus on public gender highlights the centrality of economically stratified access to space, and the jurisdictions that regulate it, to defining citizenship in Indonesia. The consequences of this history have been significant during the *reformasi* period, as cities and districts have achieved greater authority to introduce and implement their own regulations. One unintended consequence of decentralisation has been a concerted effort to govern the public comportment of women and *warias* in particular. Throughout Indonesia, regional authorities have introduced regulations that define the times of day that people can be visible, and what they can do in public space. These efforts to define access to public space and scope for mobility through the imposition of gender norms do not only reflect a preoccupation with morality. Rather, public gender authorises who can participate in public life and on what basis, reflecting its centrality to broader economic and political processes.

Public gender

A significant body of ethnographic and historical research in Indonesia and Southeast Asia has argued that gender and sexuality in the region was pluralistic where it retained a connection to broader ritual and social practices. Michael Peletz observed how, under certain settings, 'gender-transgressive behaviour was both legitimate and sanctified and could bring considerable religious merit and prestige to its practitioners' (2009: 36). One well-known example often given is that of the *bissu*, a spiritual practitioner or shaman accorded a high status within Bugis cosmology of southern Sulawesi, through their ability to 'demonstrate in

56   *Benjamin Hegarty*

dress and behavior the merging of both the male and female principles, and the replacement of profane with sacred space and time … a symbolic androgynous state that re-establishes primordial conditions' (Andaya 2000: 36; see also Davies 2007). Although human societies around the world do invoke dualisms, including those that extend to the human body (Lambek 1998), these are by no means reducible to binary models of sex and gender as they are understood on modern Euro-American terms. Concepts of male and female, as they are understood to correspond with a specific arrangement of corporeality, sexuality, psychological state and appearance, rely on an entanglement of biological and cultural processes (Atkinson 1990; Helliwell 2000). Even a cursory look at Indonesian history reveals that the meanings of what it is to be and appear as male, female or another category are not stable but are subject to change.

From the seventeenth century, the spread of secular scientific knowledge that accompanied colonisation along with the growth of modernist Islam resulted in a rearrangement in the public meanings of gender throughout Indonesia. Appearances gradually came to be understood as reflecting innate qualities of the individual, mapped onto an understanding of male and female as different types of persons, who occupy different spaces and perform different economic and social roles (Blackwood 2005). These shifts did not stand alone, but took place in a context in which public appearances had long been central to defining an individual's social position, with dress serving as a barometer of subtle shifts in racial and gendered hierarchies (Nordholt 1997; van der Meer 2020).[3] In the postcolonial period, masculinity and femininity ascended to become the primary though often unstated markers of civilised status and demonstration of the performance of a modern national identity.

The immediate post-independence period saw the beginning of concerted efforts to regulate public gender in more explicit ways. In several cases, this involved sanctions against the visibility of those who did not conform to emerging gender norms. What is notable is just how widespread efforts to enforce gender normativity in public were in the immediate postcolonial period, with similar reports emerging in different parts of the new nation. In southern Sulawesi during the Darul Islam rebellion of the 1950s, *bissu* were forced to shave their heads and renounce

---

3   It is notable that definitions of gender on binary terms borrowed much of the vocabulary and legal definitions previously granted to race as a means of managing the population in the Dutch East Indies. I discuss the way the postcolonial state's management of gender as an imposition of a monopoly on the recognition of public difference was shaped by histories of governing race in the colonial state in my book (Hegarty 2022b: chapter 1).

Chapter 4 Transgender citizenship and public gender in Indonesia

their ritual objects and practices. Similarly, in the city of Surabaya in East Java in the 1960s, the leaders of *ludruk* theatre troupes began to impose a strict boundary between on-stage and off-stage performances among actors. As one transgender performer, who both played the role of a woman on stage and dressed as a woman off stage, explained, 'like other players I once had hair halfway to my waist. I curled, arranged it like a girl—but then came embarrassment [*malu*] and progress [*madju*]. I cut it off' (Peacock 1968: 206–7). That cutting hair is mentioned specifically in events that took place in different parts of Indonesia reflects its significance, both to those subjects who experienced such violence as well as to those seeking to exert control over gender norms. These accounts of the increased regulation of public gender in the 1950s and 1960s highlight how the consolidation of the boundaries of Indonesian citizenship proceeded apace with sanctions imposed on those whose public appearance troubled the state's monopoly on recognition.

The centrality of public gender to definitions of citizenship was reflected in the state's struggle to more clearly impose a binary model of gender through definitions of heterosexuality as a natural form of human difference. Evelyn Blackwood (2007: 295) referred to the 'deployment of gender' to describe how the New Order state normalised definitions of acceptable sexuality around an ideal of heterosexual reproduction. State ideology framed the nuclear family and its gender arrangements as reflecting a natural complementarity between men and women with its origins in tradition (Boellstorff 2005; Suryakusuma 1996). As feminist scholars have demonstrated, the definition of women as belonging within the domestic sphere limited their political participation and established a gendered format for the economic doctrine of development, or *pembangunan* (Suryakusuma 2011). Femininity was, however, not as easily disciplined as the images of women as housewives within the New Order family would suggest (Jones 2010). In particular, a growing consumer capitalist economy gave rise to images of women outside the domestic realm. As Suzanne Brenner observed towards the end of the New Order, the 'tensions and anxieties that accompanied political repression, rapid and uneven modernization, and economic inequality and instability were displaced onto the figures of woman and the family' (Brenner 1999: 36). For *warias* too, femininity was a form of bodily cultivation that held an array of meanings that were distinct but not entirely separate from the femininity of women (Hegarty 2018). During the New Order, a specific configuration of binary gender that tied the accomplishment of masculinity and femininity to development was an increasingly central way to determine both the limits of participation in public life and the internal contours of citizenship.

58   *Benjamin Hegarty*

Tracing the historical position of *warias* in relation to broader efforts to regulate public gender helps to better assess the specific dynamics that generate forms of exclusion and opportunities for recognition. Rather than forms of discipline tied to women's position in the domestic sphere stemming from a unilinear state ideology, *warias* more frequently encountered exclusion from public life as regulations addressing public morality (*kesusilaan umum*) and public order (*ketertiban umum*). These regulations, gradually refined during the late 1960s and early 1970s, rested on managing access to space. As such, they highlight the historical importance of the scales of the city and the district in governing gender and sexuality in Indonesia. Looking at *warias'* encounters with the state in terms of concrete efforts to control public comportment and mobility allows for an interpretation of gender as a more dynamic, and potentially unruly, process of recognition. *Warias* highlight how efforts to control public gender from the municipal to the national level have opened new opportunities to be seen, but also for that visibility to become a target of surveillance and punishment.

A legal but nonconforming status

To better understand the possibilities and risks of the recognition and regulation of public gender, I turn to the dawn of what *warias* referred to as their 'golden age' in Jakarta at the beginning of the New Order. In August 1968, a delegation of 22 *warias* met with Ali Sadikin, the governor of Jakarta. The respected daily newspaper *Kompas* reported that a representative named Lidya had addressed the governor directly. She claimed to speak on behalf of a staggering 15,000 *warias* estimated to be resident in the city at the time. At the governor's official residence, located in an exclusive enclave in the centre of the city, Lidya made a plea for assistance. She stated that *warias* were subject to intolerable forms of exclusion and abuse at the hands of their fellow citizens. When they appeared during the day in public places wearing women's clothing, Lidya explained, they faced verbal and physical abuse. To avoid such abuse, they gathered clandestinely, meeting at night in obscure locations, such as along highways and railway tracks. In a practice that stretched back to the colonial era, municipal police detained *warias* in police raids on the public places where they gathered. Because of this, the public associated them with moral impropriety and public indecency. In response to their predicament, Sadikin—a respected former naval officer—not only declared that Lidya was a member of a group 'whose social rights must be protected' but also called on the city's residents to come together to help them (*Kompas* 1968: 2). Although gender nonconformity of various kinds

Chapter 4 Transgender citizenship and public gender in Indonesia 59

had long formed a part of Jakarta's urban fabric, the city government now evaluated it as a matter requiring official concern and action.

One of the efforts to improve the condition of *warias* concerned the introduction of new terminology. Although its use in official policy was uneven, by 1968 Sadikin himself referred to *wadam*, the new term created by combining the names of Adam and Eve (see footnote 2). The initial reason for the adoption of *wadam*, an understanding expressed by Lidya that appears to have been shared by Sadikin, was that the term served as a vehicle to articulate a desire to improve their social status. This new term, *warias* reasoned, would act as a vehicle for respectability. It served as a modern substitute for the older term *banci*, which had acquired an offensive meaning akin to an abusive term of address. These new terms of address mattered chiefly because they contributed to an improved public image. According to *warias'* own recollections of life in Sadikin's Jakarta, the adoption of these new terms was accompanied by a higher standard of modern feminine appearance and presentation among *warias* across all public settings. Together, such strategies were employed to leave behind the abusive catcalls of *banci*, which had acquired venomous force as a lewd insult. Identification with these new terms was described to me as emblematic of a new era in which *warias* strove to fashion themselves as respected citizens of the city.

This claim for recognition, one that parallels contemporary struggles among *warias*, emerged in close dialogue with regulations governing public space in the city. Although police raids continued, Ali Sadikin's intervention marked a change. For the first time, the adoption of consistent standards of modern feminine beauty could render them a more acceptable part of modern Indonesian society. This intervention was laudable but not necessarily premised on a desire to expand the visibility of *warias*. Rather, the city's interest originated from reports in the popular press that *warias'* growing visibility on city streets was a disruption of public order. Following urban studies scholar Mariana Valverde, this recognition represented belonging on conditional terms as a kind of legal but nonconforming status. According to Valverde, 'legal non-conforming use' is an ambiguous but common category of planning law which reflects how 'governing urban disorder through embodied, experiential, and relational categories is a necessary component of contemporary urban governance' (2011: 280). The ambiguous legal recognition granted to *warias* as a nonconforming status in Jakarta in 1968 can be interpreted in terms of a specific type of discipline that is characteristic of the unpredictable format of governing space. The history of *warias* in Jakarta therefore represents a different style of governance from the models of discipline usually considered more exemplary of the modern state, including

60   *Benjamin Hegarty*

that of New Order gender ideology (Suryakusuma 2011). Rather than a unilinear or top-down approach, attempts to enforce subjective standards of public gender proceeded through the uneven codification of gender nonconformity on spatial grounds. The heterogeneity of municipal governance allowed *warias* to achieve a form of recognition that rested on the fact that they did not fit the state's model of binary gender. Rather than full acceptance, therefore, this form of recognition extended concessions to *warias* to be visible only under specific conditions.

That *warias* would express a desire to pass through public space unhindered was understandable; in the 1950s and 1960s they appear to have faced fierce forms of exclusion from public life. Oral history accounts given by *warias* in the mid-2010s about the 1950s consistently included narratives that they faced the prospect of rejection from residents if they walked through city streets dressed in women's clothing during the day. As a moral concern that was addressed on spatial grounds, *warias* were ensnared in a wider logic through which the appearance of femininity on city streets was adjudicated and disciplined. *Warias* and female sex workers were drawn together through an overlapping set of spatial logics governing their appearance and movement on city streets. But although police raids on *warias* who gathered at night in dark corners of the city continued in the early years of Sadikin's tenure, this period also saw the introduction of more wide-reaching regulations that targeted the appearance of gender nonconformity in the city. These new policies did not seek to remove *warias* entirely from view, but made them more responsible for the status of their own public visibility. The municipal government encouraged them to limit their appearances to more respectable settings and to improve their appearances as a way to take charge of how they were received by the public. Far from a superficial matter, the adequate accomplishment of public gender offered access to new spaces and forms of recognition.

The legal regulations that targeted *warias* on the basis of their unwanted appearance in public, before and after 1968, were the twin concepts of *ketertiban umum* and *kesusilaan umum*, mentioned earlier. Although the concept preceded the New Order, 'public order' was a key component of military rule, serving as the initial justification for Suharto's ascendancy and key to his claims to ongoing legitimacy (Barker 2001). The twin disciplinary norms of public morality and public order overlapped on city streets, where attempts to define what public behaviour was 'moral' on categorical terms were thwarted by the ambiguity characteristic of urban life. In 1972, a regulation on public order issued by the Jakarta government stated, 'any person whose performance of moral acts that disturb public order are banned from being on the street, the park, and in public places'.

Listed among such banned behaviours were kissing and congregating in city parks at night. In line with this understanding, gender and sexual nonconformity were not subject to specific codes related to individualised forms of pathology. Rather, the city wielded public gender as a way to limit who had access to space and on what basis. Even as they were framed as a disturbance to public order, however, *warias'* visibility did provide them with access to a fragile form of recognition in the New Order city.

Governing gender in the city

The concept of the 'public' at work in regulating gender is shaped by enduring historical patterns that are tied to the capacity of district and city governments to regulate access to space in Indonesia. As described above, since at least 1972, the Jakarta government regulated *warias* and other problem bodies on spatial terms. The period since the end of the New Order in 1998 has seen the intensification of decentralisation and regional autonomy. The number of regional authorities—provinces, cities and districts—have proliferated, giving rise to new law-making bodies comprising officials elected at the local level, and concomitant regulations. This process has undoubtedly seen a rearrangement in political and economic power, in part a response by local actors against the centralising tendencies of military rule (Booth 2011). At the same time, much of the legal infrastructure for regional autonomy has been designed to ensure that entire provinces do not break away, reflected in the greater authority granted to smaller district units that do not necessarily have a unified identity (Aspinall and Fealy 2003). While certainly resulting in greater democratic participation at the local level, the sheer number of new districts created since 1999 has resulted in confusion in a range of areas, ranging from taxation to human rights. Some critics have gone so far as to describe decentralisation as resulting in 'legal disorder', a view sustained by uncertainty over the extent of law-making powers and confusion over how they are to be managed administratively (Butt 2010). Yet what appears consistent across jurisdictions is the introduction of new regulations on the grounds of protecting public order and morality, including those that explicitly target *warias'* gender nonconformity. Even as decentralisation might be seen as a period of 'disorder' from a legal and administrative perspective, the fact is that for women and transgender populations the process has resulted in an intensification of public order.

Similarities between many of these regulations highlight they do not reflect the imposition of local religious or cultural norms and traditions related to gender, sexuality or kinship. This casts doubt on the claims made by law-making bodies that justify regulations governing women and transgender populations on grounds of cultural or religious specificity. Provisions in the revised Criminal Code passed into law in December 2022 consolidated these concessions to regional authorities by purportedly recognising any 'living law' (for a description of the meaning of 'living law', see Butt 2019). Although claims to timeless tradition often conceal that efforts to craft a suitable performance of regional identity are a cultural product of the present (Long 2007), what is most notable about these district-level regulations is precisely their uniformity between districts. Given the scope available to districts and cities to create their own laws, and the diversity of understandings of gender and kinship found throughout Indonesia, one would expect quite a range of difference. To the contrary, however, almost every law is written in a similar way, with a significant majority 'wholly or partly copy-pasted from region to region across Indonesia' (Katjasungkana and Wieringa 2016: 12). Placing the historical role of the district and the city more central to examining political change during *reformasi*, I suggest, reveals the centrality of public gender to the Indonesian state's efforts to impose a monopoly on recognition.

The implications of expanded numbers of districts and cities and their scope to pass regulations targeting public gender were clear from early on in the *reformasi* period. In the immediate aftermath of the 1999 Law on Decentralisation, scholars highlighted the troubling trend towards regulations at the district level that sought to control women's appearance, comportment and movement through space (see, for example, Satriyo 2003). Since this time, several districts have introduced regulations that explicitly ban *warias* on the basis that they disrupt 'public order and morality'. While *warias* were addressed through public nuisance regulations during the New Order, in the *reformasi* period, *warias* are more explicitly addressed as social ills or in terms of sexual deviance by city and district governments. City Regulation 3/2015 of the Mayor of Bukkittingi in the Province of West Sumatra Concerning Public Peace and Order defines *waria* as 'men who prefer to play the role of women in everyday life', and states that 'persons are prohibited from behaving as *warias* who carry out activities which disturb peace and order, by gathering in public places such as parks, roads and other public facilities and engaging in prostitution'. In Banten, western Java, City Regulation 2/2010 of Serang City Concerning the Prevention and Management of Social Diseases addresses *warias*—defined as 'males with a soul or behaviour of a woman'—in terms of visibility linked to public sexuality. A round of more recent regulations targets 'sexual deviance' more explicitly, including in the City of Bogor in the Province of West Java Regional Regulation 10/2021 Concerning the Prevention and Countermeasures against Sexually Deviant Behaviours. In it, *warias* are

Chapter 4 Transgender citizenship and public gender in Indonesia   63

included in a rather peculiar list classifying 'deviant behaviours' that includes 'any sexual behaviour or activity that is religiously, culturally, socially, psychologically and/or medically defined as sexually perverse behaviour'. The wording of these regulations from geographically and culturally distinct regions is almost identical. Rather than a fragmented format of governance tied to a specific locality rooted in place-based traditions, then, the growth of regional- and municipal-level laws and regulations reflects an effort to impose a uniform national body.

Such regional regulations are not criminal but civil offences, and as a result are punishable by fines, rehabilitation, or a combination of the two. Yet this distinction is not entirely clear-cut. Components of national laws, such as the 2022 Criminal Code and 2008 Pornography Law, draw on a logic of public order. This reflects how the regulation of public gender at the level of the city has played a central role in mediating the relationship between everyday practices of recognition and emergent definitions of citizenship in the modern state. *Warias* are key to this process because they are an object of knowledge that helped to clarify the boundaries of appearances, a recognisable format for determining the relationship between binary gender and citizenship. During the New Order, binary gender was established as a locus of efforts to determine the authenticity of state citizenship. Drawing on an existing regulatory apparatus that could discipline individuals based on their appearance, city authorities made every effort to hide gender nonconformity from view on the basis that they were protecting a seeing public. The city drew on existing regulations concerned directly with spatial control to pursue this end, including the provision of additional lighting and fencing and the deployment of police to undertake raids on public places. More than this, however, a concern for the visibility of *warias* was a crucial step in establishing clearer definitions of gender normativity.

Although public gender is central to determining the boundaries of full belonging in Indonesian society, so too does the adequate performance of masculinity and femininity rest on middle-class norms. The entanglement of class and gender reflects the economic dynamics at play in generating forms of exclusion that exceed a framework of morality alone. In the mid-2010s, several districts introduced regulations concerning access to public space, particularly concerned with busking and begging. The Special Region of Yogyakarta, where I undertook fieldwork in 2014 and 2015, introduced Regional Regulation 1/2014 on the Management of Homelessness and Busking. This regulation subjected buskers and beggars to expanded punitive measures including the risk of arbitrary detention for the purposes of rehabilitation in a facility funded and run by the regional government. Following detention in a raid, the city police took those arrested to a facility for a range of assessments regarding their mental health, their residency status in the city in which they are caught, and, most importantly, their 'potential to become productive citizens'. In the case of Yogyakarta, one key criteria for evaluating who belonged in public space was whether an individual was 'dressed impolitely or inappropriately for the place'. Given how arbitrary and subjective such a standard is, *warias* found themselves detained for simply walking down the street wearing women's clothing and make-up.

At the same time, *warias* during the period of my fieldwork drew on their visibility to make distinctive claims to recognition in ways that paralleled those made during the early New Order. At one meeting between city officials and *warias* that I attended in February 2015, I observed a fierce exchange between municipal Satuan Polisi Pamong Praja (Satpol PP) officers and *warias*. When the officers asserted that, so long as *warias* did the right thing, they would not face harassment, one *waria* jumped to her feet. Drawing out small bags of snacks from her bag, she announced she had made them to sell in her neighbourhood. She explained how she had been chased by Satpol PP officers on several occasions. In tears, she raised her voice, proclaiming that all she was trying to do was make a living. In an act of political theatre, she walked around the room, throwing a bag of snacks in front of each seated official. She had cleverly demonstrated the link between public gender and economic participation in civic life: an experience shared by *warias* with many members of the urban poor, some of whom were also gathered in the room that day.

Such experiences in the *reformasi* city serve as a reminder of the role of public gender—in ways that are both explicit and implicit—in governing access to public space. These are not only a process linked to morality, but are centrally implicated in political and economic control. Nevertheless, *warias* reveal how gender is not only a site where the boundaries of belonging and state citizenship are defined and regulated, but opens new opportunities to contest exclusion and violence. After the passage of the revised Criminal Code in December 2022, which both places new limits on gendered and sexual arrangements and extends further authority to lower-level structures of governance to regulate them, it is not only *warias* who are ensnared in a regime of public gender. A range of Indonesians who do not adhere to a specific form of public gender for any number of reasons—simply for wearing the wrong clothing in the wrong place, or who cohabit with kin who are not recognised by the law—might find themselves at risk of detention, rehabilitation and even criminal charges.

Conclusion

The paradox of the recognition extended to *warias* by virtue of their legal but nonconforming status in the early New Order provides a useful framework to evaluate the enduring role of gendered appearances in the *reformasi* period. Even as *warias* narrated their movement from a golden age that started in 1968 as a success that heralded expanded possibilities for participation in public life, at night and during the day, more recent events suggest that their place in municipal and national public life is far from assured. Of particular concern is the relationship between the acceptance of *warias* and understandings of the 'public' or *masyarakat umum* that have become naturalised within Indonesian social life.

Anxieties about gender nonconformity, I suggest, have long helped to buttress a definition of the public premised on exclusion as the necessary price for the maintenance of order. The Jakarta municipal government's efforts to regulate gender nonconformity in public space during the New Order resulted in unlikely coalitions. Various actors, including charismatic *waria* leaders, the city governor, the municipal police and municipal social welfare officers made every effort to restrict gender nonconformity to certain settings under strict conditions. To *warias*, this was a new vehicle for obtaining recognition. But without an adequate set of legal and social frameworks in which *warias* could improve their position in society, such efforts to obtain belonging were fragile. The meanings of gender nonconformity remained ambiguous, representing an exemplar of feminine beauty in some contexts and posing a threat to public order in others. Living in the shadow of regulations designed to limit their visibility but which produced that visibility as one of its very effects, *warias* navigated their designation as a disturbance to public order by demanding recognition from a city governor. Similarly, even as such regulations were intended to discipline them and produce a more presentable appearance, *warias* harnessed this ambiguous recognition to accomplish respectability and belonging.

Reformasi saw the expansion of the role of districts and cities under a program of decentralisation, leading to increased concern to address public gender as a component of order. *Warias*, women, gay men and lesbians, and Indonesians from lower socioeconomic classes have all been the target of regional regulations that appear to seek to protect a middle-class seeing public. The district and the city, in turn, has served as a scale where the political mobilisation of support for the criminalisation of same-sex sexuality as a defence of public order has been tested prior to similar developments at the national level.[4] This dynamic reveals the enduring role of public gender in exercising control over the boundaries of full citizenship in Indonesia. The regulation of public gender may be one context where a sense of national unity is achieved, helping to manage or displace the effects of other potentially destabilising identities in the form of ethnic or regional difference. Districts and regions articulate what they see as a suitable and safe format for 'unity in diversity' by focusing on the regulation of public gender. This quest for a uniformity that can manage undesirable differences in the body of the nation has come at the expense of lower-class women and transgender populations. For them in particular, public space has become increasingly suffocating, as they must navigate an array of disciplinary mechanisms that limit their political and economic participation. This is one great disappointment of the *reformasi* period.

On the other hand, *warias'* historical ability to leverage ad hoc mechanisms of city governance to access forms of legal recognition at the beginning of the New Order offers a glimmer of possibility. However fragile, this history demonstrates that nonconforming individuals can claim limited forms of recognition at the scale of the city. This is not a form of acceptance, but rather an ambiguous form of rehabilitation. Ultimately, this falls short of what *warias* and other marginalised Indonesians are looking for: a form of recognition that is permanent, and exceeds the authority of local governments and their constituencies to regulate. For this, *warias* look to the central government and the dream of stable citizenship that would grant them safety everywhere they go. However, the central government appears to have no appetite to intervene in the affairs of districts to protect vulnerable citizens. *Warias'* quest for safety remains fragile while gender serves as a way to determine the boundaries of citizenship. With the passage of the revised Criminal Code, more Indonesians will encounter the impositions of these boundaries in everyday life. *Warias* help to better understand the political and economic exclusion that accompanies an intrusive gender order, as well as ways

---

4 The late 2010s saw a number of districts pass similar regional regulations related to 'the protection of the family' (*ketahanan keluarga*), effectively imposing, under threat of fines and forms of rehabilitation, the heteronormative form of the nuclear family and the biological conception of reproduction on which it is predicated. What is notable about these shifts is the way they reflect the increasing codification of gender normativity and heterosexuality. In contrast to the New Order, where such heterosexuality was simply presented as an unstated norm, the *reformasi* period has witnessed a greater emphasis to define what lies inside and outside 'belonging' to an Indonesian public.

Chapter 4 Transgender citizenship and public gender in Indonesia 67

to negotiate the ambiguous and fickle regulation of 'the public'—a scale that is not conterminous with the nation or the state but lies somewhere in-between.

Acknowledgements

I thank the convenors of the 2022 Australian National University Indonesia Update—Angie Bexley, Sarah Dong and Diahhadi Setyonaluri—for the invitation to present my paper and to my co-panellists and the audience for their questions and engagement. I would also like to thank the many *waria* and *transpuan* individuals and communities throughout Indonesia who have shared their lives with me. I also thank the *Journal of Asian Studies* for granting permission to reproduce part of an article originally published as 'Governing nonconformity: Gender presentation, public space, and the city in New Order Indonesia', *Journal of Asian Studies* 80(4): 955–74, 2021.

References

Andaya, Leonard. 2000. 'The *bissu*: Study of a third gender in Indonesia'. In *Other Pasts: Women, Gender and History in Early Modern Southeast Asia*, edited by Barbara Watson Andaya. Center for Southeast Asian Studies, University of Hawai'i.

Aspinall, Edward and Greg Fealy. 2003. 'Introduction: Decentralisation, democratisation and the rise of the local'. In *Local Power and Politics in Indonesia: Decentralisation and Democratisation*, edited by Edward Aspinall and Greg Fealy, 1–12. Institute of Southeast Asian Studies. doi.org/10.1355/9789812305237-006

Atkinson, Jane Monnig. 1990. 'How gender makes a difference in Wana society'. In *Power and Difference: Gender in Island Southeast Asia*, edited by Jane Monnig Atkinson and Shelly Errington, 59–93. Stanford University Press.

Barker, Joshua. 2001. 'State of fear: Controlling the criminal contagion in Suharto's New Order'. In *Violence and the State in Suharto's Indonesia*, edited by Benedict R.O'G. Anderson, 20–53. Cornell University Press. doi.org/10.7591/9781501719042-003

Blackwood, Evelyn. 2005. 'Gender transgression in colonial and postcolonial Indonesia'. *Journal of Asian Studies* 64(4): 849–79. doi.org/10.1017/S0021911805002251

Blackwood, Evelyn. 2007. 'Regulation of sexuality in Indonesian discourse: Normative gender, criminal law and shifting strategies of control'. *Culture, Health & Sexuality* 9(3): 293–307. doi.org/10.1080/13691050601120589

Boellstorff, Tom. 2004. 'The emergence of political homophobia in Indonesia: Masculinity and national belonging'. *Ethnos* 69(4): 465–86. doi.org/10.1080/0014184042000302308

Boellstorff, Tom. 2005. *The Gay Archipelago: Sexuality and Nation in Indonesia*. Princeton University Press. doi.org/10.1515/9781400844050

68   *Benjamin Hegarty*

Booth, Anne. 2011. 'Splitting, splitting and splitting again: A brief history of the development of regional government in Indonesia since independence'. *Bijdragen tot de Taal-, Land- en Volkenkunde* 167(1): 31–59. doi.org/10.1163/22134379-90003601

Brenner, Suzanne. 1999. 'On the public intimacy of the New Order: Images of women in the popular Indonesian print media'. *Indonesia* 67 (April): 13–37. doi.org/10.2307/3351375

Butt, Simon. 2010. 'Regional autonomy and legal disorder: The proliferation of local laws in Indonesia'. *Singapore Journal of Legal Studies* 1–21.

Butt, Simon. 2019. 'The Constitutional Court and minority rights: Analysing the recent homosexual sex and indigenous belief cases'. In *Contentious Belonging: The Place of Minorities in Indonesia*, edited by Greg Fealy and Ronit Ricci, 55–73. ISEAS Publishing. doi.org/10.1355/9789814843478-008

Davies, Sharyn Graham. 2007. *Challenging Gender Norms: Five Genders among Bugis in Indonesia*. Thomson Wadsworth.

Hegarty, Benjamin. 2018. 'Under the lights, onto the stage: Becoming *Waria* through national glamour in New Order Indonesia'. *TSQ: Transgender Studies Quarterly* 5(3): 355–77. doi.org/10.1215/23289252-6900738

Hegarty, Benjamin. 2021. 'Governing nonconformity: Gender presentation, public space, and the city in New Order Indonesia'. *Journal of Asian Studies* 80(4): 955–74. doi.org/10.1017/S0021911821000747

Hegarty, Benjamin. 2022a. 'An inter-Asia history of *transpuan* in Indonesia'. In *Queer Southeast Asia*, edited by Shawna Tang and Hendri Yulius Wijaya, 15–32. Routledge. doi.org/10.4324/9781003320517

Hegarty, Benjamin. 2022b. *The Made-Up State: Technology, Trans Femininity, and Citizenship in Indonesia*. Cornell University Press.

Helliwell, Christine. 2000. '"It's only a penis": Rape, feminism, and difference'. *Signs: Journal of Women and Culture in Society* 25(3): 789–816. doi.org/10.1086/495482

Jones, Carla. 2010. 'Better women: The cultural politics of gendered expertise in Indonesia'. *American Anthropologist* 112(2): 270–82. doi.org/10.1111/j.1548-1433.2010.01225.x

Katjasungkana, Nursyahbani and Saskia E. Wieringa. 2016. *Creeping Criminalisation: Mapping of Indonesia's National Laws and Regional Regulations That Violate Human Rights of Women and LGBTIQ People*. Outright Action International. https://outrightinternational.org/our-work/human-rights-research/mapping-indonesias-national-laws-and-regional-regulations-violate

Kompas. 1968. 'Di Djakarta terdapat 15,000 bantji' [In Jakarta there are 15,000 banci]. *Kompas*, 5 August.

Lambek, Michael. 1998. 'Body and mind in mind, body and mind in body: Some anthropological interventions in a long conversation'. In *Bodies and Persons: Comparative Perspectives from Africa and Melanesia*, edited by Michael Lambek and Andrew Strathern, 103–23. Cambridge University Press. doi.org/10.1017/CBO9780511802782.005

Long, Nicholas. 2007. 'How to win a beauty contest in Tanjung Pinang'. *Review of Indonesian and Malaysian Affairs* 41(1): 91–117.

Chapter 4 Transgender citizenship and public gender in Indonesia 69

Nordholt, Henk Schulte. 1997. 'The state on the skin: Clothes, shoes, and neatness in (colonial) Indonesia'. *Asian Studies Review* 21(1): 19–39. doi.org/10.1080/03147539708713139

Peacock, James L. 1968. *Rites of Modernization: Symbolic and Social Aspects of Indonesian Proletarian Drama.* University of Chicago Press.

Peletz, Michael G. 2009. *Gender Pluralism: Southeast Asia since Early Modern Times.* Routledge. doi.org/10.4324/9780203880043

Satriyo, Hana A. 2003. 'Decentralisation and women in Indonesia: One step back, two steps forward?' In *Local Power and Politics in Indonesia: Decentralisation and Democratisation,* edited by Edward Aspinall and Greg Fealy, 217–29. Institute of Southeast Asian Studies. doi.org/10.1355/9789812305237-019

Suryakusuma, Julia I. 1996. 'The state and sexuality in New Order Indonesia'. In *Fantasizing the Feminine in Indonesia,* edited by Laurie J. Sears, 92–119. Duke University Press. doi.org/10.2307/j.ctv1134ctq.7

Suryakusuma, Julia I. 2011. *State Ibuism: The Social Construction of Womanhood in New Order Indonesia.* Komunitas Bambu.

Valverde, Mariana. 2011. 'Seeing like a city: The dialectic of modern and premodern ways of seeing in urban governance'. *Law & Society Review* 45(2): 277–312. doi.org/10.1111/j.1540-5893.2011.00441.x

van der Meer, Arnout. 2020. *Performing Power: Cultural Hegemony, Identity, and Resistance in Colonial Indonesia.* Cornell University Press. doi.org/10.7298/h0cn-4s91

Wijaya, Hendri Yulius. 2019. 'Localising queer identities: Queer activisms and national belonging in Indonesia'. In *Contentious Belonging: The Place of Minorities in Indonesia,* edited by Greg Fealy and Ronit Ricci, 133–51. ISEAS Publishing. doi.org/10.1355/9789814843478-012

Wijaya, Hendri Yulius and Sharyn Graham Davies. 2019. 'The unfulfilled promise of democracy: Lesbian and gay activism in Indonesia'. In *Activists in Transition: Progressive Politics in Democratic Indonesia,* edited by Thushara Dibley and Michele Ford, 153–70. Cornell University Press. doi.org/10.1515/9781501742491-011

5 Gender diversity in parliament, cabinet and ambassadorial appointments: A work in progress?

Ella S. Prihatini

Women's share in public participation in the past two decades indicates promising progress. More and more women in Indonesia have been appointed as members of national parliament (Dewan Perwakilan Rakyat, DPR), cabinet ministers and ambassadors. Such progress is indicated in the United Nations Development Programme's Gender Inequality Index, which shows a decline from 0.571 in 1995 to 0.444 in 2021 (UNDP 2020). The political domain shows more progress than the two other measures. While the gender gap in politics declined by 12 points between 1995 and 2021, the gender gap in education declined by only 2 points, and labour force participation by 4.7 points. The progress in women's public participation follows a series of affirmative policies and is strongly in line with the global trend.

However, it is important to note that progress towards closing the gender gap in Indonesia is still low on a global scale. Women's underrepresentation in politics, among other professions, continues to be a persistent issue in Indonesia. Despite women comprising half the national population and the granting of suffrage in 1945, their share in politics remains insignificant.

The world average gender gap in parliamentary representation has decreased by 26.2 points in the past 27 years, while the gaps in secondary education and labour force participation have decreased by 3.8 and 1.3 points respectively (UNDP 2020). Indonesia's performance in the Gender Inequality Index has also been the lowest among other Southeast Asian countries, with a value of 0.48, ranking it 121 out of 162 countries in 2019 (ibid.). It can be argued that Indonesia has been doing well in terms of reducing gender disparity in the economic sector. Yet it continues to struggle in pursuing gender parity in politics and in education.

In another measure of the gender gap, under the political empowerment spectrum published by the World Economic Forum (2022), the percentage of women in parliament and ministerial positions in Indonesia ranked 88th. As shown in Figure 5.1, political empowerment is the weakest performing measure as it scores lower than the world average. Indonesia once sat at 41st place for this indicator when it had a female head of state—President Megawati Sukarnoputri—in 2001–2004. Nonetheless, it is interesting to note that Indonesia's overall rank is 10th in East Asia and the Pacific Region, better than China, Cambodia, Malaysia, Myanmar and Japan. The region performs poorly in political empowerment; only four countries have closed the gender gap in parliament by at least one percentage point: Vietnam, Timor-Leste, New Zealand and Indonesia. New Zealand, the Philippines and Australia are leading the region with global rankings at 4th, 19th and 43rd, respectively.

Empirical and longitudinal evidence on gender diversity in public offices in Indonesia is limited. Against this backdrop, this chapter introduces a novel dataset on female members of parliament (MPs), cabinet ministers and ambassadors in the post-Suharto era (1998 onwards). I seek to examine how women fare in prestigious positions that represent both the legislative and executive branches of government. The chapter unfolds as follows: the next section elaborates key interventions that have been implemented in order to increase gender diversity in parliament, cabinet

Figure 5.1 Indonesia's position in the Global Gender Gap Index, 2022

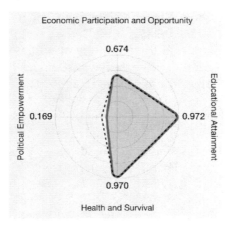

Source: World Economic Forum (2022: 15–16).

and diplomatic missions. Subsequent sections present descriptive statistics on women's presence as lawmakers, ministers and ambassadors. I further examine possible predictors of women's presence and persisting obstacles. Findings from the study suggest that Indonesia's experience offers important takeaways that contribute to the conversation about women's political representation. The conclusion contains policy recommendations that may help to improve women's political representation.

Promoting equal representation through affirmative policies

Women's political representation is often measured by their presence as presidents or prime ministers (Annesley and Franceschet 2015; Jalalzai 2018), their share in parliament (Prihatini 2019a; Stockemer 2017) and cabinet ministerial posts (Annesley et al. 2019; Breuning and Okundaye 2021). More recently, as domestic politics often shape foreign affairs, scholars also examine the share of women in ambassadorial appointments (Aggestam and True 2020; Towns and Niklasson 2018).

Drawing heavily on theories of legislative representation, barriers to women's presence in politics can be characterised into three broad explanations: socioeconomic, political and cultural/ideological (Prihatini 2019b). The first explanation focuses on how the process of modernisation, which covers socioeconomic aspects, promotes cultural change that leads to greater numerical women's representation (Shvedova 2005; Welzel et al. 2002). The second explanation is political institutional settings, ranging from electoral systems to gender quotas. The literature on gender and political recruitment (Krook 2010; Luhiste 2015; Norris and Lovenduski 1995) highlights the importance of political institution aspects in observing women in parliament. The third explanation deals with cultural or ideological barriers that often harm women's political nomination (Norris and Inglehart 2001; Paxton and Kunovich 2003; Seguino 2011). Inglehart and Norris (2003) suggest cultural attitudes and values are central to the number of female deputies. A similar conclusion was drawn by Ruedin (2012), who argues that cultural factors determine public attitudes towards women as political leaders.

In efforts to overcome the barriers in achieving gender equality, states sign and ratify international treaties, such as the 1979 United Nations Convention on the Elimination of All Forms of Discrimination against Women (CEDAW) and the 1995 Beijing Platform for Action (BPfA) (True and Mintrom 2001). Indonesia ratified CEDAW through Law 7/1984 and is a signatory to BPfA. Therefore, Indonesia has obligations to implement women's human rights as stated in these conventions, including to promote equal political representation.

Chapter 5 Gender diversity in parliament, cabinet and ambassadorial appointments 73

Khofifah Indar Parawansa, who served as state minister for women's empowerment, fought for gender equality and justice as outlined in the 1999–2004 National Medium Term Development Plan (Santoso 2016). Following that was Presidential Instruction 9/2000 on Gender Mainstreaming in National Development, which calls for gender-responsive development planning, implementation and monitoring. The 2020–2024 National Medium Term Development Plan also has sections to ensure that gender-responsive planning and budgeting are applied (Ministry of Women's Empowerment and Child Protection 2019).

A series of institutional reforms have been implemented. In the legislative branch, for example, a candidate gender quota policy was introduced for the 2004 elections, in which parties needed to consider women's representation at a minimum of 30% (Prihatini 2021). This institutional requirement was first constituted in Law 12/2003 on General Elections, which was enacted in preparation for the 2004 election. Law 2/2008 on Political Parties further required parties to appoint women to at least 30% of their national managerial positions and a similar share for the party's regional boards as a prerequisite to participate in elections. Law 8/2008 on General Elections stipulated that 30% female candidates was compulsory. Law 8/2012 on General Elections stated that parties must nominate candidates with at least 30% women using the zipper system (at least one female candidate for every three nominated candidates on each party's list), or be disqualified from running. The latter institutional requirement was stipulated by the General Elections Commission (Komisi Pemilihan Umum, KPU) in its Regulation 7/2013.

As for gender mainstreaming in the executive branch, particularly in ministerial appointments, the country has no clear affirmative policies that promote women as cabinet members. Scholars suggest that the decision in formulating cabinet has always been a complex affair influenced by many factors including party leaders and oligarchic powers (Annesley et al. 2019; Sawasdee 2018). Muhtadi (2015) asserts that the institutional settings of Indonesia's multiparty presidential system, combined with the existence of powerful interests that shape the country's politics and economy, hinder any president from forming a non-collusive administration and pushing through extensive reform such as promoting gender equality in cabinet.

The literature on women in executive power indicates that a country with a woman leader does not signify the end of gender discrimination (Jalalzai 2008). The experience in Indonesia lends support to this observation. Under the rule of Indonesia's first female president, Megawati Sukarnoputri (2001–2004), only two women were appointed for her cabinet of 37 members (state minister for women's empowerment, and minister of

74   *Ella S. Prihatini*

trade and industry), and none for the subnational decision-making level (i.e. governor or mayor) (Fleschenberg 2011).

Similarly, the government has shown a lack of distinct strategy in promoting women as ambassadors to represent the country overseas. Following constitutional amendments, the power of the DPR has increased substantially, fully matching that of the executive. Chapter 13, Article 1 stipulates that the DPR must be consulted on ambassadorial appointments, which in practice has given the DPR the right to approve or reject the government's ambassadorial candidates (Anwar 2010). This regulation was introduced to prevent the recurrence of old practices such as when Suharto used ambassadorial postings as rewards for senior military figures for services rendered or as a means to get rid of rivals, and to ensure that the ambassadors sent overseas are of sufficiently high quality.

Despite few policies that enable Indonesia to improve women's leadership in diplomatic missions, a study by Prajuli and colleagues (2021) suggests that gender mainstreaming has played a part in the increasing number of female Indonesian diplomats. The positive perception of the role of women in foreign policymaking has encouraged and motivated women to join the diplomatic corps in greater numbers. Modern gender socialisation in Indonesia reinforces the notion that being a diplomat is a professional or social role that is applicable to both genders.

Internal reforms were also carried out by reviewing all rules in the ministry that were not aligned with gender principles and by communicating gender principles within the ministry and Indonesia's representatives abroad. In 2013, the ministry released its first gender equality in foreign policy blueprint, followed by the publication of gender budgeting guidelines in 2015. Regulations have been changed to allow couples to accept diplomatic assignments abroad together or to take sabbatical leave to accompany their spouses.

The fact that there is an increasing number of women engaged as political elites, such as lawmakers, ministers and ambassadors, further indicates that gender diversity is becoming more socially acceptable in Indonesia. On the other hand, with more women attaining higher education and key competencies, the pool of talent among women has become far more competitive.

Gender equality in legislative and executive branches

This section provides longitudinal evidence on women's fare in both the legislative and executive branches of government. The data were collected from multiple sources including official websites, academic journals and media reports. All information is valid as at September 2022.

Parliament

In line with the global trend, Indonesia has achieved notable progress in efforts to improve women's political representation. For example, the share of female legislators increased 2.5-fold from 8% in 1999 to 20.52% in 2019 (Prihatini 2022). Indonesia performed slightly better than the average Asian parliament, as the region recorded the slowest growth rate, moving only 7 percentage points from 13.2% to 20.2% between 1995 and 2021. Figure 5.2 shows only a few Asian countries have surpassed the 30% mark for women's representation; the top three are Taiwan, Timor-Leste and Nepal.

Indonesia's pace in achieving gender parity in parliament is also faster than the world average, which doubled from 13% in 1998 to 25% in 2019 (IPU 2019). Additionally, Puan Maharani (the daughter of former president Megawati Sukarnoputri) currently serves as speaker of the House, making Indonesia among 41 countries with lower and unicameral chambers led by female leaders (IPU 2022).

Extensive studies have shown that women's parliamentary representation in Indonesia has been hindered by numerous factors, including institutional and cultural barriers (Aspinall et al. 2021; Prihatini 2019c; Sherlock 2010). First, political parties tend to nominate more men than women in strategic ballot list positions. As their ultimate goal is to win the most seats, parties are more inclined to prioritise winning strategies rather than long-term strategic policies in addressing public issues such as gender inequality in the political sphere.

Second, the prevalence of dynastic MPs is also critical in shaping whether Indonesian democracy will be occupied by mere elites connected with regional heads, former or current lawmakers, and party leaders (Purdey et al. 2016). The share of female dynasts continued to grow from 42% in 2009, the year when the fully open-list proportional representation system was introduced (where voters may cast their ballot for either a political party or a candidate), to 44% in 2019. As legislative elections are prohibitively expensive, it is expected that only those with strong financial and political resources are competitive (Wardani and Subekti 2021). This development along with oligarchic politics might jeopardise the efforts to create inclusive democracy that represents the vast majority of Indonesians. Women's substantive representation will also be questioned as female lawmakers will be dominated by those with limited connections to ordinary citizens.

A study on the dynastic family ties of 575 legislators in the DPR, who were elected in 2019, suggests three in every five dynasts are male, yet almost 44% of elected female MPs come from political families (Prihatini and Halimatusa'diyah 2022). Young MPs (35 years old or younger) comprise

Figure 5.2 Women's share in Asian parliaments, June 2021 (%)

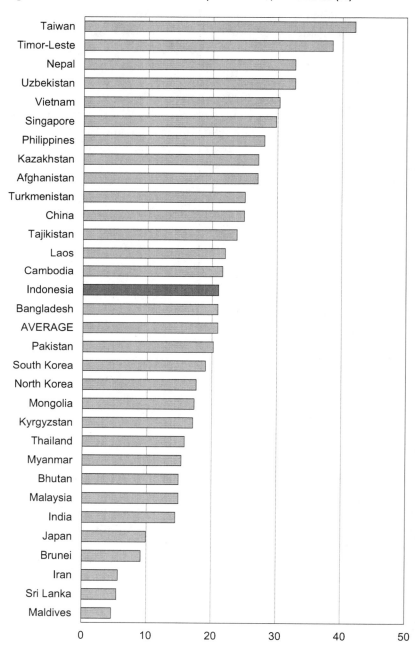

Source: Prihatini (2022).

Chapter 5 Gender diversity in parliament, cabinet and ambassadorial appointments 77

20% of all dynasts. Compared to the other age groups, the proportion is conspicuous as half of young lawmakers are dynasts. These findings corroborate Smith's (2018) assertion that legacy politicians are more likely to start their political careers earlier than their non-legacy counterparts.

Cabinet

Cabinet appointments matter because cabinets and the core executive are the most significant venues for achieving the substantive representation of women (Annesley and Franceschet 2015; Bauer and Tremblay 2011). Ministerial appointment provides additional prestige and salary benefits, as well as the opportunity to set policy agendas and make important political decisions (Annesley et al. 2019). Ministerial appointments are also gendered as most ministers have been men, as have the heads of government who appointed them.

Justifications for increasing women's presence in politics have focused on both the normative and policy implications of their inclusion in and exclusion from decision-making processes (O'Brien and Reyes-Housholder 2020). Studies indicate that the exclusion of women from politics signals that governance is primarily a male affair, discourages women citizens' participation, and ultimately erodes the legitimacy of modern democracies (Clayton et al. 2019; Mansbridge 1999). Women's share in ministerial positions signals that all citizens—women and men— can participate in executive politics and may enhance citizens' support for, and trust in, democracies (Franceschet et al. 2017).

The share of female cabinet ministers in Indonesia increased 2.6-fold from 5.6% to 14.6% in the past two decades (Table 5.1), a similar pace to the growth in the DPR. The apex took place during President Joko Widodo's (Jokowi's) first term (2014–2019), which included four cabinet shake-ups or reshuffles, where cumulatively 9 out of 50 cabinet ministers were women (Farisa 2022; Nazeer 2014). With 9 women appointed to his cabinet, there were more female cabinet ministers in Indonesia than in Australia, the United Kingdom and the United States (Diprose 2019).

A total of 23 women and 214 men were appointed as ministers during *reformasi*. On average, women's share as cabinet ministers sits at 10.02%, or half the current world average, which is 22.8% (UN Women 2023). Some female ministers worked for more than one term and/or one president. According to the portfolio characteristics, women ministers were assigned to 7 masculine (5 high prestige and 2 middle prestige), 4 feminine (2 middle prestige and 2 low prestige) and 5 neutral (4 middle prestige and 1 low prestige) portfolios.

Among the masculine and high-prestige ministries are foreign affairs, finance, state-owned enterprises and trade. These appointments suggest

78   *Ella S. Prihatini*

Table 5.1 Share of female ministers by president, 1998–2022

President (sex)	Year	Number of ministers	Number of female ministers	Women in cabinet (%)
B.J. Habibie (male)	1998–1999	36	2	5.6
Abdurrahman Wahid (male)	1999–2001	50	2	4.0
Megawati Sukarnoputri (female)	2001–2004	30	2	6.7
Susilo Bambang Yudhoyono (male)	2004–2009	42	4	9.5
Susilo Bambang Yudhoyono (male)	2009–2014	51	6	11.8
Joko Widodo (male)	2014–2019	50	9	18.0
Joko Widodo (male)	2019–2022	41	6	14.6

Source: Author's calculation.

that women ministers are considered more than capable of leading traditionally masculine fields. For example, Sri Mulyani Indrawati has served as finance minister under two presidents since 2004. Likewise, Rini Soemarno and Mari Elka Pangestu have served multiple posts in trade and investment. Indrawati, Soemarno and Pangestu are all considered as female professional ministers who receive peer recognition in their respective fields.

However, it is interesting to note that despite strong narratives by Jokowi during his presidential campaign in 2014 to not let *orang partai* (people affiliated with political parties) cramp his cabinet, the data suggest that 7 out of 15 female ministers appointed between 2014 and 2022 represent coalition parties (Table 5.2). This number is the largest of any other administration during *reformasi*. One explanation to this significant number of female political ministers lies in Jokowi's 'triple minority' position: being a newcomer to the national stage, with a government coalition that did not have a parliamentary majority, and less party authority compared to previous presidents (Sundaryani 2015). President Widodo was pushed 'to reward the main political parties and oligarchs who had supported him' in his presidential bid (Muhtadi 2015: 357).

During his first and second terms, female political ministers came from the Indonesian Democratic Party of Struggle (PDI-P), the National Awakening Party (PKB) and the National Democratic Party (NasDem). Two out three PDI-P cadres are considered dynastic politicians, namely Puan Maharani (mentioned earlier) and I Gusti Ayu Bintang Darmavati (wife of a former minister who served in the first term). Meanwhile, female

Chapter 5 Gender diversity in parliament, cabinet and ambassadorial appointments 79

Table 5.2 Distribution of female ministers by president, 1998–2022

President (sex)	Year	Number of political ministers	Number of professional ministers
B.J. Habibie (male)	1998–1999	1	1
Abdurrahman Wahid (male)	1999–2001	1	1
Megawati Sukarnoputri (female)	2001–2004	1	1
Susilo Bambang Yudhoyono (male)	2004–2009	1	3
Susilo Bambang Yudhoyono (male)	2009–2014	0	6
Joko Widodo (male)	2014–2019	3	6
Joko Widodo (male)	2019–2022	4	2

Source: Author's calculation.

ministers from other parties perceived as strong allies in the government coalition are Khofifah Indar Parawansa and Ida Fauziyah from PKB and Siti Nurbaya from NasDem. Some of the findings from Indonesia's experience confirm the literature suggesting that the electoral calendar (Borrelli 2002), the beginning of the term (Lee and Park 2018), and the size of the coalition in parliament influence a president's momentum to choose a female minister.

Overall, women's representation in the cabinet over the past two decades is a promising improvement. Yet, Finance Minister Sri Mulyani Indrawati argues the pattern is an outlier rather than breaking the glass ceiling phenomenon. She further asserts that most portfolios continue to be dominated by men while only a few female ministers are being reassigned to the same position across administrations.[1]

In an interview with the author, Minister Indrawati suggested that breakthroughs have been limited, and women remain dominant in soft politics and feminine ministries. She also mentioned that the gender ratio in the cabinet is a result of the president's preferences, hence the number of female ministers will be strongly determined by the president's interests in improving women's presence in the executive branch: 'During Susilo Bambang Yudhoyono's administration, he explicitly said that he wanted six women as cabinet ministers. With this target in mind, the president selected six women to fill the posts'.

---

1 HE Sri Mulyani Indrawati closing address to the 39th Indonesia Update conference, Australian National University, 17 September 2022.

Ambassadorial appointments

During much of the New Order period, key diplomatic posts such as ambassadors in the major ASEAN capitals, Washington, Tokyo and Canberra were held by senior military figures, mostly from the army (Anwar 2010). Powerful members of the elite whom Suharto could not simply dismiss were often sent overseas as ambassadors, popularly known by the term 'di-dubes-kan', to be made an ambassador as a punishment rather than an achievement. As another political appointment at the president's prerogative, ambassadorial posting is strongly political, hence various factors shape this decision. However, a pattern has emerged in the past couple of decades whereby politicians and former supporters (*relawan*), both male and female, are being rewarded with ambassadorial postings (Liputan6.com 2020).

To name a few, in 2016, Helmy Fauzi was appointed as ambassador to the Arab Republic of Egypt, based in Cairo. Helmy is part of the Council of Experts on International Relations of Jokowi's National Secretariat volunteer team. The PDI-P politician was a member of Commission I of the Indonesian House of Representatives for the 2009–2014 period (Akuntono 2016). In 2020, Muhammad Lutfi and Hildi Hamid were assigned to become ambassadors to the United States and Azerbaijan respectively. Muhammad Lutfi was the minister of trade and head of the Investment Coordinating Board (BKPM) under President Susilo Bambang Yudhoyono. During the presidential election, Lutfi served on the Steering Committee for Volunteer National Young Entrepreneurs (Relawan Pengusaha Muda Nasional, Repnas), one of Jokowi's volunteer groups in 2019. Meanwhile, Hildi Hamid is chair of the Jokowi-Ma'ruf Winning Team in West Kalimantan. Lena Mukti Maryana, a female politician from the United Development Party (PPP) who was also a spokesperson during Jokowi's second presidential bid, was appointed as Indonesian ambassador to Kuwait (CNN Indonesia 2021).

A total of 1,230 ambassadorial appointments were recorded between 1947 and 2022, and only 65 of them were women (5.3%). At the end of 2022, women comprised 9.3% of all ambassadors appointed during *reformasi*. This number is much bigger than women's 2.3% share during the pre-*reformasi* period. Table 5.3 displays the share of female ambassadors at its highest during Jokowi's administration (13.3%). Comparatively, a study based on a dataset containing all ambassador appointments made by the 50 highest-ranked countries in terms of gross domestic product (GDP) in 2014 concludes that women occupy only 15% of these top positions (Towns and Niklasson 2018). The Nordic countries stand out as those who appoint the most women ambassadors (35%), a share that is in sharp contrast to the female ambassadors of the Middle East (6%) and Asia (10%).

Chapter 5 Gender diversity in parliament, cabinet and ambassadorial appointments 81

Table 5.3 Distribution of ambassadorial appointments by president, 1998–2022

President (sex)	Year	Ambassadorial appointments	Women ambassadorial appointments	Women's share (%)
B.J. Habibie (male)	1998–1999	30	0	0
Abdurrahman Wahid (male)	1999–2001	47	0	0
Megawati Sukarnoputri (female)	2001–2004	75	7	9.3
Susilo Bambang Yudhoyono (male)	2004–2014	218	21	9.6
Joko Widodo (male)	2014–2022	158	21	13.3

Source: Author's calculation.

The most significant representation of Indonesian women ambassadors was in Latin American and European countries. Ecuador, Panama and Bosnia have each had only three ambassadors to date, indicating that these embassies are relatively new, yet one out of three ambassadors appointed to these countries was a female, the highest share (33%) that women have achieved in all Indonesian embassies. The second highest representation is in Denmark and Finland, where women comprise 31% of all ambassadors appointed there (Figure 5.3). This notable presence of women as envoys in relatively gender-equal societies suggests that Indonesia might consider the recipient countries' acceptance of women's leadership as one of the cues for appointing ambassadors.

On the other hand, no woman has ever been appointed to lead Indonesia's diplomatic mission in key and strategic economies like Germany, the United States, China, Japan and Australia.

The absence of women ambassadors in some countries may be a result of multiple factors, including a deep-rooted gender stereotyping believed by most MPs in the DPR. When a country is perceived as highly critical of Indonesia, lawmakers are more inclined to support a blunt, outspoken, straight-talking candidate over a soft-spoken one (Anwar 2010). Another explanation lies in the rampant practice of payback politics, *politik balas jasa*, which often sends former *relawan* in presidential elections to these strong countries.

Indonesia's experience of political appointees in ambassadorial appointments is not unique. Observations in the United States conclude that political donors are very likely to be appointed as ambassadors to European and other well-off countries (Fedderke and Jett 2017). Certain postings are deemed to be more expensive than others, hence the post will

82 Ella S. Prihatini

Figure 5.3 Percentage of female ambassadors appointed by country, 1947–2022

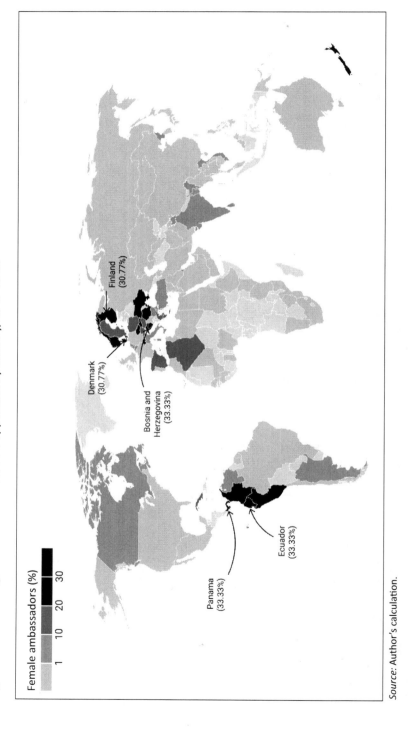

Source: Author's calculation.

Chapter 5 Gender diversity in parliament, cabinet and ambassadorial appointments 83

be given to donors with the biggest electoral funds contribution. However, further research is needed to examine the 'blackbox' of the nomination and selection of ambassadors in Indonesia. The dichotomy between career and political appointees also needs to be examined because the pattern may be gendered since electoral politics are dominated mainly by men.

Conclusion

This chapter has demonstrated progress towards achieving gender equality in Indonesia's national parliament, cabinet and ambassadorial postings in the past two decades. While women's share in the legislative branch is affected by voter preferences, socioeconomic development, institutional reforms and cultural factors, cabinet and ambassador appointments are the president's prerogative. And while the nature of what hinders women's presence as lawmakers has been studied extensively, little is known about the selection of women to serve as ministers and ambassadors.

Scholars have studied the selection of women to the cabinet and found that women are less likely to obtain a ministerial post in general, and, when they do enter cabinet, they are likely to be awarded less-prestigious posts (Escobar-Lemmon and Taylor-Robinson 2005; Krook and O'Brien 2012). Women tend to be appointed to ministerial posts that deal with softer policy issues rather than the harder and politically more prestigious positions (Allen 2016; Claveria 2014; Goddard 2019). Explaining gendered patterns in cabinet appointments across the world, Krook and O'Brien (2012) assert that women's appointments are to a large extent explained by the presence of more women among political elites, 'which they stress can partly be promoted by, for example, gender quotas' (Bäck and Carroll 2020: 323).

However, conclusions were mixed when it came to the connection between women in parliament and cabinet. Some argue that female parliamentarians act as the 'supply force for the presence of women in ministerial lines' (Whitford et al. 2007: 563). Even in presidential systems, where ministers do not have to come from the national assembly, Escobar-Lemmon and Taylor-Robinson (2005) assert that the presence of female legislators increases the number of women eligible for cabinet posts. Yet, Lee and Park's (2018) work on female ministers in East Asia and Southeast Asia concludes that women's cabinet representation has improved overall in the transition to democracy, as they found increasing the age of democracy by 10% would lead to a 2 percentage point increase in women's overall share of cabinet ministers and a 1.1 percentage point increase in women's share of professional ministers.

Other studies find the percentage of women in the legislature should have a stronger influence on the percentage of women in the cabinet in parliamentary systems than in presidential systems, because the influence is direct in the former type of governmental system, where heads of government can nominate their ministerial caucus only from the legislature (Stockemer 2017). Another observation on the connection between corruption and women's presence in ministerial positions suggests that democracies with rampant corruption will have fewer women serving in cabinets (Stockemer and Sundström 2019).

As the president determines the selection of ministers and ambassadors, his or her role is pivotal. Under Jokowi's administration, women's share in the cabinet and diplomatic postings has achieved notable progress. Yet, due to his government's 'triple minority' position, in his second term he has created multiple compromises such as appointing more female politicians than those coming from professional backgrounds. He also allocates ambassadorial positions to those who have helped him win two presidential elections.

This treatment towards diplomatic postings is not unique to Jokowi's administration, as many presidents before did the same. However, the practice of rewarding the president-elect's success team as a 'consolation gift' (Andinni 2015) should not be taken lightly as it will eventually jeopardise Indonesia's foreign policy. The need to appease those who have helped the president to get elected (domestic politics) should not be costing the country's interests in international politics.

Nevertheless, reflecting affirmative action aiming to increase the number of female parliamentarians, some policy strategies are mentioned here that may help to improve women's presence as cabinet ministers and ambassadors. First, it is crucial to build and nurture strategic partnerships in promoting gender equality values. Professional associations could provide and recommend a list of prominent females who have excelled in their respective fields. This peer recognition will help civil society organisations that promote women's political activism to further persuade the president's decision in appointing cabinet ministers and ambassadors.

Second, parties should be encouraged to openly nominate women for minister and ambassador positions. Although this might vary across parties, the talent pool in each party should serve as a starting point to make women more visible and discoverable. Lastly, the public should be made aware that gender equality will ensure not only inclusivity but also a more dynamic society, because empirical evidence has shown that female leadership offers more diverse perspectives and brings out the best from possible results.

References

Aggestam, Karin and Jacqui True. 2020. 'Gendering foreign policy: A comparative framework for analysis'. *Foreign Policy Analysis* 16(2): 143–62. doi.org/10.1093/fpa/orz026

Akuntono, Indra. 2016. 'Presiden lantik 10 dubes, salah satunya relawan Jokowi' [President inaugurates 10 ambassadors, one of them is Jokowi's volunteer]. *Kompas*, 25 February. https://nasional.kompas.com/read/2016/02/25/14510551/Presiden.Lantik.10.Dubes.Salah.Satunya.Relawan.Jokowi?page=all

Allen, Peter. 2016. 'Achieving sex equality in executive appointments'. *Party Politics* 22(5): 609–19. doi.org/10.1177/1354068816654324

Andinni, Alfani Roosy. 2015. 'PAN: Jabatan dubes bukan hadiah hiburan tim sukes Jokowi-JK' [PAN: The position of ambassador is not an entertainment prize for the Jokowi-JK success team]. SINDOnews.com, 11 August. https://nasional.sindonews.com/berita/1031690/12/pan-jabatan-dubes-bukan-hadiah-hiburan-tim-sukes-jokowi-jk

Annesley, Claire and Susan Franceschet. 2015. 'Gender and the executive branch'. *Politics & Gender* 11(4): 613–17. doi.org/10.1017/S1743923X15000446

Annesley, Claire, Karen Beckwith and Susan Franceschet. 2019. *Cabinets, Ministers, and Gender*. Oxford University Press.

Anwar, Dewi Fortuna. 2010. 'The impact of domestic and Asian regional changes on Indonesian foreign policy'. *Southeast Asian Affairs* 2010: 126–41. www.jstor.org/stable/41418562

Aspinall, Edward, Sally White and Amalinda Savirani. 2021. 'Women's political representation in Indonesia: Who wins and how?' *Journal of Current Southeast Asian Affairs* 40(1): 3–27. doi.org/10.1177/1868103421989720

Bäck, Hanna and Royce Carroll. 2020. 'The distribution of ministerial posts in parliamentary systems'. In *The Oxford Handbook of Political Executives*, edited by Rudy B. Andeweg, Robert Elgie, Ludger Helms, Juliet Kaarbo and Ferdinand Müller-Rommel, 314–35. Oxford University Press. doi.org/10.1093/oxfordhb/9780198809296.001.0001

Bauer, Gretchen and Manon Tremblay (eds). 2011. *Women in Executive Power: A Global Overview*. Routledge.

Borrelli, MaryAnne. 2002. *The President's Cabinet: Gender, Power, and Representation*. Lynne Rienner Publishers.

Breuning, Marijke and Gabriela Okundaye. 2021. 'Half of the cabinet: Explaining Ethiopia's move to gender parity in the government'. *Journal of Asian and African Studies* 56(5): 1064–78. doi.org/10.1177/00219096211007652

Claveria, Silvia. 2014. 'Still a "male business"? Explaining women's presence in executive office'. *West European Politics* 37(5): 1156–76. doi.org/10.1080/014023 82.2014.911479

Clayton, Amanda, Diana Z. O'Brien and Jennifer M. Piscopo. 2019. 'All male panels? Representation and democratic legitimacy'. *American Journal of Political Science* 63(1): 113–29. doi.org/10.1111/ajps.12391

CNN Indonesia. 2021. 'Eks jubir tim kampanye Jokowi jadi dubes RI di Kuwait' [Former spokesperson for Jokowi's campaign team becomes Indonesian ambassador in Kuwait]. CNN Indonesia, 25 October.

www.cnnindonesia.com/internasional/20211025131628-106-711963/eks-jubir-tim-kampanye-jokowi-jadi-dubes-ri-di-kuwait

Diprose, Rachael. 2019. 'Reducing barriers: Networking change from the grassroots up'. *East Asia Forum Quarterly* 11(1): 30–31. https://search.informit.org/doi/10.3316/INFORMIT.277724455229923

Escobar-Lemmon, Maria and Michelle M. Taylor-Robinson. 2005. 'Women ministers in Latin American government: When, where, and why?' *American Journal of Political Science* 49(4): 829–44. doi.org/10.2307/3647700

Farisa, Fitria Chusna. 2022. 'Riwayat "reshuffle" kabinet Jokowi sejak 2014 hingga terkini' [The history of Jokowi's cabinet 'reshuffle' from 2014 to the present]. *Kompas*, 14 June. https://nasional.kompas.com/read/2022/06/14/16524271/riwayat-reshuffle-kabinet-jokowi-sejak-2014-hingga-terkini

Fedderke, Johannes and Dennis Jett. 2017. 'What price the court of St James? Political influences on ambassadorial postings of the United States of America'. *Governance* 30(3): 483–515. doi.org/10.1111/gove.12254

Fleschenberg, Andrea. 2011. 'South and Southeast Asia'. In *Women in Executive Power: A Global Overview*, edited by Gretchen Bauer and Manon Tremblay, 23–44. Routledge.

Franceschet, Susan, Claire Annesley and Karen Beckwith. 2017. 'What do women symbolize? Symbolic representation and cabinet appointments'. *Politics, Groups, and Identities* 5(3): 488–93. doi.org/10.1080/21565503.2017.1321997

Goddard, Dee. 2019. 'Examining the appointment of women to ministerial positions across Europe: 1970–2015'. *Party Politics* 27(4): 631–43. doi.org/10.1177/1354068819878665

Inglehart, Ronald and Pippa Norris. 2003. 'The true clash of civilizations'. *Foreign Policy* 135: 62–70. doi.org/10.2307/3183594

IPU (Inter-Parliamentary Union). 2019. 'Women in national parliaments: World and regional averages'. http://archive.ipu.org/wmn-e/world.htm

IPU (Inter-Parliamentary Union). 2022. 'Women speakers of national parliaments'. https://bit.ly/3Rxsv6m

Jalalzai, Farida. 2008. 'Women rule: Shattering the executive glass ceiling'. *Politics & Gender* 4(2): 205–31. doi.org/10.1017/S1743923X08000317

Jalalzai, Farida. 2018. 'Women heads of state and government'. In *Measuring Women's Political Empowerment across the Globe: Strategies, Challenges and Future Research*, edited by Amy C. Alexander, Catherine Bolzendahl and Farida Jalalzai, 257–82. Palgrave Macmillan. doi.org/10.1007/978-3-319-64006-8_12

Krook, Mona Lena. 2010. 'Why are fewer women than men elected? Gender and the dynamics of candidate selection'. *Political Studies Review* 8(2): 155–68. doi.org/10.1111/j.1478-9302.2009.00185.x

Krook, Mona Lena and Diana Z. O'Brien. 2012. 'All the president's men? The appointment of female cabinet ministers worldwide'. *Journal of Politics* 74(3): 840–55. doi.org/10.1017/s0022381612000382

Lee, Don S. and Soonae Park. 2018. 'Democratization and women's representation in presidential cabinets: Evidence from East and Southeast Asia'. *Asian Journal of Political Science* 26(2): 161–80. doi.org/10.1080/02185377.2018.1476257

Liputan6.com. 2020. 'Deretan calon dubes RI: Dari relawan hingga politikus pendukung Jokowi di pilpres' [Rows of candidates for Indonesian ambassador: From volunteers to politicians supporting Jokowi in the presidential election]. Liputan6.com, 17 June. www.liputan6.com/news/read/4281473/deretan-calon-dubes-ri-dari-relawan-hingga-politikus-pendukung-jokowi-di-pilpres

Luhiste, Maarja. 2015. 'Party gatekeepers' support for viable female candidacy in PR-list systems'. *Politics & Gender* 11(1): 89–116. doi.org/10.1017/S1743923X14000580

Mansbridge, Jane. 1999. 'Should blacks represent blacks and women represent women? A contingent "yes"'. *Journal of Politics* 61(3): 628–57. doi.org/10.2307/2647821

Ministry of Women's Empowerment and Child Protection. 2019. *Pembangunan Manusia Berbasis Gender Tahun 2019* [Gender-based human development in 2019]. www.kemenpppa.go.id/index.php/page/read/24/2527/pembangunan-manusia-berbasis-gender-tahun-2019

Muhtadi, Burhanuddin. 2015. 'Jokowi's first year: A weak president caught between reform and oligarchic politics'. *Bulletin of Indonesian Economic Studies* 51(3): 349–68. doi.org/10.1080/00074918.2015.1110684

Nazeer, Zubaidah. 2014. 'Jokowi praised for record number of women in cabinet'. *Straits Times*, 31 October. www.straitstimes.com/asia/se-asia/jokowi-praised-for-record-number-of-women-in-cabinet

Norris, Pippa and Joni Lovenduski. 1995. *Political Recruitment: Gender, Race and Class in the British Parliament*. Cambridge University Press.

Norris, Pippa and Ronald Inglehart. 2001. 'Women and democracy: Cultural obstacles to equal representation'. *Journal of Democracy* 12(3): 126–40. doi.org/10.1353/jod.2001.0054

O'Brien, Diana Z. and Catherine Reyes-Housholder. 2020. 'Women and executive politics'. In *The Oxford Handbook of Political Executives*, edited by Rudy B. Andeweg, Robert Elgie, Ludger Helms, Juliet Kaarbo and Ferdinand Müller-Rommel, 251–72. Oxford University Press. doi.org/10.1093/oxfordhb/9780198809296.001.0001

Paxton, Pamela and Sheri Kunovich. 2003. 'Women's political representation: The importance of ideology'. *Social Forces* 82(1): 87–113. doi.org/10.1353/sof.2003.0105

Prajuli, Wendy Andhika, Richa Vidya Yustikaningrum and Dayu Nirma Amurwanti. 2021. 'How gender socialization is improving women's representation in Indonesia's foreign affairs: Breaking the ceiling'. *Australian Journal of International Affairs* 75(5): 527–45. doi.org/10.1080/10357718.2021.1893653

Prihatini, Ella S. 2019a. 'Women's representation in Asian parliaments: A QCA approach'. *Contemporary Politics* 25(2): 213–35. doi.org/10.1080/13569775.2018.1520057

Prihatini, Ella S. 2019b. 'Women's views and experiences of accessing national parliament: Evidence from Indonesia'. *Women's Studies International Forum* 74: 84–90. doi.org/10.1016/j.wsif.2019.03.001

Prihatini, Ella S. 2019c. 'Women who win in Indonesia: The impact of age, experience, and list position'. *Women's Studies International Forum* 72: 40–46. doi.org/10.1016/j.wsif.2018.10.003

Prihatini, Ella 2021. 'Explaining gender gaps in Indonesian legislative committees'. *Parliamentary Affairs* 74(1): 206–29. doi.org/10.1093/pa/gsz047

Prihatini, Ella S. 2022. 'Substantive representation of women in Indonesia'. In *Substantive Representation of Women in Asian Parliaments*, edited by Devin K. Joshi and Christian Echle, 93–116. Routledge. doi.org/10.4324/9781003275961

Prihatini, Ella and Iim Halimatusa'diyah. 2022. 'Gender, political dynasties, and committee assignments: Evidence from Indonesia'. *Parliamentary Affairs*, 1–19. doi.org/10.1093/pa/gsac019

Purdey, Jemma, Edward Aspinall and Muhammad Uhaib As'ad. 2016. 'Understanding family politics: Successes and failures of political dynasties in regional Indonesia'. *South East Asia Research* 24(3): 420–35. doi.org/10.1177/0967828X16659571

Ruedin, Didier. 2012. 'The representation of women in national parliaments: A cross-national comparison'. *European Sociological Review* 28(1): 96–109. doi.org/10.1093/esr/jcq050

Santoso, Widjajanti M. 2016. *Penelitian dan Pengarusutamaan Gender: Sebuah Pengantar* [Gender mainstreaming and research: An introduction]. LIPI Press. www.penerbit.lipi.go.id/data/naskah1479701451.pdf

Sawasdee, Siripan Nogsuan. 2018. 'A tale of two hybrid regimes: A study of cabinets and parliaments in Indonesia and Thailand'. *Japanese Journal of Political Science* 19(2): 269–92. doi.org/10.1017/S1468109918000099

Seguino, Stephanie. 2011. 'Help or hindrance? Religion's impact on gender inequality in attitudes and outcomes'. *World Development* 39(8): 1308–21. doi.org/10.1016/j.worlddev.2010.12.004

Sherlock, Stephen. 2010. 'The parliament in Indonesia's decade of democracy: People's forum or chamber of cronies?' In *Problems of Democratisation in Indonesia: Elections, Institutions and Society*, edited by Edward Aspinall and Marcus Mietzner. ISEAS Publishing.

Shvedova, Nadezhda. 2005. 'Obstacles to women's participation in parliament'. In *Women in Parliament: Beyond Numbers*, edited by Julie Ballington and Azza Karam, 33–50. International Institute for Democracy and Electoral Assistance.

Smith, Daniel M. 2018. *Dynasties and Democracy: The Inherited Incumbency Advantage in Japan*. Stanford University Press.

Stockemer, Daniel. 2017. 'The proportion of women in legislatures and cabinets: What is the empirical link?' *Polity* 49(3): 434–60. doi.org/10.1086/692491

Stockemer, Daniel and Aksel Sundström. 2019. 'Corruption and women in cabinets: Informal barriers to recruitment in the executive'. *Governance* 32(1): 83–102. doi.org/10.1111/gove.12352

Sundaryani, Fedina S. 2015. 'Jokowi must act firmly or lose trust: Expert'. *Jakarta Post*, 15 February. www.thejakartapost.com/news/2015/02/15/jokowi-must-act-firmly-or-lose-trust-expert.html

Towns, Ann E. and Birgitta Niklasson. 2018. 'Where are the female ambassadors? Gender and status hierarchies in ambassador postings'. In *Gendering Diplomacy and International Negotiation*, edited by Karin Aggestam and Ann E. Towns, 25–44. Palgrave Macmillan. doi.org/10.1007/978-3-319-58682-3_2

Chapter 5 Gender diversity in parliament, cabinet and ambassadorial appointments 89

True, Jacqui and Michael Mintrom. 2001. 'Transnational networks and policy diffusion: The case of gender mainstreaming'. *International Studies Quarterly* 45(1): 27–57. doi.org/10.1111/0020-8833.00181

UN Women. 2023. 'Facts and figures: Women's leadership and political participation'. UN Women, 7 March. www.unwomen.org/en/what-we-do/leadership-and-political-participation/facts-and-figures

UNDP (United Nations Development Programme). 2020. Gender Inequality Index. http://hdr.undp.org/en/content/gender-inequality-index-gii

Wardani, Sri Budi Eko and Valina Singka Subekti. 2021. 'Political dynasties and women candidates in Indonesia's 2019 election'. *Journal of Current Southeast Asian Affairs* 40(1): 28–49. doi.org/10.1177/1868103421991144

Welzel, Christian, Pippa Norris and Ronald Inglehart. 2002. 'Gender equality and democracy'. *Comparative Sociology* 1(3–4): 321–45. doi.org/10.1163/156913302100418628

Whitford, Andrew B., Vicky M. Wilkins and Mercedes G. Ball. 2007. 'Descriptive representation and policymaking authority: Evidence from women in cabinets and bureaucracies'. *Governance* 20(4): 559–80. doi.org/10.1111/j.1468-0491.2007.00372.x

World Economic Forum. 2022. *Global Gender Gap Report 2022*. World Economic Forum. www.weforum.org/reports/global-gender-gap-report-2022/

PART 2

Economic equality: Opportunities and limitations

6 Human capital development and gender equality in Indonesia

Sri Mulyani Indrawati

> The quality of a nation's manpower resources is the single most important factor determining national competitiveness.
>
> *Lee Kuan Yew, inaugural prime minister of Singapore*

Indonesia will celebrate a century of independence in 2045 with the aspiration—the Vision of Indonesia Maju 2045—to become a developed country. The National Development Planning Agency, Bappenas, projects that by 2045 gross domestic product (GDP) per capita will reach US$23,000 (Figure 6.1). The middle-income group will comprise 223 million people. Seventy-three per cent of people will live in urban areas, while the poverty rate will be near zero. To achieve this level of development, female labour force participation is projected to rise to 65% by 2045, demonstrating the significant role played by women in realising a more prosperous Indonesia.

To realise the 2045 vision, the government will pursue four main development agendas: improving the quality of human capital, achieving a green and sustainable economy, improving equity and common prosperity, and consistently implementing structural reforms.

Investing in human capital is critically important to advancing a country's economic development. We should draw lessons from Lee Kuan Yew's strong belief in this, as he ushered Singapore from a low- to a high-income country. Indonesia already has a promising demographic structure, dominated by productive age groups that account for around 69% of the total population. The middle class accounts for almost half of the population and is on the rise. The government has continued to enhance human capital quality in Indonesia through various policies.

94   *Sri Mulyani Indrawati*

Figure 6.1   Indonesia's growth trajectory towards 2045 (GDP per capita, US$)

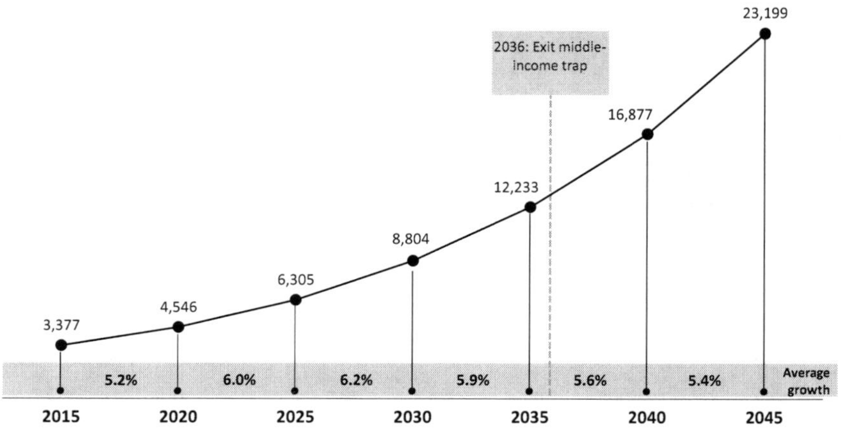

Source: Bappenas (2021).

Government spending on education and health have been mandated at a minimum of 20% and 5%, respectively, of total spending in the state budget, at both national and subnational levels. Anti-poverty policies along with social assistance programs have also been implemented by the government to improve human capital in Indonesia.

A vast amount of literature has underscored the link between human capital and economic growth. Pelinescu (2015) described human capital as the skills, knowledge or value of people. The role of human capital in economic development is illustrated through the neoclassical growth model (Solow 1956) or the endogenous growth model (Grossman and Helpman 1991; Lucas 1988; Romer 1986). These growth models have shown the significant role of human capital in driving high growth of the economy, in addition to other factors such as technology and physical capital. Bassanini and Scarpetta (2001) found from a series of OECD data for the period 1971 to 1998 that an increase of schooling by one year (equal to a rise in human capital of about 10%) leads to an average increase in GDP per capita of 4–7%.

Gender equality is crucially linked to human capital improvement. Because women make up 50% of the world population, underdevelopment, under-utilisation and misallocation of women's skills and talents is a huge lost opportunity to improve human capital and develop economies. A large body of literature states the positive impact of gender equality in increasing income and/or GDP growth (for example, Aguirre et al. 2012; Bertay et al. 2020; Kim et al. 2016; Lagerlöf 2003). Likewise, higher

Chapter 6 Human capital development and gender equality in Indonesia 95

gender inequality, particularly in education and employment, negatively affects the economy (Barro and Lee 2013; Esteve-Volart 2004; Klasen 2002; Klasen and Lamanna 2009). Pennings (2022) estimated that on average across countries, long-run GDP per capita would be almost 20% higher if gender employment gaps were closed. Madgavkar et al. (2020) observed that improvements in gender equity could add US$13 trillion to global GDP by 2030, compared with gender-regressive scenarios. Furthermore, the contribution of women to general economic welfare by performing large amounts of unpaid work, such as child-rearing and household tasks, is still poorly understood and underestimated (Kochhar et al. 2017; see also Sigiro, this volume).

According to the World Bank (2022), globally, gender equality has improved over the past decade in terms of increasing female education, declining maternal mortality rates and increasing female representation in politics. However, the World Bank argues that progress has been slow in other vital domains, such as the relatively flat female labour force participation rate (about 50% in the past three decades, and even lower in low-income countries), persistent wage gap, concentration of women in low-paying sectors and occupations with no legal contracts and lack of protection, as well as a gender digital divide. All these constraints hamper development and use of the human capital of women and in turn hamper the human capital development and growth of entire societies.

Awareness of the importance of gender equality in development has been evident in Indonesia since 2000 through Presidential Instruction 9/2000 on Gender Mainstreaming in National Development. This regulation mandated all institutions and ministries, central and regional, to carry out gender mainstreaming in the planning, implementation, monitoring and evaluation phases of policy and program development. The gender mainstreaming strategy has also been incorporated into the Indonesia National Medium Term Development Plan 2020–2024. Since women represent half of the population, the success of development goals depends on the extent to which the participation of women and men is balanced in all aspects of life. The presence of gender equality strategies emphasises the importance of women's roles in development agendas.

The World Bank (2022) estimated the benefit of eliminating gender inequality in women's workforce participation in Indonesia could be a 9% increase in GDP, or around US$135 billion by 2025. However, Indonesia faces challenges regarding the gender gap in many aspects of life, including health, education, economic livelihoods and employment. For more than two decades, progress in terms of gender equality has been slow. In addition, the COVID-19 pandemic's impact on lives and livelihoods has profoundly affected many vulnerable groups, including women.

96   *Sri Mulyani Indrawati*

In the rest of this chapter, I will discuss how the Indonesian government has used various policies to improve human capital and how those policies connect with gender equality. I also discuss what progress has been made in human capital development and how gender equality has played a role in this process. Special attention will be given to how COVID-19 has affected the development of human capital and gender equality.

Indonesia's policy journey in driving human capital and its connection to gender equality

Understanding the importance of human capital development to achieve Indonesia's Vision 2045, government policies—particularly health, education and social protection—have been heavily directed to generate healthier and productive human capital. On the health issue, the government continues to support the transformation of the health system and encourage the independence of the health sector. In the past two and a half years, we have also learned from the pandemic the urgency for strengthening health security preparedness. On the education side, the main purpose of education reform is still to improve the quality of education. Government policies to achieve these goals include improving teacher competence, providing accessible education for everyone, strengthening preschools, and developing and rehabilitating education infrastructure. Last, social protection reform is ongoing. The government continues to improve coverage and targeting, as well as striving to achieve lifelong social protection and adaptive social protection and empowerment for its citizens.

These long-term human development policies are reflected in the substantial increase in the state budget spending allocation for human capital. The budget for education, for example, has increased by more than 237% since 2007. Following the 5% mandatory allocation in 2009, health spending has risen by 137% since 2007. Last, social assistance expenditure has increased by 224% as the government continuously strengthens its efforts to alleviate poverty. The implementation of mandatory rules and budget increases have highlighted the government's preference for driving human capital quality. The budget increase is also accompanied by the improvement of the quality and effectiveness of all programs.

All of these government efforts to improve human capital are intricately connected with the advancement of gender equality. I will explain this connection by examining programs in the health, education and social protection sectors. Government policies and programs since the 1960s in these three areas are summarised in Table 6.1.

Chapter 6 Human capital development and gender equality in Indonesia

Table 6.1 Indonesia's policies in human capital since the 1960s

Decade	Health	Education	Social protection
1960s	1967 Family Planning Program		1964–1969 Massive Agriculture Credit Program (BIMAS/INMAS)
1970s	1970 Establishment of National Family Planning Coordinating Board (BKKBN)	1973 School expansion policy, including massive school construction program—Presidential Instruction on Primary Schools	
1980s	1986 Community healthcare (*puskesmas* and *posyandu*)	1984 6 years compulsory education program	
1990s		1994 9 years compulsory education program	1993 Presidential Instruction on Disadvantaged Villages
			1995 Disadvantaged Villages Infrastructure Development Program (P3DT)
			1999 Decentralisation Program
2000s	2000 Family Planning Program included as part of the National Development Program	2003 Reform on National Education System through Law 20/2003	2004 National Social Security System
	2005–2008 Healthcare for the poor (Askeskin)	2005 Schools Operational Assistance (BOS)	2007 Family Hope Program (PKH)
	2008–2013 Community Health Insurance (Jamkesmas)	2009 Mandatory 20% national budget allocation for education	2010 National Team for the Acceleration of Poverty Reduction (TNP2K)

98 *Sri Mulyani Indrawati*

Table 6.1 (continued)

Decade	Health	Education	Social protection
2000s	2009 Provision of complete immunisation for children	2010–2011 Indonesia Endowment Fund for Education (LPDP)	2012 Unified Database for Social Protection Program
	2014 National Health Insurance (JKN)	2013 • 12 years compulsory education program • First batch of LPDP awardees	2015 • Energy subsidy reform • Direct transfers to villages (Dana Desa)
	2016 Mandatory 5% national budget allocation for health	2014 Smart Indonesia Program (PIP)	2018 Food Assistance Program reform (subsidy to targeted social assistance)
	2020 Bangga Kencana Program—amplification of Family Planning Program	2019 • Education transformation through Merdeka Belajar program • Super tax deduction for industrial vocational activities	
		2021 Link and Match program for vocational education	

Health sector

Over the past 50 years, the government has committed to investing in human capital through the health sector. In the late 1960s, Indonesia introduced the Family Planning Program (Program Keluarga Berencana). It has become one of Indonesia's key policies to improving the welfare of families, especially low-income families. Its objectives are realised through empowering women and improving women's health. The National Family Planning Coordination Board (BKKBN) was established in the 1970s. This program continues to expand and amplify, such as integrating into the National Development Program and establishing the Bangga Kencana Program (a holistic program to improve the health of families, including stunting eradication).

Chapter 6 Human capital development and gender equality in Indonesia 99

Due to its broad access to and promotion of birth control provided under the Family Planning Program, Indonesia has achieved a high level of contraception prevalence, which contributed to a 38–43% reduction in maternal deaths from 1970 to 2017 (Utomo et al. 2021). Women also have a better knowledge of reproductive health, which improves their health and quality of life. The ability to control pregnancies has increased school participation and women's participation in the formal labour market (McDougal et al. 2021). At the national level, the program has also lowered the fertility rate, not only from contraceptive use but also from changing the public mindset on the nuclear family concept. Over time, Indonesia has reduced its population growth rate from 2.7% (1963) to 1.1% (2020).

In the 1980s, Indonesia established primary healthcare centres known as *posyandu* and *puskesmas*. Through these centres, Indonesia has provided a basic immunisation program for children since 2009, enabling early intervention to build quality human capital. The most renowned milestone is the mandatory allocation, introduced in 2016, of 5% of the state budget for health sector spending. Health insurance spending, especially for the poor, was introduced in the early 2000s, and is now established in the form of JKN (Jaminan Kesehatan Nasional), a national health insurance program to provide access to healthcare for all citizens.

The JKN program, introduced through legislation, aims to improve financial protection by reducing out-of-pocket health expenditure and increasing use of health facilities. Through this insurance scheme, Indonesia aspires to establish universal health coverage, improving access to healthcare, especially for women and children, in a sustainable way. Currently, 86.5% of the Indonesian population is enrolled in this program, and the government subsidises insurance for around 96.8 million people under the program for the poor and vulnerable (Penerima Bantuan Iuran). Private insurance companies exist to fill the gap. The Indonesian government is working to coordinate national and private healthcare to find the best fit for the national healthcare system.

The JKN program has also directly assisted women in improving their health outcomes. Of the 96.8 million people who receive JKN contribution assistance, based on data from the 2021 National Socioeconomic Survey (Susenas), half of the beneficiaries (50.3%) are women. The survey indicates that JKN policy, especially for the poor and vulnerable, is also inclusive in terms of gender. It allows better access to health services for women. These health services are related to pregnancy and conception, such as antenatal and postnatal care, assisted birth and access to family planning, which are important in building human capital. Given that Indonesian women generally have less paid employment and lower incomes than men, this policy is one that contributes to improving women's health and gender equality.

Education sector

Education priorities have evolved in a gradual manner over the years from primary to higher education. During the oil boom period in the 1970 and 1980s, one of the revenue allocations was dedicated to education investment. This began with a school expansion policy in the early 1970s followed by a government-mandated six years' compulsory education, introduced in the 1980s. This was lengthened to nine years of compulsory education in the 1990s, and then twelve years from 2013. The government has plans to further expand the years of compulsory schooling.

The government is not only targeting mandatory education for children, but also building adequate facilities for education and enhancing the quality of the education system as well as the quality of teachers. However, despite the mandatory allocation of 20% of the state budget for education, introduced in 2009, reforms in education policy are very much needed to better utilise this 20% state budget allocation. Many important education programs have been created, including the Smart Indonesia Program (Program Indonesia Pintar, PIP) and BidikMisi to help underprivileged students, that are intended to strengthen other previously implemented programs, such as Schools Operational Assistance (Bantuan Operasional Sekolah, BOS).

In 2010 the government established an endowment fund for education and in 2011 formed an agency—Lembaga Pengelola Dana Pendidikan (LPDP)—to administer the fund. The endowment fund and LPDP have been critical in supporting higher education and research and innovation in tandem with the provision of tax incentives for industrial vocational activities. Large tax deductions exist for companies that provide vocational activities: maximum gross income reductions of up to 200% are available for costs incurred for work practices, apprenticeships and/or learning activities.

The LPDP now manages US$7.1 billion in the endowment fund. This funding has provided more than 32,842 scholarships to young Indonesians to support their higher education in both domestic and foreign universities. The funding has also supported more than 1,668 research projects, many of which have been conducted jointly with international institutions. With this LPDP funding, many Indonesians can reach their dream of pursuing education at the best universities. The LPDP will not solve all of Indonesia's education problems, but it creates more confidence, especially among the younger generation in Indonesia.

In 2019 the Ministry of Education introduced the Merdeka Belajar program. The program is dedicated to improving students' interest in learning. In the program, teachers are also encouraged to be more

Chapter 6 Human capital development and gender equality in Indonesia 101

creative and open in delivering lessons to students. In 2021 the Ministry of Finance began to use fiscal tools more actively and innovatively for the education sector. The government wants to encourage the private sector to support the Link and Match program to support private companies to develop vocational training. Since the education budget is also disbursed through local governments, reforms and governance improvement of transfers to the regions are conducted continuously, including by using digital technology. For example, every school has an account number that is the reference for the central government to transfer the education budget directly.

Various government education programs have created more openings for Indonesian women to gain an education. Multiple indicators show that Indonesian people are increasingly better educated, including women. For instance, since the implementation of 12 years' compulsory education, expected years of schooling for women have increased from 12.13 years in 2013 to 13.22 years in 2021. In the same vein, the secondary school enrolment rate for women increased from 75.4% in 2013 to 80.7% in 2021 (Figure 6.2) (see also Dong and Merdikawati, this volume). Furthermore, in regard to the education endowment fund, 52.4% of the awardees are women, highlighting the increased competitiveness and huge potential that women have for the country's development. These expansions underscore the improving access to education and highlight considerable progress towards women's empowerment. However, Indonesia must continue to ensure equal access and quality of education across regions, keeping in mind its diverse profile.

Figure 6.2   Women's secondary school enrolment rate, 2010–2021 (%)

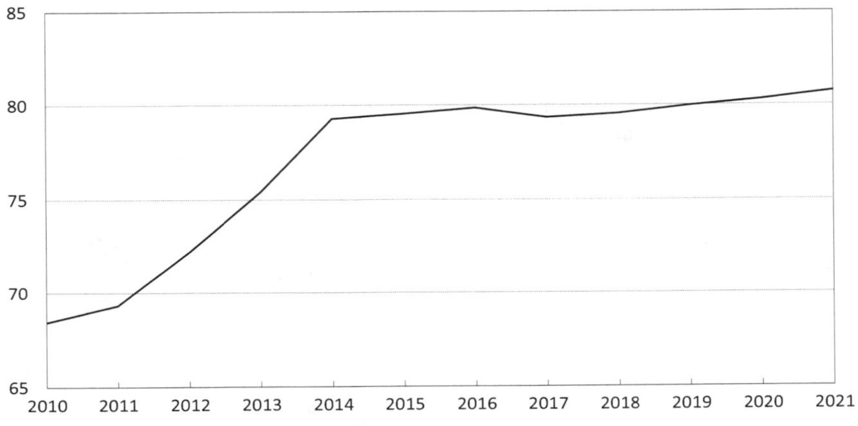

Source: Statistics Indonesia.

Social protection

Indonesia's first social protection program was more a poverty alleviation program. The Massive Agriculture Credit Program (BIMAS/INMAS) was introduced in the 1960s to improve agriculture products and productivity. In the early 1990s, the government, recognising that many villages in Indonesia were still left behind, issued presidential instructions with the aim of reducing inequality. Presidential Instruction on Disadvantaged Villages was released in 1993, followed by the Disadvantaged Villages Infrastructure Development Program (Pembangunan Prasarana Pendukung Desa Tertinggal, P3DT) in 1995. The current policy relating to village empowerment was introduced in 2015 in the form of central government direct transfers to villages, known as Dana Desa. More than 74,000 villages in Indonesia receive direct transfers, and more than 480 trillion rupiah or US$31.4 billion has been transferred to villages since 2015, helping to improve regional equality.

The poverty alleviation program today has evolved to provide more comprehensive social protection and was bolstered during the 2000s. The government introduced legislation for the National Social Security System in 2004 and continued with the implementation of the conditional cash transfer program—the Family Hope Program (Program Keluarga Harapan, PKH)—in 2007, which targets low-income families by their name, address and profile. To ensure the effectiveness and accurate targeting of various social protection programs, in 2012 the Unified Database for Social Protection Program was introduced. These programs are becoming the core reforms of poverty alleviation in Indonesia. Under President Joko Widodo's administration, the government aims to significantly reduce extreme poverty, with an ambitious target to be close to zero by 2024.

The Family Hope Program is the government's key program to alleviating poverty. It targets 10 million low-income families to be given direct cash provided they fulfil certain conditions, such as their children going to school and being immunised. The design of PKH comprises three dimensions of human capital development: health, education and social welfare. The program aims to eliminate intergenerational poverty and support families to sustain their livelihoods in a dignified way.

In addition to conditional cash transfers, the government provides economic empowerment through several programs targeting small and micro businesses. As many micro and small businesses are owned by women, these programs have direct gender equality implications. The micro credit program, Ultra Micro Credit (Umi), has been utilised by more than 5.38 million micro, small and medium enterprises (MSMEs), 95% of which belong to women. Furthermore, the Empowering Household

Chapter 6 Human capital development and gender equality in Indonesia 103

Economy program (Membina Ekonomi Keluarga Sejahtera, Mekaar), a community-based credit program dedicated to underprivileged women who want to start or develop a micro business, has reached 11.1 million women. The Kredit Usaha Rakyat (People's Business Credit) program, a subsided loan program channelled through the banking system, has benefited millions of women-owned small businesses. The government also provides support through taxation incentives. For small and medium enterprises in Indonesia, the final tax applied is only 0.5% of their gross sales.[1] MSMEs could also benefit further from training and other empowerment programs.

Social protection programs have a critical role in empowering women and improving gender equality. While the general purpose of social protection programs is to enhance the livelihoods of all citizens, many of these programs are centred around women since women tend to be more economically vulnerable. Furthermore, one of the most notable objectives of social protection programs is to reduce the inequality that can be caused by gender inequality. Many social protection programs, such as credit financing, can help empower women. Through these programs, the government aims to provide opportunities for women to access the labour market or business financing and improve women's digital literacy.

Progress and challenges in human capital development and their connection to gender equality

Progress

Government efforts over the decades to improve human capital have produced significant results. We have seen improvements in health, education and people's welfare. Women have particularly benefited from these policies. The development agenda implemented long ago has resulted in more inclusive development (Figure 6.3).

Life expectancy is one of the main indicators that reflects efforts in health sector reform. In the past two decades, life expectancy has improved from 65 years to 71.8 years (Figure 6.4a). Another critical indicator is the infant mortality rate. This indicator is vital because it also reflects the health of women and how women have better access to health facilities, which reduces the likelihood of infant mortality. This indicator has dropped from 41 to 19.5 deaths per 1,000 live births in the

---

1 Several government programs, such as Umi and Mekaar, specifically help micro businesses, while Kredit Usaha Rakyat and tax incentives apply to small and medium enterprises.

104   *Sri Mulyani Indrawati*

Figure 6.3   Gender Development Index and Gender Empowerment Measure

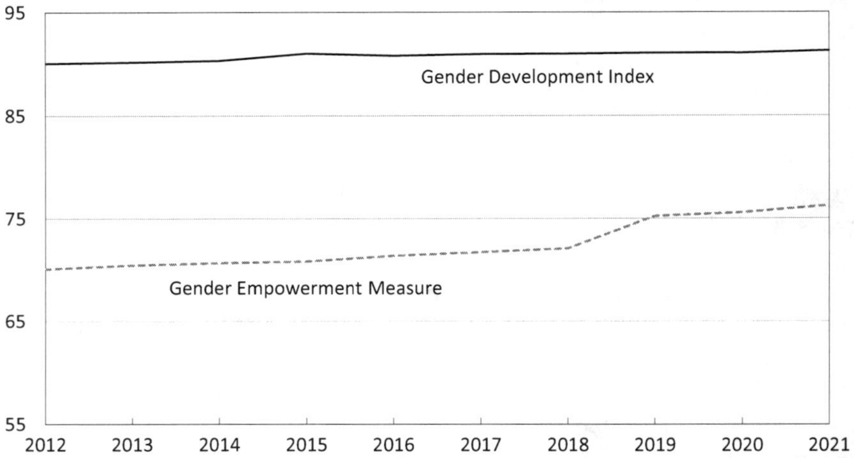

Source: United Nations Development Programme.

past two decades. It is still high, but its significant decrease is a sign that Indonesia's health policies are making a positive difference (Figure 6.4a).

In the education sector, from 2000 to 2021, the illiteracy rate has dropped to only 3.6%, and the years of schooling have increased from 6.7 years to 9 years (Figure 6.4b). If we compare the average years of schooling to the mandatory years of schooling, which is now 12 years, Indonesia is still below its target, but trending in the right direction. Another interesting trend is a decline in Indonesia's gross enrolment rate (*angka partisipasi kasar*) and an increase in net enrolment rate (*angka partisipasi murni*). This means that more people enrol in classes appropriate to their age, showing progress in fulfilling children's education rights (Figure 6.5).

At the same time as the overall increase in educational attainment in the past two decades, education of women has also caught up with that of men. For example, the enrolment rate of women in secondary school has improved from 81% to 90%. There are now more women than men in post–secondary education institutions (Figure 6.6). The improved gender equality in higher educational attainment is also reflected in the labour market, where the employment rate gap between men and women with higher education is much smaller than that for people with lower levels of education.

Figure 6.4 Indicators reflecting the improvement of human capital quality in Indonesia

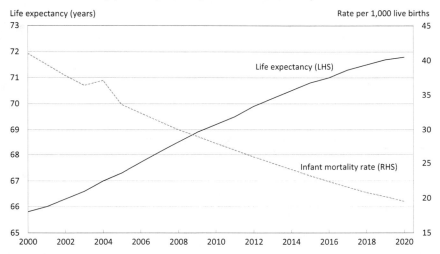

(a) Life expectancy and infant mortality rate

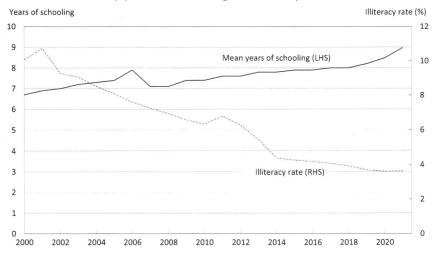

(b) Years of schooling and illiteracy rate

Note: LHS = left hand side, RHS = right hand side.

Source: Statistics Indonesia.

Figure 6.5 Educational attainment: Gross and net enrolment rates (%)

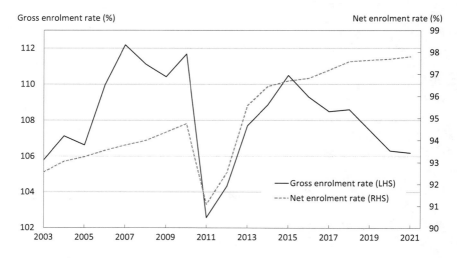

Source: Sakernas 2022 and Statistics Indonesia.

Figure 6.6 Proportion of employment by gender and education 2022 (%)

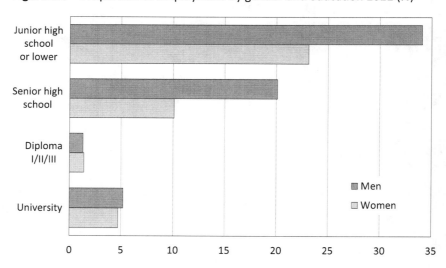

Source: Sakernas 2022 and Statistics Indonesia.

Chapter 6 Human capital development and gender equality in Indonesia 107

Aside from universal health and education policies, better-targeted social assistance has also improved people's welfare in general. The poverty rate has decreased from 19.1% to 9.5% in the past 20 years. During the COVID-19 pandemic the poverty rate rose again but decreased to single digits in 2021. This poverty reduction was followed by a decrease in inequality, which in the early 2000s had picked up strongly. This indicates that development is also more inclusive, and Indonesia now ranks as a moderate inequality country, reflected by a Gini ratio of 0.38 (Figure 6.7).

Figure 6.7   Poverty rate and Gini ratio

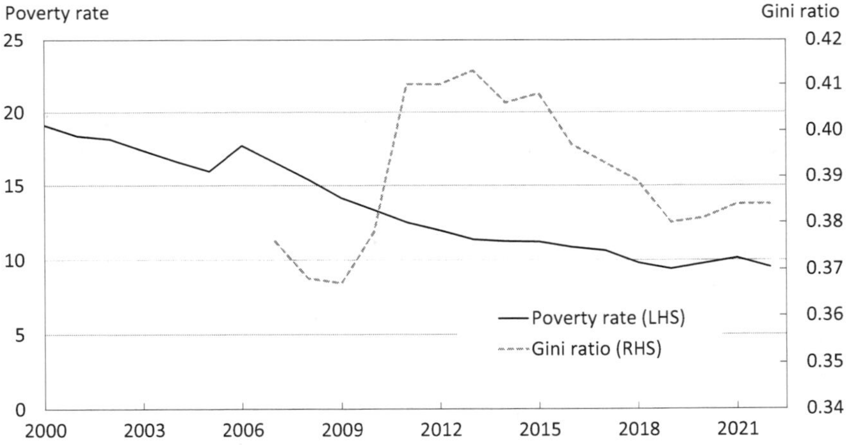

Note: The Gini ratio is a measure of income distribution across a population, and ranges from 0 (full equality) to 1 (no equality).

Source: Statistics Indonesia.

Challenges

Various policies have succeeded in making substantial progress in human capital development and at the same time improving gender equality. However, Indonesia still has many issues to solve in this regard. The COVID-19 pandemic also set back improvements in human capital development and gender equality. In the next sections, I discuss these challenges in terms of education, labour market outcomes and health. I also discuss how COVID-19 has affected the development of human capital and gender equality.

Education

Despite remarkable progress in the education sector, various learning indicators remain below government targets. In the past 20 years, Indonesia's PISA score[2] has fluctuated but generally trended flat (Figure 6.8). Among 72 countries surveyed, Indonesia's performance is lower than the OECD average in reading, mathematics and science (Table 6.2). The 2018 PISA score showed that 70% of Indonesian students scored below the minimum proficiency level for reading. Students in the lowest-income tier primarily contributed to the score, but even the highest-income student scored only 406, below minimum proficiency. Afkar and Yarrof (2021) estimated that the PISA score would worsen after the COVID-19 pandemic due to learning access difficulties during school closures. The pandemic has aggravated learning conditions for less-fortunate students, widening the learning gap between the rich and the poor.

At 20%, the Indonesian government's budget allocation for education is vast, but the low PISA scores point to inherent problems in the education system. Various programs have been implemented, such as BOS (Schools Operational Assistance), a teacher certification scheme, and School Mover Program (Sekolah Penggerak), but they have still not resolved several core issues reflected in the low PISA scores. The Knowledge Sector Initiative Indonesia has highlighted that the solution to Indonesia's problem is not more resources but rather more efficient use of resources.

There is still a gap between females and males in terms of average years of schooling. In 2021, Indonesian women's average school years (8.17) were behind men's (8.92). Even though the enrolment rate gap at all levels of education has been reduced significantly, the female enrolment rate in 2021 at tertiary level remained low at 33.4% and lagged most East Asia peers. The COVID-19 pandemic may have widened the gap between girls and boys in education. During COVID-19, out of more than 82,000 low-income families with children aged 7–18, just over 1% dropped out of school (UNICEF et al. 2021). However, girls were ten times more at risk of dropping out of school than boys, partly due to an increase in early marriage. Poverty is the main factor for children dropping out of school, where girls who are not in school are vulnerable to child marriage (see Kusumaningrum et al., this volume). This condition emphasises the lost opportunity to drive higher economic growth and better welfare.

---

2   The PISA score is the OECD's Programme for International Student Assessment. PISA measures 15-year-olds' competence in reading, mathematics and science. While Indonesia's PISA score has been flat, school enrolment has increased. In 2001, the PISA sample covered only 46% of 15-year-olds in Indonesia; in 2018, 85% of 15-year-olds were covered. In a business-as-usual scenario, more students in the data sample results in a lower performance score.

Chapter 6 Human capital development and gender equality in Indonesia 109

Figure 6.8 Indonesia's PISA score, 2000–2018

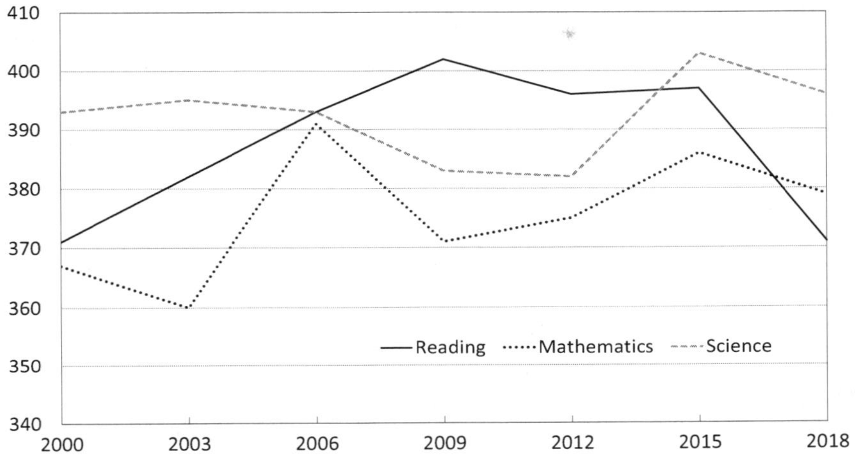

Source: OECD (2018).

Table 6.2 Average PISA scores for reading, maths and science, OECD and ASEAN countries, 2018

	OECD	ASEAN-5	Indonesia
Reading	487	434	371
Mathematics	487	432	379
Science	489	444	396

Note: PISA = OECD Programme for International Student Assessment; OECD = Organisation for Economic Co-operation and Development; ASEAN-5 = Indonesia, Malaysia, the Philippines, Singapore and Thailand.
Source: OECD (2018).

Furthermore, the pandemic has amplified the challenge of child marriage, which creates obstacles for women to pursue education. Indonesia has the highest incidence of child marriage after Cambodia in ASEAN countries. The Ministry of Women's Empowerment reported that one in nine girls below 18 years old has married, and child marriage during the pandemic escalated. Child marriage potentially disrupts future productivity and creates a welfare problem loop. Girls dragged into child marriage suffer permanent consequences, including difficulty continuing their studies, a higher risk of domestic violence and risky pregnancy, all of which potentially affect their future children. The prevalence of child marriage could worsen the situation of human capital loss in Indonesia.

Labour market

The outcome of relatively lower education levels of women translates into labour market conditions in Indonesia. One of those is reflected in the lower participation of female employment in the science, technology, engineering and mathematics (STEM) sector. Data from the National Labour Force Survey (Sakernas) show that women predominantly work in agriculture, forestry, plantations and fisheries and are mostly employed in low-skilled jobs that are at risk of future automation (ILO 2021). Consequently, women are 20% more likely than men to lose their job because of automation. In addition, the number of female internet users is still lower than male internet users (44.9% versus 50.5% in 2019), causing women to lag behind in the digital field (see Kusumawardhani, this volume). Recent entrepreneurial developments triggered by the COVID-19 pandemic have fostered a digital economy ecosystem to digitise MSMEs. Lack of access to the internet is a disadvantage for women entrepreneurs and small business owners.

Indonesia also has a significant issue with female participation in the labour market in general. Over decades, Indonesia's female participation has only marginally improved. Improvement in the education and health sectors has not resulted in more women in the workforce. Various complex issues have created barriers for women to enter the labour market, such as sociocultural gender issues, the availability of parent-friendly jobs and childcare issues.

In general, plenty of working-age women have not joined the labour force (inactivity rate). Sakernas data reveal that women's inactivity rate in Indonesia is almost triple that of men's (45.7% versus 16.4%), and women's labour force participation rate (LFPR) is also lower. In 2022, women's LFPR was 54.3%, still not back to the pre-pandemic level, while men's LFPR was 83.7%. The COVID-19 pandemic also affected women's labour force participation. In 2021, women's LFPR declined to 54% from 54.5% in 2020. Many women work in traditional service sectors and feminised sectors such as restaurants, accommodation and homeworkers, and these areas were hardest hit during the pandemic. Based on Sakernas data in 2020, more than 59% of 85 million workers in the restaurant and accommodation industries were women. Women therefore experienced a disproportionate loss of income during the pandemic. Domestic violence also intensified during COVID-19, due to increasing financial hardship, social restrictions and limited access to services for women.

The magnitude of COVID-19's impact on the working-age population and businesses was considerable. Many workers became unemployed, stopped work temporarily or had shortened working hours. In 2020, 14.3% of the working-age population was affected by COVID-19. One of the

Chapter 6 Human capital development and gender equality in Indonesia   111

reasons workers gave for ceasing work during the pandemic was to take care of the household (5% of workers who stopped working). However, 90% of workers who stopped working due to the need to take care of the household were women (Sakernas survey, August 2020). In addition, the percentage of businesses owned by women that had to terminate (7%) was twice that of men (3.4%) (UNICEF et al. 2021). This is unfortunate because women play a significant role in family businesses.

School closures put additional pressure on women regarding domestic responsibilities and caretaking. A household survey conducted by UNICEF, UNDP, Prospera and SMERU in 2020 found that mothers were the primary carers in 71.5% of households that supported their children in remote learning (UNICEF et al. 2021). The same figure for fathers was only 23.4%. Women were therefore impacted harder than men by the pandemic because women not only stopped working and lost their income but also took on more domestic chores. Moreover, women are less likely to return to work once they have been out of the workforce.

Looking deeper into economic aspects, women's income contribution to the household and per capita expenditure are also lower than men's. In 2021, women's income contribution to the household was 37.2%, just over half that of men's (62.8%). Women's income contribution is a proxy that can show how women play a role and contribute financially. It also indicates the existence of women's economic independence that can lead to more equal relationships and autonomy. Meanwhile, women's annual per capita expenditure (Rp 9 million) is significantly lower than men's (Rp 15.8 million). This can be attributed to lower workforce participation by women and the gender pay gap. For the same educational level and skills, women earn, on average, 23% less than men (BPS 2022). Most women also work in the informal sector, where average wages are much lower than in the formal sector, and job protection and health insurance are inadequate or non-existent.

A widespread view is that problems in women's workforce participation are related to the influence of sociocultural norms, stereotypes and gender roles that affect various aspects of life. While women may have employment outside the home, social norms continue to demand that women remain first and foremost committed to caring for their husbands, children and parents, which creates multiple roles for women. Sociocultural norms also affect policy support for equal access, participation, control and benefits for women, crucial variables influencing women's participation in education, health, the economy, employment and decision-making. Women's role in domestic work and caretaking (unpaid care work) has typically not been included in economic accounts. Thus, women have been seen to be less productive than men. If a financial value was calculated for the 'care economy' (domestic chores and care work, mostly performed by women), it may be treated as seriously as the value of work in the traditional economy. This is a critical element of the labour market that needs to be addressed.

Another labour force inequality is evident in political and managerial areas. Until 2020, women's representation in parliament was about a quarter of men's (21.1% versus 78.9%) (Figure 6.9). Even though policies exist to improve women's participation in politics, women's representation has not achieved the targets. In the government sector, despite the fact that the proportion of women civil servants exceeds that of men, men still dominate managerial positions and have more decision-making power. Even if women fill managerial positions, they often sit at lower levels.

The situation in private entities is similar. In 2020, the proportion of women in a managerial position was half that of men (33.1% versus 66.9%), most of which were in the administration field, such as finance and human resources. At the same time, men predominantly held more strategic and decision-making positions. This phenomenon stems from gender stereotypes and the assumption, among others, that women are not qualified enough from an educational perspective. The under-representation of women in decision-making positions in both politics and business leads to the under-utilisation of women's talents and a lack of women's voice in influencing the country's future.

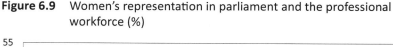

Figure 6.9 Women's representation in parliament and the professional workforce (%)

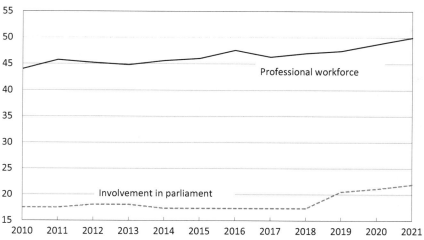

Source: Statistics Indonesia.

Health

A major problem in Indonesia's health sector is child stunting. Various social welfare programs have contributed to a reduction in stunting prevalence, from 37.2% in 2012 to 24.4% in 2021, but prevalence is still above the World Health Organization target of 20%. This number is also high compared to ASEAN-5 peers (Figure 6.10) and income-level peers. In more disaggregated data, only six provinces have a stunting prevalence below 20% but still above the Indonesian government target of 14%. There is only one province in Indonesia where the stunting prevalence is as low as 10%. There is also a gap between the rich and poor. Poor children have a higher risk of stunting than children in higher-income families, due to limited access to basic services.

Stunting is a critical problem for human capital development because of its lifelong consequences for children's future. Stunted children do not grow to their optimum potential, leading to human capital losses. While the stunting rate in Indonesia continues to decelerate, it is higher than the global average. The COVID-19 pandemic exacerbated the situation: patients' visits to health providers declined and several crucial health programs for children, such as *posyandu*, were halted. There are

Figure 6.10 Stunting prevalence, Indonesia and ASEAN countries (%)

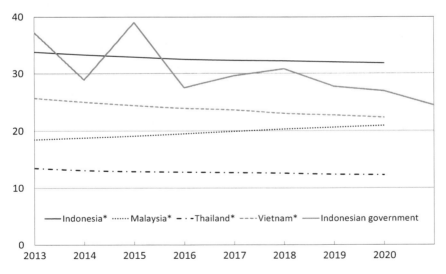

Note: * World Bank modelled.

Source: Indonesian Ministry of Health and World Bank (https://data.worldbank.org/indicator/SH.STA.STNT.ME.ZS?locations=TH-MY-ID-VN).

114   *Sri Mulyani Indrawati*

indicators that these interruptions to children's basic healthcare and lower assisted childbirth by health workers could potentially set back the stunting reduction program. Considering the urgency, the government of Indonesia has put stunting as a national priority issue and committed to significantly reduce the stunting rate to 14% by 2024.

The World Bank (2020) claims that nutrition interventions are among the most cost-effective investments for human capital. From the 5% state budget allocation for health, 1% is tagged for the stunting reduction program. However, the stunting intervention program is scattered at central, local and village levels, which complicates program coordination. This situation has again shown that implementation, efficiency and effectiveness are critical issues to be resolved beyond the high budget allocation.

In terms of gender equality in health, the unsettling fact is that the number of health complaints for women is still higher than that for men (28.3% versus 26.2% in 2021). This indicator correlates with the degree of accessibility to health knowledge and facilities, indicating that women have less knowledge and access to health services than men. Furthermore, we know that women have multiple roles that were elevated with the pandemic, such as income earner, caretaker, child tutor and domestic worker, and these extra burdens may lead to an increase in the number of health complaints by women. A survey by the National Commission on Women in Indonesia (Komnas Perempuan) found that 41% of women experienced heightened domestic violence during the pandemic (Bappenas 2021), an experience that is likely to contribute further to the deterioration of women's health.

Women's health suffers in other ways: Indonesia's maternal mortality rate in 2020 is high at 305 per 100,000 live births, comparing unfavourably to the United Nations Sustainable Development Goal 2030 target of 140. Local health services are not always able to provide the family planning, reproductive health, nutrition and other information and support that women need.

Macroeconomic and fiscal policy

To maintain budget support for the human capital development programs discussed in this chapter, sustainable macroeconomic and fiscal policies are vital. Indonesia's macroeconomic conditions have been relatively stable and resilient. These conditions have been supported by buoyant domestic demand, backed by a vibrant demographic profile. Before the COVID-19 pandemic, Indonesia's gross domestic product (GDP) growth averaged 5.3% from 2010 to 2019 (Figure 6.11), well above the global average GDP growth of 3.7%, and above the 5.1% of emerging markets and developing

Figure 6.11 Indonesia's GDP growth compared to other emerging markets, 2006–2022 (%)

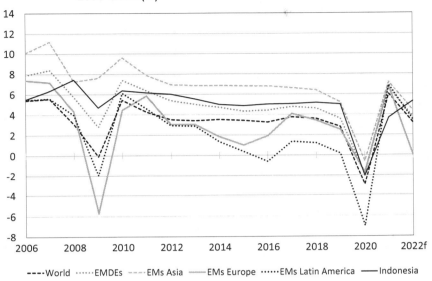

Note: EMDEs = emerging markets and developing economies; EMs = emerging markets.
Source: Indonesian Ministry of Finance and World Economic Outlook Database April 2022 (www.imf.org/en/Publications/WEO/weo-database/2022/April).

economies. Solid macroeconomic performance is also underpinned by declining inflationary pressure. From 2010 to 2019, Indonesia's average annual inflation rate was about 4.76%, significantly lower than the 2000–2009 realisation of 8.8% (Figure 6.12).

The COVID-19 pandemic created great shocks in Indonesia's economy, as it did worldwide. As a result, Indonesia's GDP growth contracted for the first time since the Asian financial crisis, by 2.1% in 2020. The large-scale mobility restrictions in response to the pandemic significantly affected both domestic and external demand sides. Nevertheless, effective health measures (including vaccine acceleration) and extraordinary economic policies (including issuing Program Pemulihan Ekonomi Nasional, National Economic Recovery Program) have led to Indonesia's relatively fast economic recovery. Indonesia's extraordinary policies during the pandemic concentrated on protecting human capital, building upon three pillars: (1) protecting health and saving lives, (2) maintaining purchasing power, mainly for vulnerable groups and (3) preventing business bankruptcies and job layoffs.

Figure 6.12 Indonesia's inflation compared to other emerging markets, 2006–2022 (%)

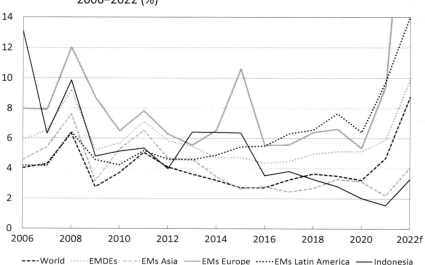

Note: EMDEs = emerging markets and developing economies; EMs = emerging markets.
Source: Indonesian Ministry of Finance and World Economic Outlook Database April 2022 (www.imf.org/en/Publications/WEO/weo-database/2022/April).

Supported by credible and extraordinary policy responses, in 2021 Indonesia's GDP growth rebounded to 3.7%, and the output level (real GDP) returned to the pre-pandemic level of 1.6%. The economy continued to gain momentum in 2022, in which GDP grew to 5.2% in the first semester, and the output level reached 7.1%. The economic recovery has improved people's welfare, as marked by the decline in unemployment from 6.3% in February 2021 to 5.8% in February 2022, as well as the poverty level that has returned to a single-digit figure (9.5%; Figure 6.7).

Indonesia's economic recovery has sustained despite elevated global risks, and policies will continue to be well calibrated to safeguard recovery and pave the way for more sustainable and inclusive economic development. The current global economic situation is challenging, and global risks are compounding due to various factors, such as the war in Ukraine that has exacerbated supply disruptions, skyrocketing commodity prices and persistently high inflationary pressures. These factors have led many countries to implement aggressive monetary policy tightening, which has increased the risk of recession. Indonesia continues to prioritise policies that protect household purchasing power amid rising prices, giving confidence to business sectors amid high uncertainty, and

Chapter 6 Human capital development and gender equality in Indonesia 117

aims to build a stronger foundation for medium to long-term development through structural reforms. Putting human capital at the centre of policies is critical because it is a core area of reform and addresses the scarring effects of the pandemic.

Indonesia's effort to prioritise human capital is also reflected in the 2023 state budget policies. The 2023 state budget is monumental, marking the return of a mandatory fiscal deficit of a maximum of 3% of GDP. Despite the consolidation trajectory, fiscal policy will remain supportive of sustaining recovery and reinforcing structural reforms but still anticipative of global dynamics. Prudent fiscal policy aims to support the core development agenda. There are several priority agendas in the 2023 state budget, including human capital, infrastructure, bureaucratic reform, industrial revitalisation and the green economy. Education, health and social protection policies are embedded in the human capital agenda.

Fiscal policy is instrumental in defending multiple goals, such as being the risk absorber during crises as well as the driver to achieve development goals. Through its functions, namely allocation, distribution and stability, fiscal policy upholds macroeconomic strength. Considering its critical role, Indonesia assiduously preserves fiscal prudence and sustainability. Fiscal management has long been disciplined, and mandatory fiscal rules were committed before the pandemic. During the pandemic, fiscal policy was adjusted to allow the deficit to rise above 3% of GDP for three years (2020–2022). Gradual consolidation has been applied, and the deficit will return to below 3% of GDP, highlighting the credible fiscal policy framework and commitment to protecting fiscal sustainability. Correspondingly, Indonesia's deficit and debt-to-GDP levels are among the lowest of its peers (Figures 6.13 and 6.14). This has shaped Indonesia's economic soundness and resilience in the past two decades.

Conclusion

As outlined in this chapter, driving human capital quality and promoting gender equality are essential to pursuing Indonesia's medium- to long-term economic development agenda. Over the past decade Indonesia has achieved significant health, education and social welfare outcomes, promoted more inclusive development and improved gender equality. Indonesia has transformed its health system, education system, poverty alleviation programs, social protection programs and gender mainstreaming strategy to improve human capital and gender equality. It has achieved a decrease in the infant mortality rate, an increase in the net school enrolment rate, a narrowing gap in the labour market between men and women with higher education, and reduced poverty to below 10%.

Figure 6.13 Government debt, 2006–2022 (% of GDP)

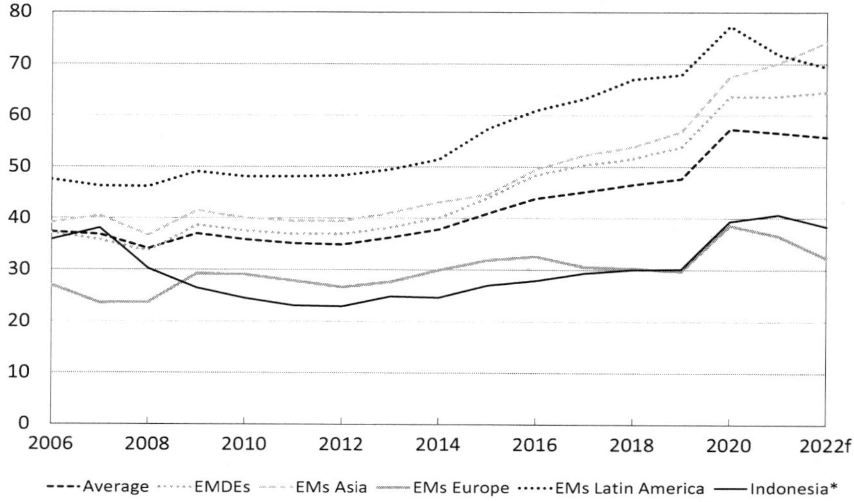

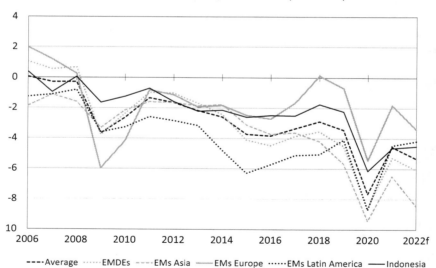

Note: * realisation until October 2022.

Figure 6.14 Government fiscal deficit, 2006–2022 (% of GDP)

Note: EMDEs = emerging markets and developing economies; EMs = emerging markets.
Source: Indonesian Ministry of Finance and World Economic Outlook Database April 2022 (www.imf.org/en/Publications/WEO/weo-database/2022/April).

Chapter 6 Human capital development and gender equality in Indonesia 119

But challenges remain, notably after the COVID-19 pandemic in 2020. For example, Indonesia's student proficiency (PISA score) is still below the minimum standard, female participation in employment is low, and child stunting and maternal mortality rates are high.

Indonesia continues to strengthen policies and strategies to address its challenges. Increasing the focus of planning and budgeting for human capital development and gender responsiveness is advancing. The spending allocation for the education and health sectors continues to be a priority. To address the COVID-19 impact, which had an uneven impact, especially for women and children, a gender-based recovery supported by gender-disaggregated data is one of the measures promoted by the national government. Encouraging learning recovery has started through a national curriculum extension. Efforts to prevent and reduce child marriage have intensified. Taking unpaid care work more seriously is a priority because the burden of domestic and unpaid care work for women has heightened since the pandemic and affected female labour force participation.

Indonesia is strongly committed to achieving its development goals and to be a prosperous country. Amid external and internal turbulence, Indonesia cannot lose sight of addressing multiple structural issues, including human capital and focusing on achieving gender equality. Human capital reforms should be accompanied by fiscal reforms and go hand-in-hand with other structural reforms. Indonesia has long been recognised as a country that pushes forward reforms amid recovery from crises, including during the episode of the COVID-19 pandemic. The launch of the omnibus law on job creation (Cipta Kerja) in 2020 was seen as a milestone to improve the investment climate and create jobs. On the fiscal front, reforms include those on taxation and fiscal decentralisation. The spirit of reform will carry on, productivity and competitiveness will be improved, and institutional frameworks will be strengthened. In all, these efforts are testimony to Indonesia's tenacity in developing the transformation of the country, supporting its people, including women, to thrive.

References

Afkar, Riftiya and Noah Yarrof. 2021. *How Indonesia's Education System Can Overcome the Losses from the COVID-19 Pandemic and Raise Learning Outcomes for All.* World Bank. https://documents1.worldbank.org/curated/en/589551630680730676/pdf/Rewrite-the-Future-How-Indonesias-Education-System-can-Overcome-the-Losses-From-the-COVID-19-Pandemic-and-Raise-Learning-Outcomes-for-All.pdf

Aguirre, DeAnne, Leila Hoteit, Christine Rupp and Karim Sabbagh. 2012. *Empowering the Third Billion: Women and the World of Work in 2012.* Booz and Company. www.booz.com/global/home/what_we_think/reports_and_white_papers/ic-display/51245276

Bappenas (National Development Planning Agency). 2021. *Tanggapan dan Masukan Terhadap Laporan Kajian 'Analisis Ketimpangan Gender Spasial dan Pengaruhnya Terhadap Perekonomian Wilayah'* [Responses and input to the study report 'Analysis of spatial gender inequality and its impact on the regional economy']. Bappenas.

Barro, Robert J. and Jong-Wha Lee. 2013. 'A new data set of educational attainment in the world, 1950–2010'. *Journal of Development Economics* 104: 184–98. doi.org/10.1016/j.jdeveco.2012.10.001

Bassanini, Andrea and Stefano Scarpetta. 2001. 'The driving forces of economic growth: Panel data evidence for the OECD countries'. *OECD Economic Studies* (33). doi.org/10.1787/eco_studies-v2001-art10-en

Bertay, Ata Can, Ljubica Dordevic and Can Sever. 2020. *Gender Inequality and Economic Growth: Evidence from Industry-Level Data.* IMF Working Paper 20/119. doi.org/10.5089/9781513546278.001

BPS (Badan Pusat Statistik). 2022. *Booklet Survei Angkatan Kerja Nasional Februari 2022* [National Labour Force Survey Booklet, February 2022]. BPS.

Esteve-Volart, Berta. 2004. *Gender Discrimination and Growth: Theory and Evidence from India.* LSE STICERD Research Paper No. DEDPS42. https://ssrn.com/abstract=1127011

Grossman, Gene M. and Elhanan Helpman. 1991. 'Trade, knowledge spillovers, and growth'. *European Economic Review* 35(2–3): 517–26. doi.org/10.1016/0014-2921(91)90153-A

ILO (International Labour Organization). 2021. 'Women in STEM Programme in Indonesia'. *Result Brief.* ILO Jakarta.

Kim, Jinyoung, Jong-Wha Lee and Kwanho Shin. 2016. *A Model of Gender Inequality and Economic Growth.* ADB Economics Working Paper No. 475. Asian Development Bank.

Klasen, Stephan. 2002. 'Low schooling for girls, slower growth for all? Cross country evidence on the effect of gender inequality in education on economic development'. *World Bank Economic Review* 16: 345–73. doi.org/10.1093/wber/lhf004

Klasen, Stephan and Francesca Lamanna. 2009. 'The impact of gender inequality in education and employment on economic growth: New evidence for a panel of countries'. *Feminist Economics* 15(3): 91–132. doi.org/10.1080/13545700902893106

Chapter 6 Human capital development and gender equality in Indonesia   121

Kochhar, Kalpana, Sonali Jain-Chandra and Monique Newiak, eds. 2017. *Women, Work, and Economic Growth: Leveling the Playing Field.* International Monetary Fund.

Lagerlöf, Nils-Petter. 2003. 'Gender equality and long-run growth'. *Journal of Economic Growth* 8(4): 403–26. www.jstor.org/stable/40215889

Lucas, Robert E., Jr. 1988. 'On the mechanics of economic development'. *Journal of Monetary Economics* 22(1): 3–42. doi.org/10.1016/0304-3932(88)90168-7

Madgavkar, Anu, Olivia White, Mekala Krishnan, Deepa Mahajan and Xavier Azcue. 2020. *COVID-19 and Gender Equality: Countering the Regressive Effects.* McKinsey & Company, 15 July. www.mckinsey.com/featured-insights/future-of-work/covid-19-and-gender-equality-countering-the-regressive-effects

McDougal, Lotus, Abhishek Singh, Kaushalendra Kumar, Nabamallika Dehingia, Aluisio J.D. Barros, Fernanda Ewerling, Yamini Atmavilas and Anita Raj. 2021. 'Planning for work: Exploring the relationship between contraceptive use and women's sector-specific employment in India'. *PLOS ONE* 16(3): e0248391. doi.org/10.1371/journal.pone.0248391

OECD. 2018. 'PISA 2018 Snapshots'. https://www.oecd.org/pisa/publications/pisa-2018-snapshots.htm

Pelinescu, Elena. 2015. 'The impact of human capital on economic growth'. *Procedia Economics and Finance* 22: 184–90. doi.org/10.1016/S2212-5671(15)00258-0

Pennings, Steven. 2022. 'How much would GDP per capita increase if gender employment gaps were closed in developing countries?' *World Bank Blogs,* 4 March. https://blogs.worldbank.org/developmenttalk/how-much-would-gdp-capita-increase-if-gender-employment-gaps-were-closed-developing

Romer, Paul M. 1986. 'Increasing returns and long-run growth'. *Journal of Political Economy* 94(5): 1002–37. www.jstor.org/stable/1833190

Solow, Robert M. 1956. 'A contribution to the theory of economic growth'. *Quarterly Journal of Economics* 70(1): 65–94. doi.org/10.2307/1884513

UNICEF, UNDP, Prospera and SMERU. 2021. *Analysis of the Social and Economic Impacts of COVID-19 on Households and Strategic Policy Recommendations for Indonesia.* Jakarta: UNICEF.

Utomo, Budi, Purwa Kurnia Sucahya, Nohan Arum Romadlona, Annette Sachs Robertson, Riznawaty Imma Aryanty and Robert Joseph Magnani. 2021. 'The impact of family planning on maternal mortality in Indonesia: What future contribution can be expected?' *Population Health Metrics* 19: 2. doi.org/10.1186/s12963-020-00245-w

World Bank. 2020. *Spending Better to Reduce Stunting in Indonesia: Findings from a Public Expenditure Review.* World Bank. doi.org/10.1596/34196

World Bank. 2022. 'Gender equality and development +10 #AccelerateEquality'. World Bank, 18 February. www.worldbank.org/en/topic/gender/brief/gender-equality-at-a-crossroads

7 New opportunities and old constraints: Gender equality in the post-Suharto era from an economic perspective

Sarah Xue Dong and Nurina Merdikawati

The advancement of gender equality is a long-term social change and can be reflected in measurable economic indicators. In the Western world, the improvement of women's status and freedom in society is accompanied by dramatic changes in economic indicators, including an increase in female labour market participation, an increase in female educational attainment, narrowing of the gender wage gap, an increase in age at first marriage, and a decline in fertility rate (Goldin 2006). Similar changes have occurred in the developing world in the past few decades where there was relatively fast economic growth. Education of girls caught up with that of boys by the mid-2010s; labour force participation of women has increased significantly, especially in Latin America and the Caribbean; and the fertility rate has dramatically declined (World Bank 2012). However, there are still persistent large gender gaps in earnings, health and asset ownership (ibid.).

The trajectory of economic gender equality in Indonesia has been consistent with that of the developing world in many aspects. Since independence, Indonesia has made great progress in increasing schooling, reducing the fertility rate and increasing life expectancy of women. Economic liberalisation in the New Order era created fast economic growth and job opportunities for women, especially in export-oriented manufacturing. The end of the New Order, however, has seen a dramatic decline in the importance of export-oriented manufacturing as a growth engine. The new driver of economic growth has mainly been the resources boom. At the same time, the change from an authoritarian and highly

Chapter 7 Gender equality in the post-Suharto era from an economic perspective 123

centralised regime to a much more democratic and decentralised regime has allowed different social and religious groups and ideologies, including gender ideologies, to surface.

Against this backdrop, how has gender equality evolved from an economic perspective during the post-Suharto era? In this chapter we will use large-scale economic data to construct trends of many of the economic indicators of gender equality. We mainly use a cohort analysis approach to show long-term generational change. We find that employment opportunities for women have significantly improved during the post-Suharto era. Each new cohort of women is more likely to join the labour force, more likely to be employed in the formal sector, and more likely to be managers and professionals in the years following completion of their education. Educational attainment of women has also caught up and surpassed that of men in recent years. On the other hand, women still face old constraints when trying to take up these new economic opportunities. Every cohort of women in urban areas, including the youngest, are likely to drop out of the formal sector and take up informal-sector jobs during child-bearing years, and are not likely to enter the formal sector again. The recent trend of marrying and having a first child earlier for women across all education groups can exacerbate this constraint as child-bearing years become earlier. We suggest that government policies should address the constraints women face in urban areas to remain and succeed in the formal sector. These policies could include better transport infrastructure, better childcare facilities, support for more flexible working arrangements and enforcement of minimum age at marriage.

Gender equality in Indonesia from an economic perspective

Gender equality from an economic perspective is often interpreted as how women's economic participation is on par relative to men's. The most common way to measure this metric is by looking at female labour force participation. In this section, we provide a review of studies examining the trends of women's participation in the labour market, various factors influencing their decisions to enter the labour market, and persistence of the wage gap between men and women in Indonesia.

Schaner and Das's (2016) study is the closest study to ours, and broadly provides a diagnostic assessment of women's economic participation in the labour market over the years, and how it is potentially shaped by changes in women's educational attainment, among other factors. Their study relies mainly on the National Labour Force Survey (Survei Angkatan Kerja Nasional, Sakernas) from 1990 to 2011 and they analyse labour market trends by age and birth cohorts, educational attainment, urban/rural residence and type of employment. They also use the 2012 Indonesian Demographic and Health Survey in order to understand the correlation between female labour force participation and education, fertility and proxies of female empowerment. They find female labour force participation is increasing among younger women in urban areas, particularly in wage employment, while the trend is reversed for younger women in rural areas as they are withdrawing from informal and unpaid work. In their correlational analysis, Schaner and Das (2016) show that married women with young children are less likely to work, especially as wage workers, in line with a finding from Comola and de Mello (2008), who use Sakernas data from 1996 and 2004.

Schaner and Das (2016) also find that female labour force participation is highest at the bottom and top of wealth distribution, most likely for different reasons. High labour market participation by poor women is more likely due to the need for additional income, while outside labour market options drive the decisions for wealthy women to work. This explanation is aligned with that of Cameron et al. (2001), who highlight the role of income and substitution effects in women's decisions to participate in the labour market. In their study, they find that women with low-educated husbands (who potentially have limited earning power) are more likely to work than women with highly educated husbands, while highly educated women are more likely engaged in the labour market. The role of income effect in dominating women's decisions to enter the labour market is even more prevalent during economic crises. Facing suddenly lower household income during the Asian financial crisis in 1997–1998, more women entered the labour force during this period, mostly to work in the informal sector (Fallon and Lucas 2002; Smith et al. 2002).

Another study by Cameron et al. (2019) sought to understand the drivers of female labour force participation using selected years of the National Socioeconomic Survey (Survei Sosio-Ekonomi Nasional, Susenas) and the Village Potential Survey (Survei Potensi Desa, Podes) from 1996 to 2013. They estimate the probability of an individual participating in the labour force, on a set of potential demand- and supply-side drivers, for which they present the results showing changes in participation probability by age and year of birth. They find that the supply-side factors are the main drivers, underlining that women's economic participation largely depends on their marital status, educational attainment and number of children. They find that younger cohorts' participation in the labour market is higher than their older counterparts, and conjecture that this reflects changing cultural norms. Studies on gender norms in Indonesia are relatively sparse, and often provide only snapshots of one period in particular areas for particular groups (Utomo 2012, 2016). The World

Chapter 7 Gender equality in the post-Suharto era from an economic perspective 125

Values Survey[1] regularly asks questions related to gender norms and the results show that, indeed, norms and attitudes towards women's participation in the labour market and higher education improved between 2001 and 2018. However, a recent survey on social norms reveals that Indonesian young adults aged 18–40 still support more traditional social norms where men's perceived role is to work and provide for their family while women are better as caretakers for their children (YouGov and Investing in Women 2020).

Further analysis tracking women across their lifecycle by Cameron et al. (2019) using five Indonesia Family Life Surveys shows that women's labour market activity changes as they get married and have children. Women with only a senior secondary school certificate experience a significant drop in their labour supply following marriage and childbirth, while tertiary-educated women continue to work as they become mothers. Cameron et al. (2019) also find that more than 40 per cent of female wage workers leave their jobs one year after marriage, and only a small fraction of them return, mostly as self-employed workers. Structural model estimates from Radhakrishnan (2010) suggest that the informal sector tends to provide greater compatibility between work and childcare responsibilities.

All the abovementioned studies are descriptive, and they are not able to answer what actually causes the stagnating female labour force participation in Indonesia. Rising women's educational attainment and fertility rate reduction have been lauded as some factors that may induce higher female labour market participation. Indeed, the gap between men and women's educational attainment has narrowed over time (Schaner and Das 2016). The total fertility rate has also reduced dramatically, from 5.9 in the 1960s to 2.6 in the early 2000s. The extensive Family Planning Program that began in 1968 has played an important role in contributing to this decline (Hull 1987). Priebe (2010) attempts to uncover a causal effect of changes in fertility rate on female labour supply in Indonesia, using Susenas data from 1993 to 2008. He postulates two opposing effects leading the female labour supply to remain unchanged. While a lower fertility rate may make some women participate more in the labour market, others may lack the incentive to do so as their budget constraints are relaxed as a result of fewer children.

In terms of other metrics of gender equality in the labour market, the wage gap between men and women in wage employment is still sizeable (Schaner and Das 2016), despite the gap decreasing over time. A large

---

1 www.worldvaluessurvey.org/wvs.jsp

share of this gender wage gap reflects the gender-based discrimination in the labour market, a conclusion drawn by AIPEG et al. (2017) using data from the 2011 Susenas. When using an earlier period of 1986 and 1997 Sakernas, Feridhanusetyawan et al. (2001) show that the declining gender wage gap is attributed to the reduction in discrimination practices, particularly for low-educated women. They further argue that education becomes the most important factor to narrow the gender wage gap. The wage gap between men and women persists not only for wage workers, but also for those who are self-employed, with lower-earning women in both types of employment experiencing the greatest gaps (Sohn 2015). Gender wage gaps are also found to be wider among younger workers, and those who work in the public sector (Taniguchi and Tuwo 2014).

Labour market policies can also have unintended consequences in exacerbating gender wage gaps. A case in point is where the minimum wage policy worsens the gender wage gap among the least-educated production workers in the manufacturing sector, illustrated by Hallward-Driemeier et al. (2017) in their analysis using Survei Industri datasets from 1995–1997 and 2006. In contrast, the gender wage gap among the higher-educated production workers narrowed. The minimum wage policy is also found to diminish women's role in household decision-making, further reinforcing traditional gender roles (Kim and Williams 2021). Despite the good intentions of minimum wage policies in improving the lives of low-wage workers, policymakers need to be aware of the potential gendered unintended consequences, in addition to potential employment loss that may disproportionately affect women (Merdikawati 2022; Suryahadi et al. 2003).

Our study contributes to the literature by providing a more comprehensive picture of women's economic participation, and changes in women's educational attainment, marriage patterns and fertility behaviour for more than two decades. Our study leverages both Susenas and Sakernas data from 1995 to 2021, which allows us to examine not only the trends of women's labour market outcomes in greater detail (i.e. types of employment, types of sectors, types of occupations), but also their marriage and fertility decisions, because all information is from the same dataset.[2] Our extensive coverage also allows us to observe longer life cycle patterns of younger cohorts born in the 1980s and 1990s. Furthermore, our study provides a more systematic assessment of changes in economic opportunities and barriers faced by women, backed by 25 years of data.

---

2 Susenas asks both labour market outcomes and detailed individual characteristics such as marital status, age at first marriage, number of children and their corresponding age.

Increased economic opportunities in the *reformasi* era

Indonesia enjoyed a period of fast economic growth during the New Order era from the late 1960s to 1996, with the gross domestic product (GDP) growth rate averaging around 7 per cent every year. This period of growth was driven mainly by export-oriented manufacturing sector growth, and was interrupted by the Asian financial crisis in 1997–1998. With the regime change and a shift in government policies, combined with increased competition from China, export-oriented manufacturing stagnated during the post-Suharto era, and the GDP growth rate has slowed compared to the New Order era. Nevertheless, Indonesian GDP continued to grow at around 6 per cent per year from the mid-2000s to the mid-2010s, driven mainly by the commodity boom generated by China's phenomenal economic growth (Garnaut 2015).

Decades of sustained economic growth has increased income levels and living standards of Indonesian households, and large numbers of households entered the middle-income class during the 2000s and 2010s (World Bank 2019). New economic opportunities were created during this process, especially for women. Goods and services demanded by the middle class, including consumption-oriented manufactured products (such as manufactured food and beverages), health, education and tourism, are mostly produced by industries that have a high concentration of women employees. Therefore, job opportunities for women have increased. At the same time, education levels and skills of women have increased because of a higher demand for education from middle-income households. The fertility rate has also decreased since the New Order, as a result of rising income levels and governments' efforts in family planning. The combined results are better-educated women with fewer children who have better economic opportunities. In the data analysis below, we will show some evidence of these developments.

Decrease in fertility, increase in education, increase in labour force participation

Using Susenas data from 1995 to 2017 we found that, over generations, there is little reduction in the number of women who have one child or two children in their lifetime, but a significant reduction in women who have three children or more in their lifetime. Figure 7.1 charts the life trajectory of women born in different cohorts in terms of the number of children they have, by their level of education. It shows the percentage of each cohort (born in five-year intervals) at each age who have three children or more. We can see there are dramatic reductions in women who have three children or more over the cohorts. The biggest drop occurred

Figure 7.1 Women who have three children or more by age, cohort and education level (%)

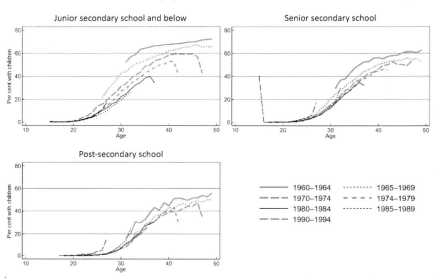

between cohorts born in earlier years (during the 1960s), and for women who have lower levels of education.

In terms of education, we look at the percentage of men and women aged at least 25 years with less than primary school, with at least primary school, with at least junior secondary school, with at least senior secondary school, and with post-secondary school qualifications, by the year they are born. In Figures 7.2 and 7.3 we can see that both men and women in rural areas have lower educational attainment than those in urban areas, but educational attainment in both urban and rural areas has risen fast for people born between 1950 and 1995. Female educational attainment started lower than male educational attainment for people born in the 1950s but caught up over four decades and surpassed that of male educational attainment in both urban and rural areas by the cohort born in 1995. There were more women than men with at least primary education in cohorts born from 1980. There were more women than men with at least junior secondary education in cohorts born from 1985 to 1990. There were more women than men with at least senior secondary education in cohorts born around 1995. From the cohort born around 1975, however, there were more women than men with post-secondary education, although for both men and women the percentage with post-secondary education remains low.

Figures 7.1, 7.2 and 7.3 show a dramatic reduction in fertility rate and increase in educational attainment for women over the past few decades.

Figure 7.2 Educational attainment in urban areas by year of birth (aged 25+), 1950–1995 (%)

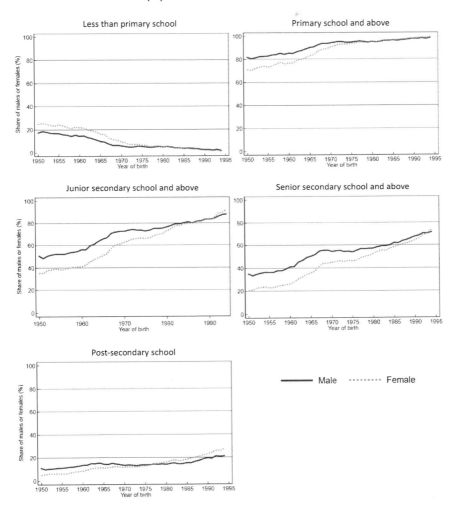

Figure 7.4 shows that these developments, combined with better economic opportunities, result in more women working in each more recent cohort, at least in the years immediately following the completion of their education. Figure 7.4 shows the percentage of women working for each cohort and age, therefore charting the lifetime trajectory of women's labour force participation for different cohorts. The most consistent long-term change is that in urban areas and for women with junior secondary education and below, each new cohort starts working earlier in their life. Although all cohorts (except the ones born in the 1950s) achieve a lifetime peak

Figure 7.3 Educational attainment in rural areas by year of birth (aged 25+), 1950–1995 (%)

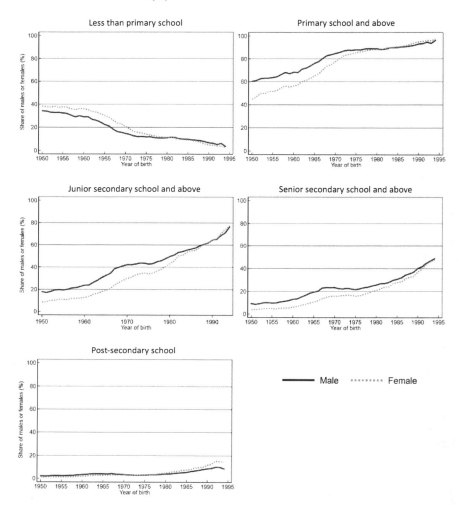

participation rate of just under 60 per cent, each new cohort reaches this peak at an earlier stage of their lives. This pattern is also observed for post-secondary educated women in both urban and rural areas, but not so much for senior secondary educated women or for junior secondary or below educated women in rural areas. For post-secondary educated women, the increase in labour force participation in the early years of women's lives occurred more prominently for more recent cohorts, namely the ones born after 1974. The increase in labour force participation in the

Chapter 7 Gender equality in the post-Suharto era from an economic perspective 131

Figure 7.4 Female labour force participation by age (aged 20–65) and cohort, urban and rural areas (%)

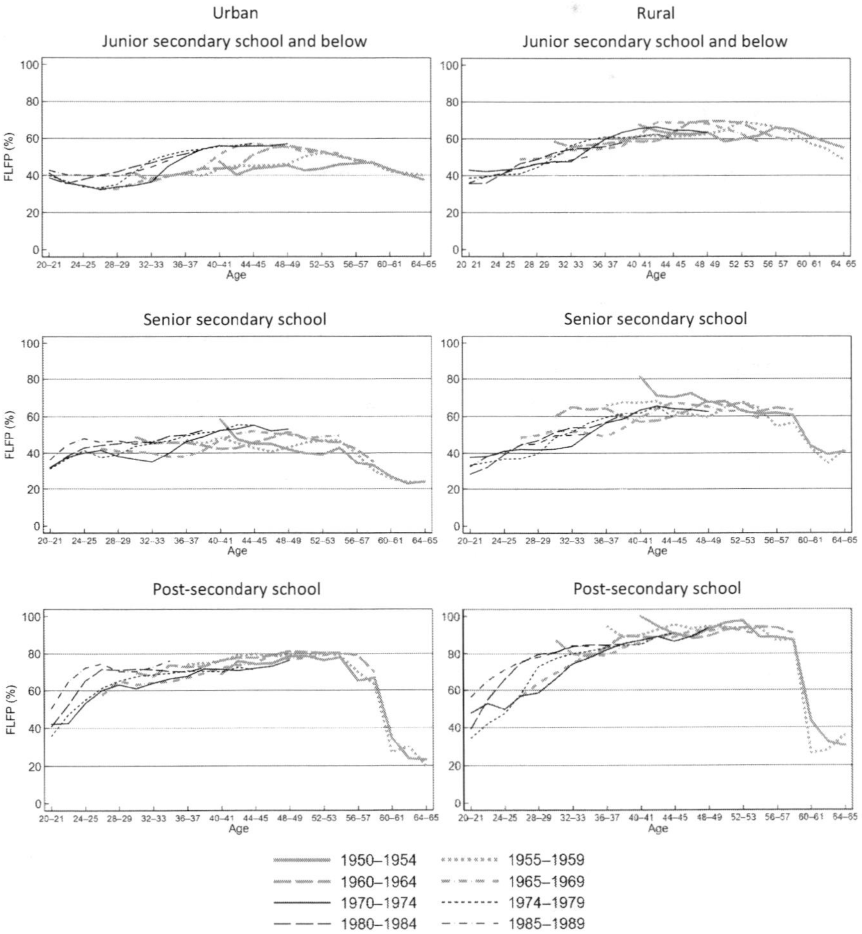

Note: Female labour force participation (FLFP) is defined as the percentage of women who worked for at least 1 hour in the past week over the population of women in the cohort age and urban/rural group.

early years of their lives for urban women with junior secondary school education or below is probably driven by both a decrease in fertility rate and an increase in economic opportunities. The increase in labour force participation in early years of their lives for both urban and rural women with post-secondary education is probably driven mainly by better economic opportunities.

Increase in formal-sector employment

In the literature on women's labour force participation in developing countries, there is a long understanding that high labour force participation does not necessarily mean abundant labour market opportunities. It could also be a sign of low income and poverty where women need to work to make ends meet for their families (Dong 2018; Goldin 2006). Therefore, one needs to look beyond labour force participation to study change in economic opportunities for women. One way to measure economic opportunities in developing countries is the number of formal-sector jobs, which is usually proxied by wage work in contrast to self-employed or unpaid family work. Figure 7.5 shows there is a dramatic increase in the percentage of women in recent cohorts who hold wage work in urban areas. Compared with the cohort born between 1970 and 1974, the cohort born between 1985 and 1989 is about five percentage points more likely to be employed as wage workers at the start of their career. This is a big increase in the number of jobs in the wage sector considering the size of the urban female population.

Figure 7.5 Female labour force participation in wage work and self-employed work by age (aged 20–65) and cohort, urban and rural areas (%)

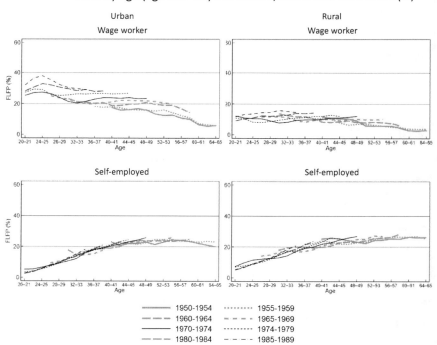

Increase in employment in high-end services

Another way to look at the increase in job opportunities for women is to look at the number of women in professional occupations in the services sector, that is, in the high-end services sector. As income levels rise in a country, high-end services are where highly paid job opportunities arise. Figure 7.6 charts the percentage of the working-age population employed in different sectors over time. We can see that the general trend for both men and women is a decline in employment in agriculture, replaced by an increase in employment in the services sector. What is noticeable about the gender difference is that, for women, there is a bigger increase in employment in manufacturing and in high-end services. The percentage of the working-age female population employed in high-end services increased from about 2 per cent in 2000 to almost 7 per cent in 2021. This is a considerable increase in the number of jobs in high-end services, again considering the size of the female working-age population in Indonesia.

Figure 7.6 Employment rate of working-age population (aged 15–65) by sector, 2000–2021 (%)

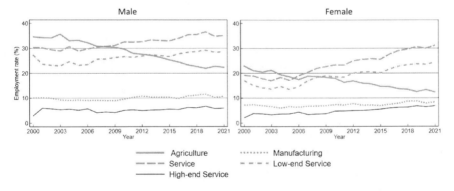

Constraints faced by women when trying to take up economic opportunities

Notwithstanding the new economic opportunities generated by income level rise, better educational attainment and lower family size, Indonesian women still face some of the old constraints when trying to take up these opportunities. Living within a traditional and dominantly Muslim society, Indonesian women are still the main caregivers in the household. Therefore, even women who are highly educated and facing good job opportunities need to balance market work and household work every day, especially after they have children. Notorious traffic jams in major cities in Indonesia resulting in hours of commuting time combined with the lack of affordable and reliable childcare for many middle-income class families makes working away from children extremely difficult, especially if there is no extended family support in the same city. These constraints make it hard for women to remain and succeed in highly paid, but at the same time demanding, jobs. Below we will show some evidence of these constraints.

Drop-out of formal sector in urban areas during child-bearing years

While Figure 7.5 shows that formal-sector job opportunities are increasing for more recent cohorts of women in urban areas, it also shows that all cohorts tend to drop out of the formal sector during the child-bearing years. The decline in participation in the formal sector happens at around age 25 for all cohorts born after 1970. It seems that some women who drop out of the formal sector enter the informal sector by taking up self-employed work, as we see in Figure 7.5. This suggests that having children is a major constraint for women to remain in the formal sector, and women take up more flexible but less formal self-employed work when they can no longer work in the formal sector. From Figure 7.5 we can also see that, in rural areas, the decline of formal-sector work during child-bearing years is lower; this shows that the shorter commute for wage workers and the existence of extended families in rural areas helps women to balance the demands of formal sector jobs and childcare.

Increasing gender wage gap in the high-end services sector

Another sign of the constraints faced by women to succeed in highly paid jobs is the decline in the gender wage ratio in the high-end services sector. Figure 7.7 shows that high-end services is the highest-paid sector among all employment sectors for men and women. In 2021, the average wage in high-end services was about 25 per cent more than the average wage in manufacturing, 50 per cent more than the average wage in low-end services, and 100–150 per cent more than the average wage in agriculture, depending on the gender of the worker. It also shows that although real wages have been rising for both men and women, men consistently earn more than women in all sectors. Therefore, it would be interesting to see if the gender wage ratio (the average of women's wages divided by the average of men's wages) has improved over time.

While gender wage ratios increased in agriculture, manufacturing and low-end services, the gender wage ratio in high-end services, the highest-paid sector, declined from 2000 to 2021 (Figure 7.8). This is in contrast with the fact that jobs in high-end services for women have grown quickly

Chapter 7 Gender equality in the post-Suharto era from an economic perspective

Figure 7.7 Log of average real wages by sector, 2000–2021

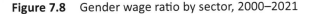

Figure 7.8 Gender wage ratio by sector, 2000–2021

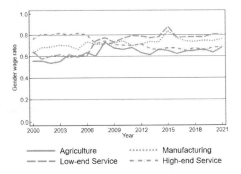

during the same period. We think these two phenomena suggest that while more women enter high-end services at the entry level at the early stage of their career, many of them are not able to remain in this sector or not able to progress into higher-paid levels in this sector. Therefore, while more women are in the sector, most of them stay at the entry level, while men are more likely to progress into higher-paid levels.

The dropping out from the formal sector during child-bearing years and the decline in the gender wage ratio in high-end services both suggest that child-bearing is a major constraint for women to remain and succeed in well-paid jobs. If women start to have children later in their lives, as has been happening in the Western world in the past fifty years, women will be able to progress further in their career before facing these constraints. We find that, however, the most recent cohorts of Indonesian women are getting married and having their first child earlier, contrary to the trend in the Western world at a similar stage of economic development. This new trend of early marriage and child-bearing is probably driven mainly by the more conservative attitudes towards dating and marriage promoted by various Muslim groups (*The Economist* 2020). Below we show some evidence of this trend.

Decreasing marriage age and child-bearing age for recent cohorts

Figure 7.9 charts the percentage of women who are married by age and by cohort. We can see there is not much change in marriage age for cohorts born between 1960 and 1979, but women born after 1980 start to get married earlier. This is the case across all education groups and in both urban and rural areas, but especially for senior secondary and

Figure 7.9 Women married by age (aged 15–49) and cohort, urban and rural areas (%)

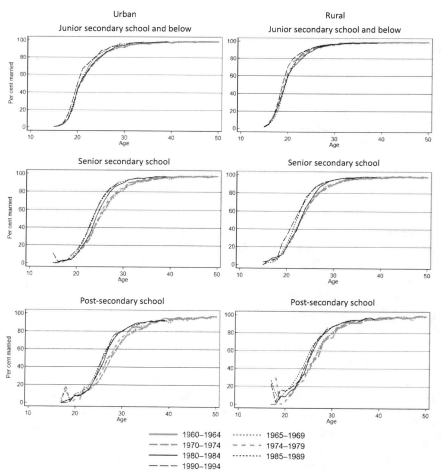

post-secondary educated women in urban areas. Earlier marriage age is accompanied by earlier child-bearing age, shown in Figure 7.10, in both urban and rural areas. This newly developed trend means that women will face childcare constraints when trying to remain and succeed in highly paid formal-sector jobs earlier in their life.

Figure 7.10 Women with at least 1 child by age (aged 15–49) and cohort, urban and rural areas (%)

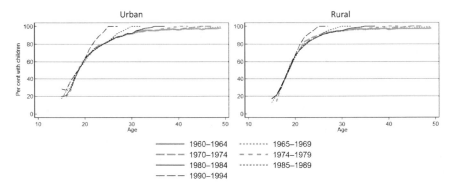

Conclusion and policy recommendations

Using National Socioeconomic Survey (Susenas) and National Labour Force Survey (Sakernas) data that cover the last few years of the New Order era and the entire post-Suharto era until right before the start of the COVID-19 pandemic in 2020, we have assessed generational change in women's labour market outcomes, education, marriage age and fertility rate in the past twenty-five years. We found that women's economic opportunities improved in the post-Suharto era, mainly due to increases in income levels and expansion of the middle class. More recent cohorts of women are more likely to start working earlier in their lives, more likely to work in the formal sector, and more likely to work in highly paid professional jobs in the services sector. But we find that women still face old constraints around family responsibilities and childcare that restrict them from fully taking advantage of the newly formed job market opportunities. Women in each cohort in urban areas are likely to drop out of the formal sector when they enter child-bearing age. The gender wage gap has widened in the high-end services sector—the most highly paid employment sector—probably because women are much less likely to stay and advance beyond entry levels in this sector when child-bearing years start. The most recent trends of marrying earlier and having their first child earlier in their lives across all education groups will exacerbate

138 *Sarah Xue Dong and Nurina Merdikawati*

the childcare constraints because many women will face these constraints earlier in their lives.

Addressing these constraints requires change in social attitudes towards division of work at home and change in workplace practice, in addition to change in government policies. While examining social attitudes and workplace practice is beyond the scope of this chapter, we discuss a few government policies that may help lessen the constraints women face when trying to participate and take up opportunities in the labour market.

Better urban transport infrastructure

Urban women may face more constraints to enter and remain in the workforce, and lack of access to reliable transport has been identified as one of the barriers (ADB 2015). Traffic is generally more congested in urban areas, translating into much longer hours being outside the home, which may put women in more challenging circumstances navigating both work and the unequal burden of domestic and childcare responsibilities. Also, women often do not have access to a private vehicle for regular use, particularly so for less-educated women from low-income households (ADB 2013; Widarti 1998). Providing efficient, affordable and safe urban public transport may relax the constraints these women have in participating in the labour market.

There have been some improvements in public transport in Jakarta, a capital city infamous for its badly congested roads. Mass rapid transit (MRT) has been operating in Jakarta since 2019 and more MRT and light rail transit (LRT) routes are under construction and development. Jakarta's network of minibuses (*angkot*) has also been integrated with other public transport modes under JakLingko. This includes its payment system where passengers can use one card to pay the fees for all transport modes, and the fees collected are regulated by Jakarta's provincial government to ensure JakLingko's affordability. Furthermore, the commuter train (KRL) serving Greater Jakarta regions provides cars reserved exclusively for female passengers and TransJakarta bus rapid transit (BRT) also reserves areas inside the buses for women.

Further improvement in public transport, not only in urban Jakarta but also in other areas, may have the potential to increase female labour force participation, particularly in addressing spatial mismatches (McKenzie 2017). This is even more pertinent for women who are at the margins of making decisions on their labour market participation (Witoelar et al. 2017). However, establishing a causal link between improvement in women's mobility and female labour market participation is empirically

Chapter 7 Gender equality in the post-Suharto era from an economic perspective 139

challenging. Nevertheless, the latest study by Field and Vyborny (2022) shows that reducing physical mobility constraints for women, in this case by providing women-only transport for pick-and-drop services to their workplaces in Pakistan, leads to a large effect on women's job search behaviour, which also includes those who are not searching for jobs initially. These results relate to broader policies improving women's mobility, of which high-quality public transport plays an important role, and how they may have the potential to improve women's labour market attachment.

Increasing access to reliable and affordable childcare services

Our findings showing declining female labour force participation during child-bearing years may indicate that these women are facing childcare constraints. Indeed, Halim et al. (2017) argue that the decision for women assuming a primary role as caretakers for their children is more likely driven by a consequence of childcare constraints, rather than reflecting their preferences. While many Indonesian women rely on informal non-parental childcare provided by grandparents or in-house domestic workers, those options are out of reach for many families and hence there is likely to be a demand for more childcare services.

Early childhood education services can be one form of childcare alternative, of which recent expansion of preschool access for children aged 3–6 years was found to increase work participation of mothers with eligible children by 7.4 per cent (Halim et al. 2022). These preschool sessions typically operate for 3 hours, and are more beneficial for women in informal sector employment who do not have full-time work commitments. Halim et al. (2022) further show that public preschools cater to lower-income groups, as proxied by mothers' education levels, as they found that public preschool expansion increases the work participation of mothers with low education.

Closing the gap of unmet demand for reliable and affordable childcare services is crucial to improving female labour force participation in Indonesia. The government may increase the duration of existing early childhood education and development programs and incentivise development of childcare services for children in other age groups, among others. It is also important that childcare services are affordable and locally based. Collaboration at the village or local-government level and financial incentives for employers to provide onsite and full-time childcare services should be explored to ensure that availability and affordability of childcare services is met for those who need them.

Flexible working arrangements

The COVID-19 pandemic has changed how people view and value flexible working arrangements. Wider adoption of these practices benefits women who also have domestic and childcare responsibilities. Women also tend to have stronger preferences for flexible work, for instance, options to work remotely (Pelta 2021). The pandemic, during which more people were required to work from home, has accelerated the offer and uptake of flexible work. This transformation took place in both the public and private sectors. The Indonesian Ministry of State Apparatus Empowerment and Bureaucratic Reform issued a number of circular letters to guide the implementation of working from home for government officials. The hybrid version combining a mix of days working at home and at an office can be a way forward post-pandemic; this option was found to increase retention, job satisfaction and productivity (Bloom et al. 2022).

Part-time work is also a flexible working arrangement often favoured by women: female part-time employment in Indonesia is nearly 50 per cent. The new government regulation 36/2021 provides a framework for calculating an hourly wage rate for part-time workers. However, worker protections for part-time employees are limited, and these can be improved by requiring employers to provide pro-rata leave and contributions to pension and worker insurance schemes for their part-time workers, for example. Policies and regulations allowing workers with young children to reduce their working hours and protecting them from retaliation are currently non-existent in Indonesia. These policy options can be considered, as the country is also pushing for more generous maternity and paternity leave in a proposed new bill. While this type of work and flexible working arrangements are often accessible only to those who work as wage workers, these more comprehensive family-friendly policies may help improve women's labour market attachment and prevent the exodus of women leaving wage employment after marriage and childbirth.

Ensuring compliance to newly legislated minimum age at marriage

Our findings show that younger cohorts are tending to marry and start child-bearing at an earlier age, in contrast to the trends in other East Asian countries of women getting married later or never marrying (Bertrand et al. 2021). It is likely that the trends of marrying and having children early contribute to the low female labour force participation in Indonesia, as our study also shows declining women's labour market participation upon marriage and child-bearing. While it is not clear if such trends are due to the prevalence of child marriage in Indonesia, it is concerning that, in 2018, one in nine Indonesian women were married as

Chapter 7 Gender equality in the post-Suharto era from an economic perspective 141

children. The harmful effects of child marriage are well documented, as child brides are more prone to complications during their pregnancy and childbirth, vulnerable to domestic violence, and less likely to remain in school (UNICEF Indonesia et al. 2020; see also Kusumaningrum et al., this volume). In a welcome change following years of pressure from advocacy groups, Indonesia's parliament amended the marriage law in 2019, raising the minimum age for girls to marry with parental permission from 16 to 19 years old, in line with boys. This change in the marriage law at least allows young women to prolong their schooling years and explore economic opportunities before they get married.

However, the amended law still contains clauses for waiving the minimum age requirement as the religious courts have retained the rights to allow underage marriage when requested by families. The number of such requests increased after the new minimum marriage age was raised. Furthermore, most of the requests are granted, often not involving the approval and without the knowledge of the underage couples (*The Economist* 2021).

While the government set an ambitious target to reduce child marriage by 40 per cent by 2030, this target is unlikely to be achieved if compliance is low. While stronger enforcement can be considered as a policy option, this path may lead to unintended consequences of higher undocumented underage marriage, a practice more common in rural areas among poor families. Instead, the government should increase its efforts to educate people about the harmful effects of child marriage. This public campaign needs to appeal to society in general, both men and women's groups, and especially to religious groups, as moral and religious arguments often dominate the debates around child marriage. Religious courts should be discouraged from granting dispensations, and should hear the opinions from the underage couples, instead of dismissing them and relying solely on the parents' requests. Further amendments to the law to eliminate loopholes or make it harder to access the special clause for dispensation should be considered.

Ensuring full implementation of 12 years' compulsory education may also help girls stay in school longer, further discouraging child marriage practices. Financial assistance targeted to young girls could also be considered, since, although public education is free, there are out-of-pocket expenses for school uniforms, worksheets and other school activities that poorer families find hard to meet. These policy options may help not only in reducing the prevalence of underage marriage, but also extending young women's attachment to the labour market as marriage and child-bearing is delayed.

References

ADB (Asian Development Bank). 2013. *Gender Tool Kit: Transport*. ADB.

ADB (Asian Development Bank). 2015. *Women in the Workforce: An Unmet Potential in Asia and the Pacific*. ADB. www.adb.org/publications/women-workforce-unmet-potential-asia-and-pacific

AIPEG, DFAT and CDES (Australia Indonesia Partnership for Economic Governance, Australian Government Department of Foreign Affairs and Trade, and Centre for Development Economics and Sustainability). 2017. *Women's Economic Participation in Indonesia: A Study of Gender Inequality in Employment, Entrepreneurship, and Key Enablers for Change*. AIPEG, DFAT and CDES.

Bertrand, Marianne, Patricia Cortes, Claudia Olivetti and Jessica Pan. 2021. 'Social norms, labour market opportunities, and the marriage gap between skilled and unskilled women'. *Review of Economic Studies* 88(4): 1936–78. doi.org/10.1093/restud/rdaa066

Bloom, Nicholas, Ruobing Han and James Liang. 2022. *How Hybrid Working from Home Works Out*. NBER Working Paper No. 30292. National Bureau of Economic Research. doi.org/10.3386/w30292

Cameron, Lisa A., J. Malcolm Dowling and Christopher Worswick. 2001. 'Education and labor market participation of women in Asia: Evidence from five countries'. *Economic Development and Cultural Change* 49(3): 459–77. doi.org/10.1086/452511

Cameron, Lisa A., Diana Contreras Suárez and Yi-Ping Tseng. 2019. 'Women's transitions in the labour market: The challenges of formal sector employment in Indonesia'. Paper presented to the Australia Gender Economics Workshop, 14 February.

Comola, Margherita and Luiz de Mello. 2008. *The Determinants of Employment and Earnings in Indonesia: A Multinomial Selection Approach*. OECD Economics Department Working Papers No. 690. doi.org/10.1787/224864812153

Dong, Sarah Xue. 2018. 'Does economic crisis have different impact on husbands and wives? Evidence from the Asian financial crisis in Indonesia'. *Review of Development Economics* 22(4): 1489–1512. doi.org/10.1111/rode.12521

Fallon, Peter R. and Robert E.B. Lucas. 2002. 'The impact of financial crises on labor markets, household incomes, and poverty: A review of evidence'. *World Bank Research Observer* 17(1): 21–45. www.jstor.org/stable/3986398

Feridhanusetyawan, Tubagus, Haryo Aswicahyono and Ari A. Perdana. 2001. *The Male-Female Wage Differentials in Indonesia*. CSIS Economics Working Paper No. 59. Centre for Strategic and International Studies, Jakarta.

Field, Erica and Kate Vyborny. 2022. *Women's Mobility and Labor Supply: Experimental Evidence from Pakistan*. ADB Economics Working Paper No. 655. doi.org/10.22617/WPS220166-2

Garnaut, Ross. 2015. 'Indonesia's resources boom in international perspective: Policy dilemmas and options for continued strong growth'. *Bulletin of Indonesian Economic Studies* 51(2): 189–212. doi.org/10.1080/00074918.2015.1061910

Chapter 7 Gender equality in the post-Suharto era from an economic perspective 143

Goldin, Claudia. 2006. 'The quiet revolution that transformed women's employment, education, and family'. *American Economic Review* 96(2): 1–21. www.jstor.org/stable/30034606

Halim, Daniel, Hillary Johnson and Elizaveta Perova. 2017. *Could Childcare Services Improve Women's Labor Market Outcomes in Indonesia?* East Asia and Pacific Gender Policy Brief Issue 1, East Asia and Pacific Gender Innovation Lab. Washington, DC.

Halim, Daniel, Hillary C. Johnson and Elizaveta Perova. 2022. 'Preschool availability and women's employment: Evidence from Indonesia'. *Economic Development and Cultural Change* 71(1). doi.org/10.1086/714439

Hallward-Driemeier, Mary, Bob Rijkers and Andrew Waxman. 2017. 'Can minimum wages close the gender wage gap? Evidence from Indonesia'. *Review of Income and Wealth* 63(2): 310–34. doi.org/10.1111/roiw.12219

Hull, Terence H. 1987. 'Fertility decline in Indonesia : An institutionalist interpretation'. *International Family Planning Perspectives* 13(3): 90–95. doi.org/10.2307/2947904

Kim, Jin Ho and Benjamin D. Williams. 2021. 'Minimum wage and women's decision-making power within households: Evidence from Indonesia'. *Economic Development and Cultural Change* 70(1): 359–414. doi.org/10.1086/711171

McKenzie, David. 2017. 'How effective are active labor market policies in developing countries? A critical review of recent evidence'. *World Bank Research Observer* 32(2): 127–54. doi.org/10.1093/wbro/lkx001

Merdikawati, Nurina. 2022. 'Employment impact of minimum wage among formal and informal manufacturing firms'. In 'Essays on the impact of labour market regulation in Indonesia'. PhD thesis. Canberra: Australian National University. doi.org/10.25911/VDE9-ES39

Pelta, Rachel. 2021. 'Survey: Men & women experience remote work differently'. FlexJobs. www.flexjobs.com/blog/post/men-women-experience-remote-work-survey/

Priebe, Jan. 2010. *Child Costs and the Causal Effect of Fertility on Female Labor Supply: An Investigation for Indonesia 1993–2008.* Courant Research Centre Discussion Paper No. 45. Georg-August-Universität, Göttingen.

Radhakrishnan, Uma. 2010. *A Dynamic Structural Model of Contraceptive Use and Employment Sector Choice for Women in Indonesia.* CES Working Paper No. 28. Center for Economic Studies, US Census Bureau, Washington, DC.

Schaner, Simone and Smita Das. 2016. *Female Labor Force Participation in Asia: Indonesia Country Study.* ADB Economics Working Paper No. 474. Asian Development Bank.

Smith, James P., Duncan Thomas, Elizabeth Frankenberg, Kathleen Beegle and Graciela Teruel. 2002. 'Wages, employment and economic shocks: Evidence from Indonesia'. *Journal of Population Economics* 15(1): 161–93. www.jstor.org/stable/20007804

Sohn, Kitae. 2015. 'Gender discrimination in earnings in Indonesia: A fuller picture'. *Bulletin of Indonesian Economic Studies* 51(1): 95–121. doi.org/10.1080/00074918.2015.1016569

Suryahadi, Asep, Wenefrida Widyanti, Daniel Perwira and Sudarno Sumarto. 2003. 'Minimum wage policy and its impact on employment in the urban formal sector'. *Bulletin of Indonesian Economic Studies* 39(1): 29–50. doi.org/10.1080/00074910302007

Taniguchi, Kiyoshi and Alika Tuwo. 2014. *New Evidence on the Gender Wage Gap in Indonesia*. ADB Economics Working Paper No. 404. hdl.handle.net/11540/1612

The Economist. 2020. 'Why more Indonesian teens are giving up dating'. *The Economist*, 2 April. www.economist.com/asia/2020/04/02/why-more-indonesian-teens-are-giving-up-dating

The Economist. 2021. 'One in nine Indonesian women marries before the age of 18'. *The Economist*, 24 June. www.economist.com/asia/2021/06/24/one-in-nine-indonesian-women-marries-before-the-age-of-18

UNICEF Indonesia, Statistics Indonesia (BPS), Universitas Indonesia's Center on Child Protection and Well-Being (PUSKAPA-UI), and National Development Planning Agency (Bappenas). 2020. *Prevention of Child Marriage: Acceleration That Cannot Wait*. www.unicef.org/indonesia/sites/unicef.org.indonesia/files/2020-06/Prevention-of-Child-Marriage-Report-2020.pdf

Utomo, Ariane J. 2012. 'Women as secondary earners: Gendered preferences on marriage and employment of university students in modern Indonesia'. *Asian Population Studies* 8(1): 65–85. doi.org/10.1080/17441730.2012.646841

Utomo, Ariane J. 2016. 'Gender in the midst of reforms: Attitudes to work and family roles among university students in urban Indonesia'. *Marriage and Family Review* 52(5): 421–41. doi.org/10.1080/01494929.2015.1113224

Widarti, Diah. 1998. 'Determinants of labour force participation by married women: The case of Jakarta'. *Bulletin of Indonesian Economic Studies* 34(2): 93–120. doi.org/10.1080/00074919812331337350

Witoelar, Firman, Alexander D. Rothenberg, T. Yudo Wicaksono, Tadeja Gracner and Bondan Sikoki. 2017. *How Jakarta's Traffic Affects Labor Market Outcomes for Women and People with Disabilities*. SurveyMETER. www.rand.org/pubs/external_publications/EP67437.html

World Bank. 2012. *World Development Report 2012: Gender Equality and Development*. World Bank. hdl.handle.net/10986/4391

World Bank. 2019. *Aspiring Indonesia—Expanding the Middle Class*. World Bank. hdl.handle.net/10986/33237

YouGov and Investing in Women. 2020. *Gender Equality Matters 2020: Social Norms, Attitudes and Practices of Urban Millennials in Indonesia, Philippines and Vietnam*. Investing in Women.

8 Women and digitisation: Promises and challenges of internet use in the Indonesian labour market

Niken Kusumawardhani

The rapid pace of digitisation has important implications not only for economic growth, but also for the labour market. Digitisation has the potential to radically transform the labour market by creating new job opportunities, improving access to job searches, changing the future of work, and making the labour market more innovative and inclusive for marginalised groups of workers. However, in the context of developing countries such as Indonesia, several barriers to harnessing the full potential of digital technology exist. Unequal access to information and communication technology infrastructure, poor digital literacy and skills, and social norms that prevent the whole population from participating equally in the digital economy may cause a winner-takes-all phenomenon that could lead to further widening of existing inequalities.

The potential effects of the internet on the labour market are multidimensional. Previous research indicates that high-skilled workers are more prone to experiencing the favourable impact of the internet on the labour market (Akerman et al. 2015; Yang et al. 2023). Meanwhile, negative employment effects for low-skilled workers are also likely as the internet replaces the performance of routine tasks through automation. Specifically for women, internet and digital technologies can offer solutions to work-related problems such as time constraints from the burdens of child care and other domestic responsibilities (ADB 2014). In patriarchal societies where job segregation is strengthened by cultural stereotypes and educational paths, digitisation might hold a promise to eliminate some gender disparities in the labour market. Evidence indicates that internet availability benefits highly educated and skilled women by providing work

146 *Niken Kusumawardhani*

flexibility, improving job searches and enabling home-based businesses (Dettling 2016; Masroor et al. 2020; Viollaz and Winkler 2021).

Widespread use of internet and digital technologies might affect lower-educated and unskilled women in the labour market in offsetting directions: obviously it creates new job opportunities, but some jobs will become obsolete since tasks originally conducted by humans face varying degrees of automation risk. Chang and Huynh (2016) estimate around 56% of employment in Indonesia is at high risk of automation in the next couple of decades, a figure that is higher than that of neighbouring countries such as the Philippines (49%) and Thailand (44%). Two sectors with the highest risk of automation are accommodation and food services, and trade (ibid.). These are also the sectors where female workers dominate employment. This implies that for women to successfully transition into the future of work, they will need to learn new skills, and labour market institutions should be designed to accommodate job switches easily.

Expanded mobile internet connectivity holds the potential to transform microentrepreneurs by expanding their access to new customers and improving the outcome of their businesses. For microbusinesses, which are generally dominated by unskilled and lower-educated women entrepreneurs, the e-commerce sector might lower barriers to market entry through reduced costs and increased accessibility. Theis and Rusconi (2019) find that a large proportion of women microentrepreneurs in Indonesia combine social media (Facebook, Instagram) and messaging platforms (WhatsApp) to help them expand their access to broader groups of customers as well as suppliers. A survey by Das et al. (2018) finds that women-owned micro, small and medium enterprises (MSMEs) in Indonesia generate 35% of e-commerce revenue, compared with only 15% of offline MSME revenue, suggesting that online commerce has the potential to improve the performance of women-owned businesses.

In this chapter I analyse the promises and challenges faced by women in the labour market amid the great transformation of the Indonesian economy towards digitisation. I start by looking at the background of digitisation and women's participation in the labour market. I then discuss what new opportunities digitisation brings to women, and barriers and challenges for women to take up these opportunities. I find that digitisation has the potential to support women to advance economically, especially by providing new job opportunities and enabling flexible working arrangements. However, the large potential benefits of digitisation on women's labour market outcomes have not materialised, since women face multiple barriers in accessing and using the internet to support their labour market activities. I argue that policymakers should prioritise initiatives that focus on removing barriers that prevent women from making the most of digitisation in the labour market, to ensure that Indonesia's digital economy is inclusive of women.

Digitisation and women's participation in the labour market
Recent developments in internet availability and accessibility in Indonesia

Internet infrastructure availability in Indonesia has undergone major improvements over the past decade. Between 2011 and 2021, the proportion of villages with base transceiver station (BTS) towers that facilitate access to the internet grew from 29% to 49% in rural areas and from 40% to 65% in urban areas (Figure 8.1). Despite the similar average growth rate of the proportion of villages with BTS towers in urban and rural areas over the past decade, rural areas continue to lag behind urban areas in availability of internet infrastructure. Stark differences in availability of BTS towers is also evident across provinces. In 2021, provinces in Java had on average 70% of villages with BTS towers, whereas eastern provinces had on average 40% of villages with BTS towers. Compared to Java and Bali Island provinces, provinces in the eastern part of the country have shown very little development in terms of availability of BTS towers during the past decade. Consequently, Indonesia's internet infrastructure availability is geographically uneven.

During the past decade, mobile broadband networks have expanded rapidly, with investments by major telecommunication providers leading this progress. Data from Telkomsel, the largest cellular network operator

Figure 8.1 Proportion of villages with BTS towers (%)

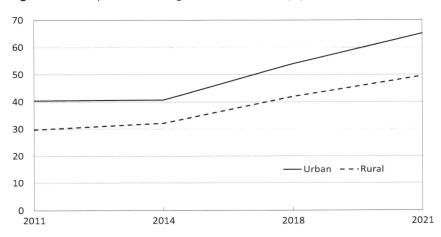

Source: Author's construction based on Podes (2011, 2014, 2018, 2021).

Figure 8.2 Deployment of BTS towers by Telkomsel (thousands)

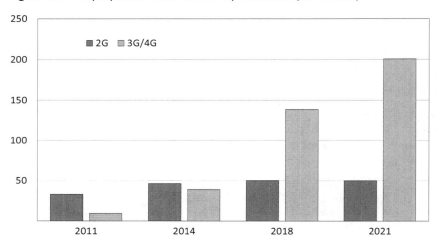

Note: Rollout of 5G began in 2021, with 113 towers, and 284 towers in 2022.
Source: Telkomsel annual reports (2011, 2014, 2018, 2021).

in Indonesia, shows that deployment of base stations during the past ten years has been driven mainly by 3G and 4G stations (Figure 8.2). Deployment of BTS towers that facilitate 5G services began in 2021.

In 2021, it was estimated that 77% of villages in Indonesia were within reach of the 4G/LTE network, the standard of cellular network that offers a better experience than 3G, especially in terms of data speed. For the past three years, the proportion of villages with access to the 4G/LTE network increased more in rural areas than in urban areas (Figure 8.3). Despite this improvement, however, access to the 4G/LTE network is still urban biased and connectivity is lacking in parts of the country where geographic contours, topography and low population density make investments relatively more costly.

With improved availability of internet infrastructure and the widespread accessibility of inexpensive phones, internet access in Indonesia has also increased significantly for people in all income classes. In 2022, individuals from the top decile of per capita consumption were almost two times more likely to be connected to the internet than individuals from the poorest decile. Meanwhile, in 2011, individuals from the wealthiest decile were forty times more likely to have internet access than individuals from the poorest decile. This comparison shows that the gap to internet access across welfare levels in Indonesia has greatly diminished during the past decade (Figure 8.4). During the same period, improvement of internet access in rural areas was even more rapid than in

Figure 8.3 Proportion of villages with access to the 4G network (%)

Source: Author's construction based on Podes (2018, 2021).

Figure 8.4 Internet access by decile of per capita consumption (%)

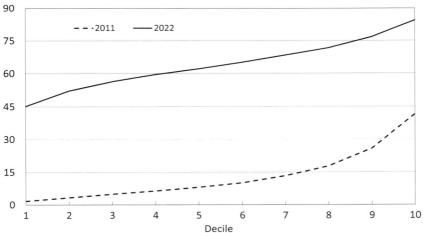

Source: Author's construction based on Susenas (2011, 2022).

urban areas. Access to the internet for rural residents jumped on average from 11% to 63% for individuals in the top five deciles, and from 3% to 49% for individuals in the bottom five deciles. Meanwhile, access to the internet in urban areas has increased on average from 26% to 77% for individuals in the top five deciles and from 7% to 60% for individuals in the bottom five deciles.

The digital economy and rise of internet-based jobs

The Indonesian digital economic landscape has seen rapid growth during recent years, reaching a gross merchandise value (GMV) of US$77 billion in 2022 or about 40% of Southeast Asia's total GMV (Figure 8.5). Indonesia's GMV expanded at an annual rate of 40% from 2020 to 2021 and 22% from 2021 to 2022, making it one of the fastest-growing digital economies in Southeast Asia. The e-commerce sector is the biggest growth driver and accounted for more than 70% of Indonesia's GMV in 2022. Increasing internet penetration rates, a growing middle class, COVID-19's influence, and increasing use of digital payments in Indonesia have created a thriving environment for the e-commerce sector that is predicted to continue for the next few years (Google et al. 2022). The e-commerce sector provides a big opportunity for the country to connect more micro and small enterprises to the digital system. Additionally, Indonesia is ranked fifth globally in start-up growth, reflecting the country's strategy in maximising the benefits of digitisation through supporting innovative entrepreneurship.

Figure 8.5 Indonesia's annual gross merchandise value (US$ billion)

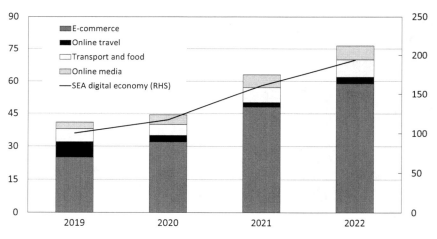

Source: Google et al. (2022).

The largest e-commerce companies in Indonesia are Tokopedia, Shopee, Lazada, Bukalapak and Blibli. By 2021, Tokopedia had more than 11 million merchants joining the platform as seller, whereas Bukalapak had 6.5 million merchant partners. As of 2023, Indonesia stands out among its ASEAN neighbours as the second-largest unicorn[1] hub with

---

1 Start-up companies that reached the value of US$1 billion.

Chapter 8 Women and digitisation: Internet use in the Indonesian labour market   151

a total of 16, reinforcing its position as a dynamic player in the regional startup ecosystem, trailing only behind Singapore with 25 unicorns.

Das et al. (2018) estimate that the digital economy in Indonesia could create 26 million new jobs in 2022 as the emergence of on-demand service platforms, e-commerce and financial technology platforms will open wider opportunities for workers to engage in better-paid jobs.

In the past couple of years, Indonesia has seen a rise in internet-based jobs, particularly in the gig economy. This trend can be attributed to the rapid growth of companies such as Gojek and Tokopedia, which have provided numerous opportunities for individuals to earn a living by providing services and selling products online. Gojek, for instance, has expanded its services from being just a ride-hailing platform (Go-Ride) to offering a wide range of services such as food delivery (Go-Food), parcel delivery (Go-Send) and grocery shopping (Go-Mart). Tokopedia, on the other hand, has become one of the largest e-commerce platforms in Indonesia, providing a platform for individuals and small businesses to sell their products online. This has not only created jobs for people to manage and run their online shops but has also provided a source of income for many who were previously unemployed or underemployed. Gojek and Tokopedia are only two examples of increasingly available internet-based jobs in the country, and the growth of Indonesia's digital economy is expected to continue, driving the rise of internet-based jobs in Indonesia in the future.

Women's participation in the labour market

Indonesia has experienced sustained economic growth over the past decades accompanied by major socioeconomic changes that include the remarkable decline in total fertility rate and massive growth in female educational attainment. The total fertility rate declined significantly from 5.6 to 2.3 children per woman of reproductive age between the late 1950s and 2018. In 2021, 67.5% of women who attended school in Indonesia completed senior high school (equivalent to 12 years of education), a rate slightly higher than the same education completion for men (64.5%).

The decline in fertility rate coupled with the increase in women's educational attainment are often regarded as factors that enable the creation of more and better opportunities for women in the labour market. However, female labour force participation (FLFP) in Indonesia remains moderate: 54% of women were active in the labour force compared to 82% of men in 2021. Interestingly, this rate has been relatively stagnant for the past two decades. Not only is greater female participation in the labour market aligned with women's empowerment, it could lead to significant macroeconomic gains for the economy. It is estimated that a country's average gross domestic product (GDP) per capita would be 20% higher if all gender employment gaps were eliminated, and the gain is predicted to be even higher for middle-income countries where GDP per capita could increase by 40–80% if women are able to develop their full labour market potential (Pennings 2022). Consequently, the fact that FLFP in Indonesia has stalled for the past two decades is of great concern to policymakers.

Figure 8.6 shows the trend of FLFP rates in various age groups over time in Indonesia. For each year from 2003 until 2021, the FLFP rate shows a consistent curve through the age groups. The rate rises quickly until around 25 years of age before slowing over the age groups that are typically associated with child-bearing (Cameron et al. 2019). The FLFP rate reaches its peak at around 45 years of age before declining. Figure 8.6 shows the extent to which a woman's decision to work is likely to be affected by her child-rearing responsibilities. The drop of FLFP in ages 55 and older indicates that women start leaving the labour force in increasing numbers from the 55–64 years age group. The decrease is even more pronounced for the group of 65 years and older.

Approximately 70% of Indonesian women work in the informal sector as self-employed, casual or unpaid family workers (Schaner and Das 2016) and they are more likely to work in low-paying sectors and labour-intensive industries compared to their male counterparts (World Bank

Figure 8.6 Female labour force participation by age group, 2003–2021 (%)

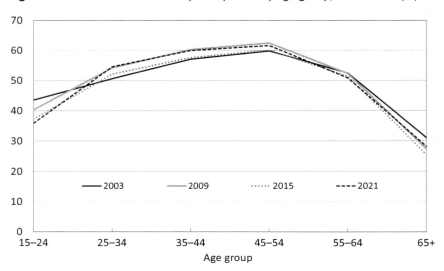

Source: Author's construction based on Sakernas data (2003, 2009, 2015, 2021).

Chapter 8 Women and digitisation: Internet use in the Indonesian labour market 153

and Bappenas 2020). The fact that women in the Indonesian labour market are concentrated in the informal sector suggests that informal jobs may be attractive in their flexibility, especially in a society in which women are primarily responsible for childcare as well as other domestic work, and formal childcare institutions are scarce.

Promises of digitisation: How does digitisation support women in the labour market?

Digitisation in Indonesia has brought several benefits to women in the labour market. With the proliferation of technology and the internet, some women are able to access more job opportunities and to have flexible work arrangements. The rise of platform-based jobs enables women to apply for and secure jobs that were previously inaccessible to them due to geographical or other constraints. Another benefit of digitisation for women in the labour market is the possibility of flexible work arrangements. With the increasing acceptance of flexible working arrangements, women are now able to balance their professional and personal commitments more effectively. This can help to reduce the gender gap in the labour market and allow more women to stay in the workforce longer.

More job opportunities: Gig workers and online merchants

The rise of internet-based jobs in the past few years has created opportunities for women to secure jobs that were previously unavailable to them. The ride-hailing industry has lowered barriers for women seeking to join the labour force, especially in a traditionally male-dominated field such as transport. The International Finance Corporation reports that female Uber drivers in Indonesia found signing up as drivers far less complicated than applying to work for a traditional taxi operator (IFC and Accenture 2018). Additionally, some jobs in the ride-hailing industry are targeted at women,[2] such as personal shoppers of grocery shopping services. Go-Mart recruits female shopping assistants and stations them at its merchant supermarkets as personal shopping assistants to Go-Mart customers. However, the number of newly created jobs for women in the digital economy remains unknown as studies on gig work in Indonesia are dominated by those focusing on workers already in the ecosystem of the platform-based industries.

---

2 In 2015 Gojek created GoLife, which offered at-home massage services (Go-Massage) and house-cleaning services (Go-Clean), mostly provided by female workers. However, GoLife was terminated in 2020.

154   *Niken Kusumawardhani*

Using data from Sakernas 2019, it is estimated there are 2.4 million gig workers in Indonesia (Table 8.1). The population of gig workers is dominated by men (74%) who live in urban areas (71%). Meanwhile, female gig workers constitute only about 26% of the gig worker population. Similarly, the population of female gig workers is dominated by urban residents (62%). Consequently, there is a higher proportion of female gig workers in sectors that are more prevalent in urban areas, including manufacturing (36%) and retail trade (44%). For female workers in general, only 16% and 34% work in manufacturing and retail trade, respectively. Additionally, there is evidence that gig workers work longer hours than workers in general. However, this pattern is evident only among male workers. Female gig workers work relatively shorter hours: 31 hours per week as opposed to female workers, who work 36 hours per week. But female gig workers and female workers have similar likelihoods of having a second job to supplement their income.

Table 8.1 Profile of female gig workers, 2019 (%)

Variables	Female gig workers	All gig workers	Female workers
Average age	39 years	39 years	40 years
Urban location	62	71	54
Use internet in main job	80	85	70
Years of schooling			
Maximum 6 years	40	31	42
Maximum 9 years	21	19	16
Maximum 12 years	29	40	26
13 years and more	8	9	16
Employment sector			
Agriculture, forestry, livestock, fishing	6	13	25
Mining and quarrying	<1	1	1
Manufacturing	36	15	16
Electricity, gas and water supply	1	1	1
Construction	1	2	1
Wholesale and retail trade, restaurants, hotels	44	23	34
Transport, storage and communications	4	40	1
Finance, insurance, real estate, business services	2	2	2
Community, social and personal services	7	4	20
Working hours per week	31 hrs	42 hrs	36 hrs
Has second job	10	14	11

Source: Author's construction based on Sakernas data (2019).

Chapter 8 Women and digitisation: Internet use in the Indonesian labour market 155

The rise of the e-commerce sector also opens up wider opportunities for women entrepreneurs to access markets or to grow their businesses. In 2021, around 10% of workers in Indonesia were identified as online merchants, defined as self-employed individuals or employers with temporary or permanent workers who sell goods or services through social media, websites or online marketplaces. Around 77% of female online merchants reside in urban areas, as opposed to 55% of female workers who are urban residents. In general, female online merchants tend to be younger and have more years of schooling than the population of female workers (Table 8.2). The average age of female online merchants is 34 years, while that of female workers is 41 years.

Table 8.2 Distribution of female online merchants and female workers (%)

Variables	Female online merchants	Female workers
Urban location	77	55
Years of schooling		
<6 years	1	2
Maximum 6 years	5	24
Maximum 9 years	12	16
Maximum 12 years	51	27
Maximum 16 years	31	16
17+ years	1	1

Source: Author's construction based on Sakernas data (2021).

Despite the rise of new job opportunities in the digital economy, the overall impact of digitisation on job opportunities for women in Indonesia seems limited. From analysing district panel data covering the years 2008 to 2018, Kusumawardhani et al. (2021) concluded that the impact of wider internet availability in Indonesia in improving women's labour market outcomes is concentrated more on the intensive margin (the number of hours worked by the worker) of women's employment. Women in areas with higher internet availability enjoy higher opportunities to work longer hours but have a lower probability of holding skilled jobs and participating in formal sectors, and these effects are concentrated among low-educated or young women. This finding is mainly explained by the rise of gig-type and platform-type work, which are classified as unskilled and informal (IFC 2021; World Bank 2021). As the informal sector is associated with undesirable characteristics such as weaker social protection, low wages and a poor career path, it may not align with the empowerment goal of facilitating greater participation of women in skilled or formal employment.

Flexibility to help women carry multiple burdens

Online platform–type work provides flexibility to set working hours, which offers a potential solution for working women who often have additional burdens of child caring and other domestic responsibilities. Evidence from a report on Uber drivers in Indonesia indicates that the ride-hailing industry offers job opportunities that provide women with flexibility, allowing them paid work around their child caring and other domestic responsibilities (IFC and Accenture 2018). Seventy-four per cent of women Uber drivers in Indonesia identify flexibility as the most valuable aspect of their work. Ability to set their own working hours is compatible with other responsibilities they carry, for example, the majority of women joining Uber are also the primary caregivers for their children. While flexibility is also cited by male drivers as a key reason to join Uber, the ability to adjust working hours around other responsibilities may benefit women more as they disproportionately carry multiple burdens.

Work flexibility can also be interpreted as having the opportunity for full-time working hours without having to be physically present at the office. In most cases, flexibility is provided through the ability to conduct work remotely or in work-from-home settings. The internet provides a platform through which people can connect to the office intranet and communicate with colleagues easily while working remotely. Kusumawardhani et al. (2021) found that a remote working policy is essential in supporting women's decisions to return to work after giving birth. Women who opt to return to work after giving birth emphasise the need to deal with child-rearing issues, especially during infancy; a remote working policy is considered supportive in their decision-making process. More importantly, office norms, both formal and informal, are vital in aiding working mothers to balance their dual responsibilities effectively.

The COVID-19 pandemic has put additional burdens on women who have to oversee their children's learning from home, which leads to a situation where many women who work from home feel that their tasks have become more troublesome and difficult to carry out. Sakernas data indicate a significantly higher proportion of female workers than male workers (10% versus 3%) cite that household responsibilities are the obstacles they have to deal with while working from home. The internet is helpful for female entrepreneurs with young children who need to juggle their multiple roles as business owner and parent, especially to assist their children with online schooling (Bachtiar et al. 2022). Additionally, digital solutions enable female business owners to better manage their domestic and family responsibilities without fully interrupting their business operations. A survey by UN Women and Pulse Lab Jakarta (2020) reveals that women entrepreneurs benefit from use of digital solutions

Chapter 8 Women and digitisation: Internet use in the Indonesian labour market 157

(e.g. MokaPOS, Selly and GoBiz)[3] in their businesses as it allows them extra time for domestic responsibilities. A qualitative study by Bachtiar et al. (2022) reveals that the internet holds the potential to alleviate numerous responsibilities faced by women. For instance, a female entrepreneur managing simultaneously her businesses and children's schooling found the internet invaluable—it helps her to stay connected through her son's class WhatsApp group during online schooling, ensuring homework completion despite her day-long absence. Another entrepreneur, burdened by aiding her children's homeschooling while handling customer orders, highlights the internet's usefulness. Through YouTube tutorials, her elder child helps his younger sisters with their maths homework, showcasing the internet's pivotal role in supporting their tasks.

However, flexible working has two opposing features related to women's economic empowerment. While it can help women carry their multiple burdens, flexible working can potentially exacerbate existing traditional gender roles in the labour market and households (Lott and Chung 2016; Sullivan and Lewis 2001). As traditional gender roles associate women more with child caring and domestic responsibilities, women are expected to conduct more domestic work simultaneously while working, leading to increased multitasking and blurred boundaries between work and domestic responsibilities. In contrast, men in flexible working situations are expected to enhance their work performance by increasing their working hours, and are rewarded through income premiums (Lott and Chung 2016). Therefore, the question of whether flexible work arrangements made possible by digitisation align with women's empowerment agendas should be examined more carefully.

Challenges faced by women in accessing and using the internet for labour market activities

There are several barriers that prevent Indonesian women from fully harnessing the potential of digitisation in the labour market. One major barrier is lack of access to the internet. Another barrier is a lack of digital literacy due to poor education or training that prevents women from using the internet productively for job searching and participating in internet-based jobs. Additionally, the double burden of work and caring

---

3 GoBiz is a business management application that enables mobile connectivity, digital payments and other financial services for small and individual merchants. Selly is a keyboard application that facilitates customer service and transactions via messaging apps for online sellers. MokaPOS is a cloud-based cashier application for managing transactions and online payments.

responsibilities often leaves women with little time to invest in acquiring the necessary digital skills. Consequently, these barriers limit the extent to which women can fully benefit from the opportunities afforded by digitisation.

Barriers to internet access

As in the case of many developing countries, women's access to the internet in Indonesia has grown over the past decade but is yet to catch up with men's access (Figure 8.7). Unless women are able to close the existing gap in internet access, the gender disparity puts them at risk of losing opportunities in the labour market where digitisation rapidly changes the nature of work and increases demand for digital skills.

Within-group inequality of access to the internet among women is also evident. Obviously young, highly educated women and women who live in urban areas have better internet access compared to older, less-educated women or women living in rural areas. Figure 8.8 shows the progress of women's access to the internet during the past decade by age, education and area of residence. The gap is most pronounced between education groups: the proportion of highly educated women with access to the internet is more than two times higher than that of less-educated women.

Women face a variety of barriers to internet access, with ownership of handheld devices topping the list. As the fourth-largest smartphone market worldwide after China, India and the United States, the majority

Figure 8.7 Gender gap in internet access (%)

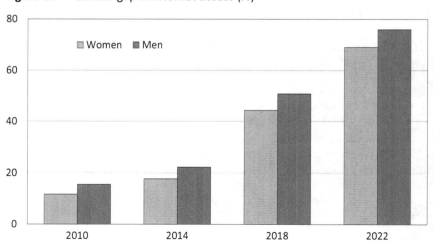

Source: Author's construction based on Susenas data (2010, 2014, 2018, 2022).

Figure 8.8 Women's access to the internet by age, education and area of residence (%)

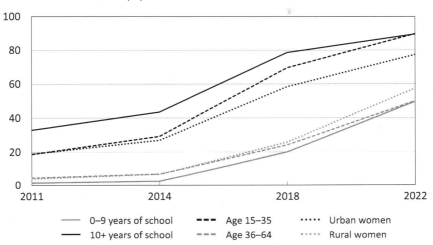

Source: Author's construction based on Susenas data (2011, 2014, 2018, 2022).

(98%) of internet users in Indonesia access the internet through their mobile phones. However, a global trend shows that women are more likely to borrow mobile phones and to have phones with simpler features that might prevent internet use (GSMA 2015). This trend applies to Indonesia, as the share of females aged 15 or older who do not own a mobile phone (30%) is almost twice that of males aged 15 or older who do not own a mobile phone (17%), indicating that women are more likely to use shared phones in a household. Although availability of inexpensive phones has increased in recent years, handset cost is cited by women as the main reason for not having a mobile phone (Table 8.3). Setiawan et al. (2022) estimate that the least expensive internet-enabled phone would still cost one-fifth of the monthly expenditure of a low-income person. As women are more likely to have limited financial independence and poorer access to external sources of finance, the barriers to mobile phone ownership among women are likely to be driven by cost considerations.

Challenges when using the internet for work-related activities

The SMERU Research Institute et al. (2022) estimate that, with respect to digital literacy, the Indonesian labour force is dominated by unskilled workers or those with basic skills: 87% and 86% of the labour force was unskilled or had basic digital literacy in 2018 and 2020, respectively

160   *Niken Kusumawardhani*

Table 8.3 Reasons cited by women for not having a mobile phone (%)

Handset cost	38
Data cost	29
Internet is not relevant for me	19
Don't know how to use internet on a mobile	16
No time to learn how to use internet on a mobile	12
Reading /writing difficulties	10
Information security	9
Family does not approve	8
Harmful content	8
Slow connection / cannot do what I want	7
Network coverage	6

Source: Statista Research Department (2019).

(Figure 8.9).[4] Limited digital skills and digital literacy among women leads to non-productive and minimal use of the internet, undermining the potential benefit that women could obtain from digitisation. This can be due to a lack of access to training or education on how to effectively use digital tools and platforms, or a lack of confidence in their ability to navigate and utilise these resources. As a result, women may be unable to take advantage of the many opportunities for career advancement and economic development that the internet offers. For example, there is no evidence that the internet has been used to improve job searches among women, even though the internet can potentially reduce direct costs of searches for jobseekers. More than 90% of women jobseekers in the labour force prefer to seek jobs by contacting their acquaintances. Meanwhile, less than 40% use other methods, such as directly contacting firms to find out about job opportunities, registering with a job-search service, or self-advertising in print or electronic media. In 2021, among women jobseekers in the labour force, only 13% of women self-advertised for work using the internet. This figure was an increase from about 8% in 2018. Unfortunately, further information on self-marketing activities in the freelance talent marketplace, for example, Upwork or Fastwork, is not available.

---

4 The estimation is conducted using Sakernas data to roughly predict the supply of a digitally competent workforce in Indonesia based on four dimensions: employment and unemployment status; use of the internet in an individual's main job; the highest level of educational attainment; and information and communication technology background for those in vocational, diploma and university-level education.

Chapter 8 Women and digitisation: Internet use in the Indonesian labour market   161

Figure 8.9   Digital skills of the labour force

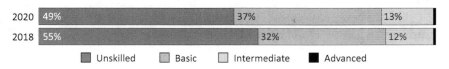

Source: SMERU Research Institute et al. (2022).

The majority of female internet users in Indonesia enjoy using the internet to access social media and to read news (Table 8.4). Indonesia is one of the largest social media markets as the number of Facebook users in the country is among the largest in the world. However, the proportion of highly educated women who use the internet to obtain information or to read news is triple the proportion of less-educated women who do so. Similarly, the proportion of younger women who use the internet to obtain information or to read news is more than double the proportion of women in the older age group. Table 8.4 reveals that the use of the internet for relatively more productive activities such as financial purposes or selling goods or services is limited. The internet is especially used by younger and highly educated groups to obtain resources needed to complete schoolwork, while the share of older or less-educated groups performing this activity on the internet is significantly lower.

Table 8.4 Women's internet use by age and education (%)

Activity	Age 15–35	Age 36–64	Education 0–9 years	Education 10+ years
Social media	82	41	36	84
To obtain information or to read news	67	31	24	72
Entertainment purposes	56	21	19	55
To buy goods or services	30	9	6	32
To send or receive email	19	7	2	25
To obtain information about products/services	21	7	5	23
To obtain resources for schoolwork	19	9	5	22
Financial (ebanking)	13	6	1	18
To sell goods or services	11	4	3	12
Other activities	4	2	1	5

Source: Author's construction based on Sakernas data (2021).

162 *Niken Kusumawardhani*

Female workers use the internet mainly for communication with consumers, followed by promotion activities. Across sectors, it is evident that female workers in the formal sector are more likely to use the internet compared to female workers in the informal sector. Approximately 63% of female workers in the formal sector used the internet for work in 2021, while only 21% of female workers in the informal sector used the internet for work (Table 8.5). Across age groups, a significantly lower proportion of female workers in the older group use the internet for work, and the pattern holds for both formal and informal sectors. Similarly, the proportion of female workers in lower-educated groups who use the internet for work is far below that of higher-educated groups. Additionally, the proportion of female workers who use the internet for communication and transactions (either through email and social media or websites and marketplaces) is higher in the formal sector. The data also reveal that only a very small proportion of female workers use websites and marketplaces for transactions, while a higher share of female workers use email and social media, especially in the younger and higher-educated groups. This pattern persists for both formal and informal sectors.

The combination of functions, benefits and ease of uptake makes social media the more attractive internet platform to support work-related activities. From a survey of micro and small enterprises (MSEs) in Jogjakarta, Bachtiar et al. (2022) found that social media is the most widely used platform by microentrepreneurs, followed by email, marketplaces

Table 8.5 Internet use at work among women workers, 2021 (%)

Activity		All women	Age		Education	
			15–35	36–64	0–9 years	10+ years
Use internet for work	Formal	62.7	68.7	55.4	23.7	76.9
	Informal	21.5	34.6	16.1	12.0	44.6
Promotion activities to consumers	Formal	17.0	21.3	11.6	4.1	21.6
	Informal	12.0	22.2	7.8	5.3	28.6
Communication with consumers	Formal	61.8	67.5	54.7	23.5	75.7
	Informal	21.1	34.0	15.8	11.8	43.9
Transactions through email and social media	Formal	14.6	17.6	10.9	3.2	18.7
	Informal	9.4	17.9	5.9	3.9	22.7
Transactions through websites and marketplaces	Formal	3.6	4.9	2.1	0.6	4.7
	Informal	1.8	4.1	0.8	0.5	5.0

Source: Author's construction based on Sakernas data (2021). The samples in rows 2–5 are conditional on row 1.

Chapter 8 Women and digitisation: Internet use in the Indonesian labour market 163

and websites. Among MSEs who use the internet, 90% use social media, compared to 10% who participate in marketplaces. Specifically, 95% of MSEs in the sample who use social media utilise WhatsApp as their preferred application to support their work. Combined with data from Table 8.4, this finding reflects several points. First, social media is considered relatively easy to access using smartphones and requires less technological savvy, whereas websites and marketplaces require more skills to operate, and/or access to a computer. Second, internet adoption for work-related activities does not always translate to productive and deep use of technologies. Especially for microentrepreneurs with a lack of interest in growing their business,[5] internet adoption could be interpreted as simply as using WhatsApp. This reality finds resonance in the experiences of two female entrepreneurs. One entrepreneur's attempts at promoting products on Facebook and within WhatsApp groups were met with stiff competition, leading her to discover the efficacy of using WhatsApp status updates for more successful promotion. Another entrepreneur noted that while increased sales weren't a direct outcome of WhatsApp use, the platform significantly improved her communication with both customers and suppliers of raw materials, showcasing its pragmatic role in refining business operations (Bachtiar et al. 2022).

As women invariably bear a disproportionate burden of household and family responsibilities, they are often left with little time to invest in acquiring the digital skills needed to excel in the digital economy. GSMA (2015) reveals that the limited time women have leads to basic and minimal use of the internet exclusive to applications that women are already familiar with, such as Facebook or WhatsApp, even if women have mobile phones with internet access. Based on a series of interviews with young women in Indonesia with access to shared or personally owned mobile phones and basic awareness of mobile internet, GSMA (2015) noted that women generally start their internet journey with one or two popular applications, become proficient at using them, but then are not motivated to learn or explore other applications. Instead, they look for ways to have their needs met through those applications, for example, posting questions to their acquaintances on WhatsApp groups instead of Google search, or selling goods and services on their Facebook posts instead of joining an online marketplace as sellers. Although basic

---

5 Some microentrepreneurs do not wish to grow their business; their business fulfils their daily needs and growing their business is simply not something they wish to do or feel they can do. For these microentrepreneurs, their internet adoption practices are often limited to using WhatsApp to communicate with their customers and not exploring any other digital platforms.

internet education has been included in junior and senior high school curriculums since 2006, the curriculum covers basic concepts only and omits specific use of the internet (e.g. job searches) that would be more valuable for women.

Data from Sakernas reveal that the proportion of women who conduct both paid work and domestic work is always higher than that of men, in both the formal and informal sectors (Figure 8.10). Approximately 35% of women engage in formal work while still doing domestic work, as opposed to 29% of men. The difference is more striking for jobs in the informal sector: 56% of women with informal jobs also perform domestic work, compared to only 39% of men. These data reflect that in addition to their paid employment, most women come home to a second shift of unpaid work that primarily includes domestic chores and child care. Consequently, women have little free time to learn or to experiment with new technologies such as the internet.

Figure 8.10 Proportion of men and women performing paid and domestic work, 2021 (%)

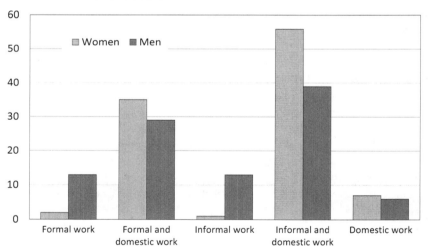

Source: Author's construction based on Sakernas data (2021).

Chapter 8 Women and digitisation: Internet use in the Indonesian labour market   165

Conclusion

Indonesia's expanded internet availability during the past decade and its fast-growing digital economy create tremendous opportunities for the country to gain maximum benefits from digitisation in the labour market. The Government of Indonesia has prepared the 2021–2024 Digital Nation Roadmap as a guide to develop digitally literate citizens and a digitally competent workforce in order to ensure that no one is left behind in benefiting from the digitised economy. This chapter documents the most recent developments of digitisation in the Indonesian labour market by focusing on women, a group of workers who are at a disadvantage in the traditional economy. As female labour force participation in Indonesia has stalled for the past two decades and women continue to lag behind men in terms of internet access, it is important to examine if the latest developments of digitisation in the Indonesian economy are inclusive of women.

Digitisation in Indonesia holds the potential to support women in the labour market. With the proliferation of technology and the internet, many women are now able to access more job opportunities and have flexible work arrangements. The rise of internet-based jobs has the potential to enable women to stay in the workforce, which could increase the overall participation and productivity of women in the labour market. However, the benefit of digitisation is unequally distributed among women and tends to be concentrated in subgroups of young, highly educated and urban women. This is mainly because these groups of women enjoy better access to the internet and are more likely to possess the digital literacy and skills required to secure the kinds of new jobs in the digital economy. The overall impact of digitisation on job opportunities for women in Indonesia seems limited, as women still face significant barriers in accessing and using the internet to support their labour market activities.

The potential for women to benefit from digitisation and advance economically depends on their possession of digital skills and other capabilities required for success in the digital economy. Several factors hinder Indonesian women from fully utilising the benefits of digitisation in the labour market. One major issue is a lack of access to the internet, which is lower for women than for men in Indonesia. Another barrier is a lack of digital literacy due to inadequate education or training, which prevents women from effectively using the internet for job searching or participating in internet-based jobs. Furthermore, the dual responsibilities of work and caring for others often leave women with little time to develop the necessary digital skills. These barriers limit the extent to which women can fully benefit from the opportunities presented by digitisation.

As Indonesia's digital economy grows, it is crucial to ensure that women are able to fully participate and benefit from this growth. To address the barriers that prevent women from harnessing the full benefit of digitisation, it is important for policymakers to prioritise initiatives that increase internet access and provide education and training programs to improve digital literacy among women. Additionally, addressing the dual responsibilities of work and caregiving that often fall disproportionately on women can help to create more time and opportunities for women to develop digital skills. By addressing these issues, policymakers can ensure that no one is left behind in benefiting from the digitised economy and that women are able to fully participate in and contribute to Indonesia's growing digital economy.

References

ADB (Asian Development Bank). 2014. *Information and Communication Technologies for Women Entrepreneurs: Prospects and Potential in Azerbaijan, Kazakhstan, the Kyrgyz Republic, and Uzbekistan.* ADB. www.adb.org/sites/default/files/publication/42869/ict-women-entrepreneurs.pdf

Akerman, Anders, Ingvil Gaarder and Magne Mogstad. 2015. 'The skill complementarity of broadband internet'. *Quarterly Journal of Economics* 130(4): 1781–824. doi.org/10.1093/qje/qjv028

Bachtiar, Palmira, Niken Kusumawardhani and Veto Indrio. 2022. *Dampak Penggunaan Internet oleh Perempuan Pelaku Usaha Mikro dan Kecil pada Kesejahteraan Rumah Tangga: Studi Kasus di Daerah Istimewa Yogyakarta* [The impact of internet use by female micro and small business owners on household welfare: A case study in the Special Region of Yogyakarta]. https://smeru.or.id/id/publication-id/dampak-penggunaan-internet-oleh-perempuan-pelaku-usaha-mikro-dan-kecil-pada

Cameron, Lisa, Diana Contreras Suárez and William Rowell. 2019. 'Female labour force participation in Indonesia: Why has it stalled?' *Bulletin of Indonesian Economic Studies* 55(2): 157–92. doi.org/10.1080/00074918.2018.1530727

Chang, Jae-Hee and Phu Huynh. 2016. *ASEAN in Transformation: The Future of Jobs at Risk of Automation.* International Labour Organization.

Das, Kaushik, Toshan Tamhane, Ben Vatterott, Phillia Wibowo and Simon Wintels. 2018. *The Digital Archipelago: How Online Commerce Is Driving Indonesia's Economic Development.* McKinsey & Company. https://www.mckinsey.com/~/media/McKinsey/Featured%20Insights/Asia%20Pacific/The%20digital%20archipelago%20How%20online%20commerce%20is%20driving%20Indonesias%20economic%20development/FINAL_The-digital-archipelago-How-online-commerce-is-driving-Indonesias-economic-development.pdf

Dettling, Lisa J. 2016. 'Broadband in the labor market: The impact of residential high-speed internet on married women's labor force participation'. *ILR Review* 70(2): 451–82. doi.org/10.1177/0019793916644721

Chapter 8 *Women and digitisation: Internet use in the Indonesian labour market*

Google, Temasek, and Bain & Company. 2022. *E-conomy SEA 2022*. https://services. google.com/fh/files/misc/e_conomy_sea_2022_report.pdf

GSMA. 2015. *Bridging the Gender Gap: Mobile Access and Usage in Low and Middle-Income Countries*. GSMA Connected Women. www.gsma.com/ mobilefordevelopment/wp-content/uploads/2016/02/Connected-Women-Gender-Gap.pdf

IFC (International Finance Corporation). 2021. *Women and E-commerce in Southeast Asia*. www.ifc.org/content/dam/ifc/doc/mgrt/202105-digital2equal-women-and-e-commerce-southeast-asia.pdf

IFC (International Finance Corporation) and Accenture. 2018. *Driving Toward Equality: Women, Ride-Hailing, and the Sharing Economy*. www.ifc.org/wps/ wcm/connect/62a2871b-271b-4256-b426-65b2012d00f7/00418+IFC+DTE+Rep ort_Complete_Layout+Final2-pxp.pdf?MOD=AJPERES&CVID=m9ksr4q

Kusumawardhani, Niken, Rezanti Pramana, Nurmala Saputri and Daniel Suryadarma. 2021. *Heterogeneous Impact of Internet Availability on Female Labour Market Outcomes in an Emerging Economy: Evidence from Indonesia*. WIDER Working Paper No. 49. www.wider.unu.edu/publication/heterogeneous-impact-internet-availability-female-labour-market-outcomes-emerging

Lott, Yvonne and Heejung Chung. 2016. 'Gender discrepancies in the outcomes of schedule control on overtime hours and income in Germany'. *European Sociological Review* 32(6): 752–65. doi.org/10.1093/esr/jcw032

Masroor, Nida, Muhammad Asim and Saman Hussain. 2020. 'E-commerce: A gateway to mobilizing female entrepreneurs in the digital era'. *International Journal of Advanced Science and Technology* 29(10s): 1–17.

Pennings, Steven Michael. 2022. *A Gender Employment Gap Index (GEGI): A Simple Measure of the Economic Gains from Closing Gender Employment Gaps, with an Application to the Pacific Islands*. World Bank. http://hdl.handle.net/10986/37062

Schaner, Simone and Smita Das. 2016. *Female Labor Force Participation in Asia: Indonesia Country Study*. ADB Economics Working Paper No. 474. Asian Development Bank.

Setiawan, Imam, Utz Pape and Natasha Beschorner. 2022. 'How to bridge the gap in Indonesia's inequality in internet access'. *World Bank Blogs*, 13 May. https://blogs.worldbank.org/eastasiapacific/ how-bridge-gap-indonesias-inequality-internet-access

SMERU Research Institute, Digital Pathways at University of Oxford and UNESCAP. 2022. *Diagnostic Report: Digital Skills Landscape in Indonesia*. SMERU Research Report No. 2. SMERU Research Institute. https://smeru.or.id/en/ publication/diagnostic-report-digital-skills-landscape-indonesia

Statista Research Department. 2019. 'Main reasons for not having a mobile phone among adults in Indonesia as of 2019, by gender'. Statista. www.statista.com/ statistics/1168638/indonesia-main-reasons-for-not-having-mobile-phone-among-adults-by-gender/

Sullivan, Cath and Suzan Lewis. 2001. 'Home-based telework, gender, and the synchronization of work and family: Perspectives of teleworkers and their co-residents'. *Gender, Work & Organization* 8(2): 123–45. doi.org/10.1111/1468-0432.00125

Theis, Sophie and Giudy Rusconi. 2019. 'Social commerce entrepreneurship and new opportunities for women's financial inclusion in India and Indonesia'. Women's World Banking. www.womensworldbanking.org/insights-and-impact/social-commerce-report-2019/

UN Women and Pulse Lab Jakarta. 2020. 'Leveraging digitalization to cope with COVID-19: An Indonesia case study on women-owned micro and small businesses'. https://data.unwomen.org/sites/default/files/documents/Publications/Indonesia-Digitalization-Women-MSBs-COVID19-EN.pdf

Viollaz, Mariana and Hernan Winkler. 2021. 'Does the internet reduce gender gaps? The case of Jordan'. *Journal of Development Studies* 58(3): 436–53. doi.org/10.1080/00220388.2021.1965127

World Bank. 2021. *Beyond Unicorns: Harnessing Digital Technologies for Inclusion in Indonesia*. World Bank. www.worldbank.org/en/country/indonesia/publication/beyond-unicorns-harnessing-digital-technologies-for-inclusion-in-indonesia

World Bank and Bappenas. 2020. 'Indonesia's occupational employment outlook. Technical report'. World Bank and Bappenas. www.worldbank.org/en/country/indonesia/publication/toward-a-world-class-labor-market-information-system-for-indonesia

Yang, Gongyan, Shujie Yao and Xinran Dong. 2023. 'Digital economy and wage gap between high- and low-skilled workers'. *Digital Economy and Sustainable Development* 1: 7. doi.org/10.1007/s44265-023-00009-y

9 Deconstructing care work in Indonesia

Atnike Nova Sigiro

Women's participation in the economy has been considered one of the key strategies for achieving gender equality. The reasoning is that by entering the labour market or earning their own money, women will achieve wider opportunities, such as to participate in public life, improve their personal wellbeing, improve their family's welfare, contribute to the country's economic development, and have their capability in professional and public works recognised. In the past two decades in Indonesia, women's labour force participation has slowly but steadily increased. However, this trend has not changed the gendered role of care work at home. Social norms continue to prevail: that care work is women's natural role and family duty. This chapter explores how women are encouraged to participate in the economy, while at the same time still expected to fulfil their duty in care work in the family. I also analyse that care work has been underappreciated, which is reflected in the marginalisation of paid care work in the domestic worker profession.

Backdrop: The progress of gender equality in economic participation in Indonesia

Since the 1970s, Indonesia has witnessed improving indicators of women's economic participation. A rapid decline in the fertility rate after the implementation of government-led family planning during the New Order era and increase in educational attainment has resulted in better economic opportunities for women. More women have post-secondary education, and more women in each recent cohort have been working, particularly during the early years after completing school (Dong and Merdikawati, this volume).

170   *Atnike Nova Sigiro*

Over the past few decades, the female labour force participation rate in Indonesia has remained low, at around 52% in 2019, and still relatively low compared to the East Asia and Pacific region, Thailand and China (all more than 60%) and Vietnam and Cambodia (both nearly 80%) (World Bank 2020: 16). Women's contribution to household income has, at the same time, increased slowly (Table 9.1). However, whether women's increased financial contribution to family livelihoods has also contributed to gender equality in the family is unclear. This is because, while women continue to pursue participation in the economy, they also continue to bear the burden of domestic work in the household.

Table 9.1 Women's income contribution in the family in Indonesia (%)

Year	2011	2013	2015	2017	2019	2021
Income contribution (%)	34.16	35.17	36.03	36.62	37.10	37.22

Source: BPS (2022a).

Indonesia's National Medium Term Development Plan (Rencana Pembangunan Jangka Menengah Nasional, RPJMN) 2020–2024 has set a key development agenda 'to increase the quality and competitiveness of human resources'. The RPJMN also lays out plans for the improvement of gender equality and women's empowerment, with enhancement of women's role and participation in development as one of its policy and strategic directions. The RPJMN noted that women's participation in formal jobs in 2018 was still very low compared to men's participation (34.3% versus 65.8%) (Bappenas 2020). Therefore, the development plan also set enhancement of the quality and competitiveness of women in the workforce as a target.

The RPJMN 2020–2024 includes a gender equality perspective. It notes the important role of family as the key institution for childcaring and education, and emphasises the equal responsibility of men and women in educating and caring for children (Bappenas 2020). It also identifies several problems concerning family development, such as the high rates of child marriage, divorce and unintended pregnancy. However, little was mentioned regarding the heavy load of care work that is borne by women.

The Family Development Index (Indeks Pembangunan Keluarga) was referred in the RPJMN 2020–2024 as a tool to measure achievement and targets of development on family welfare. The index measures family quality through several dimensions, namely, family peacefulness, independence and happiness; and describes the role and function of the family for all regions in Indonesia (BKKBN 2020). However, the concept of an equal gender role in the family in the Family Development Index refers only to shared responsibilities in childcaring, and not to other care work activities in the family.

This situation discloses that the government's development agenda and strategy on gender equality in Indonesia puts much of its focus on efforts to enhance women's participation in the economy, while lacking in strategy for addressing women's role and burden in care work. In reality, when women participate in the workforce, they also take more responsibility for care work activities, such as taking care of children, family and households.

In this chapter I explore how the gender-based division of labour on care work, and the exclusion of care work's contribution to the economy, have created a double burden for women and a lack of appreciation for paid care work. This chapter will support its argument by exploring data and information around women's role and situation concerning care work in Indonesia. The data examined for this chapter cover the period 2001–2021 and sources include Statistics Indonesia (BPS) surveys, the National Socioeconomic Survey (Survei Sosio-Ekonomi Nasional, Susenas) and the National Labour Force Survey (Survei Angkatan Kerja Nasional, Sakernas), as well as International Labour Organization research.

The hidden burden and contribution of unpaid care work in Indonesia

Care work, particularly unpaid care work, has been excluded from the economy. Unpaid care work refers to activities that are necessary to maintain households and care for family members, and includes cooking, cleaning, child-rearing and care of the elderly; unpaid care work takes the largest share of time allocation for women around the globe (Charmes 2019). The burden borne in doing care work and also its contribution to the economy are often disregarded. According to Razavi (2007) the reason for this exclusion can be traced from the emphases towards the monetary contribution of work, while ignoring the social reproduction contribution. Furthermore, mainstream economic analyses usually ignore power relations and inequality between men and women that place the obligation of care work upon women.

The International Labour Organization broadly defines care work as activities and relations involved in meeting the physical, psychological and emotional needs of adults and children, old and young, frail and able-bodied, in households and in institutions (such as schools, nurseries and hospitals). It consists of direct, face-to-face care activities such as feeding,

172   Atnike Nova Sigiro

nursing and helping with personal care, and indirect care activities such as housing cleaning, laundry and other household maintenance (ILO 2018).

The concept of care work is gaining recognition in international policy discourse. This can be seen in the inclusion of care work in the United Nations Sustainable Development Goal 5 'Achieve gender equality and empower all women and girls' (UN Women 2018). Aside from ensuring women's full and effective participation and equal opportunities in economic and public life, Goal 5 also sets a target to recognise and value unpaid care work and domestic care work, including promoting shared responsibilities within households and the family.

A compilation of time-use survey data from 64 countries reveals several less-visible facts concerning women's contribution of care work worldwide (Charmes 2019; ILO 2018). First, 16.4 billion hours are spent in unpaid care work every day. Second, women perform three-quarters of the unpaid care work. Third, compared to men, women dedicate on average 3.2 times more time on care work. The huge amount of time spent on care work globally shows that women's contribution in care work is an important activity for many countries.

The unequal distribution of unpaid care work has several consequences. One is the traditional gender roles that assign caregiving responsibilities to women. Another is the lack of public policies and infrastructure to support families with caregiving responsibilities, such as affordable childcare and care services for the elderly. These factors can create a 'care penalty' for women, where they have to choose between caring for their families and participating in paid work.

In Indonesia, recognition of the contribution of care work to the economy is limited. In the national labour force statistics, unpaid care work activities, particularly the time allocated for them, has not been measured. Tables 9.2 and 9.3 compare indicators from Sakernas that illustrate the importance of unpaid care work. The current national statistics still exclude care work from the category of productive economic activity. The activity 'housekeeping'—a form of care work—is treated as a non–labour force activity, under the same category as attending school or studying. The mode of data presentation reveals how care work has been disregarded as productive work in economic terms.

Despite there being no measurement of unpaid care work, Sakernas data provide an indication that women bear the brunt of unpaid care work in Indonesia. From the overall population aged 15 and older, nearly 31 million individuals reported housekeeping as a reason for them being out of the labour force in 2004 (Table 9.2). This figure increased to 40.6 million in 2021. Among those who did housekeeping, more than 97% were women in 2004 (Table 9.3). While their share of housekeeping

Chapter 9 *Deconstructing care work in Indonesia*   173

Table 9.2 Population aged 15 years and over (male and female) by the type of main activity in urban and rural Indonesia

Main activity	Year		
	2004	2011	2021
Population aged 15 years and above	153,923,648	171,756,077	206,708,299
Labour force/economically active	103,973,387	117,370,485	140,152,575
Labour force participation rate (%)	67.55	68.30	67.80
Employed	93,722,036	109,670,399	131,050,523
Unemployed	10,250,351	7,700,086	9,102,052
Unemployment rate (%)	9.86	6.56	6.49
Non–labour force/not economically active	49,950,261	54,385,592	66,555,724
Attending school	11,577,230	13,104,294	14,644,442
Housekeeping	30,877,274	32,890,423	40,577,943
Other	7,495,757	8,390,875	11,333,339

Source: BPS (2004, 2011, 2021).

Table 9.3 Female population aged 15 years and over by the type of main activity in urban and rural Indonesia

Main activity	Year		
	2004	2011	2021
Population aged 15 years and above	77,290,430	86,045,248	103,400,058
Labour force/economically active	38,046,223	45,118,964	55,157,803
Labour force participation rate (%)	49.23	52.44	53.34
Employed	33,140,525	41,680,456	51,787,209
Unemployed	4,905,698	3,438,508	3,370,594
Unemployment rate (%)	12.89	7.62	6.11
Non–labour force/not economically active	39,244,207	40,926,284	48,242,255
Attending school	5,544,018	6,485,255	7,521,722
Housekeeping	30,234,772	31,252,814	36,726,944
Other	3,465,417	3,188,215	3,993,589

Source: BPS (2004, 2011, 2021).

declined to 95% in 2011 and 90% in 2021, women continued to take on the burden of unpaid care work.

Unpaid care work is also understudied in Indonesia. Among the few studies, one survey on the care economy and burden of homemakers conducted in 34 provinces in Indonesia found that women—particularly

174   *Atnike Nova Sigiro*

female homemakers[1]—had undertaken most of the care work in the family (Sigiro et al. 2018). The survey reported that 78% of the female homemakers interviewed spend more than 12 hours on unpaid care work per day, 16% of them spend 8 to 12 hours per day, and 6% work up to 8 hours per day. On average, the women in the study allocated time for care work for about 13.5 hours per day. The research also captured the form of care work activities that women do for families. These activities covered both direct and indirect care, such as taking care of children, sending children to school, cooking, laundry, shopping, house cleaning, gardening, participating in their neighbourhood association and house maintenance.

A more recent pilot study on women's time-use agency in Greater Jakarta and Surabaya also confirmed the high burden of unpaid care work for women (Prospera et al. 2023). Unlike the study by Sigiro et al. (2018), the Prospera study took into account supervisory care as a form of unpaid care work.[2] It found that married women spent 3.9 hours per day and married men spent 1.4 hours per day doing unpaid care work (as distinct from domestic work). As has been argued in previous studies (for example, Cameron et al. 2019; Setyonaluri 2013; Widarti 1998) that the presence of young children is a barrier for women to participate in paid work, the time-use pilot study confirmed it by showing that married women with young children spent 8.5 hours per day on unpaid care work (Prospera et al. 2023).

The COVID-19 pandemic revealed the reliance of the formal economy and people's daily lives on the invisible unpaid labour of women and girls on care work. Before the global outbreak of COVID-19, women did three times more unpaid care and domestic work than men (United Nations 2020). During the pandemic, many countries witnessed the intensified need for care work, such as taking care of sick family members, children's education and other domestic work. Indonesia experienced a similar situation.

Women in Indonesia have borne a heavier burden of care work due to the impact of COVID-19 on families and households. A national survey in 2020 found that the COVID-19 pandemic has caused widening

---

1   A person in charge of managing the household, and who is not usually employed outside the home.

2   Supervisory care or indirect care refers to the time a person is 'available and in close proximity' to provide active care for a child or a dependent adult should the need arise (UNSD 2022). The amount of time spent on supervisory care is typically higher than on active care, but is often overlooked. It limits time allocation as well as the type of productive work that can be done close to the dependent (Folbre 2018).

Chapter 9 Deconstructing care work in Indonesia 175

gender inequalities in households, as women take on additional caring responsibilities (UNICEF et al. 2021).

Other research also found an increasing care work burden for women during the COVID-19 pandemic in Indonesia (Sigiro et al. 2020). Due to the closing of schools, offices and other public services, most family members were compelled to do their daily activities at home. This change of family daily routine consequently brought additional care work responsibilities upon women. Aside from the usual care work such as taking care of children, cooking and cleaning, women undertook additional care work tasks, such as caring for family members who were exposed to COVID-19. The pandemic also required women to master additional skills on information and communication technology in order to support their children to use the internet during online learning.

During the pandemic, households in Indonesia also experienced economic hardship due to income loss, increasing health costs and increasing household expenditure. A national survey in Indonesia found almost three-quarters of households interviewed in October–November 2020 were earning less than they were in January 2020 (UNICEF et al. 2021). The survey also found that almost a quarter of the respondents experienced increasing household expenses, due to increasing costs of groceries and other essentials, and for internet and mobile phones charges. Similar findings regarding household budget pressures due to the loss of income and increasing household expenses were also captured by Sigiro et al. (2020). For example, electricity bills were one of the most affected costs, since most family activities were done at home and consumed more electricity.

Women's unpaid care work entails a broad range of activities, resources and skills. First, women—particularly homemakers—dedicate the majority of their time for care work above normal working hours in formal employment. Second, care work activities are varied, from direct care work such as childcare and caring for sick family members, including during the COVID-19 pandemic; and indirect care work such as cooking, house cleaning, laundry and shopping. Lastly, women's role in care work also includes managing the household budget and expenses.

The exclusion of unpaid care work from the economy hides these dimensions of unpaid care from its contribution to the family and the economy. It is not surprising that development strategy such as the RPJMN could not sufficiently formulate policy responses to address women's burden in care work due to gender inequality at home. The exclusion of care work from the economy not only hides women's contributions, but it also correlates with underappreciation of paid care work, which I will elaborate next.

The undervalued paid care work

Based on its monetary compensation, care work can be categorised into unpaid and paid care work. Unpaid care work usually happens in households or within families, while paid care work can take place in wider settings—from private individuals to households, and also institutions such as hospitals, nursing homes and schools (ILO 2018). This section will analyse the marginalisation of paid care work that happens in Indonesia, that is, the marginalisation of the domestic worker profession.

The domestic worker has been a gendered occupation around the globe, including in Indonesia. Similar to unpaid care work, paid care work has also been underestimated in national statistics. Suhaimi and Farid (2018) estimated there were 4 million domestic workers in Indonesia in 2015. Around 92% of domestic workers in Indonesia are women, and most of them come from rural areas and have low levels of education (ILO n.d.). More than 80% of domestic workers were not live-in maids (*pekerja pulang-pergi*) and around 60% worked for more than 40 hours per week (Suhaimi and Farid 2018). In the national labour force statistics, 'domestic worker' is not recognised as formal employment. Due to the lack of legal status of their occupation, most domestic workers in Indonesia are not entitled to employment contracts, minimum working hours, overtime pay, pensions and other labour rights entitlements (Sofiani et al. 2014).

Online media has released unofficial figures that show the salary ranges of domestic workers in several provinces (Qothrunnada 2022). Figure 9.1 compares domestic workers' salaries to the minimum wage in several provinces in Indonesia. The comparison shows that domestic workers' salaries in most provinces are lower than the provincial minimum wage, except in provinces that are anecdotally famous for being the exporters of domestic workers to other regions: Central Java, East Java and Banten. However, official statistics released by Statistics Indonesia in 2022 show that the nominal wages of domestic workers in December 2022 were much lower, at 426,588 rupiah per month (BPS 2022b). Many domestic workers also worked in low- to middle-income households. Suhaimi and Farid (2018) estimated that 75% of domestic workers worked in households with monthly spending of less than 5 million rupiah. It is also important to note that employers often set the salary level for domestic workers based on subjective considerations. Pelupessy (2017) describes the practice of determining salary standards for domestic workers based on the employers' calculation of the work burden, and behavioural preferences.

The unequal power relations between domestic workers and their employers results in unfair work treatment against domestic workers. The job descriptions of domestic workers are usually not fixed. Domestic

Chapter 9 Deconstructing care work in Indonesia   177

Figure 9.1   Comparison between minimum monthly wages and domestic workers' salaries in selected provinces, 2022 (rupiah)

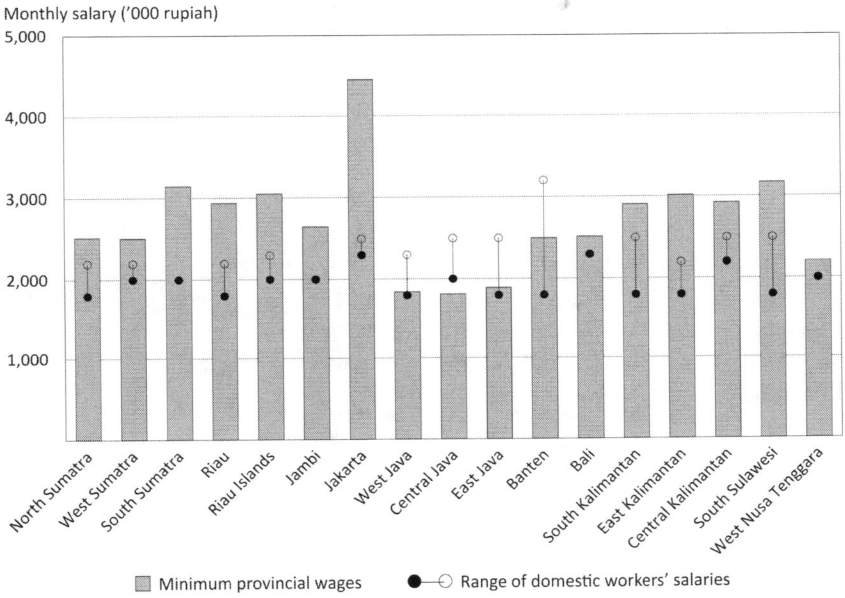

Monthly salary ('000 rupiah)

Minimum provincial wages ●—○ Range of domestic workers' salaries

Source: Minimum provincial wages: BPS (2022c); domestic workers' salaries: Qothrunnada (2022).

workers are required to do various activities such as cleaning the house, ironing, laundry, washing dishes and childcare (Pelupessy 2017). When asked to do additional work or to work late, they do not always receive overtime pay, and there is no fixed standard wage for working overtime (ibid.). Because their workplace is isolated, domestic workers are also vulnerable to domestic violence. A report on violence cases against domestic workers indicated it is difficult to find reliable data about violence against domestic workers, because most cases of violence are under-reported (Jala PRT et al. 2017).

Research on employers' perceptions of decent work for domestic workers in three cities in Indonesia revealed ambiguous ideas about the domestic worker profession that correlate with the lack of rewards and protection for domestic workers (Ruwaida 2017). The respondents in this research see domestic workers as workers who are entitled to salary and other labour standards and protection. However, they do not see domestic work as a formal job, but rather as a family relational interaction and/or as a form of help to the less fortunate. The employers have the perception

178   *Atnike Nova Sigiro*

that they should not be restricted by regulations on labour standards concerning domestic workers. Most of the surveyed employers also think that the minimum wage is not applicable to domestic workers.

Domestic workers bear multiple layers of inequalities, including gender inequality and class exploitation. The work of domestic workers allows members of families to enter the labour market. As a replacement to women's care work, domestic workers take on household tasks and care work for family members, from adults to children, the elderly, disabled and sick. The perception of care work as woman's natural role and ability serves an underlying assumption that caregiving work is not a job that requires skills and abilities. Further, domestic work is a subordinate position in the workplace, within a family or household. Marginalisation of domestic workers has uncovered the underappreciation of care work and has resulted in the denial of domestic workers' rights to labour protections.

Conclusion

The discussion in this chapter reaffirms the care work contribution, done mostly by women, to family welfare and the economy in Indonesia. However, society and policymakers still fail to recognise the economic contribution of care work. The National Medium Term Development Plan 2020–2024, for example, has recognised the importance of women's quality and competitiveness in the labour market, but it has not recognised the social expectations of women to do care work activities in the family while entering the workforce.

The data and research findings concerning the situation of care work in Indonesia highlight how women's contribution and burden in care work are still invisible from society and policymakers. The mainstream economy and policy approach has considered human productivity based only on monetary output and rewards. The fact that women in Indonesia spend more than eight hours a day to do unpaid care work is rarely recognised in the economy.

Women's unpaid care work entails a broad range of activities, resources and skills. The COVID-19 pandemic should have become a reminder to society that the economy and education and healthcare systems would be dysfunctional without the support of women's contribution in households and families. During the pandemic, women had to handle the common household chores, monitor children's education from home, care for sick family members, and manage economic hardship due to income loss and increasing household expenditure.

The invisible contribution of unpaid care work to families and society is also reflected in the conditions of paid care work in the domestic worker profession. Domestic work is not yet recognised as a formal job. As the profession is generally carried out by women, it is commonly associated as unskilled feminine work. Working without an official employment contract, no fixed working hours, wages below the minimum standard and the lack of labour rights protection is experienced by many domestic workers in Indonesia.

The key findings from the experience of women in Indonesia show that the marginalisation of care work not only reproduces gender inequality in the family, it also results in gender inequality in the economy. Within the family, house chores and caregiving remain the responsibility of women. Women continue to face a double burden of entering the workforce and at the same time continuing to do care work in the family. Marginalisation of care work has caused paid care work professions, which are also mostly done by women, to be economically valued lower than other jobs. In addition, the paid care work profession has no protection of labour rights, such as wages, pensions and leave.

In conclusion, the marginalisation of care work and the domestic worker profession stem from two main reasons. The first is the gender-based division of labour of care work in the family. The second is the exclusion of care work's contribution to the economy. Therefore, deconstruction of the gender-based division of labour and dismantling the marginalisation of care work should be considered as key factors towards achieving gender equality within the family and in society.

References

Bappenas. 2020. 'Lampiran Peraturan Presiden Republik Indonesia Nomor 18 Tahun 2020 Tentang Rencana Pembangunan Jangka Menengah Nasional 2020–2024' [Appendix to Regulation of the President of the Republic of Indonesia 18/2020 concerning the National Medium Term Development Plan 2020–2024]. https://perpustakaan.bappenas.go.id/e-library/file_upload/koleksi/migrasi-data-publikasi/file/RP_RKP/Dokumen%20RPJMN%202020-2024/Lampiran%201.%20Narasi%20RPJMN%202020-2024.pdf

BKKBN (Badan Kependudukan dan Keluarga Berencana Nasional). 2020. 'Buku saku pengenalan Indeks Pembangunan Keluarga' [Pocket book introduction to Family Development Index]. BKKBN. http://siperindu.online/dokumen/Ebook_iBangga.pdf

BPS (Badan Pusat Statistik). 2004. 'Keadaan angkatan kerja di Indonesia Agustus 2004' [The state of the labour force in Indonesia, August 2004]. BPS.

BPS (Badan Pusat Statistik). 2011. 'Keadaan angkatan kerja di Indonesia Agustus 2011' [The state of the labour force in Indonesia, August 2011]. BPS. www.bps.

180 *Atnike Nova Sigiro*

go.id/publication/2011/11/28/de1341bc43b62015fe8f6bb3/keadaan-angkatan-kerja-di-indonesia-agustus-2011.html

BPS (Badan Pusat Statistik). 2021. 'Keadaan angkatan kerja di Indonesia Agustus 2021' [The state of the labour force in Indonesia, August 2021]. BPS. www.bps.go.id/publication/2021/12/07/ee355feea591c3b6841d361b/keadaan-angkatan-kerja-di-indonesia-agustus-2021.html

BPS (Badan Pusat Statistik). 2022a. 'Sumbangan pendapatan perempuan (persen), 2021–2022' [Women's income contribution (per cent), 2021–2022]. BPS. https://bps.go.id/indicator/40/467/1/sumbangan-pendapatan-perempuan.html

BPS (Badan Pusat Statistik). 2022b. 'Perkembangan upah pekerja/buruh Januari 2022' [Development of wages for workers/labourers, January 2022]. *Berita Resmi Statistik*, 16/02/Th.XXV. BPS. www.bps.go.id/pressrelease/2022/02/15/1936/upah-nominal-harian-buruh-tani-nasional-januari-2022-naik-sebesar-0-72-persen-.html#:~:text=Upah%20nominal%20harian%20buruh%20tani%20nasional%20pada%20Januari%202022%20naik,kenaikan%20sebesar%200%2C28%20persen

BPS (Badan Pusat Statistik). 2022c. 'Keadaan ketenagakerjaan Indonesia Agustus 2022' [Indonesian employment conditions, August 2022]. *Berita Resmi Statistik*, 82/11/Th.XXV. BPS. www.bps.go.id/pressrelease/2022/11/07/1916/agustus-2022—tingkat-pengangguran-terbuka—tpt—sebesar-5-86-persen-dan-rata-rata-upah-buruh-sebesar-3-07-juta-rupiah-per-bulan.html

Cameron, Lisa A., Diana Contreras Suárez and William Rowell. 2019. 'Female labour force participation in Indonesia: Why has it stalled?' *Bulletin of Indonesian Economic Studies* 55(2): 157–92. doi.org/10.1080/00074918.2018.1530727

Charmes, Jacques. 2019. *The Unpaid Care Work and the Labour Market: An Analysis of Time Use Data Based on the Latest World Compilation of Time-Use Surveys.* International Labour Organization.

Folbre, Nancy. 2018. *Developing Care: Recent Research on the Care Economy and Economic Development.* International Development Research Center. www.iaffe.org/media/cms_page_media/788/Folbre_Nancy.pdf

ILO (International Labour Organization). n.d. 'Factsheet: Domestic workers in Indonesia'. www.ilo.org/wcmsp5/groups/public/---asia/---ro-bangkok/---ilo-jakarta/documents/publication/wcm_041844.pdf

ILO (International Labour Organization). 2018. *Care Work and Care Jobs: For the Future of Decent Work.* International Labour Office. www.ilo.org/wcmsp5/groups/public/---dgreports/---dcomm/---publ/documents/publication/wcms_633135.pdf

Jala PRT, LBH Jakarta and YLBH Apik Jakarta. 2017. *Kompilasi Penanganan Kasus: Pekerja Rumah Tangga (PRT) dan Pekerja Rumah Tangga Anak (PRTA)* [Compilation of case handling: Domestic workers (PRT) and child domestic workers (PRTA)]. International Labour Organization. www.ilo.org/wcmsp5/groups/public/---asia/---ro-bangkok/---ilo-jakarta/documents/publication/wcms_559226.pdf

Pelupessy, Purnama. 2017. 'Effort of domestic workers to realize decent work: Learning, organizing and fighting'. *Jurnal Perempuan* 22(3).

Prospera, Universitas Indonesia and Investing in Women. 2023. *Piloting the Measurement of Time Use, Supervisory Care and Women's Agency in Indonesia.* Prospera.

Qothrunnada, Kholida. 2022. 'Daftar gaji ART per bulan tahun 2022 di sejumlah wilayah di Indonesia' [Monthly household member salaries in a number of regions in Indonesia, 2022]. detikFinance, 21 March. https://finance.detik.com/berita-ekonomi-bisnis/d-5994084/daftar-gaji-art-per-bulan-tahun-2022-di-sejumlah-wilayah-indonesia

Razavi, Shahra. 2007. *The Political and Social Economy of Care in a Development Context: Conceptual Issues, Research Questions and Policy Options.* Gender and Development Programme Paper No. 3. United Nations Research Institute for Social Development.

Ruwaida, Ida. 2017. 'Kondisi kerja layak bagi PRT di mata majikan: Hasil studi di Makassar, Surabaya dan Bandung' [Decent working conditions for domestic workers in the eyes of employers: Results of studies in Makassar, Surabaya and Bandung]. *Jurnal Perempuan* 22(3): 191–200.

Setyonaluri, Diahhadi. 2013. 'Women interrupted: Determinants of women's employment exit and return in Indonesia'. PhD thesis. Canberra: Australian National University. doi.org/10.25911/5d5e7727dad2c

Sigiro, Atnike Nova, Alfindra Primaldhi and Bagus Takwin. 2018. 'Ekonomi perawatan dan beban kerja ibu rumah tangga di Indonesia' [The economics of care and workload for housewives in Indonesia]. *Jurnal Perempuan* 23(4): 249–58.

Sigiro, Atnike Nova, Abby Gina and Dewi Komalasari. 2020. 'Potret dampak pembatasan sosial berskala besar di masa pandemi COVID-19 terhadap perempuan dan kelompok marginal melalui pendekatan feminisme interseksional' [Portrait of the impact of large-scale social restrictions during the COVID-19 pandemic on women and marginalised groups through an intersectional feminism approach]. *Jurnal Perempuan* 25(4): 296–308.

Sofiani, Triana, Sudarsono, Rachmat Syafa and Muhammad Ali Syafa. 2014. 'Legal status of domestic workers in Indonesia in labor law and the implication on employment relationship'. *Journal of Law, Policy and Globalization* 30: 33–47. www.iiste.org/Journals/index.php/JLPG/article/view/16335/16853

Suhaimi, Uzair and Muhammad N. Farid. 2018. *Toward a Better Estimation of Total Population of Domestic Workers in Indonesia.* International Labour Organization. www.ilo.org/wcmsp5/groups/public/---asia/---ro-bangkok/---ilo-jakarta/documents/publication/wcms_628493.pdf

UN Women. 2018. *Promoting Women's Economic Empowerment: Recognizing and Investing in the Care Economy.* Issue Paper. UN Women. www.unwomen.org/sites/default/files/Headquarters/Attachments/Sections/Library/Publications/2018/Issue-paper-Recognizing-and-investing-in-the-care-economy-en.pdf

UNICEF, UNDP, Prospera and SMERU Research Institute. 2021. *Analysis of the Social and Economic Impacts of COVID-19 on Households and Strategic Policy Recommendations for Indonesia.* UNICEF.

United Nations. 2020. *The Impact of COVID-19 on Women*. Policy Brief, 9 April. www.un.org/sexualviolenceinconflict/wp-content/uploads/2020/06/report/policy-brief-the-impact-of-covid-19-on-women/policy-brief-the-impact-of-covid-19-on-women-en-1.pdf

UNSD (United Nations Statistics Division). 2022. 'Minimum harmonized instrument for the production of time-use statistics'. UNSD.

Widarti, Diah. 1998. 'Determinants of labour force participation by married women: The case of Jakarta'. *Bulletin of Indonesian Economic Studies* 34(2): 93–120. doi.org/10.1080/00074919812331337350

World Bank. 2020. *Indonesia Country Gender Assessment: Investing in Opportunities for Women*. World Bank. doi.org/10.1596/35310

PART 3

Social policy reforms and agendas: Challenges to policy implementation

10 In anticipation of perennial contestation: Progress and challenges to national laws and by-laws concerning sexual violence and sexuality in the *reformasi* era

Andy Yentriyani[1]

Twenty-five years of *reformasi* has seen progress in the development of policies towards various types of gender inequality. The most recent was the Sexual Crime Law, after twelve years of rigorous advocacy facing ferocious objection in the name of religion and morality. Nevertheless, more than two decades of *reformasi* has also seen regression and stagnation that hinder more advanced progress towards the fulfilment of women's human rights. This chapter will discuss the conflicting policy frameworks where progress towards gender equality, as well as the gaps, contradictions and setbacks, are all consequences of deficits within the *reformasi* process, while contestations around gender equality, sexuality and sexual violence also serve as a focus of the perennial struggle for

---

1 Chairperson of the National Commission on Violence against Women, Komnas Perempuan, 2020–2025. Komnas Perempuan is a national human rights institution in Indonesia and was the first independent institution set up in the *reformasi* era in the aftermath of the May 1998 riots. Established by presidential decree, Komnas Perempuan's mandate focuses on the elimination of all forms of violence against women and on the advancement of women's human rights. Komnas Perempuan works independently to monitor, fact find and document cases of violence against women. It conducts strategic studies as the basis to provide policy recommendations and to develop materials for public education. Komnas Perempuan has a website written in Bahasa Indonesia.

186 *Andy Yentriyani*

power in Indonesia. It will also highlight the role of women's groups, their challenges and future priorities in their efforts to promote fulfilment of women's rights.

The breakthrough of the Sexual Crime Law

The Sexual Crime Law, the first of its kind in Indonesian history, was passed by the Indonesian parliament in April 2022. Issuance of the Sexual Crime Law has been highly commended by national and international communities for its adoption of a victims-centred perspective. The law was passed amid a background of continuously increasing reported cases of sexual violence. According to Komnas Perempuan's annual report, at least 26,117 cases of sexual violence were reported between 2017 and 2021 (Figure 10.1). The increase of sexual violence cases reported to Komnas Perempuan from 2017 to 2021 is almost sixfold, from 369 cases in 2017 to 2,204 cases in 2021. Rape, which includes marital rape and incest, is the main type of sexual violence reported.

The Sexual Crime Law addresses gaps in the 1946 Penal Code,[2] and in legal provisions regarding sexual violence in general. It is noteworthy that rape (*perkosaan*) according to the 1946 Penal Code is limited to acts of forced sexual intercourse through vaginal penetration by male genitals. Other acts of forced sexual intercourse are categorised as molestation (*pencabulan*). There is also a category of intercourse (*persetubuhan*), defined as sexual intercourse perpetrated against a woman who is unconscious, or towards girls. While these three acts are all indisputably rape, due to their different classifications, perpetrators of *persetubuhan* will get the lightest punishment, while *pencabulan* is lighter than *perkosaan*.

The 1946 Penal Code doesn't have any provisions regarding sexual harassment or many other kinds of sexual violence experienced by women in Indonesia. One is forced marriage, which is justified mostly by cultural and religious arguments. However, according to Law 1/1974 on Marriage, a marriage is only legitimate if both parties enter the marriage voluntarily. Meanwhile, in some cases, sexual violence not covered in the 1946 Penal Code is partially regulated under other laws. For example, forced sterilisation, sexual slavery and sexual torture are recognised only when they are conducted in relation to an act of crime against humanity according to Law 26/2000 on the Human Rights Court. Another example is sexual exploitation; it is prohibited only in relation to people trafficking as

---

2 The 1946 Penal Code adopted the archaic Criminal Code enacted during the Dutch colonial era. This law was revised by Law 1/2023 on the Criminal Code that will be further discussed in this chapter.

Chapter 10 Progress and challenges to national laws concerning sexual violence 187

Figure 10.1 Number of sexual violence cases reported to Komnas Perempuan and to community service organisation–based service providers, 2017–2021

(a) Sexual violence cases reported to Komnas Perempuan

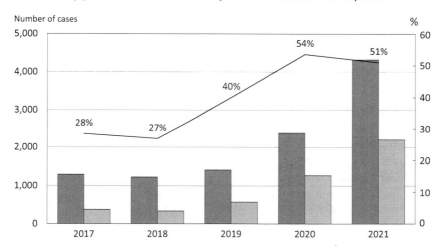

(b) Sexual violence cases reported to community service organisation–based service providers

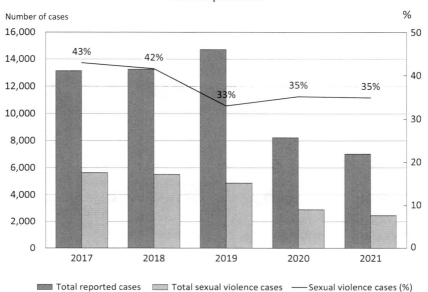

■ Total reported cases ■ Total sexual violence cases — Sexual violence cases (%)

Source: Komnas Perempuan annual reports, 2017–2021.

regulated by Law 21/2000. However, Law 44/2008 on Pornography treats sexual exploitation not as a form of assault against another, but as an act of a person exhibiting their sensuality and sexuality. This is considered to be a violation against social norms or an obscenity. Hence, one can be criminalised for consensually exposing their body in a particular manner considered obscene. Likewise, Law 11/2008 on Electronic Information and Transactions has the potential to criminalise victims of sexual exploitation. It tends to refer to the Pornography Law, and thus it means anyone who consensually produces sexual material for private consumption can be prosecuted if the materials are then transmitted electronically without their consent.

Gaps in legal provisions mentioned above—inadequate definitions, partial regulation and contradictions—have been the main reasons for advocating for a Sexual Crime Law. Another reason is to improve the current law on legal procedures that places a burden on victims to provide adequate evidence for their reports. The Sexual Crime Law is expected to address the persistent complaints that the perspective and behaviour of law enforcers and the state's service providers have been the main obstacles for victims seeking justice.

More specifically, breakthroughs have been made in at least eleven areas of the Sexual Crime Law that show the adoption of the victims' perspective:

- Criminalisation of nine types of sexual violence experienced widely but unrecognised or partially recognised by previous laws: non-physical sexual harassment, physical sexual harassment, forced contraception, forced sterilisation, forced marriage, sexual torture, sexual exploitation, sexual slavery and electronics-based sexual crime.
- Recognition of sexual crimes (e.g. rape, molestation, trafficking, child pornography) that are regulated in other laws.
- Provision of prerequisite criteria for law enforcers, which includes integrity and competence training in handling sexual crime cases.
- Adoption of human rights principles in handling sexual violence cases, in which it is compulsory for law enforcers to uphold human rights and where they are prohibited to behave in a way that intimidates or re-victimises the victims.
- Prohibition of settling cases outside court, except in the case of perpetrators who are minors, and for complaint-based offences (e.g. non-physical sexual harassment).
- Improvement in the rule of evidence, including acknowledging the role of related testimony, medical reports, certificates from clinical

Chapter 10 Progress and challenges to national laws concerning sexual violence 189

psychologists, psychiatrists or other mental health specialists to corroborate the victim's testimony, recognition of electronic evidence or electronic recordings, and testimony of witnesses who are family members of the perpetrator.

- Recognition of the testimony of victims and witnesses with disabilities and the obligation for adequate facilities for the disabled to access justice and recovery.
- Affirmation of victims' rights in the handling of their report, including the right to have protection such as access to a safe house, privacy and anonymity from the public, and the right to immunity. Victims also have the right to legal aid, information, physical and mental health services, compensation and restitution, employment, empowerment and assistance for social integration.
- Adoption of an integrated operational approach to the handling of sexual violence cases, in which comprehensive and quality services to support victims must be provided from the beginning of the report until the trial ends.
- Endorsement of the role of family, community and other institutions in preventing and handling cases.
- Enforcement of the role of national human rights institutions in monitoring the implementation of the law: National Commission on Human Rights, National Commission on Violence against Women, National Commission on Child Protection, and National Commission on Disability.

The relationship between the passing of the Sexual Crime Law and the women's rights movement

Reflecting on the process and the breakthroughs achieved, it is arguable that the Sexual Crime Law is a pinnacle of women's rights leadership in the quarter century of the *reformasi* era. This leadership is evident in the bill, the effort to ensure a participatory and inclusive process, and the frameworks and operational approach, based on women's experiences.

Policy formulation for the Sexual Crime Law was initiated and led by women's rights activists, partly in response to the stalled attempts to revise the 1946 Penal Code. Reforming the criminal justice system to include the experiences of female victims of sexual violence was one of the main recommendations for the newly established government of Indonesia during the *reformasi* era.

While revision of the Penal Code has proceeded slowly, since 1998 organisations providing services for female victims of violence have

190 *Andy Yentriyani*

increased dramatically. In fact, the number has tripled: from 37 women's crisis centres in 2003 to more than 112 in 2019. The police set up a special unit for investigating cases of violence against women and children at provincial and district/municipality levels. In 2019 more than 427 units had been set up throughout the country. There are also around 350 integrated units at health facilities, coordinated by the Ministry of Health, for handling cases concerning women victims of violence. To date, there are also more than 400 integrated service units for women's empowerment and child protection (P2TP2A) at provincial and district/municipality levels. These are coordinated by the Ministry of Women's Empowerment and Child Protection. The establishment of these institutions was enabled through the passing of the Law on the Elimination of Domestic Violence in 2004. The growth of these institutions has relied heavily on the activism by defenders of women's human rights.

Established in 1998, Komnas Perempuan, the National Commission on Violence against Women, is a symbol of triumph of the women's movement in Indonesia. It has successfully compelled the state to take special measures for the elimination of all forms of violence against women in the aftermath of the May 1998 tragedy, when ethnic Chinese women were sexually assaulted during riots in Jakarta and several other big cities in Indonesia. Since its inception, Komnas Perempuan has worked closely with all the aforementioned organisations for women victims of violence. The work that Komnas Perempuan has been building with service providers focuses on the development of systems to prevent violence against women and to fulfil victims' rights with a gender-balanced perspective.

Part of this cooperation involves the compilation of national data on cases reported to service providers, which began in 2001. The compilation is published annually in a document called CATAHU or *Catatan Tahunan*. It provides information regarding the trend of reported cases of violence against women, as well as the development of responses to the cases, both in terms of policy and implementation. In 2010, Komnas Perempuan conducted a review of ten years of CATAHU and found a shocking trend of an increasing number of reports of sexual violence against women and girls. The review result was introduced in a national consultation of Komnas Perempuan with service providers for the preparation of the 16 Days' Campaign against Violence towards Women 2010. The consultation recommended further study on sexual violence throughout the country, including a review on the need to have a specific law regarding this matter. So began the journey of the Sexual Crime Law.

Komnas Perempuan and its networks dedicated five consecutive years to document and further study reported cases of sexual violence. It also

Chapter 10 *Progress and challenges to national laws concerning sexual violence*   191

introduced the nationwide campaign 'Recognising and Handling Sexual Violence'. The availability of data and vehement discussions on issues related to sexual violence around the country led to the adoption of the Sexual Violence Bill as a priority item promised by almost all political parties and presidential candidates in the 2014 election.

In 2015, a bill on sexual crime was drafted. It strongly advocated for a shift in paradigm from sexual violence as a morality issue, as set out in the 1946 Penal Code, to a human rights issue. It also requested a more thorough examination on gendered and intersectionality-based vulnerabilities to sexual violence and its impacts. In order to do so, it adopted feminist legal theory and practice (FLTP) as a framework.

Explicitly mentioning use of the FLTP framework, the initial draft earned strong opposition in 2016–2019, mostly from Islamist groups, who used hoax and hate speech to claim the draft was against Islamic norms and intended to change Indonesian societal values regarding consensual sexual relations outside marriage. These claims were reminiscent of hatred against feminists during the New Order and linked to the black campaign against Gerwani,[3] a women's organisation affiliated with the Indonesian Communist Party. The black campaign was part of the New Order regime's attempts to incite hatred against communism and bolster its own power. Feminists were portrayed as promiscuous women and hence feminism promoted promiscuity. Opponents of the draft advocated extending the bill to cover prohibition of adultery, cohabitation and homosexuality. In pursuit of their demands, opponents mobilised rallies and instigated attacks using social media.

However, the bottom-up process of policy advocacy of the bill from the regions and ongoing data collection and massive campaigns served as a solid foundation for development of the Sexual Crime Law. Vibrant advocacy, offline and online, was led by women's rights movements and joined by many sectors and across generations, including the labour and environmental movements, private sectors, students, mass media and those working in the arts, cultural and entertainment sector, as well as members of parliament and government officials. Thus, although the draft was not adopted until the last parliamentary session in 2019, the agenda

---

3 Gerwani was accused as being responsible for the sexual torture of military generals kidnapped by communist forces. A film was made showing that, prior to the torture, Gerwani members performed sensual dances, apparently in a trance. Autopsy results showed no evident of sexual torture against the military generals prior to their murder on 30 September 1965. The depiction of sexual torture was a deliberate false accusation to heighten the hate against communism (Wierenga 2002).

192   *Andy Yentriyani*

to have a specific law on sexual violence prevailed as a national priority in the newly elected parliament of 2019–2024.

The leadership of the women's movement in policy formulation is also seen in the promotion of the concept of integrated services for women victims of violence in response to the multidimensional needs of victims. The concept encourages and requires cooperation of multiple responsible stakeholders and was adopted in the 2004 Law on the Elimination of Domestic Violence and 2007 Anti Trafficking Law. In relation to this, Komnas Perempuan signed a memorandum of understanding in 2008 with seven ministries and institutions to implement an integrated criminal justice system for handling cases of violence against women (SPPT PKKTP).[4] In this integrated system, services for victims are provided throughout the legal process, from the time the case is reported until after the case is settled by the court. Strengthened based on the review of ongoing implementation, this concept was adopted by the Sexual Crime Law.

Lastly, the public was able to substantively and actively participate in the advocacy, and the Sexual Crime Law arguably serves as a role model for a democratic legislation process. This was made possible due to the persistence of women's groups to encourage participation through various avenues, and to include aspirations from other groups. This kind of legislation-making process was inspired by the reformists as a correction to the centralised and exclusive process during the New Order regime and in many other legislation processes during the *reformasi* era.

Crucial issues remaining after the issuance of the Sexual Crime Law

While the breakthroughs are commendable, there are at least four priority follow-up areas, as well as gaps and possible pushbacks that need to be addressed to ensure the immediate implementation of the Sexual Crime Law and for the law to meet its objectives.

The first of the follow-up areas is the provision of derivative regulations. The government, Komnas Perempuan and other national human rights institutions as well as women's organisations and networks are working together to draft these derivative regulations. Second is the need to set a standard for capacity building of law enforcers and service providers. According to the Sexual Crime Law, attending specific training

---

4   The memorandum of understanding was signed by Komnas Perempuan with the police, the High Prosecutor's Office, the Supreme Court, the Ministry of Women's Empowerment and Child Protection, the Ministry of Health, the Ministry of Social Welfare, and the Advocate Association (Peradi).

Chapter 10 Progress and challenges to national laws concerning sexual violence 193

on sexual violence is mandatory for law enforcers and service providers to implement the law.

Third is the need to expedite the development of infrastructure to provide quality service throughout the country. One of the main priorities is to change the status of the police unit for handling cases of violence against women and children to be an autonomous directorate, rather than as a sub-unit of the general criminal directorate, as at present. In the regions, particularly in remote areas, service infrastructure needs improvement. According to Komnas Perempuan's 2020 study of 285 regional regulations on services for women victims of violence, only 30 per cent of the regulations ensure the establishment of safe houses, around 30 per cent guarantee the provision of psychological recovery services, and less than 10 per cent have measures to protect the identity of women victims with specific vulnerabilities. Furthermore, while the law guarantees that all services are freely available, most regions reported that the budget allocated is inadequate to provide quality and sustainable service.

The fourth follow-up item is to develop more effective prevention measures, accompanied by accountable monitoring mechanisms throughout the process. This item is also one of the recommendations of the United Nations' Committee of the Convention on the Elimination of All Forms of Discrimination against Women (CEDAW) to the Indonesian government in its last session in 2021. The Sexual Crime Law has nine areas of focus for prevention,[5] with attention to specific situations such as geography, conflict and disaster, and to education, social rehabilitation and other high-risk settings.

In addition to the four priority follow-up areas, there are gaps in legal protection that need to be addressed. Some of the gaps are the result of the political negotiation during the legislating process. One is that several provisions regarding sexual violence, including rape and forced abortion, were retained in the revised Penal Code. I will discuss the issues related to the new Penal Code in more detail in the next section.

A possible pushback is posed by the risk of reinforcement into legislation of a protectionist and domestication perspective against women, through the Mother and Child Welfare Bill (Rancangan Undang-Undang Kesejahteraan Ibu dan Anak), which some suspect as a substitute to the infamous Family Resilience Bill (RUU Ketahanan Keluarga) that promotes patriarchal norms in family settings. There is also a threat of

---

5   The nine areas are education, public facilities and infrastructure, governance and organisational management, economy and labour, social welfare, culture, information technology, religion and family.

194 *Andy Yentriyani*

the proliferation of discriminatory by-laws that criminalise sexuality and limit freedom of expression, targeting women and other minorities in the name of religion, morality and majority. While the number of by-laws had decreased to 305 in 2021, in comparison to 421 in 2016, another 20 newly issued by-laws in 2021 had similar content to the objected discriminatory by-laws (Komnas Perempuan 2022). This fact highlights the need to expedite review and improvement in prevention measures.

The 2023 Criminal Code: Another battleground on sexuality

As mentioned earlier, the government retained the provision of rape in the revision of the 1946 Penal Code. When later issued in early 2023, the revised Criminal Code adopted a definition of rape that meets international standards, namely, to include broader forced sexual activity including vaginal, oral and anal penetration and also the use of other instruments besides male genitals for the act. Rape is no longer regulated as a crime against morality but as a crime against bodily integrity. The 2023 Criminal Code also prohibits marital rape, and no longer differentiates between the act of rape (*perkosaan*) with intercourse (*persetubuhan*) with a person who is unconscious or unable to give consent. The maximum penalty for rape is 12 years jail with a possible additional 3 years when perpetrated against a child or if it causes severe injury, and an additional one-third of the maximum sentence when it causes the death of the victim or is perpetrated against the assailant's own child or a child in their care.

Progress can also be observed in the provision on abortion. Though generally abortion is still illegal, the new law strengthens access for women to a safe abortion, previously governed by the Law on Health. It expands the eligibility of safe abortion services to all victims of sexual crime and the service can be accessed to a maximum of 14 weeks after conception. Previously, safe legal abortion was available only to rape victims or mothers with pregnancy complications that risked the life of the mother or the child, whose pregnancy was a maximum of 12 weeks. This expanded provision is crucial since many rape and other sexual crime victims only report their case when their pregnancy is known.

The revised Criminal Code also halves the previous punishment for mothers who abandon their newborn or child under five years old. This is due to an understanding that a woman may feel compelled to abandon her child because of social pressures related to sexual relations outside marriage, or as a victim of sexual exploitation or rape. The understanding of this gender-based vulnerability is a significant shift of paradigm from

Chapter 10 Progress and challenges to national laws concerning sexual violence 195

the previous provision that applied a heavier punishment because the act is considered an abandonment of the responsibilities of motherhood.

While the progress is commendable, the new Criminal Code, as predicted, has potential to infringe upon the Sexual Crime Law. Even with the progressive definition of rape, the 2023 Criminal Code includes in its definitions an act of sexual intercourse with people with mental or intellectual disability by offering or promising money or other goods, or by manipulating the imbalance in power relations. This definition is similar to the definition of sexual exploitation as regulated under the Sexual Crime Law, which imposes a sanction of up to 15 years jail, compared to the Criminal Code penalty of 12 years.

The 2023 Criminal Code also maintains prohibition of molestation (_cabul_), which is defined as any sexual contact other than rape. This broad definition can be easily confused with many acts of sexual crimes, including sexual harassment, as regulated under the Sexual Crime Law.

The Criminal Code also contradicts the Sexual Crime Law in the provision of forced marriage. The sanction in the Criminal Code is up to 7 years jail when the victim is a minor and 9 years jail when the victim is an adult. In the Sexual Crime Law, the act of forced marriage is punishable with up to 9 years jail and an additional one-third of the maximum punishment when conducted against a minor.

Furthermore, the 2023 Criminal Code reduces legal protection for children from sexual abuse by annulling some articles in the 2014 Law on Child Protection (LCP). The annulment of articles 81(1) and 82 of the LCP risks the protection of children from any sexual activity by an adult. The LCP regulates a minimum of 5 years to a maximum of 15 years imprisonment for perpetrators of molestation, rape or any act involving sexual intercourse against a child, and an additional third of the maximum penalty if the perpetrator is a guardian. However, the Criminal Code differentiates the sexual assaults against minors and reduces the punishments for perpetrators. For example, the code provides a maximum of only 9 years for perpetrators of molestation against a child, reduces the minimum punishment for perpetrators of rape and any other sexual intercourse against children from 5 years to 3 years and reduces the maximum punishment for incest against a minor from 15 years to 12 years. The LCP's sanction of a maximum of 10 years for anyone facilitating any sexual activity against a child is also reduced to a maximum of 7–10 years depending on the crime committed (sexual intercourse, molestation or sexual exploitation). This change in punishment provisions is arguably influenced by a growing perception of teenagers' desire to be sexually active. In addition, while the Criminal Code regulates extensively with a variety of punishments for child molestation, article 622(6) instructs the use of article 473(4) on rape against a child when handling cases of molestation or sexual intercourse. This could create confusion since there is an article regulating a maximum of 9 years imprisonment for molestation, while article 473(4) calls for a maximum of 15 years.

In addition, the new law has no regulation on forced abortion, despite women group's expectations, since this issue was dropped from discussions on the Sexual Crime Law. Some groups also protested against the persisting prohibition against abortion. Strong objections to abortion by religious-based groups has been a reason given for minimal change to the abortion law.

Lastly, a large setback has occurred through expansion of the prohibition of sexual relations outside marriage. The new law expands the provision of adultery and also prohibits cohabitation of an unmarried couple. While the previous definition of adultery applied to sexual relations between people where one or both parties were legitimately married to others, the new law expands the definition to apply even when both parties are single. Although it maintains the case as a private matter, it expands the category of plaintiff from only the spouse of a pair who is accused of adultery to also their parents or children. These provisions reduce a woman's autonomy to decide for herself whether to report a case of adultery by her husband, since it may risk her marriage; now, the adultery can also be reported by her parents or children. In addition, the prohibition for singles to have a sexual relationship outside wedlock is considered regressive as it undermines one's autonomy to consensually engage in sexual relations outside marriage. Religious and social norms were arguments deployed to justify this change in the law.

Perennial contestation

For many who have been in policy advocacy on sexual violence and sexuality over the past twenty years, the struggle to bridge the gaps and to anticipate pushback, as seen in the Sexual Crime Law and the 2023 Criminal Code, is undoubtedly another chapter of this perennial contestation of political power in Indonesia between nationalist and Islamist groups. The nationalists are those advocating for respect of diversity and secularism in the legal system, while the Islamists are those with a political agenda to establish explicit references to Islam in the legal system, if not the proclamation of the Islamic State of Indonesia. In the *reformasi* era, this contestation can be observed in the trajectory of laws and by-laws according to their year of issuance that display the dynamics of the struggle (Table 10.1).

Chapter 10 *Progress and challenges to national laws concerning sexual violence* 197

Table 10.1 Policies and by-laws regulating sexual violence and sexuality in the *reformasi* era

1998	May 1998 tragedy leads to reform of criminal justice system, e.g. provision of special police unit for women victims to report their cases, establishment of Komnas Perempuan as specialised national human rights institution on violence against women
1999	Law on human rights, specific articles on women's rights Initiation of anti pornography bill
2000	Second amendment of constitution to reaffirm human rights Law on Human Rights Court acknowledges sexual violence and other gender-based violence as part of crimes against humanity
2001	First regional law (Aceh) obliging veil and criminalising intimacy
2004	Law on the Elimination of Domestic Violence—criminalises marital rape
2007	Constitutional Court's decision affirming conditions for polygamous marriage Anti Trafficking Law and sexual violence in derivative regulations on handling Disaster Law
2008	Law on Elimination of Race and Ethnic Based Discrimination—criminalises ethnic/racial-based rape Pornography Law—protection from pornography industry but also criminalisation of sexuality Law on Electronic Information and Transactions—ambiguous provision on obscenity potentially criminalises women victims of sex exploitation
2009	Komnas Perempuan recorded 154 discriminatory by-laws in the name of religion, morality and majority
2012	Sexual violence in derivative regulations on handling social conflict law
2014	Sexual violence as a specific category in Law on Victim and Witness Protection Qanun Jinayat—local regulation in Aceh that criminalises intimacy, adultery and homosexuality
2016	Special attention to sexual violence in Law on Disabilities 421 discriminatory by-laws documented by Komnas Perempuan
2017	Supreme Court guidelines to prohibit gender bias of judges, including use of women's sexual-related background to undermine their rights Constitutional Court decision to deny request for expansion of criminalisation of adultery to cover all sexual relations out of wedlock
2019	Revision of Marriage Law to increase marriage age to 19 years old Ministry of Religion's circular on prevention and handling of sexual violence in Islamic educational institutions
2021	Joint decree of three ministries on prohibition to impose or ban religious attire at school annulled by Supreme Court Ministry of Education's regulation on prevention and handling of sexual violence in higher education, affirmed with Ministry of Religion circular and the Supreme Court
2022	Sexual Crime Law passed Presence of 305 discriminatory by-laws documented by Komnas Perempuan
2023	Revision of Criminal Code passed, with improved definition on rape

198   *Andy Yentriyani*

As mentioned earlier, *reformasi* was established in the aftermath of the May 1998 riots, in which sexual assaults were committed. The exposure of this incident allowed other cases of sexual violence committed by the state apparatus to also be publicly visible, particularly those committed in special military operation zones, such as Aceh, Papua and Timor Leste. Ratification of the Convention on Anti Torture and partial adoption of the Rome Statute into the Law on the Human Rights Court are arguably responses to this situation. So are the ratifications of other primary international conventions or covenants in human rights, for example, on civil and political rights; on economic, social and cultural rights; and on rights of migrant workers and their families.

Furthermore, the constitution was amended to strengthen the state's commitment to arrest the abuse of power that led to human rights violations. Elaboration of human rights as constitutional rights can be seen in the addition of articles 28A to 28J, and articles related to the division of power in the governance of Indonesia. At the same time, vehement discussion regarding a demand to explicitly acknowledge Islam as the country's main religion took place in the discussion of constitutional amendment. This was reminiscent of similar debate during Indonesia's transition to independence in 1945. While the demand was dismissed, the idea successfully crept into the Indonesian constitution. For example, in the amended constitution, article 31 on education mentions *akhlak* (piety) as one of the objectives of national education. *Akhlak* is an Arabic word that has been adopted into the Indonesian language and its usage is strongly associated with values of Islamic teachings. Hence, inclusion of the term *akhlak* in the constitution can serve as a marker of this perennial contestation.

Debate around the amendment of the constitution, as noted by Indrayana (2007), reinvigorated the tension between the Islamist and nationalist groups that shapes the direction of Indonesia's reformation. Another battleground of the Islamist and nationalist groups is in the formulation of various legislation, primarily laws relating to sexual acts and sexuality.

In 2004, Indonesia issued Law 23/2004 on the Elimination of Domestic Violence, which recognises sexual violence in the family and marital rape. While considered a triumph for women's rights, this law is still often criticised as a feminist agenda to encourage the dissolution of the family, and for some the concept of marital rape is objectionable, if not heretical. A particular interpretation of Islamic teaching is to prefer male dominance and total subordination of women in marriage; traditional family relations were deployed in objecting to the Law on the Elimination of Domestic Violence. Hence, almost as a response to this law, there was

Chapter 10 Progress and challenges to national laws concerning sexual violence   199

a submission for judicial review at the Constitutional Court in 2007 to revoke the conditions for polygamous marriage, which were considered a violation to freedom of religion. Although the Constitutional Court dismissed the request, its considerations were very much influenced by the debate around the interpretation of the Qur'an regarding the arrangement of polygamous marriage.

2008 is remembered as a turning point for the women's rights movement in the *reformasi* era. Just when it seemed that women's human rights were progressing, as indicated by the prohibition of sexual crimes under the Law on the Elimination of Racial and Ethnic Discrimination, parliament issued the infamous Law on Pornography. The law was first discussed in 1999, when the Human Rights Law was introduced. The law was originally called the Anti-Pornography and Pornoaksi Bill, and promoters claimed it was intended to rescue Indonesia from *demokrasi kebablasan* ('too much' democracy) (Arnez 2005). It is noteworthy that *demokrasi kebablasan* was mostly directed at women, since it originally referred to so-called *sastrawangi* or 'fragrant literature', a derogatory term for the writings of women who gained public attention for exploring body autonomy and sexuality as their topic.[6]

The Law on Pornography was issued following huge rallies of both contesting camps, the first open division of Indonesian society into those for sharia-inspired legislation and others for secular, diversity-promoting legislation (Ikkaracan 2000). There was a small group of women advocating for the bill to reduce the risk of child pornography. But the heart of the debate centred on the adoption of a particular Islamic interpretation of sexuality into Indonesian legislation. Most of the promoters pushed for prohibition of sexual and sensual acts, including exposing one's sensuality and sexuality according to a particular Islamic teaching called *aurat*, which is commonly referred to as areas of the body that can be publicly seen, and are different for men and women. Since women are considered as a symbol of morality, as well as the origin of sin, the regulation of *aurat* targets women more than men.

Although the 'Pornoaksi' was dropped and so was the term *aurat*, the idea remained in the regulation. Article 10 of the Pornography Law states that public nudity, sexual exploitation and possession of pornographic material is illegal. According to the law, pornographic materials constitute 'elements of sexual intercourse, including those of deviant sexual intercourse, sexual violence, masturbation, nudity or impressions of nudity,

---

6   According to Arnez (2005), this term conveyed a derogatory message, namely that 'the female writers have not much to offer besides distraction' and hence they were condemned for regression or degrading the essence of democracy.

genitals, and child pornography'. Deviant intercourse is then elaborated as 'intercourse with a corpse, animal, oral sex, anal sex, lesbianism and homosexuality'. This prohibition is considered necessary by its promoters since the law states that it aims to, among other things, provide guidance and education for the morality and *akhlak* of wider society.

Since its implementation, the Pornography Law has put women victims of sexual exploitation and other sexual violence at risk of being criminalised. This situation is exemplified by the case of a woman who was found guilty for being in a video of her having sexual intercourse; she was non-consensually videotaped by her husband, who sold the video to another man without her knowledge. The risk is also heightened by the Law on Electronic Information and Transactions, also issued in 2008. One of the most prominent cases involved Baiq Nuril, a teacher who was imprisoned for exposing sexual harassment against her, perpetrated by her supervisors. She was found guilty for breaching the law for electronically transmitting the sexual remarks made by her supervisor that she considered as harassment. Gaining support from the public, Nuril was later released under presidential clemency.

While national laws regarding sexual violence continued to progress from 1998, with the Sexual Crime Law being the latest, by-laws discriminatory against women, non-binary groups and religious minorities in the name of morality and majority rule continued to grow. As seen in Table 10.2, the number of discriminatory by-laws increased almost threefold between 2009 (Komnas Perempuan 2009) and 2016. By 2022, there were still 305 discriminatory by-laws. Almost 40 per cent of the regulations target women.

Among the 305 discriminatory by-laws, 62 regulate wearing of the veil. In 2002, Aceh issued the Qanun Aqidah or local regulation on Obedience to Islamic Teaching that introduced the obligation to wear 'Muslim attire'. It arguably encouraged other regions to issue similar regulations. Attire is considered as a marker that publicly denotes one's religion. It is also heavily linked to the concepts of sensuality and sexuality, that vary

Table 10.2   Number of discriminatory policies in the name of religion and morality, 2009–2022

Year	Number of policies
2009	154
2014	381
2016	421
2022	305

Chapter 10 Progress and challenges to national laws concerning sexual violence   201

even within Islamic tradition. Hence, this kind of policy preferences a particular interpretation of the holy text as to which parts of the body are to be hidden from public eyes; this applies particularly to the female body through the use of the veil.

Another local regulation in Aceh, the Qanun Jinayat, issued in 2014, criminalises intimacy, consensual extramarital sex and homosexuality. It likely played a significant role in encouraging other regions to also adopt more '*kaffah*/comprehensive' Islamic norms in regulating sexuality. To justify the policy those regions referred to their history in relation to the induction of Islam and the composition of the population, the majority of which is Muslim. However, this kind of policy is not only influenced by Islamic politicians and others with a specific Islamist agenda, but also from those claiming to belong to the nationalist party.

In line with this, in 2017 there was a submission for a judicial review by the Constitutional Court requesting *zina* (adultery) in the 1946 Penal Code to include prohibition of cohabitation and to change the case from a complaint-based case to a public offence. The submission was made by a group called Aliansi Cinta Keluarga Indonesia (AILA, Family Love Alliance Indonesia), whose argument relied heavily on Islamic teachings. It complained that the existing provision violated rights of individuals and communities. The court dismissed the request and suggested the parties challenge the provision within the process to revise the Penal Code. AILA then took up the issue in both the drafting of the Sexual Crime Bill and revision of the 1946 Penal Code. While the parliamentary legislation working group on the Sexual Crime Bill refused to integrate prohibition of adultery and cohabitation, the prohibition was partially adopted in the new 2023 Penal Code as explained above.

While debate on prohibition of consensual sexual relations outside marriage was ongoing, in 2021 Indonesia witnessed a contestation in relation to the discriminatory policy that obliged wearing 'Muslim attire'. This was the first time an objection to the rule was made public. It was posted by a Christian female senior high school student in West Sumatra, one of the first areas that had issued such discriminatory by-laws. Her protest against wearing the veil was later joined by students from other areas; some were also from Muslim families who were bullied by teachers and peers for refusing to wear the veil. In response, the Ministry of Education, Ministry of Religion and Ministry of Home Affairs issued a joint decree to prohibit the obligation to wear a veil at school. The decree was later challenged in the Supreme Court by a group claiming to be the guardians of social norms in West Sumatra, based on the Qu'ran. The Supreme Court agreed with the challenge and annulled the decree. The Ministry of Education then issued a 2022 Regulation on Uniforms but it

202   *Andy Yentriyani*

had a vague prohibition to the obligation to wearing the veil in school. It is noteworthy that this latter law to allow an exception to wearing the veil in school is almost impossible to regulate when the local by-law obliges veil wearing for all women in all institutions.

Reflecting on the ongoing contestation that has been taking place for more than two decades, it becomes clearer how policymaking on sexual violence and sexuality serves as a battleground for political struggle and for manufacturing the Indonesian identity. There are at least four elements to this contestation.

First, there is always a deployment of the narrative that the women's rights movement is the villain of Indonesian democracy and Indonesian ideals in general. This narrative is reminiscent of the New Order regime's narrative against human rights, and women's human rights in particular. As observed, both the rise and fall of the New Order was signified with sexual violence (Komnas Perempuan 2019). In 1965, as part of the campaign against communism to argue for the need for the New Order regime, there was a vast demonising campaign against Gerwani, a women's organisation closely related to the Communist Party. When Suharto, who led the New Order for more than 32 years, stepped down following the May 1998 tragedy, the sexual assault cases were denied and depicted as an anti-nationalism campaign against Indonesia.

These two stigmas—of belonging to Gerwani and of being anti-nationalist—have been perpetually utilised in the contestation during *reformasi* against women's rights groups. At the same time, the women's rights groups bear a further stigma—that of being 'feminist': women brainwashed with Western ideas, anti-family and anti-tradition.

Second, anti–women's rights campaigns, particularly on debates related to sexual violence and sexuality, is used as a convenient strategy to seize public support for the revival of the Islamist Indonesian Movement, once suppressed during the New Order era. Proponents use Islam as a unifying symbol and to argue for policy reform. In parliament, the narrative is mostly uttered by the Prosperous Justice Party (Partai Keadilan Sejahtera, PKS), an Islam-based political party set up in 2002 as a reconstituted Justice Party, which was linked to the Muslim Brotherhood Movement in Egypt. PKS, for example, named the Pornography Law as a gift of Ramadan to attract voters in the 2009 election. It is noteworthy though, that in many areas and at national levels the support for discriminatory legislation also comes from political elites not necessarily of any religious-based political party.

In addition, since 2014 AILA has emerged as a crucial actor in promoting Islamist ideals to direct legislation. It exercises this through active influence in the drafting of policies related to sexual and sexuality

Chapter 10 Progress and challenges to national laws concerning sexual violence 203

issues, as well as whenever the narrative of protection of the family and communal interest is possible. In its arguments, AILA invests in co-opting human rights language from a protectionist perspective and cultural relativism approach. Its advocacy can be seen in the call to criminalise consensual sexual relations outside marriage. As mentioned above, AILA's advocacy yielded a partial success through a revision of the 2023 Criminal Code.

Third, the agenda around the debate for criminalisation of sexuality is linked directly with the prolonged tension in democratising Indonesia, namely on the relationship between the state and religion, on the relationship between the majority and minority in particular areas or even at national level, and on the relationship between central and regional authorities in law making. This tension dates back to pre-independence Muslim Indonesia, when the nationalists succeeded in pushing for no preference of Islam in the constitution, although it is the religion adhered to by the majority of the population.

Fourth, deployment of 'in the name of the majority or public aspiration' in loopholes in the monitoring mechanisms in the executive, legislative and judiciary systems make it possible, in policymaking, to undermine human rights that are guaranteed in the constitution. There is also growing sophistication in utilising democracy mechanisms to claim power and reinforce spheres of influence on a new identity of Indonesia based on a particular interpretation of Islam.

Conclusion

Being in the position of activist/practitioner, taking note of the historical contestation pattern and heading to the next battle, I would like to conclude this chapter by requesting support for five priorities to advance the current achievements in policymaking in Indonesia:

- The first is to strengthen women's rights movement leadership, including through more strategic studies on relevant issues, data gathering, and opportunities for capacity building such as in writing and communication skills

- Second is to grow alliances at local, national and international levels using all possible communication and coordination means, online and offline

- Third is to continue raising public awareness on the critical problems in Indonesian democracy and its relevance to our daily lives

- Fourth is to amplify the modes of resilience that have enabled the progress achieved to date, including historical evidence, progressive religious movements such as Kongres Ulama Perempuan Indonesia (KUPI, Indonesian Congress of Women Religious Scholars), and young people

- Fifth is to expedite improvement of the monitoring system in policymaking.

Reflecting on the lessons learned from the Sexual Crime Law and revision of the 2023 Criminal Code, being vigilant to policy suggestions on issues relating to the family and to sexuality, including the recent Mother and Child Welfare Bill, serves as a crucial key to ensuring progress on human rights for all within the perennial contest between Islamists and nationalists in the democratising of Indonesia.

References

Arnez, M. 2005. 'Provocative women's literature: The case of *sastra wangi*'. Paper presented to the international symposium Islam and Gender in Southeast Asia, Institute for Southeast Asian Studies, University of Passau, Germany, September 2005.

Ikkaracan, Pinar, ed. 2000. *Women and Sexuality in Muslim Societies*. Women for Women's Human Rights.

Indrayana, Denny. 2007. *Amandemen UUD 1945: Antara Mitos dan Pembongkaran* [Amendment 1945: Between myth and demolition]. Mizan.

Komnas Perempuan. 2009. 'Kita bersikap: Empat dasarwarsa kekerasan terhadap perempuan' [We stand: The four principles of violence against women]. Komnas Perempuan.

Komnas Perempuan. 2019. 'Atas nama otonomi daerah: Pelembagaan diskriminasi dalam tatanan negara bangsa Indonesia' [In the name of regional autonomy: Institutionalisation of discrimination within the Indonesian nation-state]. Komnas Perempuan.

Komnas Perempuan. 2022. 'Bayang-bayang stagnansi: Daya pencegahan dan penanganan berbanding peningkatan jumlah, ragam dan kompleksitas kekerasan berbasis gender terhadap perempuan' [The shadow of stagnancy: The power of prevention and management compared to the increase in number, variety and complexity of gender-based violence against women]. Komnas Perempuan.

Wierenga, Saskia. 2002. *Sexual Politics in Indonesia*. Palgrave Macmillan.

11 Indonesia's social protection landscape: Women, exclusion and deservingness in social assistance

Vania Budianto

In 2018, the Indonesian government scaled up its conditional cash transfer program called the Family Hope Program. Approximately 10 million poor women became entitled to social assistance programs.[1] This reflects a trend across the global South: social assistance programs have increasingly provided women with new social entitlements. Despite significant achievements in the expansion of social assistance, issues of exclusion and gender inequality in Indonesia persist (OECD 2019).[2]

Although public discourse has focused on issues of exclusion and inclusion errors due to mistargeting,[3] the debate tends to overlook 'exclusion by design'—omission of particular population groups due to their lack of legal entitlements (Leisering 2019). While in Indonesia social assistance or social insurance has extended considerably, it tends to overlook some vulnerable population groups such as the elderly, people with disability and those in the informal sector (Holmemo et al. 2020; OECD 2019; TNP2K 2018). This lack of coverage for these vulnerable populations also has a gender dimension.

---

1 Indonesia's current social protection arrangements include a non-contributory system, social assistance in the form of cash or in-kind transfers, and a contributory system known as social insurance.
2 The problem of exclusion tends to affect women more than men.
3 An 'exclusion error' occurs when a household or individual meets the criteria to receive social assistance but does not receive it. Conversely, an 'inclusion error' occurs when someone does not meet the criteria or does not need assistance but receives it.

206 *Vania Budianto*

While Indonesia's approach parallels other social assistance policies that target women as the primary recipient, gender equality and women's empowerment are not priority objectives of the country's social protection strategy (Sabates-Wheeler and Kabeer 2003). While scholars have discussed how social assistance programs overlook the structural barriers faced by women (Bradshaw 2008; Holmes and Jones 2013), researchers also need to examine how different notions of deservingness shape and influence the pattern of exclusion and inclusion.

In this chapter, I examine how the notion of deservingness leads to a pattern of exclusion (Leisering 2019) in Indonesia's social assistance. Notions of deservingness influence policy around social assistance, such as which groups to target and the rationale and framing that government uses to justify its policy choices. Historically, the idea of the 'deserving poor' emerged at the time of the English Poor laws, when overseers of the poor would differentiate between the deserving and the undeserving. This involved categorising those seeking assistance into different groups according to specific moral or ideological judgements (Alcock et al. 2002). The 'deserving poor' were those entitled to resources because they could not work due to no fault of their own (Watkins-Hayes and Kovalsky 2016). Overseers considered others as undeserving due to their lack of virtue, including their 'unemployed' status. As notions of deservingness change over time, different categories of vulnerable people can move in and out of social assistance programs (ibid.). Such notions of deservingness are also at work in Indonesia.

Drawing on interviews with policy actors and relevant literature, I examine how Indonesia's social assistance programs see particular types of women as 'deserving'. The aim here is to explain what has changed since Indonesia introduced the social protection system twenty years ago, exploring implications for the gender equality agenda in Indonesia.

I explore how notions of deservingness and gender norms shape patterns of inclusion and exclusion in social assistance. Indonesia's social assistance has evolved from a 'gender-blind' program design to one targeting women as beneficiaries of social assistance programs. The latter approach sees women as instrumental to the goal of social development rather than pursuing gender equality goals per se. Further, this approach reinforces existing gender norms. It overlooks the specific vulnerabilities women face throughout their life cycle, particularly by insufficiently recognising female-headed households, women in the informal sector and women in their old age.

This chapter is structured as follows: first, I will discuss the evolution of Indonesia's social assistance and how gender relations and women are considered. Second, I will discuss how targeting women can have intended and unintended outcomes. Third, I will examine which groups of

Chapter 11 Indonesia's social protection landscape   207

women are excluded through lack of legal entitlement to social protection. I then turn to the reasons behind Indonesia's notion of deservingness. Finally, I consider how Indonesia's social assistance can be more inclusive towards the different conditions of women, and how gender-sensitive social assistance programs that empower women might be designed.

The emergence of Indonesia's social assistance programs: A case of a gender-blind intervention?

Indonesia's social assistance programs have evolved as the government has responded to various crises (Table 11.1). The state began to assist Indonesia's very poor households during severe crises. First, the Asian financial crisis in 1997–1998 triggered the introduction of the first-in-kind social assistance program, Rice for the Poor or Raskin (Beras untuk Keluarga Miskin), in the form of rice subsidies for 15.5 million poor households. Subsequently, the increase in global fuel prices required the Indonesian government to remove fuel subsidies, forcing the government to introduce a temporary unconditional cash transfer program, Bantuan Langsung Tunai (BLT), in 2005. As a key government official at that time recalled, 'it was not that we were so good that we had the idea to give cash transfers, but we just had to' (retired senior official, 2022). The Indonesian government also introduced BLT to reduce conflict due to increased fuel prices and to make these policy changes more socially tolerable (Kwon

Table 11.1 History of Indonesia's main social assistance programs

Before 1999	Traditional social protection systems (family and community based)
1999	Raskin (Rice for the Poor)
2005	Bantuan Langsung Tunai, BLT (temporary unconditional cash transfer program)
2007	Program Keluarga Harapan, PKH (Family Hope Program)
2018	PKH scales up to 10 million households Raskin becomes Kartu Sembako (Staple Food Card)
2020–2022	COVID-19 assistance: BLT Dana Desa (Village Funds Direct Cash Assistance) Bantuan Upah (Wages Assistance) Bantuan UMKM (Usaha Mikro, Kecil, dan Menengah)/Bantuan Produktif (Assistance for Micro, Small and Medium Enterprises) Kartu Prakerja (Pre-employment Card)

Source: Compiled by the author.

and Kim 2015). A total of 19.2 million poor and near-poor households were eligible to receive the BLT program.

Initially, as the policy design ignores gender relations within poor households, we might consider the policy 'gender blind'. The government identified men as the head of households as the primary recipients of Raskin and BLT and deserving of assistance. Wives could collect social assistance benefits when their husbands were unavailable (Arif et al. 2010). While 'poor households' were 'deserving' of social assistance, benefits were explicitly given to the head of the household to reflect existing gender norms where men are the primary breadwinners in the family. However, the policy had yet to consider gender relations within a household.

At this stage policy actors neglected the inequality inherent in social protection targeting. In interviews, government officials tend to see gender equality as meaning that men and women have the same access to services, such as equal access to education opportunities and health services. Similarly, in social protection, government officials tend to view social protection policy as 'gender neutral' where men and women have equal access. One official commented that 'the condition of gender equality has improved, there are many programs, men and women have equal access' (TNP2K interview, 2022). However, government officials have yet to acknowledge the gendered nature of poverty, such as gender earning gaps or women being time poor, or realise this in targeting programs.

To bring the gender dimension into policy, social programming also needs to acknowledge the critical intra-household dynamics. We need to avoid assuming that benefits will be divided equally within a household. The Raskin program tends to assume that the food or rice is divided equally within the household, without considering the different needs of the household or the household's consumption patterns (Arif et al. 2010). This is because the government aimed to ensure that low-income families have access to food, without considering age-specific food security needs. Raskin did not specifically target women; however, Raskin helped women meet their needs because women manage the purchasing and cooking of food for the family (ibid.). Here, the program needed to acknowledge the critical intra-household dynamics that dictate food consumption: food consumption inside a household is unequal.

During the early years of social assistance no government programs targeted women specifically. While Raskin and BLT targeted poor households, they lacked specific criteria for more vulnerable households, such as 'women-headed households'. Yet, women-headed households are more vulnerable to poverty, particularly income poverty. Female-headed households rely mainly on government or family assistance as these households have 'substantially lower earned income' (Schaner 2012: 4).

A policy that assumes men are the heads of households can also discriminate against more vulnerable women-headed households seeking social assistance. Due to the program's requirements, women-headed households often lack access to social assistance. The legal status of their marriage and the possession of a Family Card (Kartu Keluarga) determines whether poor Indonesian women are eligible for social assistance programs. According to one study, 'informal marriage' or de facto marriage with no legal documentation disadvantages women seeking access to social assistance (World Bank 2020). Not having a marriage certificate, for instance, because the woman is not the first wife, or is a divorcee, means that women are not eligible to qualify as a 'female-headed' household to receive social assistance programs (ibid.). The main administrative requirement for social assistance in Indonesia is having the Family Card.

Even when social assistance targets women specifically, a lack of a gender lens in social assistance can have unintended consequences for women, as discussed in the next section.

From gender blind to 'mothers in service of the state'? Evolving approaches to targeting in Indonesia's social assistance

After the national government introduced a conditional cash transfer (CCT) program, Indonesia's social programs considered poor families with children as particularly deserving of social assistance. The Family Hope Program (Program Keluarga Harapan, PKH), targeted ultra-poor families, following the CCT model that originated from Latin America. Since 2018, PKH has expanded to target the poorest 10 million households (Figure 11.1). The program deemed only very poor families with children or pregnant mothers as entitled to PKH benefits. This entails a particular conception of deservingness.

PKH advances a concept of deservingness based on the idea that poor families can escape poverty if they receive regular income. It provides incentives to change their behaviour. Poor families receive a particular amount based on the number of eligible recipients in the family. The original criteria included pregnant and breastfeeding mothers, babies to children aged five years, and school-aged children (up until high school).[4] The program also assumes they are poor because they lack access to

---

4 Since 2017, PKH criteria have included the elderly and people with disability. Yet this is still a family-based cash transfer where the benefit is given to mothers or female caregivers.

Figure 11.1 Family Hope Program (PKH) coverage, 2007–2020

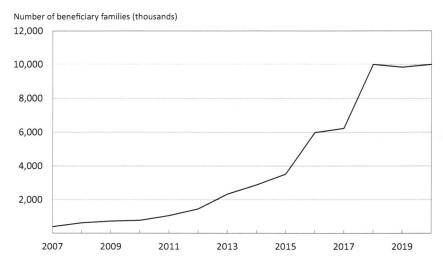

Source: Syamsulhakim and Khadijah (2021: 9).

education and health facilities. PKH aims to increase poor families' consumption and break intergenerational poverty. Women, in their role as mothers, have been identified as the primary recipient and targeted explicitly on behalf of their families.

The program logic considers women as more deserving of social assistance for a number of reasons. First, Indonesian government officials tend to believe that giving benefits to women or mothers will be more effective in achieving program objectives than helping men. 'We learned from the BLT study that the men as the head of the household used the money to buy phone credit or cigarettes. In 2007 we introduced CCT, conditional ones, and we learned from BLT that the recipients should not be men but women' (interview with Bappenas 2, 2022). This suggests that the program mainly targets women to ensure that the money is used for the family rather than because women are more vulnerable than men.

The government uses women in 'the service of the state' to achieve its poverty reduction and human development objectives (Molyneux 2007). According to Molyneux, 'where women's needs were specifically acknowledged, entitlements were gained principally by virtue of their place within the family as wives and mothers whose main legally enforceable responsibility was the care of husbands and children' (ibid.: 5). In other words, the government utilises the mother's role in caring for her family to ensure that programs such as CCT achieve policy objectives. With PKH, the main aim is to break intergenerational poverty; here, targeting mothers ensures that PKH families are achieving program conditions.

Furthermore, the program sees women because they both receive a cash payment and take part in capacity-building programs. The program requires PKH mothers to attend monthly training, known as a family development session (FDS), to build their capacity. Despite being referred to as a 'family', only mothers and not fathers are expected to attend FDSs. In this monthly meeting, PKH facilitators deliver training modules on parenting, family health and financial management. The FDS aims to empower women as mothers and help them influence their children and husbands. As a government official noted, the program designed modules to make the women 'great moms for the children, to motivate them [the children] to go to school, so they don't just end up in the kitchen' (interview with Bappenas 1, 2022). When I asked why only women needed to attend the FDS, a government informant told me that men or fathers are the primary breadwinners.

We see here an assumption that women, as 'housewives', have time to attend the FDS and hence only women or mothers need to attend the training. This fails to recognise that women play economic and other roles in the family. When I spoke to PKH facilitators, they noted that in areas where PKH recipients rely on farming, they find it challenging to organise the monthly FDS session, especially during the planting season, as the women will be in the paddy field during the daytime. The program design needs to acknowledge women's economic role in the family.

While PKH has achieved positive results for children and women, especially with respect to health and education outcomes, there are several unintended negative implications. In terms of achieving these health and education outcomes, impact studies on PKH have shown that PKH increased school enrolment for children and more women delivered babies in health facilities (Cahyadi et al. 2018). However, this is at the expense of gender equality and women's empowerment agendas.

First, PKH conditionalities reproduce existing gender norms that confine women to their reproductive and domestic roles within the family. As the main recipients of the program, the women in the PKH family are responsible for providing their children with health check-ups and ensuring they go to school. Women must perform their unpaid caring role to ensure that their family can continue to receive social assistance and achieve the government's intended objective. According to one of the key government officials who designed PKH:

> We learned from our other programs that women's role was crucial to changing mindsets and ensuring that the next generation continued education. So, we need their capacity to build. So, we educate the mothers, but if the mother is not around in the case of where she became a migrant worker, other caregivers in the family like the aunt or grandmother can attend the session. (Interview with Bappenas 1, 2022)

While government officials acknowledged that some women can be the main breadwinner of poor families, such as women working as migrant workers, caring for children has always been the responsibility of the 'female' member of the family, such as the aunt or grandmother. Consequently, this reinforces the gender stereotype that women in the family are responsible for caring for children. As Chopra (2018) highlighted, by ignoring issues such as unpaid care work and women's time, social assistance programs can perpetuate power imbalances and reproduce gender stereotypes based on traditional gender roles.

Further, PKH adds tasks to the workloads of poor women who already juggle multiple domestic and economic responsibilities. Women worldwide, including in Indonesia, are time poor because they must carry out unpaid caregiving duties as well as economic activities. Compared to men, poor women spend more time on paid or unpaid work (Bessell and Bexley 2021). Moreover, women often perform caring tasks as part of their daily routines. Hence, the requirement of PKH beneficiaries to attend monthly FDSs means that the session can be a burden on women. Fieldwork interviews revealed that many women receiving PKH must work to support their families, as the cash transfer is insufficient to meet their daily needs. However, their work may only provide an irregular and unstable income; this includes farming, working as a daily-wage home worker or selling food at markets.

Critics have suggested that CCTs like PKH are limited in another way: CCTs in Indonesia do not address the structural barriers for women, for instance by improving women's bargaining power. A study in Brazil revealed how women who receive CCTs increased their bargaining power (de Brauw et al. 2014). Yet, in Indonesia, there is little evidence regarding how receiving social assistance influences intra-household dynamics. A SMERU study (Arif et al. 2013) on PKH in West Java and East Nusa Tenggara found that while receiving cash transfers helped women to meet their immediate needs, receiving PKH changed neither intra-household relations nor the relative position of women in the household. PKH targets the family, but most if not all interventions are aimed at mothers, not fathers. To transform the existing intra-household family dynamics, Arif et al. (2013) suggest that husbands and fathers should be involved in the program, thereby achieving a more transformative result. This would

Chapter 11 *Indonesia's social protection landscape* 213

contribute to the broader ideals for gender equality by challenging the status quo of gender roles in households.

The introduction of PKH has shifted the notion of deservingness: families with children, specifically women as mothers, were deemed as deserving of social assistance. However, this notion of deservingness does not advance gender equality and women's empowerment. PKH aims to achieve the state's main objectives of poverty reduction and human development. More needs to be done to make the program design gender-sensitive and to contribute more meaningfully to the gender equality agenda. Furthermore, this notion of deservingness also has consequences, especially for other vulnerable groups of women who are not entitled to receive social assistance.

Who is left behind: Women in the informal sector and elderly women

Women in the informal sector

As 60 per cent of women work in the informal sector (World Bank 2020), social assistance for informal workers disproportionately affects women. Most women working informally are 'self-employed, home-based ..., casual, or family workers', often unpaid (ibid.: 21). Further, women also make up 64 per cent of Indonesia's small-to-medium enterprises (Salyanti and Askar 2022). Informal workers are either unable or unwilling to contribute to social insurance and are ineligible for social assistance (OECD 2019). Before COVID-19, only 25 per cent of poor households were entitled to social assistance. Consequently, most informal sector women missed out on social assistance. This has several negative implications.

First, women working informally rely particularly on social assistance or cash transfer programs, especially during crises. A recent study on ultra-micro entrepreneurs found that 95 per cent are women, and around 60 per cent of these women depended on cash assistance from the government during the COVID-19 pandemic (Salyanti and Askar 2022). However, when it comes to social assistance to help medium and small enterprises, such as Productive Assistance (Bantuan Produktif), women lack access to these programs compared to men. This is despite the reality that women work in more vulnerable micro, small and medium enterprises (ibid.). This research also found that while programs for ultra-micro entrepreneurs such as savings and loans do not systematically discriminate against women, the program design lacks a gender lens and consequently women lack easy access to program benefits.

214　Vania Budianto

Second, women face systematic obstacles to accessing 'gender-neutral' policies that ostensibly target informal sector workers. This is because of women's legal status as 'housewives' or *ibu rumah tangga*. While gender-neutral policies do not discriminate against women in the informal sector, women face difficulties accessing them. This became apparent when an activist from non-government organisation KAPAL Perempuan shared her experiences advocating for women fishers seeking access to KUSUKA, a program for those in the maritime and fisheries sector:

> The female fishermen we worked with cannot access KUSUKA because of legal identity and data issues. In their national ID card [Kartu Tanda Penduduk, KTP], their occupation is written as 'housewife' [*ibu rumah tangga*], so it made them ineligible to receive the program.
> (KAPAL Perempuan activist, 2022)

Even after KAPAL Perempuan advocated the issue to the Ministry of Women's Empowerment, at the time of the interview, only 4 out of 160 women in KAPAL Perempuan's data could access KUSUKA. This example shows that women can still be systematically excluded even when a government program gives 'equal access' to men and women. Many government policies assume that men are the main breadwinners and hold occupations like farmers and fishermen and that women play a supporting role as housewives.

Third, as programs inadequately recognise that poor women play an instrumental economic role in their families, women are entitled to receive social assistance only if they have the status of 'women-headed households'. During COVID-19, only women who are identified as 'women-headed households' are specifically targeted by the Village Funds Direct Cash Assistance program (BLT Dana Desa). Yet, the Minister of Villages maintained that in 2022 out of 6.38 million program recipients, many recipients were 'women-headed households' (UPDESA 2022).

Elderly women

Programs also leave behind a second vulnerable group of women, elderly women. In general, both elderly men and women need access to social assistance. Yet social assistance covers just 2 per cent of Indonesia's elderly (TNP2K and SMERU 2020), despite the older population being prone to poverty and facing various types of vulnerabilities such as disability and deteriorating health conditions. Further, Indonesia's ageing population sits predominantly in the bottom 40 per cent by expenditure (ibid.) and 36 per cent of the elderly are either in the poor or vulnerable category (Holmemo et al. 2020). Nevertheless, elderly women are disproportionately affected by the lack of social assistance.

First, working mostly in the informal sector, women remain vulnerable in their old age as they lack contributory social insurance, which would provide old-age savings. While having no access to social insurance or social assistance affects both elderly women and men, 53 per cent of the population aged 65 and over in Indonesia are women and women tend to live longer than men (TNP2K 2018). Further, women are 14 per cent more likely to be extremely poor, and widowed (56 per cent compared to 14 per cent of men), and 15 per cent of women live alone compared to 5 per cent of men (ibid.). Lack of access to social assistance in old age affects more women than men.

Second, women continue to work in the informal sector in their old age in larger numbers than men. The large number of elderly women working in the informal sector indicates their poor livelihood choices. Poor elderly women cannot rely on government or family assistance. Eighty-nine per cent of elderly women compared to 81.4 per cent of men are informal workers (TNP2K and SMERU 2020), and women are 'more likely to work informally and to be informally employed the older they are' (OECD 2019: 115).

While the Indonesian government strives to increase elderly social assistance, the notion of deservingness that prioritises families with children hampers this effort. In 2018, the Indonesian government added 'elderly' as an eligibility component for PKH, increasing coverage for the elderly (OECD 2019). According to the latest survey conducted by Statistics Indonesia, only 11.9 per cent of the elderly received PKH. However, the elderly PKH entitlement does not go to the individual, but to the family receiving the PKH benefit (Holmemo et al. 2020). Adding an elderly component to the PKH assumes a family norm that elderly parents must live with their children to receive entitlements.

Although the Indonesian government has committed to increasing coverage of social assistance for the elderly, its approach is based on a residual approach: entitlements can only go towards the 'very poor elderly'. Presidential Decree 88/2021 on a National Strategy for the Elderly aims to increase coverage of 'poor elderly', those in the bottom 30 per cent of the population. Non-government organisation activists advocate for a more universal social pension not dependent on poverty or income level: 'all elderly should receive social assistance, whether they are poor or rich. For social assistance, all elderly should be entitled as the elderly have worked all their life, it is a way for the government to thank the elderly' (interview with PEKKA, 2022). However, advocating for more universal social assistance will be challenging in the Indonesian context, especially given the embedded but implicit ideas of deservingness that shapes Indonesia's social assistance.

Explaining Indonesia's notion of deservingness in social assistance: Social values meet international ideas

We also need to consider how sociocultural values, limited fiscal space and the hegemony of social investment ideas affect notions of deservingness. First, Indonesia's social assistance policy reinforces a particular gender construct that determines deservingness: women as 'mothers' are more deserving of receiving social assistance, compared to women in the informal sector or elderly women. Indonesia's gender ideology, what Suryakusuma called 'state ibuism' (Hyunanda et al. 2021; Jakimow 2018), guides this idea of deservingness. Here, the role of a woman is to be a dutiful wife and mother who serves her family, community and the state. This gender construct of state ibuism prevails in Indonesia's poverty programs like PKH, even though it emerged during the New Order regime and arguably needs to be updated. As pointed out by Hyunanda et al. (2021), this 'domestication of women' is an official state construction of the ideal Indonesian women. With the 'gender mainstreaming' agenda in development, including in poverty reduction, the conditions of women deteriorate as women 'enter a precarious labour market while still having unpaid domestic responsibilities, as demanded by society' (ibid.: 10). Hence, the CCT approach that sees women as mothers as more deserving of social assistance is generally acceptable in Indonesia, as it does not challenge the existing social values and gender norms.

The state ibuism ideology has also underwritten the lack of recognition of women's economic roles and their status as informal sector workers. The gender construct of state ibuism came from upper-class or elite Javanese women (Jakimow 2018) and does not match the reality of lower-economic-income working women. A woman activist interviewed during this study suggested that Indonesia has an outdated marriage law (from 1974). This law, still in force, recognises the husband as the head of the household and the wife as 'housewife'. A UNDP and UNICEF (2021) study of Southeast Asian adolescents and young people found that sociocultural and religious norms influence the high value of marriage and children, limiting women's opportunities to participate in the economy. Hence, advocating for policy that supports women to work or have opportunities in the formal labour force (e.g. childcare benefits or improving childcare services) gains limited traction: this does not fit with the ideal concept of ibuism or the virtue of good Indonesian women. When policy ideas fail to align with a country's collective 'world view', it will be difficult for a new policy or approach to be introduced (Bessell 2016).

Second, the issue of limited fiscal space constitutes a major constraint to expanding Indonesia's social assistance, including to more vulnerable

Chapter 11 *Indonesia's social protection landscape* 217

groups such as women, the elderly or those in informal work. When asked why Indonesia has adopted household-based social assistance rather than based on individual vulnerabilities, most government officials I interviewed raised the issue of budget constraints and the government's limited fiscal capacity. Indonesia has a low tax ratio and the government does not have enough resources for social protection. As a result, the government needs to prioritise and thus focuses social assistance towards 'poor and vulnerable' families. This notion of deservingness reflects a particular political commitment to a particular social group that is entrenched in politics and society (Leisering 2019). Consequently, this view of deservingness is both the perspective of the government and an unwritten common belief in society.

The dominant view of who are deserving of social assistance reflects the Islamic concept of *fakir miskin* (the destitute, or 'poorest of the poor') found in zakat almsgiving (McCarthy et al. 2022). Indonesia's constitution observes that '*Fakir Miskin* and abandoned children are protected by the state', which signals that the poor deserve assistance from the state. While Indonesia's legal framework lacks a specific law on social assistance, Law 13/2011 on Handling the Destitute explicitly uses the *fakir miskin* concept. Article 7 of the law mentions 'social protection and social security' (not social assistance) as 'rights' but the detailed explanation of the article specifies that social protection is given when *fakir miskin* face adversity such as disaster, negative impacts of economic crises or social conflict. In Indonesia, promoting 'social protection' or 'social assistance' as an individual right has been challenging, as it is still considered based on 'needs' not 'rights'.

Third, the idea of deservingness in targeting the poor family also matches the international agenda—the 'social investment' hegemony in social policy promoted by the World Bank. According to this framing, the state should invest in human capital and future generations. Accordingly, as mentioned in the CCT discussion, the Indonesian government prioritises helping the children of poor families in breaking 'intergenerational' poverty. Even though women are poorer than men across the life cycle, the dominant discourse still focuses on poor families, who are seen as the 'most deserving' of social assistance. This dominant discourse of the 'poor' overlooks the insights provided by applying a gendered and intersectionality lens. Hence, policy actors struggle to advocate for women or ensure that policy considers women's specific vulnerabilities across the life cycle, thinking beyond their domestic role as mothers.

Conclusion

The notion of 'deservingness' in Indonesia's social assistance policy has evolved over time. It started with gender-blind social assistance programs such as Raskin and BLT, in which policy design ignores gender relations within poor households. With the introduction of the conditional Family Hope Program, a new notion of deservingness arose, where women as mothers were deemed as deserving to receive social assistance. This approach sees women as instrumental to the goal of social development rather than pursuing gender equality goals. Though women became recipients of social assistance programs, this notion of deservingness reinforces existing gender norms. It also excludes other groups of women including women-headed households, women in the informal sector and elderly women.

Three main reasons influence the notion of deservingness towards women and social assistance. First, Indonesia's sociocultural values are influenced mainly by the gender ideology 'state ibuism', in which there is a lack of recognition of women's roles outside the domestic sphere. Second, limited fiscal space compels the Indonesian government to target only the poorest or the *fakir miskin*. Third, the 'social investment' hegemony brought by the World Bank made Indonesia focus on investing in human capacity and future generations.

This chapter recommends that the next step for the Indonesian government is to embed a gender equality and women's empowerment agenda in Indonesia's social protection policy beyond targeting women only as 'mothers'. First, the Indonesian government needs a gender analysis in designing and implementing social assistance programs. Gender-sensitive social assistance programs ensure that programs do not have unintended consequences for women. Further, policymakers could consider social assistance programs that contribute to remediating the unequal gender relations in Indonesian society. Second, Indonesian policymakers need to adopt intersectionality as a critical consideration for social protection policy, with the elderly and informal sector women needing special attention. Instead of treating women as a homogenous group, policymakers need to consider women's vulnerabilities across their life cycles.

References

Alcock, Pete, Angus Erskine and Margaret May, eds. 2002. *The Blackwell Dictionary of Social Policy*. Blackwell.

Arif, Sirojuddin, Muhammad Syukri, Rebecca Holmes and Vita Febriany. 2010. *Gendered Risks, Poverty and Vulnerability: Case Study of the Raskin Food Subsidy Programme in Indonesia*. Report to AusAID. Overseas Development Institute.

Arif, Sirojuddin, Muhammad Syukri, Widjajanti Isdijoso, Meuthia Rosfadhila and Bambang Soelaksono. 2013. *Is Conditionality Pro-Women? A Case Study of Conditional Cash Transfer in Indonesia*. Working Paper. SMERU Research Institute.

Bessell, Sharon. 2016. 'Good governance, gender equality and women's political representation: Ideas as points of disjuncture'. In *The Public Law of Gender: From the Local to the Global*, edited by Kim Rubenstein and Katharine G. Young, 273–95. Cambridge University Press. doi.org/10.1017/CBO9781316481493.013

Bessell, Sharon and Angie Bexley. 2021. 'Deepening multidimensional poverty: The impacts of COVID-19 on vulnerable social groups'. In *Economic Dimensions of COVID-19 in Indonesia: Responding to the Crisis*, edited by Blane D. Lewis and Firman Witoelar, 190–207. ISEAS Publishing.

Bradshaw, Sarah. 2008. 'From structural adjustment to social adjustment: A gendered analysis of conditional cash transfer programmes in Mexico and Nicaragua'. *Global Social Policy* 8(2): 188–207. doi.org/10.1177/1468018108090638

Cahyadi, Nur, Rema Hanna, Benjamin A. Olken, Rizal Adi Prima, Elan Satriawan and Ekki Syamsulhakim. 2018. *Cumulative Impacts of Conditional Cash Transfer Programs: Experimental Evidence from Indonesia*. NBER Working Paper No. 24670. National Bureau of Economic Research. www.nber.org/papers/w24670

Chopra, Deepta. 2018. 'Initiating women's empowerment; achieving gender equality: Interlinkages amongst social protection, infrastructure and public services'. Background paper for Expert Group Meeting at Sixty-Third Session of the Commission on the Status of Women, 13–15 September, UN Women, New York. www.unwomen.org/en/csw/csw63-2019/preparations/expert-group-meeting

de Brauw, Alan, Daniel O. Gilligan, John Hoddinott and Shalini Roy. 2014. 'The impact of Bolsa Família on women's decision-making power'. *World Development* 59: 487–504. doi.org/10.1016/j.worlddev.2013.02.003

Holmemo, Camilla, Pablo Acosta, Tina George, Robert J. Palacios, Juul Pinxten, Shonali Sen and Sailesh Tiwari. 2020. *Investing in People: Social Protection for Indonesia's 2045 Vision*. World Bank. https://openknowledge.worldbank.org/handle/10986/33767

Holmes, Rebecca and Nicola Jones. 2013. *Gender and Social Protection in the Developing World: Beyond Mothers and Safety Nets*. Zed Books. doi.org/10.5040/9781350220300

Hyunanda, Vinny Flaviana, José Palacios Ramírez, Gabriel López-Martínez and Victor Meseguer-Sánchez. 2021. 'State ibuism and women's empowerment in Indonesia: Governmentality and political subjectification of Chinese Benteng women'. *Sustainability* 13(6): 3559. doi.org/10.3390/su13063559

Jakimow, Tanya. 2018. 'Beyond "state ibuism": Empowerment effects in state-led development in Indonesia'. *Development and Change* 49(5): 1143–65. doi.org/10.1111/dech.12374

220 *Vania Budianto*

Kwon, Huck-Ju and Woo-Rim Kim. 2015. 'The evolution of cash transfers in Indonesia: Policy transfer and national adaptation'. *Asia & the Pacific Policy Studies* 2(2): 425–40. doi.org/10.1002/app5.83

Leisering, Lutz. 2019. *The Global Rise of Social Cash Transfers: How States and International Organizations Constructed a New Instrument for Combating Poverty.* Oxford University Press.

McCarthy, John F., Andrew McWilliam and Gerben Nooteboom, eds. 2022. *The Paradox of Agrarian Change: Food Security and the Politics of Social Protection in Indonesia.* NUS Press. https://nuspress.nus.edu.sg/products/the-paradox-of-agrarian-change-food-security-and-the-politics-of-social-protection-in-indonesia

Molyneux, Maxine. 2007. *Change and Continuity in Social Protection in Latin America: Mothers at the Service of the State?* Gender and Development Programme Paper No. 1. United Nations Research Institute for Social Development.

OECD (Organisation for Economic Co-operation and Development). 2019. *Social Protection System Review of Indonesia.* OECD Publishing. doi.org/10.1787/788e9d71-en

Sabates-Wheeler, Rachel and Naila Kabeer. 2003. *Gender Equality and the Extension of Social Protection.* ESS Paper No. 16. International Labour Organization.

Salyanti, Agnes and Media Wahyudi Askar. 2022. *Economic Resilience and Digital Adoption among Ultra-micro Entrepreneurs in Indonesia.* Women's World Banking. www.womensworldbanking.org/insights-and-impact/report-economic-resilience-and-digital-adoption-among-ultra-micro-entrepreneurs-in-indonesia/

Schaner, Simone. 2012. 'Gender, Poverty, and Well-Being in Indonesia: MAMPU Background Assessment'. Department of Foreign Affairs and Trade. www.dfat.gov.au/about-us/publications/Pages/gender-poverty-well-being-indonesia-mampu-background-assessment

Syamsulhakim, Ekki and Nurzanty Khadijah. 2021. *Graduating from a Conditional Cash Transfer Program in Indonesia: Results of a Household Survey of Prosperous-Independent Graduates of the Family Hope Program (PKH) in 2020.* World Bank.

TNP2K. 2018. *The Future of the Social Protection System in Indonesia: Social Protection for All.* National Team for the Acceleration of Poverty Reduction. http://tnp2k.go.id/download/24864181129 SP Exe Summary ENG-web.pdf

TNP2K and SMERU. 2020. *The Situation of the Elderly in Indonesia and Access to Social Protection Programs: Secondary Data Analysis.* National Team for the Acceleration of Poverty Reduction. https://tnp2k.go.id/downloads/the-situation-of-the-elderly-in-indonesia-and-access-to-social-protection-programs-secondary-data-analysis

UNDP and UNICEF. 2021. *Addressing Gender Barriers to Entrepreneurship and Leadership among Girls and Young Women in South-East Asia.* Bangkok: UNDP Bangkok Regional Hub and UNICEF East Asia and the Pacific Regional Office.

UPDESA. 2022. 'BLT Dana Desa 2022 telah disalurkan kepada 6,38 juta KPM, PEKKA mendominasi' [BLT Village Funds 2022 distributed to 6.38 million KPM, PEKKA dominates]. https://updesa.com/blt-dana-desa-2022-telah-disalurkan/

Watkins-Hayes, Celeste and Elyse Kovalsky. 2016. 'The discourse of deservingness: Morality and the dilemmas of poverty relief in debate and practice'. In *The Oxford Handbook of the Social Science of Poverty*, edited by David Brady and Linda M. Burton, 193–220. Oxford University Press.

World Bank. 2020. *Indonesia Country Gender Assessment: Investing in Opportunities for Women*. World Bank. http://hdl.handle.net/10986/35310

12 Leaving no girls behind: Inclusive ways to address child marriage in Indonesia

Santi Kusumaningrum, Ni Luh Putu Maitra Agastya and Andrea Andjaringtyas Adhi

Indonesia is committed to combating child marriage as part of the country's multiple international commitments, from the United Nations Convention on the Rights of the Child we ratified in 1990 to the Sustainable Development Goals we pledged to achieve by 2030. Joko Widodo's administration has also identified child marriage as one of the challenges it must tackle in the National Medium Term Development Plan 2020–2024. Most recently, in 2022, the president signed a decree to end violence against children that assigns inter-ministerial priority to, among other initiatives, preventing child marriage. Given over 80 million children will benefit from this protection effort, the impact of such policies is potentially significant.

Beyond international and national promises, there seems to be a cross-institutional consensus that ending child marriage is a worthy cause, as marriages involving an individual or a couple below the age of 18 can cause long-lasting negative consequences on children's lives, especially girls. In Indonesia, women who marry early are less likely to access health services during pregnancy, and their utilisation of medically assisted birth and antenatal care is limited (BPS 2016; Bruno et al. 2021). Moreover, women in early marriages have weaker decision-making power. They are less likely to have marriage certificates, and their children are less likely to obtain birth certificates (Cameron et al. 2022). In contrast, women who marry after the age of 18 have higher average educational attainment (BPS et al. 2020).

Chapter 12 Inclusive ways to address child marriage in Indonesia   223

The impact of child marriage is also long term and may be passed on to the next generation. Child marriage poses a risk of poverty to families, which in turn influences girls' decision to marry before adulthood (SMERU 2013). Among children whose parents were married before age 18, there are higher risks of infant (under 12 months) mortality, stunted growth and being underweight at birth. Children with young mothers have also demonstrated lower cognitive scores (Cameron et al. 2022).

Child marriage has negative consequences for both women and men who marry early. There is a higher chance of divorce in households with underage marriages (Cameron et al. 2022). Additionally, individuals who marry before turning 18 have low participation in the formal labour market and live in households with lower living standards (BPS 2017).

In this chapter, we first discuss the state of child marriage in Indonesia, the progress made through relevant policies, and the challenges to addressing child marriage. We then take a deeper look into the different forms and drivers of child marriage, unpacking the complexities of childhood adversity, gender-biased religious and social norms, teen pregnancy and children's agency. Lastly, we conclude by discussing the main policy takeaways informed by our analysis.

The state and drivers of child marriage in Indonesia

Data from Indonesia's National Socioeconomic Survey (Susenas) show that child marriage prevalence[1] in Indonesia has decreased over the past 10 years and was at 9.23% in 2021 (Table 12.1). There was a 1.12% decline in child marriage prevalence in 2021 compared to 2020. Based on the figures from 2021, we estimate that over one million girls were still affected by child marriage in Indonesia.[2]

Susenas data give further insight into which women were most affected by child marriage. In 2021, 61% of women who experienced child marriage lived in rural areas and 58% belonged to poor and vulnerable households in the bottom two income quintiles (PUSKAPA analysis). West Sulawesi, West Nusa Tenggara and Central Kalimantan were the three provinces with the largest proportion of child marriages (ibid.). In another study that used Susenas data, we discovered that child marriage in rural areas had decreased between 2015 and 2019 (Kusumaningrum et al. 2021). During 2015–2019, the prevalence of child marriage in urban areas was

---

1   Female respondents aged 20–24 years who were married before 18.
2   Obtained by multiplying child marriage prevalence with 2015 SUPAS population projections for the female population aged 20–24 (BPS 2020).

Table 12.1   Child marriage prevalence in Indonesia, 2012–2021

Year	Prevalence (%)	Difference compared to the year before (percentage points)
2012	14.02	+0.05
2013	13.59	-0.43
2014	13.55	-0.04
2015	12.14	-1.41
2016	11.11	-1.03
2017	11.54	+0.43
2018	11.21	-0.33
2019	10.82	-0.39
2020	10.35	-0.47
2021	9.23	-1.12

Source: PUSKAPA analysis from Susenas data.

relatively stable, but the practice was higher in urban slum households than in non-slum households (ibid.).

Poverty, poor access to education, remoteness and lack of socioeconomic opportunities are the main factors driving the practice of child marriage (Rumble et al. 2018; BPS et al. 2020). However, other external factors also contribute to child marriage. Research has found that disasters contribute to child marriage because marrying girls off is considered to lighten a family's economic burden in the aftermath of a disaster (Kumala Dewi and Dartanto 2019). Some communities still exercise harmful traditions such as *merariq*, where girls are abducted and forced into an arranged marriage (Benedicta et al. 2017). There is also a stigma around girls who reject a marriage proposal and remain single (UIN Alauddin 2017), driving girls to early marriage to avoid being stigmatised.

Legal reform and policy milestones

The amendment of Law 1/1974 on Marriage was a significant victory in 2019 that preceded the articulation of Indonesia's national anti–child marriage technical policies. One especially remarkable reform was made in the increase of the minimum age of marriage from the previous 16 years old for women and 19 years old for men to 19 years old for all. This change affirms that no girls should be married before they become adults, and it also confirms that they are equal to their male counterparts.

Chapter 12 Inclusive ways to address child marriage in Indonesia   225

Although the new marriage law still allows a marriage dispensation route through the courts for anyone under 19 to be married legally, the exemption comes with a warning that dispensation should be granted only as a last resort when no other alternatives are available for the child(ren).

In 2020, the government launched a cross-sectoral national strategy that detailed ways to end child marriage in Indonesia. The priorities include strengthening children's awareness of sexual reproductive health, child participation in child marriage prevention, changing of norms, promoting positive parenting and caregiving, improving access to services for girls, and reinforcement of social institutions and law enforcement (Bappenas 2020).

The most recent milestone was the adoption of Law 12/2022 on Sexual Crime, in which forced child marriage can be charged with a maximum of nine years imprisonment and a fine of 200 million rupiah.

Remaining challenges

The courts continue to hear and approve child marriage dispensation cases

After the 2019 marriage law became more progressive in determining the legal marriage age, the Supreme Court observed a jump in petitions for marriage dispensation, from 23,900 cases in 2019 to 64,200 in 2020 (Jayani 2021; Parikesit 2021; Pranita 2021). Some have speculated that the COVID-19 pandemic contributed to an increase in child marriage (Fulazzaky 2022; Jayani 2021). In 2021, however, the total number of such petitions reportedly decreased to 59,700 (Dihni 2022).

It is important to note that the surge in marriage dispensation since 2020 was somewhat expected due to the establishment of the higher marriage age. Moreover, the numbers may include dispensation petitions requested for individuals above 18 years old (adults) who have not yet reached the legal marriage age of 19. In our assessment of 367 randomly selected marriage dispensation decisions from 2019 available on the Supreme Court website, we found that 60% (n = 216) of the total court decisions (n = 360, with seven documents dropped due to missing data) were child marriage cases. These cases had either one or both applicants who were under 18.[3] The remaining cases were marriage dispensation cases in which both applicants were adults above 18 (Table 12.2).

---

3 In practice, most marriage dispensation cases were submitted by the parents. For practical purposes, this chapter will use the term 'applicant' to refer to the couple who are the subjects of the petition.

Table 12.2 Court decisions based on applicant characteristics and situations

Application cases	Number of court analyses	Total of court analyses	Percentage
Either or both parties are children or child marriage case	216	360	60.00
Both parties are adults	144	360	40.00
Only girl as child applicant (in child marriage cases)	173	216	80.09
Only boy as child applicant (in child marriage cases)	18	216	8.33
Both parties are children (in child marriage cases)	25	216	11.57
Pregnant female applicant (all ages)	119	360	33.06
Pregnant female applicant (in child marriage cases)	79	216	36.57
Pregnant girl applicant (in child marriage cases)	70	216	32.41

What's more, almost all (94%, n = 337) of the applications for marriage dispensation were approved by judges; only 6% resulted in a refusal (n = 23; Table 12.3). Among the refused petitions, 4 were disqualified due to no appearance in court, and 12 were withdrawn by the applicants.[4] Only 7 of 23 refusals carried a legal rejection by the judge.[5]

Girls and the most vulnerable children continue to characterise child marriage cases brought to court for dispensation

While we see a downward trend in Indonesia's child marriage prevalence from Susenas data, girls and the most vulnerable individuals remain at risk of falling into child marriage. Our court decision analysis reveals

---

4 The reasons for application withdrawal include the parents and children deciding to postpone the marriage after considering the judge's advice.

5 Judges' arguments for rejecting a marriage dispensation petition included that the applicants were not represented by their biological parents or legitimate caregivers, the judge felt the applicants could exercise sexual restraint and 'avoid the forbidden thing', the judge did not find that any violation of religious law was performed, the applicants were seen as emotionally and economically unstable, or the applicants lacked knowledge of basic religious practices (i.e. failed to recite prayers and post-coital ablution prayer according to Islamic teaching). In one case, the petition was rejected due to a technicality (religious marriage had been performed, thus rendering the marriage dispensation moot).

Chapter 12 Inclusive ways to address child marriage in Indonesia 227

Table 12.3 Results of the total sample of court decisions

Court decisions	Number of court analysis	Total of court analysis	Percentage
Cases disqualified	4	360	1.11
Cases withdrawn	12	360	3.33
Cases rejected	7	360	1.94
Cases approved	337	360	93.61

that girls remain more vulnerable to child marriage than boys. Around 80% (n = 173) of child marriage cases included girls who were subject to marrying an adult man. Only 8% (n = 18) of child marriage cases registered boys who were to marry an adult woman. The rest of the child marriage cases (12%) featured both applicants under the age of 18 (Table 12.2).

The majority of applicants were 17-year-old females and 21-year-old males, and girls and boys as young as 13 were among the marriage dispensation requests heard in court. On average, the age of female and male applicants in our sample was 16.8 years old and 21.7 years old, respectively, with the youngest female and male at 13.3 years old and the oldest at 29 for female and 40 for male applicants. The average mean age difference[6] between female and male applicants in child marriage cases was 4.9 years overall and 3.2 years for cases involving pregnancy (Table 12.4).

From the same court decisions dataset, we found that most applicants' education consisted of partially or fully completed elementary or junior secondary school. More female applicants had completed junior secondary schooling compared to their male counterparts. However, male applicants were more likely than female applicants to have continued or finished senior secondary school (Table 12.5).[7]

Lastly, 94% (n = 197) of male applicants self-reported as working (Table 12.6), and most listed labourers[8] (*buruh*), farmers (*petani*) or private

---

6 We found similar age differences through singulate mean age and average matched age difference.

7 Information on education status was not always available in the decisions. We had to comb each document to see if any school diploma was submitted by the applicants as one of the supporting documents of the petition. When the list included a diploma, we categorised the education status as 'completed'. In other cases where the level of education was mentioned but the diploma was not listed, we categorised the applicant as 'ever having been in' some form of education. In some cases, both pieces of information were not available.

8 Casual labour not in farming.

228 *Santi Kusumaningrum, Ni Luh Putu Maitra Agastya and Andrea A. Adhi*

Table 12.4 Age among applicants in child marriage cases, by sex

Descriptive statistics among child marriage cases	Average (year)	Std dev (year)	Minimum (year)	Maximum (year)	Sample (number)
Age of female applicant	16.8	1.26	13.3	29.0	216
Age of male applicant	21.7	4.38	13.3	40.0	216
Age of pregnant female applicant	16.9	1.29	13.3	20.6	79
Age of male applicant among pregnant girls cases	20.1	3.60	13.3	29.2	79
Matched age difference (age of male applicant—age of female applicant) per cases, then summarised	4.9	4.79	-4.7	24.0	216
Matched age difference among pregnant girls cases (age of male applicant—age of female applicant) per cases, then summarised	3.2	4.01	-3.8	12.5	79
Age difference (average age of male applicant—average age of female applicant)	4.9	n/a	n/a	n/a	n/a
Age difference among pregnant girls cases (average age of male applicant—average age of female applicant)	3.2	n/a	n/a	n/a	n/a

Table 12.5 Education of applicants among child marriage cases, by sex

Education of applicant among child marriage cases	Male applicant		Female applicant	
	Number	Percentage	Number	Percentage
Ever been in primary school	27	17.42	25	14.88
Finished primary school	28	18.06	30	17.86
Ever been in junior high school	29	18.71	42	25.00
Finished junior high school	32	20.65	53	31.55
Ever been in senior high school	26	16.77	12	7.14
Finished senior high school	10	6.45	5	2.98
Ever been in college	1	0.65	n/a	n/a
Not in school	2	1.29	1	0.59
Total	155	100	168	100

Chapter 12 Inclusive ways to address child marriage in Indonesia   229

Table 12.6   Applicants' employment status, by sex

Employment status	Male applicant		Female applicant	
	Number	Percentage	Number	Percentage
Working	197	93.8	37	20.1
Not working	13	6.2	147	79.9
Total	210	100	184	100

Note: 6 missing data points in boys'/men's data and 32 missing data points in girls'/women's data.

Table 12.7   Applicants' employment type among child marriage cases

Employment type	Male applicant		Female applicant	
	Number	Percentage	Number	Percentage
Labourer / *buruh*	75	39	14	38
Farmer / *petani*	44	23	5	14
Private worker / *swasta*	41	21	13	35
Trader / *pedagang*	14	7	1	2
Online driver / *ojek online/ supir*	10	5	0	0
Fisherman / *nelayan*	6	3	0	0
Teacher / *guru*	3	2	0	0
Helping parents / *membantu orang tua*	0	0	4	11
Total	193	100	37	100

workers (*swasta*) as their occupation (Table 12.7). Only 20% (n = 37) of female applicants reported having a job (Table 12.6); of these, most reported working as labourers, private workers or farmers (Table 12.7).

The conundrums of child marriage

It takes more than legal reform and policy changes to address complex problems like child marriage. To gain more insight into what underpins the remaining challenges and how to address them better, we systematically scoped the literature to learn from research done in the past three years and juxtaposed this with our court decision analysis whenever appropriate.

Child marriage occurs in many forms

Since child marriage is discussed as a form of violence against children, especially girls, we found that most research has focused on forced or arranged child marriages (Judiasih et al. 2020; Latifiani 2019; Marcoes and Putri 2019). Fewer studies have considered child marriage as a 'voluntary' situation that the child enters willingly (Rahiem 2021).

In most forced or arranged child marriages, researchers have noted that children lack the power to defy the decision made by their parents or families (Judiasih et al. 2020; Latifiani 2019; Marcoes and Putri 2019). In cases where a marriage was of the child's own choosing, studies warned that it may have resulted from uninformed consent, where the child may have consented but only because they had no other viable options for a better life or to escape adversity (Abebe 2019; Marcoes and Putri 2019; Maulidar et al. 2021; Rahiem 2021).

In all forced, arranged and 'voluntary' child marriages, studies have observed that village, religious affairs or court officials may have played facilitation roles. These officials did not comply with the latest regulation due to a lack of capacity or refused to comply due to personal views. Forms of facilitation include local religious leaders supporting and officiating child marriages or local officials helping to fabricate the child's age so that a marriage can be registered and legalised (Julianto et al. 2022; Marcoes and Putri 2019; Rofika and Hariastuti 2020; Susanti et al. 2021).

Gender-biased norms and parental worries about children's moral transgressions also drive child marriage

Parents' concerns over children's premarital sexual activities, adultery and promiscuity is common across different regions in Indonesia. Such perceived risks for children's moral transgression seem to be influenced by gender-biased social norms and religious values and have shaped parents' support for early marriage (Judiasih et al. 2020; Marcoes and Putri 2019; Rofika and Hariastuti 2020). Out of fear of their children committing sin by having premarital sex (*zina*), parents prefer to wed their children as soon as possible (Hamidah 2019; Kusmayanti and Mulyanto 2020; Marcoes and Putri 2019; Rofika and Hariastuti 2020; Susanti et al. 2021). During the COVID-19 pandemic, parents reported increased worries over their children's private behaviour online and, as a result, encouraged their children to get married to prevent religious desecration (Julianto et al. 2022). In some situations, children choose marriage to avoid impiety (Marcoes and Putri 2019; Maulidar et al. 2021).

Some parents also view children as ready to marry once they hit puberty (*akil baliq*) (Nurmala et al. 2020; Rahiem 2021; Wibowo et al. 2021). Several

Chapter 12 Inclusive ways to address child marriage in Indonesia 231

studies found that girls who remain single at a certain age following puberty are labelled spinsters and seen as burdens to their families (Rahiem 2021; Rofika and Hariastuti 2020; Wibowo et al. 2021). According to previous research, being a divorcee is more socially acceptable than being a spinster in some regions in Indonesia (Latifiani 2019; Susanti et al. 2021). Moreover, studies revealed that girls are also perceived as economic liabilities, which has led to a common understanding that marrying girls off will reduce the financial burdens born by the family (Kumala Dewi and Dartanto 2019; Marcoes and Putri 2019).

Practices of arranged marriage also put girls at more risk than boys. A study in Bone, South Sulawesi, confirmed that child marriage was treated as a form of 'upholding the family's honour' when this so-called honour was seen as at risk because someone's daughter started dating someone's son (Wibowo et al. 2021). In some communities in East Java, marriages may be arranged before a child is born or when children are toddlers to secure family lineage or to fulfil a pact between two families (Nurmala et al. 2020; Rofika and Hariastuti 2020). Customary law has also been used to justify harmful traditions against girls, such as *merariq* in West Nusa Tenggara, for forced child marriages (Marcoes and Putri 2019; Rahiem 2021).

Studies have further determined that gender-biased religious and social norms condoning child marriage are not specific to a small number of groups or families but are instead often shared within the larger community and reinforced by local or religious leaders (Kusmayanti and Mulyanto 2020; Latifiani 2019; Marcoes and Putri 2019; Rofika and Hariastuti 2020; Susanti et al. 2021). These harmful norms can seem abstract but manifest in child marriage practices, as evidenced by the court's marriage dispensation decisions. According to the child marriage court cases, the majority of the arguments for petitioning a marriage dispensation for children included parents' opinions that their children were ready to start a family (89% of the reasons cited by applicants), followed by parents' belief that marrying their children did not violate any religious law (85%) and parents' worries about their children committing religious violations (72%) (Table 12.8). The same arguments were also found to be what judges used to justify their dispensation approvals (Table 12.9).

Pregnancy leaves girls with no feasible solution other than marriage

Teen pregnancy is still strongly stigmatised in Indonesia, and the stigma applies to both the mother and the child. In some cultures, single mothers cannot claim their land or property rights (Horii 2020a). Studies have confirmed that parents almost always force their pregnant daughters into

Table 12.8 Reasons for dispensation application among child marriage cases

Reasons for dispensation application	Number of court decisions	Percentage (out of 216 marriage cases)
Ready to start a family / *Sudah siap berumah tangga*	193	89
Does not violate religious law / *Tidak melanggar hukum agama*	184	85
Worried/afraid to commit religious violations / *Khawatir / Takut untuk melanggar agama*	156	72
[They] have been too familiar/intimate / *Sudah terlalu akrab / intim*	155	72
Already engaged / *Sudah bertunangan*	120	56
The family approves of their child's marriage/relationship / *Keluarga merestui pernikahan / hubungan anaknya*	116	54
Been in a relationship for a long time / *Sudah lama berhubungan*	102	47
Have loved each other / *Sudah saling mencintai*	81	38
Already pregnant / *Sudah hamil*	78	36
Families are willing to help their children's livelihood / *Keluarga bersedia membantu penghidupan anak-anaknya*	70	32
Have often gone together / *Sudah sering pergi bersama*	40	19
Have already stayed/slept together / *Sudah pernah menginap / tidur bersama*	31	14
Fear of being gossiped about by neighbours/community / *Takut digunjingkan tetangga / masyarakat*	26	12
Does not violate state law / *Tidak melanggar hukum negara*	25	12
Families are willing to fulfil their children's education rights / *Keluarga bersedia memenuhi hak pendidikan anak-anaknya*	18	8
Have received a recommendation from a psychologist/ counsellor / *Sudah mendapat rekomendasi dari psikolog / konselor*	1	1
Must follow the prospective husband who will go out of town or abroad / *Harus ikut calon suami yang akan merantau*	0	0

marriage so the child they carry can obtain legal and social certainty (Horii 2020a; Marcoes and Putri 2019; Rofika and Hariastuti 2020). Similarly, the authorities also justify child marriage in cases that involve a pregnancy by citing 'protecting the girls from stigma' (Hamidah 2019; Horii 2020b; Julianto et al. 2022; Latifiani 2019).

Chapter 12 Inclusive ways to address child marriage in Indonesia 233

Table 12.9 Reasons for dispensation approval (by the judge) among child marriage cases

Reasons for dispensation approval	Number of court decisions	Percentage (out of 216 marriage cases)
Does not violate religious law / *Tidak melanggar hukum agama*	176	81
Ready to start a family / *Sudah siap berumah tangga*	144	67
Worried/afraid to commit religious violations / *Khawatir / Takut untuk melanggar agama*	137	63
[They] have been too familiar/intimate / *Sudah terlalu akrab / intim*	132	61
The family approves of their child's marriage/relationship / *Keluarga merestui pernikahan / hubungan anaknya*	70	32
Families are willing to help their children's livelihood / *Keluarga bersedia membantu penghidupan anak-anaknya*	63	29
Already pregnant / *Sudah hamil*	57	26
Already engaged / *Sudah bertunangan*	51	24
Have loved each other / *Sudah saling mencintai*	40	19
Fear of being gossiped about by neighbours/community / *Takut digunjingkan tetangga / masyarakat*	31	14
Been in a relationship for a long time / *Sudah lama berhubungan*	30	14
Does not violate state law / *Tidak melanggar hukum negara*	30	14
Have already stayed/slept together / *Sudah pernah menginap / tidur bersama*	17	8
Families are willing to fulfil their children's education rights / *Keluarga bersedia memenuhi hak pendidikan anak-anaknya*	15	7
Have often gone together / *Sudah sering pergi bersama*	11	5
Have received a recommendation from a psychologist/counsellor / *Sudah mendapat rekomendasi dari psikolog / konselor*	2	1
Must follow the prospective husband who will go out of town or abroad / *Harus ikut calon suami yang akan merantau*	0	0

In Indonesia, accidental pregnancy can only result in a marriage. Abortion is illegal, and moral disgrace is attached to premarital sex. Children, particularly girls, are often viewed as non-sexual, passive or vulnerable (Beta and Febrianto 2020), making any suggestion of them being involved in sexual intimacy even more unacceptable. At the same time, parents, schools and society often do not value the importance of sexual and reproductive health knowledge and services for children, and studies have indicated that girls experiencing pregnancy have poor comprehension of reproductive issues, including the risks of pregnancy (Fitriana et al. 2021; Nurmala et al. 2020; Rofika and Hariastuti 2020; Susanti et al. 2021).

Furthermore, pregnancy derails girls from their future. In Indonesia, pregnant girls are expelled from school, must take on child caregiving immediately after giving birth, are burdened with domestic responsibilities in their household, and can only access non-formal schooling if they want to continue their education (Arifin et al. 2020; Judiasih et al. 2020; Latifiani 2019; Marcoes and Putri 2019; Rofika and Hariastuti 2020).

Globally, comprehensive sexual and reproductive health education has been positively associated with protective factors against child marriage, shown by a higher age of marriage and first pregnancy, use of contraception and higher participation in health services (Svanemyr et. al. 2015). Consequently, lack of access to information and services on sexual reproductive health—as in Indonesia—contributes to the risk of child marriage due to pregnancy. In the analysed court decisions, 37% of child marriage cases involved pregnancy (Table 12.2). Among the approved child marriage dispensation cases, a third stated pregnancy as one of the reasons for the petition, and 94% of child marriage dispensation applications that involved pregnancy obtained the judge's approval (Table 12.10).

Children perceive marriage as an escape or a better option

Children can initiate marriage, and they have been doing so. However, we need to be careful in rushing to the conclusion that when children express their wish to be married, the intent comes from a full agency. Studies suggest that 'voluntary' child marriage stems from three primary conditions: pregnancy (as discussed in the previous section), perceived hardness or restrictions in life, and socioeconomic adversity.

Studies found that children often had no options other than marriage due to their family's economic constraints, a lack of access to schooling (Latifiani 2019; Rofika and Hariastuti 2020) and limited employment opportunities (Arifin et al. 2020; Fitriana et al. 2021; Hamidah 2019; Susanti et al. 2021). Ironically, child marriage may provide a false sense of economic security when marriage is thought to be a way out of poverty but, in the end, individuals who marry early remain impoverished (Beta and Febrianto 2020).

Poverty can also compromise the caregiving capacities of parents. Inadequate parenting, lack of parental affection, the low perceived value

Chapter 12 Inclusive ways to address child marriage in Indonesia 235

Table 12.10 Court decisions among child marriages by pregnancy cases

Court decisions	Pregnant		Total	Reasons for the decisions
	No	Yes		
Withdrawn/ *Dicabut*	2	2	4 1.8%	The applications were withdrawn after hearing judge's advice
Approved/ *Dikabulkan*	131	74	205 94.9%	n/a
Rejected/ *Ditolak*	3	1	4 1.8%	• children's best interest, the applicants are still young (F 14y, M 25y), judge has not seen the desire to do *zina* is really urgent, the potential of not finishing school when they got married, the applicants have not known each other long enough, the girl is too young and is vulnerable to health risks • prospective couple seemed able to exercise sexual restraint, no indication they will do forbidden things (*perbuatan terlarang*) • after processing the application, it turned out that they were already married (*did akad*), so the urgency of dispensation is no longer needed • the rejected pregnant case was because the applicants were not the biological parents of the soon-to-be wife and husband, nor the ones appointed
Disqualified/ *Gugur*	1	2	3 1.4%	The applicants did not come to the court (*sidang*)
Total	137 63.4%	79 36.6%	216	

of education, and physical and verbal violence experienced in the home have been found to exacerbate children's desire to escape (Fitriana et al. 2021). Marriage is often the only avenue available.

Socioeconomic adversity also aggravates the sense of restrictions in children's lives where children's need for social interactions and explorations of intimacy may be unmet. Lack of social and recreational infrastructure due to remoteness or natural disasters (Kumala Dewi and Dartanto 2019; Maulidar et al. 2021; Oktriyanto et al. 2019), frustrations with online learning and restrictions on physical movement during the COVID-19 pandemic (Rahiem 2021), and the lack of socially acceptable mediums for dating and social interactions (ibid.) have led youths to see marriage as a better option to live a more engaged life.

More recently, a few studies have examined access to digital technology as a contributing factor to children's desire to marry young and catalysing children's false ideas about the joys of marriage. Some studies have viewed exposure to excessive digital media as providing new dating spaces for teenagers (Kusmayanti and Mulyanto 2020, Horii 2020a), and encouraging risky premarital behaviour as well as creating a false association between happiness and marriage (Julianto et al. 2022; Kusmayanti and Mulyanto 2020; Nurmala et al. 2020; Rahiem 2021). However, we need a further examination of how access to digital technology interacts with the risks of child marriage by controlling socioeconomic characteristics.

Married girls are left without marriage certificates

Though there is no research on child marriage and marriage registration yet, we have enough knowledge to predicate that when child marriage is done informally without a marriage dispensation from a judge through a religious ceremony only or *sirri*, it runs the risk of leaving girls without a marriage certificate. However, women can only access reproductive healthcare and some social protection services when they produce proof of marital status. Some studies confirmed that the absence of a marriage certificate prevents parents from registering their child's birth despite available alternatives to do so without legal proof of marriage because the birth certificate will print only the mother's name (Kusumaningrum et al. 2016, 2020; Sumner and Kusumaningrum 2014).

While there is an argument for making forced child marriage punishable by law and marriage dispensation procedures stricter, the evidence also indicates that the consequences of unregistered marriage might be harsher for girls and women. We need more investigation to carefully assess the efficacy and unintended consequences of the current incentive/disincentive practices, such as local religious offices withholding marriage certificates for couples of child marriages until they become adults (Hartarto and Triwibowo 2022).

Policy takeaways

There is almost no doubt that Indonesia has reached a cross-sectoral consensus that child marriage is happening, harmful and preventable. All regulatory achievements so far must not go unrecognised, and they reflect the power of collective action that uses evidence, advocacy, policy development and community services effectively. However, while they provide valuable legal protection for women and girls and signify gender equality, amending the legal age for marriage and penalising the practice of child marriage increase the risk that child marriages are

Chapter 12 Inclusive ways to address child marriage in Indonesia   237

carried out secretly without being formally registered or recorded on the statistical radar.

As a result, official child marriage prevalence masks the actual magnitude of the problem. Moreover, married girls and children born from child marriages will be hidden and at risk of not having adequate legal identities, which may further hinder them from accessing services. The national strategy needs to be transformed into policies; programs need prioritisation amid limited resources; and the process can leave the most marginalised behind.

The evidence supports that parents' worries about children's moral transgression results in forced or arranged marriages underpinned by gender-biased religious and social norms. Such norms also intertwine with the notion that children are pure, and parents and state institutions position themselves as the guardians of children's innocence. At the same time, concerns over children exercising risky sexual behaviour have blocked children from safe spaces to enjoy social interactions. Changing these norms requires sustainable reform efforts. Meanwhile, children continue to be at risk of falling pregnant and either face or willingly enter marriage as the only solution.

Irrespective of whether marriage is forced or entered into voluntarily, pregnancy, perceived difficulty and restrictions in life, socioeconomic adversity related to access to quality education, the perceived value of education and parenting capacity underlie the occurrence of child marriage. Cultural norms and stigma surrounding single parenthood— especially for girls—may act as a strong incentive to opt for child marriage when a pregnancy is involved. Therefore, investments should be made to mitigate the risks of teen pregnancy and its immediate consequences through measures that will break the intergenerational trap of child marriage.

Child marriage prevention should aim to minimise the implications faced by the children involved. Changing perceptions about child marriage must not stigmatise married children. Prevention should prioritise services to mitigate the consequences of child marriage that affect girls directly, namely the disruption of formal education, risks of domestic violence, and poverty. In addition, programs need to include the prevention of pregnancy complications and maternal mortality and risks of child stunting, morbidity and mortality. Furthermore, child marriage prevention must assist married children with livelihood and childcare support.

Policymakers and civil society must be more willing to consider and engage in conversations about 'voluntary' child marriages. Children who exercise their agency—no matter how thin—must be supported so that their decision does not rob them of their education, basic services and life opportunities. Moreover, the policy and advocacy spheres must address their reluctance to discuss children as having sexual curiosity and needing intimacy.

Finally, marriage dispensation may increase the chances for child marriage to be registered, thereby cushioning the negative impacts of legal identity deficiency for women and girls. Courts, village offices and religious offices are the frontline in identifying the needs for comprehensive reproductive health, caregiving and livelihood support that must be made available to married children, pregnant girls and minor heads of households.

Drawing from our reflections based on the scope of evidence and our takeaways above, we see the need to explore the impacts of marriage registration. Understanding the relationship between marriage certificate ownership and wellbeing outcomes of women and children, as well as access to services, will provide important insights to inform child marriage prevention policies. Adding a question on marriage and divorce certificate ownership in Susenas will be an important first step.

Moreover, the complexity of the child marriage issue warrants deeper considerations around ways to implement the laws without further excluding the most vulnerable. In this case, we need to know how to approach marriage registration as a protective measure without further harming individuals who, until today, cannot register their marriage due to the structural barriers they face.

Lastly, the evidence around support for married children is lacking. We need to continuously examine the consequences of providing support for married children. The assumption, if any, that supporting girls who are now already married will send the wrong message and build the wrong incentives necessitates a thorough investigation and, more importantly, whether such moral hazard outweighs the benefits for the supported children.

Concluding remarks

For Indonesia to have a chance of meaningfully lessening the prevalence of child marriage, priorities must include preventing girls from being forced to marry secretly, entering unregistered matrimony, and supporting those who fall into marriage and pregnancy.

Child marriage prevention should not leave any girl behind.

Authors' contribution

SK was the principal investigator and led the conceptualisation and implementation of this research and the development of this paper. SK oversaw the overall analyses, with NLPMA co-leading the scoping review and AAA the court decision analysis. All authors contributed equally to the writing and finalisation of the paper. All authors read and approved the final draft.

Acknowledgements

This work was supported by the ANU Indonesia Project and the Center on Child Protection and Wellbeing PUSKAPA, FISIP Universitas Indonesia. We thank PUSKAPA research assistants Aisyah Assyria and Rayfienta Khairannisa Gumay, who supported the data collection for this paper. Lastly, we would like to thank all the girls and families who shared their stories in the publications we read and everyone working in child marriage prevention with whom the authors have interacted and from whom we have gained insights and inspiration.

References

Abebe, Tatek. 2019. 'Reconceptualising children's agency as continuum and interdependence'. *Social Sciences* 8(3): 81. doi.org/10.3390/socsci8030081

Arifin, Ridwan, Rodiyah Rodiyah and Fadhilah R.A. Putri. 2020. 'The legal and social aspect for underage marriage: Women's education rights in the perspective of human rights: Contemporary issues and problems'. *Sawwa: Jurnal Studi Gender* 15(2): 219–40. doi.org/10.21580/sa.v15i2.5165

Bappenas (National Development Planning Agency). 2020. *Strategi Nasional Pencegahan Perkawinan Anak* [National Strategy for the Prevention of Child Marriage]. Bappenas. www.unicef.org/indonesia/media/2851/file/Child-Marriage-Report-2020.pdf

Benedicta, G.D. et al. 2017. 'Studi kualitatif "Yes I Do Alliance" (YID). Faktor penyebab dan konsekuensi perceraian setelah perkawinan anak di Kabupaten Sukabumi' [Qualitative study of the 'Yes I Do Alliance'. Factors causing and consequences of divorce after child marriage in Sukabumi Regency]. Rembang dan Lombok Barat.

Beta, Annisa R. and Ryan Febrianto. 2020. 'Are Indonesian girls okay? An examination of the discourse of child marriage, victimization, and humanitarian visuality of Global South girls'. *Jurnal Studi Pemuda* 9(2): 163–76. doi.org/10.22146/studipemudaugm.57432

BPS (Statistics Indonesia). 2016. *Child Marriage in Indonesia: Progress on Pause.* Research Brief. UNICEF Indonesia. www.girlsnotbrides.org/resource-centre/unicef-indonesia-child-marriage-research-brief/

BPS (Statistics Indonesia). 2017. *Child Marriage in Indonesia (2013 and 2015).* BPS. www.bps.go.id/publication/2017/08/02/a89a2789e9ff45b2bc4e4cb5/child-marriage-in-indonesia-2013-and-2015-.html

BPS (Statistics Indonesia). 2020. *Proyeksi Penduduk Indonesia 2015–2045 Hasil SUPAS 2015* [Indonesian population projection 2015–2045: 2015 SUPAS results]. BPS. www.bps.go.id/publication/2018/10/19/78d24d9020026ad95c6b5965/proyeksi-penduduk-indonesia-2015-2045-hasil-supas-2015.html

BPS, PUSKAPA, UNICEF and BAPPENAS 2020. *Pencegahan Perkawinan Anak: Percepatan Yang Tidak Bisa Ditunda* [Prevention of child marriage: Acceleration that cannot be delayed]. BPS, PUSKAPA, UNICEF and BAPPENAS. www.unicef.org/indonesia/media/2851/file/Child-Marriage-Report-2020.pdf

Bruno, Shirley K.B., Hermano A.L. Rocha, Sabrina G.M.O. Rocha, David A.B.S. Araújo, Jocileide S. Campos, et al. 2021. 'Prevalence, socioeconomic factors and obstetric outcomes associated with adolescent motherhood in Ceará, Brazil: A population-based study'. *BMC Pregnancy and Childbirth* 21(1): 616. doi.org/10.1186/s12884-021-04088-7

Cameron, Lisa, Diana Contreras Suárez and Susan Wieczkiewicz. 2022. 'Child marriage: Using the Indonesian Family Life Survey to examine the lives of women and men who married at an early age'. *Review of Economics of the Household* 21: 725–56. doi.org/10.1007/s11150-022-09616-8

Dihni, Vika Azkiya. 2022. 'Selama 2021, angka dispensasi pernikahan anak menurun 7%' [During 2021, the child marriage dispensation rate decreased by 7%]. Databoks. https://databoks.katadata.co.id/datapublish/2022/03/08/selama-2021-angka-dispensasi-pernikahan-anak-menurun-7#:~:text=Dispensasi%20adalah%20pemberian%20hak%20kepada,awal%20bagi%20pencegahan%20perkawinan%20anak

Fitriana, Dessy, Rize Budi Amalia and Nur Ainy Fardana. 2021. 'A qualitative study: The phenomena of child marriage in urban areas of Surabaya City reviewed from comprehension of reproductive health'. *Indian Journal of Public Health Research & Development* 12(1). doi.org/10.37506/ijphrd.v12i1.13859

Fulazzaky, T. 2022. 'Meroketnya kasus perkawinan anak di masa pandemi COVID-19, Knowledge Hub Kesehatan Reproduksi Indonesia' [Skyrocketing cases of child marriage during the COVID-19 pandemic, Indonesian Reproductive Health Knowledge Hub]. https://rhknowledge.ui.ac.id/id/articles/detail/meroketnya-kasus-perkawinan-anak-di-masa-pandemi-covid-19-fb2199

Hamidah, T. 2019. 'Religious heads' perspectives towards the abolition of child marriage: A study in Malang, East Java, Indonesia'. *Pertanika Journal of Social Science and Humanities* 27(4): 2703–19.

Hartarto, Romi Bhakti and Wahyu Triwibowo. 2022. 'Conditional cash transfer and early marriage: A case study of Mataram City, West Nusa Tenggara'. Forum Kajian Pembangunan, ANU Indonesia Project, 18 August. www.youtube.com/watch?v=EplT8CC-hK0andlist=PL3VE_Ir91MdWTEuihuMYZsdaiQkhVR1SMandindex=11andt=3306sandab_channel=ANUIndonesiaProject

Horii, Hoko. 2020a. 'Child marriage as a "solution" to modern youth in Bali'. *Progress in Development Studies* 20(4): 282–95. doi.org/10.1177/1464993420977793

Horii, Hoko. 2020b. 'Legal reasoning for legitimation of child marriage in West Java: Accommodation of local norms at Islamic courts and the paradox of child protection'. *Journal of Human Rights Practice* 12(3): 501–23. doi.org/10.1093/jhuman/huaa041

Chapter 12 Inclusive ways to address child marriage in Indonesia   241

Jayani, Dwi Hadya. 2021. 'Dispensasi perkawinan anak meningkat 3 kali lipat pada 2020' [Child marriage dispensation will triple in 2020]. Databoks. https://databoks.katadata.co.id/datapublish/2021/03/20/dispensasi-perkawinan-anak-meningkat-3-kali-lipat-pada-2020

Judiasih, Sonny D., Betty Rubiati, Deviana Yuanitasari, Elycia F. Salim and Levana Safira. 2020. 'Efforts to eradicate child marriage practices in Indonesia: Towards sustainable development goals'. *Journal of International Women's Studies* 21(6): 135–49. https://vc.bridgew.edu/jiws/vol21/iss6/8

Julianto, Very, Kamsi Kamsi, Arin Haq and Raydinda Laili Shofa. 2022. 'Tick tick boom: The rise of child marriage in Indonesia during the COVID-19 pandemic'. Preprint. https://doi.org/10.31234/osf.io/m6der

Kumala Dewi, Luh P.H. and Teguh Dartanto. 2019. 'Natural disasters and girls' vulnerability: Is child marriage a coping strategy of economic shocks in Indonesia?' *Vulnerable Children and Youth Studies* 14(1): 24–35. doi.org/10.108 0/17450128.2018.1546025

Kusmayanti, Hazar and Dede Mulyanto. 2020. 'Problematics culture of child marriage in Indramayu: A legal and cultural perspective'. *JPH: Jurnal Pembaharuan Hukum* 7(2). doi.org/10.26532/jph.v7i2.9297

Kusumaningrum, Santi, Cyril Bennouna, Clara Siagian and Ni Luh Putu Agastya. 2016. *Back to What Counts: Birth and Death in Indonesia.* Bappenas, PUSKAPA, Australian Aid and KOMPAK.

Kusumaningrum, Santi, Sandra Dewi Arifiani, Widi Laras Sari, Feri Sahputra, Rahmadi Usman, et al. 2020. *Strong Institutions, Resilient Communities: An Assessment of the Basic Services Governance and Results in CRVS, Education, and Health in KOMPAK Areas.* PUSKAPA, Bappenas and KOMPAK. https://puskapa.org/en/blog/publication/5677/

Kusumaningrum, Santi, Clara Siagian, Widi Sari, Andrea Andjaringtyas Adhi, Wenny Wandawari, et al. 2021. *The Situation of Children and Young People in Indonesian Cities.* PUSKAPA, UNICEF and Bappenas. http://rgdoi.net/10.13140/RG.2.2.36250.36803

Latifiani, Dian. 2019. 'The darkest phase for family: Child marriage prevention and its complexity in Indonesia'. *Journal of Indonesian Legal Studies* 4(2): 241. doi.org/10.15294/jils.v4i2.34708

Marcoes, Lies and Fadilla Dwianti Putri. 2019. 'Testimony of child brides: Child marriage and the role of institutions in nine regions in Indonesia'. *Intersections: Gender and Sexuality in Asia and the Pacific* (43). http://intersections.anu.edu.au/issue43/marcoes_putri.html

Maulidar, Juli Amira, Aliasuddin and Chenny Seftarita. 2021. 'The early-age marriage in Indonesia: Comparison between urban and rural areas'. *International Journal of Advanced Research in Economics and Finance* 3(3): 196–204.

Nurmala, I., F. Astutik and Y. Devi. 2020. 'Surrounding the reason for women to continue the tradition of child marriage'. *Utopia y Praxis Latinoamericana* 25(2): 24–32.

Oktriyanto, Oktriyanto, Hilma Amrullah, Dwi Hastuti and Alfiasari Alfiasari. 2019. 'Persepsi tentang usia pernikahan perempuan dan jumlah anak yang diharapkan: Mampukah memprediksi praktek pengasuhan orang tua?'

[Perceptions of women's age at marriage and expected number of children: Can it predict parenting practices?]. *Jurnal Ilmu Keluarga & Konsumen* 12(2): 145–56. doi.org/10.24156/jikk.2019.12.2.145

Parikesit, G. 2021. 'Permohonan dispensasi perkawinan anak meningkat' [Applications for child marriage dispensation increase]. *Tempo*, 1 August. https://koran.tempo.co/read/topik/466742/permohonan-dispensasi-perkawinan-anak-meningkat

Pranita, Ellyvon. 2021. 'Pernikahan dini meningkat selama pandemi, BKKBN gencarkan edukasi reproduksi' [Early marriages increased during the pandemic, BKKBN intensified reproductive education]. *Kompas*, 1 October. www.kompas.com/sains/read/2021/10/01/100000523/pernikahan-dini-meningkat-selama-pandemi-bkkbn-gencarkan-edukasi

Rahiem, Maila D.H. 2021. 'COVID-19 and the surge of child marriages: A phenomenon in Nusa Tenggara Barat, Indonesia'. *Child Abuse & Neglect* 118: 105168. doi.org/10.1016/j.chiabu.2021.105168

Rofika, Ainur Mila and Iswari Hariastuti. 2020. 'Social-cultural factors affecting child marriage in Sumenep'. *Jurnal Promkes: The Indonesian Journal of Health Promotion and Health Education* 8(1): 12–20. doi.org/10.20473/jpk.V8.I1.2020.12-20

Rumble, Lauren, Amber Peterman, Nadira Irdiana, Margaret Triyana and Emilie Minnick. 2018. 'An empirical exploration of female child marriage determinants in Indonesia'. *BMC Public Health* 18: 407. doi.org/10.1186/s12889-018-5313-0

SMERU 2013. 'Child poverty and social protection conference: Prevalence of child marriage and its determinants among young women in Indonesia'. http://cpsp.smeru.or.id/index_konferensi%20CPSP%202013.htm

Sumner, Cate and Santi Kusumaningrum. 2014. *AIPJ Baseline Study on Legal Identity: Indonesia's Missing Millions*. Australia Indonesia Partnership for Justice.

Susanti, Vinita, Reni Kartikawati, Irwan M. Hidayana, Ida Ruwaida and Lusiana Rumintang. 2021. 'Preventing child marriage: The role of strategic actors in South Kalimantan'. *Jurnal Antropologi: Isu-Isu Sosial Budaya* 23(1): 110–17. doi.org/10.25077/jantro.v23.n1.p110-117.2021

Svanemyr, Joar, Avni Amin, Omar J. Robles and Margaret E. Greene. 2015. 'Creating an enabling environment for adolescent sexual and reproductive health: A framework and promising approaches'. *Journal of Adolescent Health* 56(1 Suppl): S7–14. doi.org/10.1016/j.jadohealth.2014.09.011

UIN Alauddin. 2017. *Dinamika Perkawinan Anak di Kabupaten Gowa dan Kota Makassar Sulawesi Selatan* [The dynamics of child marriage in Gowa Regency and Makassar City, South Sulawesi]. Universitas Islam Negeri Makassar.

Wibowo, Heribertus Rinto, Muliani Ratnaningsih, Nicholas J. Goodwin, Derry Fahrizal Ulum and Emilie Minnick. 2021. 'One household, two worlds: Differences of perception towards child marriage among adolescent children and adults in Indonesia'. *Lancet Regional Health – Western Pacific* 8: 100103. doi.org/10.1016/j.lanwpc.2021.100103

PART 4

Gender expression, representation and practice

13 *Perempuan mengkaji seni*: Gender, activism and Indonesian visual arts

Wulan Dirgantoro

On a breezy Friday night on 12 August 2022, five women wearing all-white dresses walked into a gallery space. They sat on white chairs arranged in a clockwise direction; in the middle of the circle, a digital clock was set on a small stool. A small pile of fabric was positioned on the floor. Each performer then placed a small, portable sewing machine on their lap. For twenty minutes, the performers sewed small pieces of cloth from a small cardboard box next to their chairs and added their contributions to the existing pile in the centre of the circle.

The performance art was titled *Rotary*. It was performed by an all-women art collective, Perempuan Pengkaji Seni, based in Surabaya. The venue where they performed the piece was Lawangwangi Creative Space, one of the premier contemporary art spaces in the city, located in the hilly northern part of Bandung. The event was the announcement evening of the seventh Bandung Contemporary Art Awards, a biennial contemporary art prize in Indonesia. Earlier in the evening, the jury comprising FX Harsono (visual artist), Aaron Seeto (director of Museum MACAN), Tom Tandio (founder of IndoArtNow Foundation), Evelyn Halim (CEO of Sarana Global Finance Indonesia) and Wiyu Wahono (entrepreneur) announced that Perempuan Pengkaji Seni had won the money prize of 100 million rupiah. In addition, two other artists, Patriot Mukmin and Victoria Koesasi, were the winners of the three-month art residency in France and travel prizes to Europe (Siswadi 2022; Surya 2022).

The description of the performance work by Perempuan Pengkaji Seni serves as a starting point to discuss a significant shift in the Indonesian art world in the past two decades, namely the production and reception of visual arts framed through the lens of gender activism. Since the fall

246   *Wulan Dirgantoro*

of the authoritarian regime, Indonesia has achieved some noteworthy progress towards gender equality, such as ratifying all major international conventions that uphold principles of gender equality and empowerment, for example, the 2004 Law on the Elimination of Domestic Violence and the 2009 Law on the Protection of Women and Gender-Based Violence. However, gender inequality remains a systemic problem in the Indonesian art world. Koalisi Seni, a non-government organisation that focuses on arts and cultural policy advocacy in Indonesia, observed that women continue to be under-represented in leadership positions in the cultural sector and in collections and exhibitions in major institutions (Koalisi Seni 2021a).

This chapter will discuss how creative practices by individual artists and art collectives, both women and gender-diverse artists, have demonstrated innovation, resilience and hope in the face of democratic regression in Indonesia. Relatedly, it will focus on the thematic shift and strategies in the post–New Order era when engaging with the issues of gender and its attendant politics and activism in the current generation of Indonesian women and gender-diverse artists.

Production: Themes and methods

Indonesian women artists' active contributions to the development of Indonesian modern art and art history, loosely defined as starting in the mid-nineteenth century, have long been overshadowed by male artists and writers. Scholars and researchers have argued that in Indonesian art and art history, women's participation tends to be linked with male figures, from husband, brother or father, within the art world (Dirgantoro 2017; Swastika 2019). This was particularly prevalent during the New Order (1966–1998), when the state promoted and elevated women's *kodrat* (destiny) as mothers and supporters for their spouses (Suryakusuma 1996). As a result, while women were active in the public sphere as professional artists, their career was often circumscribed by domestic life and sociocultural expectations at the same time. For example, they often had to prioritise or manage their husband's career (artistic or otherwise) on top of their own artistic career. Despite these challenges, women actively formed professional groups and participated in group exhibitions (Swastika 2019).

After the fall of the New Order in May 1998, to further address the lack of visibility of women artists, senior journalist Carla Bianpoen, along with two co-authors, began the task of compiling a profile of Indonesian women artists in the book *Indonesian Women Artists: The Curtain Opens* (2007). This book was subsequently followed by two more: *Into the Future:*

Chapter 13 Gender, activism and Indonesian visual arts   247

Indonesian Women Artists (2019) and *Indonesian Women Artists: Infusions into Contemporary Art* (2022), with a range of writers that reflect the diversity of practices and perspectives of Indonesian women.[1]

Notably, the thematic shift in the artworks also mirrored the changes in Indonesian society post–New Order. In contrast to the apolitical and formalist aesthetics that most women artists favoured during the New Order, those who built their careers from the mid-1990s onwards celebrated the freedom to challenge gender norms, such as representing the female body and critique of patriarchy, while some were less comfortable with this type of political emphasis by male curators on their work. Bianpoen noted that feminism remained a contested term for many Indonesian artists, even after the fall of the New Order regime. As she observed, 'ironically for a generation that should have experienced a greater degree of freedom to follow its calling, the gender issue seems to be a constant preoccupation' (Bianpoen 2002: 125).

As will be discussed more extensively in this chapter, the current generation of women and gender-diverse artists that developed their careers from the mid-2000s onwards have been working intensely with diverse themes and artistic strategies. Themes such as an examination of history, challenges to gender diversity and environmental concerns are the dominant issues that have preoccupied this generation of artists in the past two decades. While the current generation of artists also employ feminist critiques in their art, in contrast to the previous generation they are less constrained by the term and in doing so acknowledge the diversity of feminism and women's voices through their creative practices.

Examining history

A strong interest in research and creating narratives that have generally been the domain of historians distinguishes the current generation of artists from the mid-career artists mentioned above. The raw materials of the past, such as archives, oral history, and individual and collective memories, are reworked into the present to question past assumptions of history.

---

1 Importantly, in parallel with these publications on contemporary art from the 1990s onwards, researchers have also begun to address gaps in the modern era. One recent example is the research on Oei Sian Yok (1926–2002). The Chinese Indonesian art critic regularly wrote for the popular magazine *Star Weekly* from 1956 to 1961, and her writings provided a stark contrast to the nationalist, Java-centric writings of male art critics of the time (Isabella 2020; see also Dewan Kesenian Jakarta 2020).

248 *Wulan Dirgantoro*

For Citra Sasmita (born 1990, based in Denpasar), a reappraisal of the past began with critically examining the ancient *kakawin* text. Her work focuses on unravelling myths and misconceptions of Balinese art and culture. She is deeply invested in questioning a woman's place in the social hierarchy and seeks to challenge normative constructs of gender (Wah 2022). One of her long-term projects, *Timur Merah Project, Harbour of Restless Spirits* (2017, ongoing), features female figures, fire and natural elements. The scenes are rooted in Hindu and Balinese mythological thinking, but according to a curatorial text in an exhibition in Sydney, 'they also represent the contemporary process of imagining a secular and empowered mythology for the future' (16albemarle project space 2022).

For artist Tamarra (born 1986, based in Yogyakarta), Indonesia's premodern history is a utopian ideal that speaks about Indonesia's challenges in implementing its state motto Bhinneka Tunggal Ika (Unity in Diversity) in the present day. The artist, who identifies as non-binary, created an installation work titled *Tantular* (2021) for ARTJOG MMXXI, one of the major events in the Indonesian contemporary art calendar. The installation is centred on a child-sized figure wearing a colourful dress, a floor-length skirt and an oversized collar. The dress is woven from different fabrics by the artist and collaborators to symbolise the diverse voices and communities in Indonesia. The title referenced Mpu Tantular, a 14th-century poet whose work *Kakawin Sutasoma* is the source of the Indonesian state motto. According to Tamarra, the small figure is deliberately selected as a symbol of hope for the future of diversity in Indonesia.[2]

Accompanying the installation, the artist also presented twelve single-channel videos that documented the artist's collaboration with a British artist, Emma Frankland, titled *Trans Performance Exchange* (2019). Tamarra and Frankland worked together for six months to sketch a shared trans history across different geographies, resulting in a digital exhibition on social media platforms.[3] The artists articulated their art as a means 'to speak out, to enjoy life and create platforms for others' (Tamarra 2021). The latter point is particularly poignant as they explain that they conceived their art projects as a way to foster a sense of belonging for trans communities and be an exemplar for the government, which continues to turn a blind eye to the history of queer and gender-diverse communities in Indonesia (ibid.).

---

2 ARTJOG, www.artjog.id/mmxxii/artist.php?id=56#2
3 @trans_performance_exchange, Instagram, 13 March – 27 October 2021. www.instagram.com/trans_performance_exchange/?hl=en

Chapter 13 Gender, activism and Indonesian visual arts   249

The use of the past to hold a critical mirror for the present is also used in Yaya Sung's (born 1986, based in Jakarta) body of work. The Chinese Indonesian artist regularly references historical violence, from the event that has become Indonesia's founding trauma, the 1965–1966 anti-communist mass killings, to the anti-Chinese violence of 1998. For *#perempuan* exhibition in Melbourne in 2018, Sung created an installation that referenced and visualised a critical historical document that exposed one of the biggest myths created by the New Order about a progressive women's group, Gerwani, affiliated with the Indonesian Communist Party.

The Future (Lies) (2018, 7-channel video installation, dimensions variable) installation consisted of seven flat-screen televisions on vertical frames. The screens were arranged in a semicircle facing away from the gallery entrance. The videos in the installation depict seven rotating naked male bodies accompanied by mournful music sung by female survivors of the 1965–1966 events, Pujiati, Sri Sulistiawati, Lestari and Sri Suprapti, played on a loop. Working with a team of make-up artists, videographers and talents, Sung carefully and meticulously reconstructed the bodies' condition based on the forensic report translated in Benedict Anderson's 1987 article 'How Did the Generals Die?'. Her team vividly re-created bleeding gunshot wounds and bruises that had resulted from blunt trauma injuries.

In this work, ambiguity and nuance are not Sung's primary concerns in depicting the impact of 1965–1966. In her artist's journal, Sung states that Gerwani's gender equality and education achievements are still very relevant for contemporary Indonesian women. She feels strongly that her work should speak about the injustices many Gerwani women experienced during the 1965–1966 events.[4] Based on the artist's belief in the body's ability to convey a 'truthful' account of events, the installation represented visual evidence of the New Order's propaganda about Gerwani.[5]

For the generation of visual artists who emerged after the fall of the New Order regime, their strategies are to examine the past from imaginative spaces that often reveal a version of the past that may not be available to historians. Importantly, their reappraisal of Indonesian history from precolonial and colonial times to the anti-communist genocide of 1965–1966 and the anti-Chinese violence in May 1998 comes from a gendered perspective that is critical of history's ongoing impact on the representation of gender and sexuality in present-day Indonesia.

---

4 Sung continues to make works about Gerwani. In 2019 she exhibited a small series of works titled *Present Measures* at Project Space, RMIT Melbourne, 4 April – 3 May, www.intersect.rmit.edu.au/-ps-sr-st-/present-measures

5 For a detailed discussion of this work see Dirgantoro (2022a).

Environment and technology

In parallel with the focus on re-examining the past, Perempuan Pengkaji Seni's winning performance marked another thematic shift in the development of Indonesian visual arts. The collective, which consisted of Shalihah Ramadhanita, Syska La Veggie, Ambawani Gelar, You Winda Dona W and Nabila Warda Safitri, was established in 2021 as a response to the lack of awareness about women's issues in the arts in East Java. La Veggie stated that the collective 'believe that art can be a part of [community] and represent how we feel about issues around women and gender equity' (La Veggie 2022).

The theme of labour or, more precisely, female labour, that the collective represented in their performance is connected to the collective's focus on female subjectivity and a subject matter that has long been perceived as a 'woman's only' topic. As a result, women artists in Indonesia and around the world have brought attention to this subject matter in intimate and revealing ways; thus it is an apt focus for the performance in the aforementioned contemporary art award.

Rotary highlighted how social norms around gender roles dictate that certain labours such as cooking, cleaning and sewing are primarily associated with women. The repetition in the performance mimics the relentless routine chores done mainly by women. At the same time, the performance also speaks of another form of labour, namely women's participation in Indonesia's garment industry. As the collective noted in an interview, 'women are often accused as the main consumers in fast fashion, but female workers dominate the garment industry around our hometown in East Java. They are also the most badly treated and have the worst working conditions' (Artopologi 2022). The performance thus highlights the plight of female workers, following the trajectory of Indonesian artists who championed the rights of working-class communities.

The collective described that they collected the fabric they use in the performance from the waste of the garment industry. They stated that women are not the only losers in the capitalist system but also the environment, as waste continues to build and the industry has done very little to process it. The collective's strategy to link creative practice with environmental awareness, particularly through a gendered lens, is another critical shift that scholars have noted in the past five years (Jurriëns 2020; Kent 2020).

An example of this thematic focus on the relationship between gender, artmaking and environmental awareness can be seen in the practice of XXLab, which consists of Irene Agrivinna, Atinna Rizqiana, Eka Jayani

Ayuningtyas, Asa Rahmana and Ratna Djuwita, an all-female collective based in Yogyakarta. Their practice reveals that when art collaborates with science and technology, the results could go beyond the bounds of the gallery space and laboratory walls. *SOYA C(O)U(L)Ture* (2015) is an installation art piece comprising a dress accompanied by petri dishes with live bacteria culture and a documentation video of the process. The work won several international awards, notably Art and Technology Grant voestalpine 2015 for artistic, scientific, technological and social entrepreneurship innovations and Singapore Art Museum's Dana SAM for art and environmental projects in 2015 (Sick-Leitner 2015).

Using everyday objects and open-source software and hardware, the collective turned wastewater from Yogyakarta's intensive tofu production into an alternative form of tanned leather. The process involved bacteria (*Acetobacter xylinum*) turning the glucose into a cellulose sheet known as *nata de soya*. The sheet was further processed through pressing, drying and dyeing to make it suitable for clothing and craft materials. Notably, the collective explained that in addition to eliminating waste and water pollution, their projects also aimed to provide an alternative source of income for women of lower socioeconomic backgrounds in Yogyakarta.

Gender and transnational connectivity

While Indonesian artists historically have worked alongside cultural and political activists, in the shifting landscape of post–New Order Indonesia this partnership often just scratched the surface of what it means for visual artists and activists working together to enact change. With some notable exceptions of activist artists who rely on raising social consciousness through direct actions—such as the Taring Padi collective, the late Semsar Siahaan, Moelyono and Alit Ambara—Arahmaiani's recent projects seek an alternative way to initiate change through a more inclusive and empathic approach that came from a gendered subjectivity. Arahmaiani (born 1961, based in Yogyakarta and Denpasar) is one of the most renowned Indonesian contemporary artists, and she has represented Indonesia in prestigious global art events. The artist is known for her strong feminist statements in performance and installation art. Arahmaiani's body of environmental work could be seen as a connecting point between gender activism more broadly in Indonesia and in the Indonesian art world more specifically.

Despite geographical differences, the seed for Arahmaiani's Tibet project (2010, ongoing) came from a closer place. Following the devastating earthquake that shook the city of Yogyakarta in 2006, the artist worked with an Islamic boarding school, Pondok Pesantren Amumarta, to rebuild

252   *Wulan Dirgantoro*

the traumatised community. Arahmaiani applied a similar approach to the project in Tibet, where she worked with religious leaders and the Tibetan community to reconnect and rebuild the community's connection with the environment. The artist's initiative in Tibet triggered a series of community projects. Together with monks from the Lab monastery and community members from sixteen villages, Arahmaiani has initiated waste management, mass tree planting, clean water projects and yak coops over the past ten years. In addition, the artist focused on participation and transversal dialogue to rebuild ecological awareness within communities (Hylands 2013).

Arahmaiani's projects in Tibet can be seen to be dealing with processes of belonging outside normative citizenship. Her engagement with local communities, from Yogyakarta to Tibet, speaks of the artist's effort to connect within and beyond the nation's boundaries. Importantly, as also demonstrated by the other artists in this section, the relationship between gendered subjectivity and artmaking has shifted from a focus on the personal towards more collaborative, participatory and community-based projects (not only on individual artmaking). The current shift also appeared to embrace feminism as a driver in these artists' works, while acknowledging the diversity of approaches in formulating their own understandings of the term.

Networks

As women and gender-diverse artists in the post–New Order era continue strengthening their voices and developing their practice, they are also becoming more aware of collective power. Historically, women artists have worked together in the forms of *perkumpulan*, from groups that promote career development for professional artists and amateurs, such as Nuansa Indonesia (established in Jakarta, 1984) and Ikatan Wanita Pelukis Indonesia (IWPI, Association of Women Painters, established in 1985), to social groups such as IKAISYO (Ikatan Istri Senirupawan Yogyakarta, Association of Artist Wives, established in 1982) (Low 2015). Yvonne Low argues that despite the lack of explicit feminist statements in establishing these groups, the founding of the groups marked the beginning of 're-modelling the male-dominated Indonesian art world' (ibid.: 212). In an echo from the previous generation, the current generation of artists sees the collective as a way to regenerate communal spirit through diverse creative and activism platforms.

Citra Sasmita, for example, is an active member of Futuwonder, an all-female collective based in Denpasar. Together with Ruth Onduko, Savitri Sastrawan and Putu Sridiniari, who form the collective, they map the issues surrounding the writing and understanding of works by Balinese women artists. Their statement of the issues they perceive is worth quoting in length (my translation):

1. The lack of appreciation for female artists in Bali, in the forms of exhibition opportunities and acknowledgement of their contribution in artmaking.

2. The lack of archival projects, from documentation and writing about the creative processes of female artists.

3. The lack of discussion in mapping the art world, community movements and enlivening alternative spaces in Bali.

4. The lack of regeneration in artists, curators and writers in Bali makes it difficult to achieve a healthy and progressive art world.[6]

In addition to exhibitions, Futuwonder also organised Puan Empu Seni Edit-a-thon in July 2018, inviting participants to edit Wikipedia entries for Indonesian women artists at Rumah Sanur Creative Hub. Collaborating with Wikimedia Indonesia, the project was intended to raise the visibility of women artists in general and, specifically, reveal how Indonesia's art historical canon has long favoured Javanese and male artists and writers (Horstman 2019). Futuwonder's initiative was inspired by a similar project conducted in March 2018 by the Indonesian Visual Art Archive, Kunci Cultural Studies Centre and Wikimedia Indonesia, with a comparable aim of increasing the visibility of Indonesian women artists on the internet database (IVAA 2018).

Another collective based in Yogyakarta has taken similar steps to address the points above. Inkubator Inisiatif (IIN) was co-founded by visual artists Karina Roosvita, Lashita Situmorang and Venerdi Handoyo in 2019. The collective aims to be a platform to share ideas and knowledge that, in return, nurture contemporary art practices in Indonesia (Dirgantoro 2022b). Kelas Seni Terbuka is their annual program with the aim of raising gender awareness and equity issues in the art world. Employing feminist pedagogy, the classes are built upon knowledge co-creation, community and empowerment.

IIN released an open call and selected a number of young artists from diverse backgrounds and different cities in Indonesia who were otherwise unable to gain access to formal art academies. The collective then facilitated a mentoring program where the artists met regularly with experts on gender and activism, such as ALB (Aliansi Laki-laki Baru, New Men's Alliance), Peretas (Perempuan Lintas Batas, Women across

---

6 Futuwonder, https://futuwonder.wordpress.com/about/

254 *Wulan Dirgantoro*

Borders), RUAS (Ruang Arsip dan Sejarah Perempuan, Women's History and Archive Collective) and Koalisi Seni. The mentoring program in 2022 was led by senior artist FX Harsono and myself, with the outcome of an exhibition.[7] The mentoring program and subsequent dialogue with the experts are both illuminating and revealing. For many of the female participants, their ideas and aspirations are aligned with the current intersectional feminism dialogue. On the other hand, for some of the male participants, it was a confronting experience as they reflected on issues such as toxic masculinity and male privilege.

Notably, the collaborators in IIN's project, namely Peretas, RUAS and Koalisi Seni, are all working from transdisciplinary areas that share a similar trajectory. For example, Peretas utilises feminist solidarity in all fields of cultural production to support all females and female-identifying art workers through gatherings, research, publication and advocacy projects across different parts of Indonesia, not just Java or Bali.[8] At the same time, RUAS turns its focus to the critical rebuilding of Indonesian history from a gendered lens (Bas 2020). In addition, Koalisi Seni, a non-profit organisation advocating for the development of a healthy art ecosystem in Indonesia, has made gender equity in the arts one of its main portfolios (Koalisi Seni 2021b).

These examples reflect how the current generation of women artists, writers and curators in Bali and Yogyakarta has taken critical steps to address the patriarchal legacy of the New Order and post–New Order Indonesia. Their practice, either as individual artists or as collectives, utilises the growing space for Indonesian women in using digital media and engagement to creatively express themselves, contest gendered ideals and organise social and political activism (Winarnita et al. 2022). In doing so, they recontextualise and expand their artmaking with activist networks outside and inside the Indonesian art world.

Reception: Longitudes and latitudes

Perempuan Pengkaji Seni's win points to another shift in the reception of art in Indonesia. Reception in art refers to how the intended audience reacts to an artwork in public viewing. First, Perempuan Pengkaji Seni, as a collective from Surabaya, reaffirms the development of Indonesian contemporary art outside the main art centres of Jakarta, Bandung, Yogyakarta and Denpasar. Indeed, artists, curators and researchers have

---

7 Inkubator Inisiatif [@inkubatorinisiatif]. Instagram profile. www.instagram. com/inkubatorinisiatif/

8 Peretas, https://peretas.org/tentang/

Chapter 13 Gender, activism and Indonesian visual arts 255

long pointed out this trend, with visual artists from West Sumatra and South Sulawesi particularly active in developing their artistic network within their area, in Indonesia and overseas (Bruhn 2020; Campbell 2022). Yet Java and the main art centres remain the desired destination for tertiary art education, production and circulation of visual art practices.

Second, that a collective (all women) won a contemporary art prize where prizes are usually handed out to a single medium, and to what so far has been dominated by male artists, is indicative of how the latest development of gender politics has impacted the Indonesian art world. For example, the preference for performance art (Victoria Koesasi, the winner of the travel prize, also presented a performance art piece), in which the artist uses their body as the medium and artistic vehicle to express themselves, over more conventional mediums such as painting, is also noteworthy because women artists have long had a specific interest in this medium due to its capacity to explore both personal and political issues (Dirgantoro 2019).

The path towards more visibility and positive reception of works by women and gender-diverse artists in the past few years has been paved by the increase in women's activism since 1998. While this chapter has discussed the production of art by individuals and collectives that challenge gender norms in the field of representation, the relative success of such visibility is even more remarkable against an increase in censorship with regard to freedom of expression.

Koalisi Seni reported that, based on data collected from 2010 to 2020, there had been a clear increase in censorship in the arts since 2015 (Gumay et al. 2020). According to the report, visual arts had the second-highest censorship (film being number one) between 2010 and 2020. One notable incident was in 2016 in Yogyakarta, where a female-led art and music community festival called Lady Fast was forcefully disbanded by the local police and religious mass organisations (Forum Umat Islam, Forum Jihad Indonesia) because the festival allegedly promoted 'communism and LGBT issues' (ibid.: 48; BBC Indonesia 2016).[9] The incident highlighted that expression of gender politics in Indonesia is still fraught; many female artists and gender-diverse communities are silenced through accusations of communism, LGBT, blasphemy and/or violation of cultural norms in their creative practices (Wijaya 2022a; see also Puspawardhani 2021).

The incident above does not stop the mainstreaming of feminism in the visual arts. For example, in recent contemporary art events such as the Yogya Biennale, feminist tours were run for the general public in its last

---

9 The second Lady Fast festival was held in 2017 in Bandung without incident.

256   *Wulan Dirgantoro*

two iterations (2019, 2021). Alia Swastika, curator and director of the Yogya Biennale Foundation, remarked that the tours aim to bring awareness about how feminism inspired artmaking in the biennale. Similarly, in ARTJOG 2022, an annual art festival in Yogyakarta, anecdotal data suggested a higher number and visibility of female and non-binary artists participating. Tamarra, for example, gave an artist talk to a rapt audience where they spoke about the need for greater tolerance for diversity of (gender) identity.[10]

In contrast with the controversy surrounding the censorship of murals in 2021 (Pasaribu 2022; Puspawardhani 2021; also see Rahmawati and Napitupulu 2021), exhibition spaces continue to provide an enabling space for artists to speak about difficult issues in the past and present. The 2021 edition of Yogya Biennale, titled *roots <> routes*, which was centred on the connection between Indonesia and Oceania, is a case in point. A collective from Papua, Udeido, garnered plenty of media attention for its work. Yanto Gombo (born 1996, based in Jayapura), a member of Udeido, painted a large mural on the entrance of the main venue to signal the direction of the curatorial framing of the biennale, namely addressing the impact of colonialism including Indonesia's own.

However, the work by Betty Adii (born 1998, based in Yogyakarta and Papua), the only female member of the collective, demonstrated how gender and activism in Indonesian contemporary art remain highly relevant today. Adii's installation was titled *Dystopian Reality: The Agony of Existence* (2021, mixed media installation, dimensions variable). The installation consisted of large bullet-shaped penises with skulls imprinted on the testicles, placed on the wall and the floor. In addition, Adii wrote texts that referenced Indonesian military codes encircling the objects on the wall, while female underwear was scattered and draped around the objects. Along with the objects were a series of drawings consisting of quotes, testimonies and figures and a large painting depicting a Papuan woman with an open chest shaped like a coffin while a small child watched nearby.

The message was direct and unambiguous: Papuan women suffered heavily from the ongoing military conflicts in Papua. Sexual violence and the sociocultural stigma in the aftermath of the violence they experienced is a raw wound for many Papuan women and communities (Komnas Perempuan 2010). Adii further stated that the collective's work is a statement of solidarity for other women in conflict areas (Maharani 2021). Importantly, the artist is also keen to emphasise that despite the

10   See Tamarra's profile at ARTJOG, www.artjog.id/mmxxii/artist.php?id=56#2

Chapter 13 Gender, activism and Indonesian visual arts 257

challenging subject matter, she felt that the exhibition space is a safe space for her to speak out and build a community with other Papuan women in Yogyakarta.[11] There was no reported incident or intimidation against the collective or the biennale.

In parallel with the achievements of many artists based in Indonesia, outside Indonesia mid-career artists are gaining recognition. Melati Suryodarmo (born 1969, based in Solo, Java) recently held her first solo exhibition in Europe, at the Bonnefanten Museum in the Netherlands. The museum awarded Suryodarmo the Bonnefanten Award for Contemporary Art (BACA) on 12 June 2022.[12] Suryodarmo is considered an influential figure in performance art in Indonesia as well as a curator, educator and renowned festival organiser. In another example, on the intersection between research and creative practice, multimedia artist Tintin Wulia (born 1972, based in Gothenburg) recently won the prestigious European Research Council Grant for an examination of drone warfare's impact on conflict societies (HDK-Valand 2022).

Finally, IGAK Murniasih's (1966–2006) works increasingly attracted the interest of many regional museums and galleries. Her inclusion in exhibitions such as *Contemporary Worlds: Indonesia* at the National Gallery of Australia in 2019 and a posthumous exhibition at Gajah Gallery Singapore in 2021 highlighted how a successful reception of contemporary art by women artists could be developed from feminist-inspired research. As a result, Murniasih's works have now been collected by institutions such as the National Gallery of Singapore and National Gallery of Australia, and by private collectors.

Conclusion

So how to situate the positive reception of works by women and gender-diverse artists within broader societal change in Indonesia? The cliché about works by female artists in Indonesia, such as challenging subject matter, non-mainstream mediums, and the perceived lack of career longevity due to adherence to *kodrat*, are currently being redefined by the younger generation of artists. The recent development of gender politics in Indonesian visual arts reflects the global #metoo movements and post–New Order women's activism (Setiawan and Tomsa 2022a). For many women, particularly, being an artist allows them to channel their

---

11 Nggalu (2022); see also interview with Adii, 'Profil Perempuan Papua: Betty Adii' in Kikikolab, https://www.youtube.com/@kikikolab2739

12 Bonnefanten Museum, *Melati Suryodarmo: I am a ghost in my own house*, www.bonnefanten.nl/en/exhibitions/melati-suryodarmo-i-am-a-ghost-in-my-own-house

ideas and aspirations. Artmaking gives them a platform to speak about issues considered taboo or sensitive, especially in light of the increasing censorship of freedom of expression and limitations of gender expression in Indonesia (Setiawan and Tomsa 2022b). This remains a cornerstone of their practice.

The current generation is also less rigidly defined in its approach to gender activism. It actively seeks to learn and collaborate with activist groups while maintaining a sense of autonomy as artist. The latter is an important distinction for the current generation because, in the previous generation, artists either maintained a strict separation between their practice and their political view or placed activism at the core of their practice and set aside their autonomy as artist.

Importantly, the initiatives mentioned throughout this chapter largely came from the non-government sector, with steady support from local governments (particularly in Java and Bali) and, increasingly, the national government. Since the 1990s, Indonesia's dynamic art scene has been driven by independent art spaces and individuals (Supangkat et al. 2001); the Ministry of Culture and Education is a relatively new player in this field. When parliament passed the Law on Advancement of Culture in April 2017, the law shifted the government's role from enforcer to facilitator to 'position the community as the owner and driving force of culture, and make culture the guidelines for national development' (Koalisi Seni 2022).

While the Directorate of Culture has released important initiatives, such as the Dana Abadi Kebudayaan, a 3-trillion-rupiah fund for arts development, concerns over freedom of expression and gender inequality remain high among female art practitioners. For example, there is no policy to protect and provide institutional support from the state and within the arts industry to women and gender-diverse artists (Maharani et al. 2022; see also Wijaya 2022b). Combined with a weak mechanism in the prosecution of gender-based violence in Indonesia, women and gender-diverse artists remain vulnerable to exploitation, violence and censorship in Indonesia today.[13]

Yet, as the discussion above has demonstrated, artmaking based on the lived perspectives of Indonesian women and gender-diverse communities offers a sense of hope. As female artists, researchers and curators continue to *mengkaji seni* (learn about art), their initiatives show a strong belief in art's capacity to raise gender awareness, bring visibility for women and gender-diverse artists and advocate for social change in Indonesia today.

---

13 For Indonesia's gender equality report card, see Bexley and Bessell (2022).

References

16albemarle project space. 2022. 'Seni baru: New art from Bali and Bandung'. 16albemarle project space, 23 Apr – 22 May 2022, Sydney. www.16albemarle. com/ex-9-citra

Anderson, Benedict. 1987. 'How did the generals die?' *Indonesia* 43: 109–34. doi.org/10.2307/3351215

Artopologi. 2022. 'Perempuan bukan buruh gratisan' [Women are not free labour]. www.youtube.com/watch?v=XxKsmfp3aF0

Bas, Fira. 2020. 'Gerakan perempuan Indonesia dalam melawan penjajahan' [Indonesian women's movement against colonisation]. Perempuan Mahardhika, 30 December. https://mahardhika.org/gerakan-perempuan-dalam-melawan-penjajahan/

BBC Indonesia. 2016. 'Polisi dan ormas bubarkan acara Lady Fast di Yogyakarta' [Police and mass organisations break up Lady Fast event in Yogyakarta]. BBC Indonesia, 3 April. www.bbc.com/indonesia/berita_indonesia/2016/04/160403_indonesia_diskusi_perempuan_bubar_ormas

Bexley, Angie and Sharon Bessell. 2022. 'Indonesia's gender equality report card'. *Policy Forum*, 7 March. Asia & the Pacific Policy Society. www.policyforum. net/indonesias-gender-equality-report-card/

Bianpoen, Carla. 2002. 'Indonesian women artists: Transcending compliance'. In *Women in Indonesia: Gender, Equity and Development*, edited by Kathryn Robinson and Sharon Bessell, 113–29. Institute of Southeast Asian Studies. doi.org/10.1355/9789812305152-017

Bianpoen, Carla. 2019. *Into the Future: Indonesian Women Artists.* Cemara Enam Foundation.

Bianpoen, Carla. 2022. *Indonesian Women Artists: Infusions into Contemporary Art.* Cemara 6.

Bianpoen, Carla, Farah Wardani and Wulan Dirgantoro. 2007. *Indonesian Women Artists: The Curtain Opens.* Yayasan Seni Rupa Indonesia.

Bruhn, Katherine. 2020. 'Traversing Alam Minangkabau: Tradition, identity and art world making in Indonesia'. *World Art* 10: 239–58. doi.org/10.1080/215008 94.2020.1810752

Campbell, Siobhan. 2022. 'The art of seafaring'. *di'van* 11(June): 110–19. https:// artdesign.unsw.edu.au/unsw-galleries/divan-issue-11

Dewan Kesenian Jakarta. 2020. *Dari Pembantu Seni Lukis Kita: Bunga Rampai Tulisan Oei Sian Yok 1956–1961* [From our painting assistants: Anthology of Oei Sian Yok's writings 1956–1961]. Jakarta Arts Council.

Dirgantoro, Wulan. 2017. *Feminisms and Contemporary Art in Indonesia: Defining Experiences.* Amsterdam University Press. doi.org/10.1515/9789048526994

Dirgantoro, Wulan. 2019. 'Transformative territory: Performance art and gender in post–New Order Indonesia'. *Ideas Journal,* Asia Art Archive, 18 December. https://aaa.org.hk/en/ideas-journal/ideas-journal/shortlist-transformative-territory-performance-art-and-gender-in-post-new-order-indonesia

Dirgantoro, Wulan. 2022a. 'After 1965: Historical violence and strategies of representation in Indonesian visual arts'. In *Living Art: Indonesian Artists Engage Politics, Society and History,* edited by Elly Kent, Virginia Hooker and Caroline Turner, 273–93. ANU Press. doi.org/10.22459/LA.2022.09

Dirgantoro, Wulan. 2022b. 'Conversation with Inkubator Inisiatif: On gender, pedagogy and artmaking in Yogyakarta'. In *CHECK-IN 2022*, edited by Nadya Wang, 134–38. Margins Print. https://artandmarket.net/publications/checkin-2022

Gumay, Hafez, Reisky Handika, Eduard Lazarus and Ratri Ninditya. 2020. *Kebebasan Berkesenian di Indonesia 2010–2020: Studi Pustaka* [Artistic freedom in Indonesia 2010–2020: A literature review]. Koalisi Seni.

HDK-Valand. 2022. 'Research on how aesthetic objects instigate socio-political change receives prestigious ERC grant'. University of Gothenburg, 10 January. www.gu.se/en/news/research-on-how-aesthetic-objects-instigate-socio-political-change-receives-prestigious-erc-grant

Horstman, Richard. 2019. 'Empowering Balinese women artists – Futuwonder'. Life as Art Asia, 23 January. https://lifeasartasia.art/2019/01/23/empowering-balinese-woman-artists-futuwonder/

Hylands, Peter. 2013. 'Arahmaiani in Tibet'. *Creative-i*, April (4): 18–28. www.creativecowboyfilms.com/publications/creative-i-4

Isabella, Brigitta. 2020. 'Situated formalism in the art of encounters: A brief introduction to the selected writings of Oei Sian Yok'. *Southeast of Now: Directions in Contemporary and Modern Art in Asia* 4(2): 285–309. doi.org/10.1353/sen.2020.0013

IVAA (Indonesian Visual Art Archive). 2018. 'Tangannya putus satu: Edit-a-thon Wikipedia seni dan perempuan' [One detached hand: Wikipedia edit-a-thon art and women]. https://ivaa-online.org/program/past/tangannya-putus-satu-edit-a-thon-wikipedia-seni-dan-perempuan/

Jurriëns, Edwin. 2020. 'Gendering the environmental activism: *Ekofeminisme* and *unjuk rasa* of Arahmaiani's Art'. *Southeast of Now: Directions in Contemporary and Modern Art in Asia* 4(2): 3–29. doi.org/10.1353/sen.2020.0006

Kent, Elly. 2020. 'Critical recycling: Post-consumer waste as medium and meaning in contemporary Indonesian art'. *Southeast of Now: Directions in Contemporary and Modern Art in Asia* 4(1): 73–94. doi.org/10.1353/sen.2020.0003

Koalisi Seni. 2021a. 'Perspektif gender dalam kebijakan kesenian: Usulan agenda advokasi' [Gender perspective in arts policy: Proposed advocacy agenda for the arts coalition]. Koalisi Seni. https://koalisiseni.or.id/advokasi/keadilan-gender/ (see 'Dokumen')

Koalisi Seni. 2021b. 'Advokasi: Keadilan gender dalam seni' [Gender justice in the arts]. Koalisi Seni. https://koalisiseni.or.id/advokasi/keadilan-gender/

Koalisi Seni. 2022. 'Pemajuan kebudayaan' [Cultural advancement]. Koalisi Seni. https://pemajuankebudayaan.id/en/actions/

Komnas Perempuan. 2010. 'Stop sudah! Kesaksian perempuan Papua korban kekerasan dan pelanggaran HAM 1963–2009: Hasil pendokumentasian bersama kelompok kerja pendokumentasian kekerasan dan pelanggaran HAM perempuan Papua 2009–2010' [Enough! Testimony of Papuan women victims of violence and human rights violations 1963–2009: Results of joint working group on documentation of violence and human rights violations of Papuan women 2009–2010]. Komnas Perempuan.

Chapter 13 *Gender, activism and Indonesian visual arts* 261

La Veggie, Syska. 2022. 'Perempuan dan kesetaraan dalam seni' [Women and equality in the arts]. Greatmind, 5 March. https://greatmind.id/article/perempuan-dan-kesetaraan-dalam-seni

Low, Yvonne. 2015. 'Becoming professional: Feminisms and the rise of women-centred exhibitions in Indonesia'. *Australian and New Zealand Journal of Art* 15(2): 210–24. doi.org/10.1080/14434318.2015.1089820

Maharani, Annayu, Hafez Gumay and Oning Putri, eds. 2022. *Merawat Seni dengan Hati: Kondisi Kerja Emosional Perempuan* [Caring for art with the heart: The emotional working condition of women]. Koalisi Seni Indonesia.

Maharani, Shinta. 2021. 'Kekerasan Papua dan Highlight Biennale' [Papuan violence and Highlights of the Biennale]. *Tempo*, 24 October: 42–43.

Nggalu, Eka Putra. 2022. 'Papua dalam Koreri Projection' [Papua in the Koreri Projection]. *Lau Ne* [Knowledge through Art], 29 April. https://laune.id/papua-dalam-koreri-projection/

Pasaribu, Adrian Jonathan. 2022. 'Censoring the pandemic in Indonesia'. *Arts Equator*, 25 August. https://artsequator.com/censoring-pandemic-indonesia/

Puspawardhani, Stania. 2021. 'Indonesia: Painted politics'. *The Interpreter*, 30 September. Lowy Institute. www.lowyinstitute.org/the-interpreter/indonesia-painted-politics

Rahmawati, Maidina and Erasmus AT Napitupulu. 2021. 'Mural controversies expose the poor health of Indonesian democracy'. *Indonesia at Melbourne*, 23 August. https://indonesiaatmelbourne.unimelb.edu.au/mural-controversies-expose-the-poor-health-of-indonesian-democracy/

Setiawan, Ken M.P. and Dirk Tomsa. 2022a. 'Gender equality and sexual politics'. In *Politics in Contemporary Indonesia: Institutional Change, Policy Challenges and Democratic Decline*, 135–50. Routledge. doi.org/10.4324/9780429459511-9

Setiawan, Ken M.P. and Dirk Tomsa. 2022b. 'Human rights'. In *Politics in Contemporary Indonesia: Institutional Change, Policy Challenges and Democratic Decline*, 158–60. Routledge. doi.org/10.4324/9780429459511

Sick-Leitner, Magdalena. 2015. 'SOYA C(O)U(L)Ture—useful things arise out of waste'. *Ars Electronica*, 30 September. https://ars.electronica.art/aeblog/en/2015/09/30/soya-coulture/

Siswadi, Anwar. 2022. 'Kelompok Perempuan Pengkaji Seni raih hadiah Bandung Contemporary Art Awards Rp 100 Juta' [Perempuan Pengkaji Seni wins the Bandung Contemporary Art Awards prize of 100 million rupiah]. *Tempo*, 13 August. https://seleb.tempo.co/read/1622466/kelompok-perempuan-pengkaji-seni-raih-hadiah-bandung-contemporary-art-awards-rp-100-juta

Supangkat, Jim, Sumartono, Asmudjo Jono Irianto, Rizki A. Zaelani and M. Dwi Marianto. 2001. *Outlet: Yogyakarta within the Contemporary Indonesian Art Scene*. Cemeti Art Foundation.

Surya, Denny. 2022. 'Perempuan Pengkaji Seni jadi pemenang Bandung Contemporary Art Award 2022' [Perempuan Pengkaji Seni wins the 2022 Bandung Contemporary Art Award]. madania.co.id, 14 August. https://madania.co.id/perempuan-pengkaji-seni-jadi-pemenang-bandung-contemporary-art-award-2022/

262   *Wulan Dirgantoro*

Suryakusuma, Julia. 1996. 'State and sexuality in New Order Indonesia'. In *Fantasizing the Feminine in Indonesia,* edited by Laurie J. Sears, 92–119. Duke University Press. doi.org/10.1215/9780822396710-004

Swastika, Alia. 2019. *Membaca Praktik Negosiasi Seniman Perempuan dan Politik Gender Orde Baru* [Reading the negotiation practices of female artists and New Order gender politics]. Tan Kinira Books.

Tamarra. 2021. 'Hello my name is Tamarra'. In *Post: Notes on Art in a Global Context,* translated by Ferdiansjah Thajib. Contemporary and Modern Art Perspectives (C-Map), Museum of Modern Art, 17 March. https://post.moma.org/hello-my-name-is-tamarra/

Wah, Ho See. 2022. 'Conversation with Balinese artist Citra Sasmita'. *A&M* (Art and Market), 9 March. https://artandmarket.net/dialogues/2020/3/9/conversation-with-balinese-artist-citra-sasmita

Wijaya, Hendri Yulius. 2022a. 'Digital homophobia: Technological assemblages of anti-LGBT sentiment and surveillance in Indonesia'. *Indonesia & the Malay World* 50(146): 52–72. doi.org/10.1080/13639811.2022.2010357

Wijaya, Hendri Yulius. 2022b. 'My own words: Queerness in motion'. In *CHECK-IN 2022,* edited by Nadya Wang, 46–51. Margins Print. https://artandmarket.net/publications/checkin-2022

Winarnita, Monika, Nasya Bahfen, Adriana Rahajeng Mintarsih, Gavin Height and Joanne Byrne. 2022.'Gendered digital citizenship: How Indonesian female journalists participate in gender activism'. *Journalism Practice* 16(4): 621–36. doi.org/10.1080/17512786.2020.1808856

14 Feminist intervention in cultural activism

Intan Paramaditha

Examining the development of feminist thought and practice in Indonesian arts and culture since the early 2000s, this chapter argues that new forms of cultural activism are emerging; they are feminist, trans-archipelagic and moving towards a decolonial approach. In the first decade of Indonesia's *reformasi*, feminist discourses became visible through high-profile media debates and spectacles from the rise of women writers who write openly about sex and sexuality (writing labelled by the media as *sastrawangi* or fragrant literature), to the controversial Rancangan Undang-Undang Pornografi (Pornography Bill), which became law in 2008. Women in the arts have challenged traditional gender roles prescribed by the New Order regime by reclaiming their agency as creators and decision-makers in literary, music, film, performance and visual art scenes. The two most prominent trajectories of feminist thought, liberal feminism and Islamic feminism, have shaped the discussions around women, gender and feminism, and these influences have continued to thrive in the subsequent decades. With the prevalent use of digital technology, liberal and Islamic feminist ideas have travelled through digital platforms, circulated by the younger generation of feminist activists, often in response to the increasing religious conservatism that attempts to confine women and discriminate against sexual and gender minority groups.

Yet more feminist directions have emerged. The Joko Widodo (Jokowi) administration, which began in 2014, has led to a new development in feminist articulations that fit more with free market logic. Centred on the idea of *kerja* (work) within a neoliberal framework, the Jokowi regime flaunts successful female ministers as well as millennial staff and spokespersons—many of whom are women—as the icons

264   *Intan Paramaditha*

of Indonesia's assertive move towards a global digital economy and creative entrepreneurship. This development, coinciding with global feminist movements, paved the way for the rise of neoliberal feminism that frames women's struggles as individual endeavours to break the glass ceiling. There has also been an emerging feminist movement that focuses on forging feminist connections across borders in the *nusantara* (archipelago) while making interventions to the Jakarta/Java-centric feminist thought and practice. This chapter focuses on the latter movement and highlights its trans-archipelagic and decolonial characteristics. My scope is limited to feminist cultural activism, a specific site within the feminist movement in which collectives use culture as a site for political intervention. Individuals involved in feminist cultural activism are writers, artists, performers, filmmakers and musicians, and many of them connect themselves with networks of human rights activists and labour activists, as well as feminist academics. I draw attention to the trans-archipelagic feminist spaces created by initiatives such as Puan Seni, Peretas, Sekolah Pemikiran Perempuan and Perkawanan Perempuan Menulis. Focusing on encounters and learning processes in the feminist collective Sekolah Pemikiran Perempuan, I will discuss how women across the archipelago collaborate while acknowledging difference rather than erasing it to dismantle colonial, capitalist and heteropatriarchal knowledge production.

The New Order contexts

In her 2002 article about feminism in Indonesia, scholar and activist Saparinah Sadli writes that 'the term "feminism", "feminist" and even "gender" are still questioned by the majority of Indonesians' (2002: 81). As a feminist who built a foundation for women's studies and activism throughout the 1980s and 1990s and witnessed how the institution she set up, Komnas Perempuan (National Commission on Violence against Women), influenced policymaking in the 2000s, Saparinah Sadli embodies what feminism looked like under the New Order. Feminists had to be careful in navigating their political agenda through patriarchal institutions, and compromises often had to be made. In developing a women's studies curriculum in the 1990s, Saparinah Sadli and her colleagues adopted the term 'women's perspective' rather than 'feminist perspective' to avoid backlash from the academic community. Sadli acknowledges, however, that in the 1990s younger feminists—who established feminist non-government organisations (NGOs) such as Kalyanamitra—criticised the approach and struggled for 'subversive' spaces to discuss feminist ideas despite restrictions imposed by the Suharto regime (Sadli 2002: 82–83).

Chapter 14 Feminist intervention in cultural activism 265

Scholarly works on women in Indonesia have discussed how Suharto regulated women by discouraging their participation in politics and institutionalising their roles within organisations that positioned women as appendages of their husbands. Julia Suryakusuma (2004) used the term 'state ibuism' (state motherism) to describe how gender ideology of the state was encapsulated in the figure of the *ibu*, whose role is to raise children, support her husband, and maintain harmony between the family and the state. Feminists therefore often had to operate in small spaces or cracks within the New Order structure. For instance, the feminist NGOs advocated, through tactical ways, 'alternative perspectives' that challenged the institutionalisation of women via Dharma Wanita (an organisation for civil servants' wives) and PKK (Pembinaan Kesejahteraan Keluarga, Guidance for Family Welfare, an organisation to increase women's domestic skills). Saparinah Sadli's feminist legacies such as Komnas Perempuan and the University of Indonesia's Women's Studies Department, the first of its kind in the country, resulted from negotiations that she had to make with bureaucratic frameworks and institutions. Her writings in the 1980s and early 1990s reflect these negotiations; her critique of the patriarchal structure, including the idealisation of motherhood as a prevalent norm of the New Order regime, is conveyed through an engagement with a developmentalist paradigm. In her collection of essays *Berbeda tetapi Setara: Pemikiran tentang Kajian Perempuan* (2010), she proposes that women be viewed as the subject and not just the object of development and that there should be a balance between career and family so that women can be an equal partner to men.

One thing that was absent from Sadli's book is an observation that the New Order ideology of ibuism was established upon the destruction of Gerwani (Gerakan Wanita Indonesia) as an organised political women's movement and that this has had a tremendous impact on twenty-first century feminisms in Indonesia. In 1963, Gerwani was one of the world's largest women's organisations with a membership of some 1.5 million women. Affiliated to the Indonesian Communist Party, Gerwani was known for its anti-imperialist focus on issues of gender, labour and family, but in 1967 the organisation was disbanded, followed by the stigmatisation and imprisonment of leftist women. In the *reformasi* era, there has been an effort from women artists and activists to engage with the issues of violence against leftist women, including Faiza Mardzoeki's play *Nyanyi Sunyi Kembang-Kembang Genjer* (The Silent Song of Genjer Flowers), which focuses on women survivors of the communist purge telling their own stories (Sabarini 2016), and the documentary *You and I* (2020) by Fanny Chotimah, which revolves around the friendship between two women who were accused as communists. However, when Indonesian feminists rebuilt the movement after the fall of Suharto, socialist feminist thinking as a legacy of leftist women was largely absent from public conversations. This means that, first, there is a gap in the trajectories of feminist thought that became visible in the early years of *reformasi* and, second, Indonesian feminists still need to deal with the repercussions of ruptures in Indonesia's feminist genealogy.

Post-Suharto feminist discourses

Since the early 2000s, certain forms of feminism have become part of the mainstream imagination in Indonesian public culture and influenced the ways in which gender and sexuality are expressed in arts and culture. If we delve into the question of feminist visibility, the mapping of post-Suharto feminism offered by feminist scholar and activist Gadis Arivia in her report co-written with Nur Iman Subono, *A Hundred Years of Feminism in Indonesia* (2017), provides an interesting view of which feminist voices are heard and where. In a chapter titled 'The emergence of contemporary feminist thought', Arivia and Subono outline some markers in which contemporary feminist thought emerges: NGOs and universities, *Yayasan Jurnal Perempuan* (Women's Journal) and Suara Ibu Peduli (The Voice of Concerned Mothers), and feminist novelists who reject patriarchy (with a focus on Ayu Utami and Djenar Maesa Ayu). Arivia and Subono also acknowledge the rise of women's institutions funded by the government, including Komnas Perempuan.

Arivia and Subono's map is a window to look at highly visible feminist individuals and groups in the early years of *reformasi*. Drawn by prominent elite figures in the movement, the map demonstrates that dominant feminist voices that shape Indonesian feminist discourses are centred in Jakarta/Java, secular and liberal. In 1998, Suara Ibu Peduli, a group of feminist activists that took to the streets to protest Suharto's policies and supported the student movement, reappropriated the term *ibu* (mother) to push for their feminist agenda. The group received media attention after three women activists—Gadis Arivia, Karlina Leksono and Wilasih Noviana—were arrested for rallying, and this visibility further contributed to more attention to discourses of women's rights and feminism. Conversations around feminism intensified in the early 2000s as the media highlighted a group of women writers such as Ayu Utami, Fira Basuki and Djenar Maesa Ayu, who broke New Order restrictions and taboos around gender and sexuality through their overt writings about sex and the autonomy of the body.

Due to the rhetoric of freedom of expression attached to the *reformasi*, it is not surprising that liberal feminism served as the dominant framework

Chapter 14 Feminist intervention in cultural activism 267

in various post–New Order narratives. Liberal feminism has influenced the women's movement in Indonesia since the 1920s (Blackburn 2010), yet it was only after the 1998 *reformasi* that its articulations became more prominent, shaping public conversations around contentious national issues, and increasingly attached to the questions around women's bodies and sexuality as well as institutions—the state, religion, family—that regulate them. With its emphases on individual rights, equality, freedom of expression and bodily autonomy, liberal feminism permeated the middle-class public sphere as a highly visible discourse, represented by high-profile urban feminists such as Gadis Arivia, author Ayu Utami and, later, film director Nia Dinata, who was acclaimed for her 2006 film, *Berbagi Suami* (Love for Share), that criticised the polygamy phenomenon. The value of individualism is highlighted, as demonstrated by Gadis Arivia's reading of the work of Ayu Utami and Djenar Maesa Ayu: 'The description of women in their work is that of a confident woman, who is able to decide her own life as a strong individual' (Arivia and Subono 2017: 18). With this dominant feminist framework, reclaiming feminist thought was often synonymous with reclaiming the body. The performance of Eve Ensler's *Vagina Monologues* in Jakarta was adapted to incorporate Indonesian stories regarding taboos and repression around women's sexuality. Performed on 8 March 2002 at the established art centre Taman Ismail Marzuki, it featured famous Indonesian actresses Jajang C. Noer, Niniek L. Karim, Ayu Azhari, Cornelia Agatha and Ria Irawan, who claimed, 'Why should we be afraid of talking about vagina? This is a word that describes women's problems' (*Liputan6* 2002).

Liberal feminist thought frames public conversations around high-profile media cases from the controversy of *dangdut*[1] singer Inul in 2003 to the Pornography Bill that became law in 2008. Inul's sensuous gyrating dance, deemed as *haram* (forbidden, unclean) by the Indonesian Council of Islamic Scholars (Majelis Ulama Indonesia, MUI), evoked moral panic among conservative groups on one hand, and on the other hand garnered support from feminists who took to the street to protest the attempts to control women's bodies (Abhiseka 2003). The Pornography Bill was expected to regulate production, distribution and consumption of pornographic materials, but it ended up focusing on women's bodies and behaviour. The bill was supported by women's factions of Islamic conservative groups and rejected by secular and feminist Muslim activists for its patriarchal logic.

---

1 A genre of Indonesian popular dance music that combines local traditions, Indian and Malay musical styles, and Western rock.

While liberal feminist thought dominated media attention, Islamic feminist groups have also drawn more support since the 1990s with the emergence of feminist NGOs such as Rahima and Rifka Annisa as well as the more feminist wings of major Islamic organisations Muhammadiyah and Nahdlatul Ulama. A women's faction within Muhammadiyah has been active since the colonial period (Blackburn 2010), but it was in the 1990s that Islamic feminist thought became more overt with the translations of global Muslim feminist works (Nurmila 2011). While Muslim feminist scholars such as Musdah Mulia and Lily Zakiyah Munir emerged as public intellectuals, women have also been fighting for authority within male-dominated Islamic organisations. Kongres Ulama Perempuan Indonesia (KUPI, Indonesian Congress of Women Religious Scholars) was organised to foreground the voices of women *ulama* as authority figures who issue important, gender-sensitive fatwa regarding various matters from violence against women to environmental issues. In arts and culture, by the late 2000s, scholars started noticing that with conversations and debates focusing on *sastrawangi* writers, many women writers who engaged with other topics were overlooked, including those who focus on Islamic discourses (Hellwig 2011). Writers such as Abidah El Khalieqy have vigorously challenged patriarchal interpretations of Islam and perceptions of Muslim women in society (Arimbi 2009; Hellwig 2011).

A common agenda that has brought secular feminists closer to Islamic feminists in the past two decades has been the rise of conservative Islam that led to campaigns to return women to the domestic sphere. Women's activism also emerged from conservative Islamic circles such as AILA (Aliansi Cinta Keluarga Indonesia, Family Love Alliance Indonesia), which claims itself anti-feminist and upholds what it perceives as the standard morality. In combating the rise of conservatism that discriminates against women, Indonesian feminists have increasingly been taking advantage of digital media to claim their voice. For instance, musician and activist Kartika Jahja wrote a song for her band, Tika and the Dissidents, titled 'Tubuhku Otoritasku' (My Body My Authority, 2016) and produced a music video that brings awareness to violence against women and the importance of respecting women's authority over their bodies. The video, which became viral via social media, features women with various body types and dresses (including women with hijab) who show off writings scrawled across their bodies, including bold statements such as 'My Body, My Rules'. The discourse of the body in the music video carries the echo of the celebration of the body via Ayu Utami and other liberal feminist writers, but here the video speaks directly to the rise of conservatism and makes an attempt to connect to Islamic feminism by incorporating the image of hijabi women who represent progressive Muslim women. The

Chapter 14 Feminist intervention in cultural activism 269

younger generation of Islamic feminists also uses digital media platforms to disseminate their ideas, as exemplified by Muslim feminist writer and activist Kalis Mardiasih, who produces regular content on her Instagram page to engage with her women followers. Alternative liberal and Islamic media such as Magdalene.co and Mubadalah.id serve as platforms that circulate feminist knowledge to a younger audience.

In another direction, we have also been witnessing the rise of neoliberal feminism, shaped by various shifts in Indonesia's politics and culture including neoliberal directions with emphases on digital/creative economy and entrepreneurship under President Joko Widodo as well as the mainstreaming of feminism through popular culture. With the government's increased investment in creative industries, we see more incentives for creatives to attend international festivals abroad, and local festivals such as IDEAFEST often present conversations on the creative industry, neoliberal ethos and activism on the same table. Global feminist movements such as Women's March and #MeToo attracted more public figures—similar to what has happened in the West—to embrace feminism and thus contribute to the mainstreaming of feminist discourses.[2] Neoliberal feminism, as described by Catherine Rottenberg, criticises the structures that marginalise women but situate women as individual agents who 'lean in' to achieve success; she is responsible for her own wellbeing and self care, turning 'gender inequality from a structural problem into an individual affair' (2014: 420). Former minister and entrepreneur in the Widodo government, Susi Pudjiastuti, exemplifies this brand of feminism with her capacity to blend entrepreneurial skills, individual discipline and feminist articulations. Neoliberal feminist language informs expressions of creatives, celebrities and influencers that frame feminism as a tool to break the glass ceiling and attain individual success. Singer and influencer Maudy Ayunda, appointed by Joko Widodo as Indonesia's official G20 spokesperson in 2022, is another example of how neoliberalism, creative industry and feminism are linked together. Maudy is a celebrity with over 16 million followers on Instagram and has been cited as the icon of millennials and Gen Z (Yuniar 2022) as well as Indonesia's modern Kartini who champions women's empowerment. Graduated from both Oxford and Stanford and named in Forbes Asia's 30 under 30, she often speaks of entrepreneurial skills, personal growth and the importance of education for women to achieve success (Yuristiawan 2018).

---

2 #MeToo was initiated by black activist Tarana Burke but it became viral after Hollywood actresses deployed the movement to speak of their problems. For a critique of the co-option of #MeToo by white feminists, see Phipps (2020).

The map of post-Suharto feminist discourses reveals that *reformasi* has paved the way for more public discourses around gender and sexuality and inspired new feminist initiatives in arts and culture. In the past twenty years, women have organised women's art festivals, filmmaking workshops, public lectures and discussion forums. While the secular liberal framework underpins many feminist initiatives, Islamic feminist ideas have also shaped certain expressions in arts and culture. Yet despite the increasing awareness of feminism, highly visible feminist voices and movements have been largely centred or rooted in Java. Many prominent organisations, feminist thinkers and feminist artists are part of the Jakarta elite environment, or they are embedded in artistic environments in cities with strong cultural traditions and infrastructure, like Yogyakarta or Solo. As a result, women's initiatives and concerns outside major cities or the island of Java remain on the margins as they do not align with feminist concerns in the centre. There has been a growing concern with the idea of feminism as an individual affair, which is the core of liberal feminists' notion of individual freedom of expression, and is understood through the neoliberal framework as the agency in entrepreneurial freedom and personal responsibility. These issues raise questions: How do women reach out to other women beyond borders and make a meaningful connection beyond feel-good multiculturalism? What feminist framework is important to create a space that is critical of geographical, cultural and class differences and power relations within feminist collaboration?

Trans-archipelagic feminist spaces in arts and culture

In the past decade, a new direction of feminism has emerged in arts and culture. More women writers, artists and cultural activists work within collectives, organisations and networks and engage in cultural activism, which could be defined as claiming political agency to speak to power structures and make cultural intervention (Ginsburg 2016). Women collaborate and strategise to respond to the ongoing exclusion of women in arts and culture, which manifests in all-male panels or all-male nominees for prizes. A blatant example of persisting patriarchal views in the arts is the 2020 nominations for national literary awards of Badan Bahasa (the Indonesian language and book development agency), which drew protests for publishing a list of all-male nominees for fiction, poetry, literary criticism and plays.[3] Cultural activism in Indonesia is not

---

3 The awards were open to works published between 2015 and 2020. This means that within five years, no women writers were considered worthy of nomination. For more about the Badan Bahasa scandal, see Indirani (2020).

new, as communities in arts and culture have been mushrooming since the fall of Suharto's dictatorship, stimulated by a freer climate for new initiatives to grow. Yet many of these seemingly progressive communities are male dominated, relegating female members to administrative labour, and cases of sexual violence are rampant. What differentiates the new forms of cultural activism in arts and culture from the more established ones is that they are feminist, trans-archipelagic and moving towards a decolonial approach. The new feminist movement is trans-archipelagic in scope: feminists create efforts to expand meeting spaces for women across the Indonesian archipelago, taking advantage of the development of digital technology. Further, decolonial thought and questions complicate these feminist projects and affiliations, resulting in a more critical view of the archipelago or *nusantara* as an orientation. I will discuss the trans-archipelagic nature of connection and elaborate on the decolonial frame in the next section.

When COVID-19 hit in 2020, many artists and activists turned to virtual meetings and public discussions, and opportunities for women from different geographical locations to meet online increased significantly. Technology-supported virtual spaces had emerged a few years before the pandemic, such as the simple WhatsApp technology, which was used as a meeting space to create and maintain connections. While the WhatsApp application has been used by conservative groups to disseminate ideas, it has also been used to strengthen feminist networks to transcend geographical borders. In the past five years, organisations and collectives such as Puan Seni, Peretas, Sekolah Pemikiran Perempuan and Perkawanan Perempuan Menulis have amplified the digital platform to facilitate encounters for feminists living in different islands and interrogate not only patriarchy but also colonialism, Javacentrism and heterosexism that are often embedded in feminism itself.

Puan Seni, the Association of Women Art Workers, started as a network in 2015 called Jaringan Seni Perempuan (Art Network for Women) and became an official association in 2021, led by Ama Ahmad from Banggai, South Sulawesi, who was elected through voting. Concerns of Puan Seni include sexism in art communities, the lack of support in the arts for women, and inequality of access for women creators outside Java. The organisation's vision highlights women's contributions to arts and culture, gender equality and diversity for all, including marginalised and minority groups (Alsair 2021). Puan Seni organises regular events on YouTube, including Beranda Seni, where women discuss gender issues in arts and culture, from the effects of the pandemic on women to mental health, and Parade Karya, which showcases works by women artists from different parts of the archipelago.

272   *Intan Paramaditha*

The organisation Perempuan Lintas Batas, or Peretas (Women across Borders), was founded in 2017. It focuses on building feminist solidarity among women art workers with an intersectional perspective to 'expose the plurality of women subjectivities that cross and disrupt borders between nations, races, ethnicities, classes, sexualities, religions, and disabilities' (https://peretas.org/about/), a paradigm that echoes Chandra Talpade Mohanty's (2003) idea of feminism without borders. Peretas aims to 'move towards social transformation and knowledge distribution instead of centralizing in creative industry productivity-driven or individual career', which indicates a clear rejection of the neoliberalisation of arts and creativity that has become more prevalent under the Jokowi administration. Its members met for the first time in Sulawesi, which could be seen as an effort to de-centre the feminist movement, and it has been using online platforms for discussions and dissemination of ideas since then.

Sekolah Pemikiran Perempuan (School of Women's Thought), a collective in which I am involved, grew from a small group of women who managed the Ford Foundation grant for women in the arts called Cipta Media Ekspresi in 2018–2019. In 2020, Cipta Media Ekspresi organisers created the independent collective Sekolah Pemikiran Perempuan as an initiative that intervenes in the processes of knowledge production that marginalise, invalidate and erase women. Departing from an awareness that knowledge produced by women is often devalued at all levels— from the level of *adat* (traditional custom) to the state, from local arts communities to the global politics of knowledge production, Sekolah Pemikiran Perempuan situates Third World women as knowing subjects and engages in epistemic disobedience to the colonial, capitalist and heteropatriarchal knowledge system. Sekolah Pemikiran Perempuan's two main activities are the *sekolah* (school) or informal classes that run for twenty weeks—focusing on anti-colonial feminist thought via women of colour feminisms, gender politics in arts and culture, and feminist cultural activism—and the annual feminist festival called Etalase Pemikiran Perempuan or ETALASE. The festival has featured, among others, Papuan women thinkers Rode Wanimbo, Elvira Rumkabu and Els Tieneke Rieke Katmo addressing colonialism and racism in West Papua, Muslim trans male activist Amar Alfikar reclaiming the concept of *hijrah* from the dominant interpretations of conservative Islam, and transwoman/human rights activist Rully Malay interrogating the concept of *ibu* by looking at transwomen's engagement with care work. Since 2022, ETALASE has been designed with alumnae of the school, based in various locations in Indonesia including Java, Kalimantan, West Nusa Tenggara, East Nusa Tenggara and Papua.

Chapter 14 Feminist intervention in cultural activism 273

Other feminist initiatives include small group meetings organised by Makassar International Writers Festival, which supports literary voices with a feminist perspective from eastern Indonesia, and Let's Talk, an online space for feminist discussions that often brings together the 1990s generation of feminists with the younger generation. The collective Perkawanan Perempuan Menulis (Women Writers Collective, or Comradeship) is a notable example of a trans-archipelagic feminist space created to respond to male-dominated literary communities that alienate women. Initiated by six women writers—Raisa Kamila (Aceh), Ruhaeni Intan Hasanah (Central Java), Amanatia Junda Solikhah (East Java), Armandhany (South Sulawesi), Maria Margareth R.F. (East Nusa Tenggara) and Astuti N. Kilwouw (North Maluku)—the collective creates a virtual feminist literary space to connect women writers in the *nusantara*. Their first project, supported by a Cipta Media Ekspresi grant, is the publication of a collection of short stories, *Tank Merah Muda* (The Pink Tank), which explores the memories, trauma and voices of women outside the centre/Jakarta during the transitional period from the New Order regime to the *reformasi*.

Technology plays an important part in virtual feminist border crossing, but other factors have also contributed to this new direction of feminism. First, trans-archipelagic feminist spaces can be seen as an iteration of the pluralism movement—ways of thinking about plural society and diversity—that started in the late 1990s and early 2000s among feminist groups. However, women involved in these spaces are critical of the persisting 'centralist' view in which ideas from Jakarta are disseminated to the rest of Indonesia in the name of pluralism. Second, global social justice movements helped amplify local resistance, particularly Black Lives Matter. The interwoven connection between global social justice movements and local resistance heightened the politics of 'passing the mic'. For example, there has been an increased awareness among feminist and pro–human rights organisations about the importance of creating more platforms for eastern Indonesian speakers in public events, drawing attention to the question of not only which story should be told but also who has the right to tell the story. Finally, trans-archipelagic feminist spaces are influenced by the discourses of decolonising feminism. The rhetoric of decolonising travelled globally since the Rhodes Must Fall protest at the University of Cape Town in 2015. Many groups have tried to engage with decolonial thinking as well as with indigenous feminism as tools to examine specific structures of oppression in Indonesia. An example of this is the project of West Papuan activist Rode Wanimbo and her colleagues in creating a feminist reading group to decolonise the Bible. At the 2021 ETALASE, Rode Wanimbo presented how the group aims to

274   *Intan Paramaditha*

create new ways of reading the Bible to reclaim faith, using a decolonial feminist lens, with an awareness of gender and colonial oppressions experienced by Papuan women (SPP 2021a).

Towards a decolonial feminism

The word *nusantara* is highly contested. It has been used by the state to claim unity and assert territorial authority, and often when *nusantara* is evoked, what follows is a seamless, sanitised image of multiculturalism where borders, difference and friction are flattened or erased. In transarchipelagic feminist meeting spaces, encounters between feminists from different parts of the archipelago often lead to difficult and uncomfortable questions about one's position. How is one's location and privilege implicated in an unequal power relation? Women within the networks of feminist cultural activism are moving towards solidarity by confronting rather than erasing borders. The decolonial frame is therefore an important element in its emphasis on coloniality and knowledge production. While liberal feminism in the early 2000s often referred to white liberal feminist thought such as that of Simone de Beauvoir, women in trans-archipelagic spaces have been referring to the decolonial/anti-colonial thinking of Chandra Talpade Mohanty and Audre Lorde. In Sekolah Pemikiran Perempuan, we try to reflect on our daily practice by reading the feminist thought of bell hooks, Linda Tuhiwai Smith, Gloria Anzaldua and Indonesian feminist theologian Marianne Katoppo.

In Indonesia, trans-archipelagic decolonial feminism addresses two forms of coloniality. The first is the Western imperial power that dominates knowledge production, including knowledge about feminism, and the second is the political and cultural dominance of another 'West', in this case western Indonesia or Java. In their meetings, women need to constantly address the notion of Javanese cultural superiority and privilege and its impact on economic and cultural gaps between eastern and western Indonesia, including how it legitimised settler colonialism in West Papua. For instance, in Sekolah Pemikiran Perempuan, the initiators—including myself—must acknowledge that most of us grew up and work on the island of Java, and a decolonial lens requires us to interrogate power relations that result from our privileged locations. We need to make sure that we facilitate exchange without falling into the trap of merely inclusion or neoliberal multiculturalism. Questions around knowledge production have become more pressing. Who produces the knowledge? For whom is the knowledge? And who benefits from it? These questions frame our discussions of potential feminist collaborations that aim to transcend borders.

Chapter 14 Feminist intervention in cultural activism 275

I will discuss some case studies of this new direction of feminism based on encounters facilitated by Sekolah Pemikiran Perempuan as a hub in which women study feminist thought, learn from one another and pursue their individual or collective projects with the support of other members of the group. Women who are featured at ETALASE often become part of a network and continue their involvement as colleagues or guest teachers of Sekolah Pemikiran Perempuan. I will focus on the narratives of three feminists—Erni Aladjai, Septina Layan and Martha Hebi—that show how feminists across the archipelago collaborate while acknowledging difference, rather than erasing it, to dismantle colonial, capitalist and heteropatriarchal knowledge production.

Erni Aladjai, a novelist and non-fiction writer from Banggai, Central Sulawesi, focuses her work on capturing the experiences of women in eastern Indonesia as a way to interrogate the exclusion of eastern Indonesian women from knowledge production. She became part of the Sekolah Pemikiran Perempuan network after receiving a grant from Cipta Media Ekspresi to collect recipes for traditional medicine and publish them as a book titled *Ramuan Nenek* (Grandma's Herbs). In this project, she interviewed elder women in Banggai about how they use traditional medicine for reproductive health and pass the knowledge through oral tradition from generation to generation. Erni's project shows her attempt as a feminist writer to recognise the roles of women to produce local knowledge in their community. Erni is often referred to in the media as a woman writer or an eastern Indonesian woman writer, yet she reminds us that despite the 'woman' label, not all women writers are the same. Growing up on Labobo Island, a remote area in Banggai Islands, Erni's access to books was limited and she could connect to communities only after she studied in Makassar, a hub of arts and culture in eastern Indonesia. Erni uses the opportunities to speak at public forums and literary events to draw attention to inequalities of access to literature (Gramedia Pustaka Utama 2020).

Martha Hebi, a writer and activist from Sumba, East Nusa Tenggara, published *Perempuan (Tidak) Biasa di Sumba Era 1965–1998*, a book about fifteen women artists/activists in Sumba who have made important contributions to society but who have been overlooked by their male-dominated culture as well as the Jakarta/Java-centric cultural field and feminist discourses. In interviewing women figures, from Salomi Rambu Iru, who has been fighting the practice of kidnapping women for marriage (*kawin tangkap*—capture and wed), to Kahi Ata Ratu, a *jungga* artist and singer/songwriter, Martha identifies local feminist tactics used by women activists to push for change in the community while adhering to or negotiating with their culture. As a rare work that documents the roles of women in the Sumba community, written by a Sumbanese, Martha's book can be seen as an attempt to decolonise the writing of Indonesian feminist history that is largely centred in Jakarta and Java.

Martha received a Cipta Media Ekspresi grant to support her book research, participated in the 2022 Sekolah Pemikiran Perempuan classes, and has been involved in ETALASE as a speaker and co-organiser since 2020. In 2021, she co-organised a panel in ETALASE titled 'Manifesto Mama' in which she interviews Salomi Rambu Iru, one of the women she writes about in her book, about the violence against women in Sumba (SPP 2021b). Martha's active involvement in the event is an intervention to the common practice of cultural activism, in which women and minority groups outside the cultural centres are incorporated as tokens rather than as decision-makers. Further, it contributes to the discourse on sexual violence in Indonesia. The discourse around the Sexual Violence Bill, which became the centre of national feminist struggles for many years before it became law in 2022, might have re-centred the struggles of feminist groups that engaged in the process of lobbying the government in Jakarta as well as the experiences of middle-class women through the anti–sexual violence media campaigns supported by brands such as The Body Shop and L'Oreal (Aurelia 2021). The ETALASE panel co-organised by Martha pushes for a non-urban narrative of sexual violence; it addresses the challenges of anti–sexual violence activists in dealing with people and institutions who use *adat* to justify discrimination against women.

Another feminist who works within a trans-archipelagic decolonial feminist trajectory is composer and ethnomusicologist Septina Layan, who participated in the 2022 Sekolah Pemikiran Perempuan and has been involved in the music panel at ETALASE since 2020. Septina has been focusing on the lament tradition of Papuan music for her research and creative project as a musician. After several discussions and encounters facilitated by Sekolah Pemikiran Perempuan, she mentioned she had learned to critically view how her identity complicates her practice and research. Septina's parents were originally from Maluku, but she was born and raised in Merauke, Papua, and her Papuan-influenced music has travelled nationally and internationally. She asks questions about who benefits from the circulation of Papuan music and culture and how to make sure that the process of cultural production is fair for the Papuan people. In particular, Septina learned from Papuan feminist scholar Els Tieneke Rieke Katmo, who spoke at ETALASE about colonialism in the Papuan context and taught in the anti-colonial module of Sekolah Pemikiran Perempuan. Through Els Tieneke Rieke Katmo's presentations, Septina was introduced to the writings of indigenous scholar Linda Tuhiwai Smith (1999) on decolonising research methodology. Reflecting on the relation

Chapter 14 Feminist intervention in cultural activism　　277

between feminist knowledge and her own practice, Septina is committed to exploring ethical, non-colonial and non-capitalist ways of circulating Papuan knowledge and ideas outside Papua. Septina's case reveals the trajectory of feminist knowledge connecting herself, Els Tieneke Rieke Katmo and Linda Tuhiwai Smith, enabled by trans-archipelagic decolonial feminist spaces. Cosmopolitan, decolonial feminist thinking circulates in a way that situates women in the Global South as sources of knowledge production.

Conclusion

It has been twenty years since Saparinah Sadli claimed that 'feminism' is not widely accepted in Indonesia. Her statement is still relevant if we consider the patriarchal manoeuvres of the conservative groups, but feminist discourses have become part of the national imagination through contentious debates around bodies and sexuality regarding the Pornography Law and the Sexual Crime Law. More women identify as feminists and circulate feminist discourses through various channels, through writing, public discussions, street rallies and digital platforms. The backlash against feminism shown by conservative anti-feminist movements demonstrates a growing anxiety around the visibility of feminism.

In this chapter, I have focused on the latest developments in feminist thinking and practice in Indonesia in the field of arts and culture. Indonesian women are still trying to deal with the knowledge gap left by the destruction of socialist feminism and the massive feminist organisation Gerwani. The rise of neoliberal feminism, which demonstrates an intimate relationship between feminism and capitalism, can be viewed as an implication of this gap. However, a trans-archipelagic decolonial feminist trajectory is emerging as a new direction: women are working collectively to dismantle the structural exclusion of and invalidation of women's knowledge and interrogate the domination of the West as well as western Indonesia/Java in the processes of knowledge production. Drawing attention to geographical and cultural differences that shape women's experiences, they reject the universalising notion of feminism that often characterises the rhetoric of liberal and neoliberal feminisms. While conversations around feminism have re-emerged globally via movements such as #MeToo and Women's March, it is important to remind ourselves that feminism is not singular anywhere. Indonesian feminisms show that women continue to find ways to dismantle structures of colonial and patriarchal oppression while acknowledging difference and ruptures within the feminist movement.

278   *Intan Paramaditha*

References

Abhiseka, Arya. 2003. 'Attack on Inul is against freedom of expression'. *Jakarta Post*, 3 May.

Alsair, Ach Hidayat. 2021. 'Sikapi masalah gender, seniman perempuan bentuk perkumpulan Puan Seni' [In response to gender issues, female artists form an Association of Women of the Arts]. *IDN Times*, 9 March. https://sulsel.idntimes.com/news/indonesia/ahmad-hidayat-alsair/sikapi-masalah-gender-seniman-perempuan-bentuk-perkumpulan-puan-seni

Arimbi, Diah. 2009. *Reading Contemporary Indonesian Muslim Women Writers: Representation, Identity and Religion of Muslim Women in Indonesian Fiction.* Amsterdam University Press. www.jstor.org/stable/j.ctt46n07t

Arivia, Gadis and Nur Iman Subono. 2017. *A Hundred Years of Feminism in Indonesia: An Analysis of Actors, Debates and Strategies.* Friedrich Ebert Stiftung Indonesia. https://library.fes.de/pdf-files/bueros/indonesien/13830.pdf

Aurelia, Joan. 2021. 'Yang tersembunyi di balik misi produk kecantikan mendukung RUU PKS' [What's hidden behind beauty brands campaigning for the Sexual Violence Bill] *Tirto.id*, 23 July. https://tirto.id/yang-tersembunyi-di-balik-misi-produk-kecantikan-mendukung-ruu-pks-ghYG

Blackburn, Susan. 2010. 'Feminism and the women's movement in the world's largest Islamic nation'. In *Women's Movements in Asia: Feminisms and Transnational Activism*, edited by Mina Roces and Louise Edwards, 21–33. Routledge.

Ginsburg, Faye. 2016. 'Indigenous media from U-Matic to YouTube: Media sovereignty in the digital age'. *Sociologia & Antropologia* 6(3): 581–99. doi.org/10.1590/2238-38752016v632

Gramedia Pustaka Utama. 2020. 'Perempuan penulis dan ruangnya' [Women writers and their space]. 11 November. www.youtube.com/watch?v=qmnrLrF6pkA

Hebi, Martha. 2019. *Perempuan (Tidak) Biasa di Sumba Era 1965–1998* [Extraordinary women in Sumba, 1965–1998]. Alteras Publishing.

Hellwig, Tineke. 2011. 'Abidah El Khalieqy's novels: Challenging patriarchal Islam'. *Bijdragen tot de taal-, land- en volkenkunde/Journal of the Humanities and Social Sciences of Southeast Asia* 167(1): 16–30. doi.org/10.1163/22134379-90003600

Indirani, Feby. 2020. '"All male authors" di nominasi penghargaan sastra 2020 Badan Bahasa' ['All male authors' in the Language Agency's 2020 literary award nominations]. *MAGDALENE*, 3 September. https://magdalene.co/story/all-male-authors-di-nominasi-penghargaan-sastra-2020-badan-bahasa

Liputan6. 2002. 'Ria Irawan: Membicarakan vagina jangan dianggap tabu' [Ria Irawan: Talking about vaginas should not be taboo]. *Liputan6*, 11 March. https://www.liputan6.com/news/read/30478/ria-irawan-membicarakan-vagina-jangan-dianggap-tabu

Mohanty, Chandra Talpade. 2003. *Feminism without Borders: Decolonizing Theory, Practicing Solidarity.* Duke University Press. doi.org/10.1515/9780822384649

Nurmila, Nina. 2011. 'The influence of global Muslim feminism on Indonesian Muslim feminist discourse'. *Al-Jami'ah: Journal of Islamic Studies* 49(1): 33–64. doi.org/10.14421/ajis.2011.491.33-64

Chapter 14 *Feminist intervention in cultural activism* 279

Phipps, Alison. 2020. *Me, Not You: The Trouble with Mainstream Feminism.* Manchester University Press.

Rottenberg, Catherine. 2014. 'The rise of neoliberal feminism'. *Cultural Studies* 28(3): 418–37. doi.org/10.1080/09502386.2013.857361

Sabarini, Prodita. 2016. '"The Silent Song of Genjer Flowers": Against despair through storytelling'. *Jakarta Post*, 22 August. www.thejakartapost.com/news/2016/08/22/the-silent-song-genjer-flowers-against-despair-through-storytelling.html

Sadli, Saparinah. 2002. 'Feminism in Indonesia in an international context'. In *Women in Indonesia: Gender, Equity and Development*, edited by Kathryn Robinson and Sharon Bessell, 80–91. ISEAS Publishing. doi.org/10.1355/9789812305152-014

Sadli, Saparinah. 2010. *Berbeda tetapi Setara: Pemikiran tentang Kajian Perempuan* [Different but Equal: Thought's on Women's Studies]. Penerbit Buku Kompas.

SPP (Sekolah Pemikiran Perempuan). 2021a. 'Rantau: Settler colonialism and transnational solidarity'. Etalase Pemikiran Perempuan, 25 July. www.youtube.com/watch?v=h_FW2q08zqI&t=7s

SPP (Sekolah Pemikiran Perempuan). 2021b. 'Manifesto Mama: Kekerasan seksual dan komunitas adat' [Mama's manifesto: Sexual violence and indigenous communities]. Etalase Pemikiran Perempuan, 25 July. www.youtube.com/watch?v=-KTGG3Pwle0&t=4s

Suryakusuma, Julia. 2004. *Sex, Power and Nation: An Anthology of Writings, 1979–2003*. Metafor Publishing.

Tuhiwai Smith, Linda. 1999. *Decolonizing Methodologies: Research and Indigenous Peoples*. Zed Books.

Yuniar, Resty Woro. 2022. 'Indonesia's Oxford, Stanford-educated influencer Maudy Ayunda faces heat over G20 role as Russia debacle grows'. *South China Morning Post*, 20 April. www.scmp.com/week-asia/people/article/3174874/indonesias-oxford-stanford-educated-influencer-maudy-ayunda-faces

Yuristiawan, Rivan. 2018. 'Ubah stigma kuno, Maudy Ayunda berbicara tentang women empowerment' [Challenging age-old stigma, Maudy Ayunda talks about women's empowerment]. *Fimela.com*, 19 November. www.fimela.com/entertainment/read/3695029/ubah-stigma-kuno-maudy-ayunda-berbicara-tentang-women-empowerment

15 Male caregiver protagonists on the silver screen: A middle-class biased shift of ideal masculinity

Evi Eliyanah

In the first two decades of the twenty-first century, Indonesia was recovering from multiple crises. It struggled to recover its economy after the Asian financial crisis of 1997–1998. When the economy stabilised, the COVID-19 pandemic hit hard in 2020–2021. The global health disaster led to crises in various sectors, including again in the economy, with businesses dwindling and many people losing their jobs due to mobility restrictions. The period also saw the country re-establish itself as a democratic country after the demise of the New Order (1966–1998) authoritarian regime. The democratisation of the public sphere led to the flourishing of civil society movements and an intensifying Islamisation. Among the civil society movements were feminist and LGBTQI movements, which previously had been carefully controlled by the authoritarian regime. In addition, Islamisation became the most striking feature in politics, the economy and culture of the period. Interactions between these movements triggered major changes and debates within Indonesian gender politics. They partly called into question the patriarchal gender order (see Robinson, this volume) and thus the legitimacy of *bapakism*, which is mainly premised in men's breadwinning, leadership in family and society, and heteronormativity as the official and dominant ideal of masculinity (Suryakusuma 2011: 5).

During the period, Indonesian cinema flourished, with emerging filmmakers seeking to engage with various sociocultural transformations in the post-authoritarian landscape. Indonesian cinema was reinvigorated by the emergence of a new generation of filmmakers (Sasono 2012)

Chapter 15 Male caregiver protagonists on the silver screen 281

who were eager to take part in the country's democratisation process through cinema. During the COVID-19 pandemic, the film industry was also affected. Production and consumption declined due to mobility restrictions. Yet, alternative screening methods through on-demand platforms flourished. Once the restrictions were eased in 2021, production increased, albeit with new rules in place to prevent the spread of the disease among crew. Consequently, Indonesian cinema became one of the most important arenas for gender politics, including the struggle to secure a new form of ideal masculinity in Indonesia. Filmmakers who were critical of the patriarchal gender order and hegemonic masculinity experimented and innovated with alternative ideal masculinities in their works.

My study examines the nexus between gender politics and cinema. I look at commercial filmmakers' roles in the broader struggles to steer the gender order through the cinematic representation of ideal masculinity. I unpack filmmakers' choices, negotiations and compromises in shaping what could and could not be represented, thus also idealised, on screen during this period in Indonesia. Combining textual analysis on three selected films—*7/24* (7 days 24 hours, 2014, directed by Fajar Nugros), *Hijab* (2015, directed by Hanung Bramantyo) and *Cinta Pertama, Kedua dan Ketiga* (First, Second and Third Love, 2021, directed by Gina S. Noer)— and media discourse analysis, I discuss how the filmmakers behind the selected films engaged with contemporary gender politics as they challenged the hegemony of *bapakism*, and what these cinematic examples can tell us about the transformations in Indonesia's gender order during the *reformasi* era.

In the cinematic arena, 'new man' masculinity, characterised by emotional sensitivity and a willingness to compromise breadwinning roles, share day-to-day domestic and caring responsibilities, and foster equal gender relations of power, emerged as one of the most prevalent alternative ideals. I use the filmmakers' efforts to legitimise the new man through commercial cinema as my investigative lens. The selected films emphasise a renegotiation of gender relations of labour at the household level and recast men's domestic and caring responsibilities as imperative and favourable.

I reveal that while promoting such alternative masculinity that values more fluid and equal gender relations, the films were riddled with middle-class biases. The cinematic idealisation of domestically involved and caregiving men can be seen as an attempt to break away from *bapakism's* rigid and unequal gender relations of labour: the breadwinning men and homemaking women. Yet, these depictions cater heavily to the world view and experience of Indonesian middle-class professionals, rather

282   *Evi Eliyanah*

than the lower class, who can barely choose who gets to stay at home. I reflect on the consequence of these representations, while arguing for more inclusive cinematic representation in challenging the enduring gender ideals.

My study contributes to the existing literature on Indonesian gender politics of the twenty-first century by offering a different vantage point: the efforts of filmmakers to challenge the existing hegemonic masculinity ideal through commercial cinema. In this niche study, discussion on men and masculinity, let alone in pop culture, is still scant. I engage with the works of Tom Boellstorff (2004), Rebecca Elmhirst (2007), Pam Nilan (2009), Kathryn Robinson (2015) and Sonja van Wichelen (2009) in exploring the masculine dimension of Indonesian gender politics in the post–New Order period. I also contribute to this scholarship by exploring the class dimension of the struggle. Commercial filmmakers are a representation of urban-based and highly educated middle classes. Their political expressions may differ from that of lower-class men, who were likely to resort to violence against the growing involvement of women in paid work, as they themselves faced dwindling income and employment opportunities (Elmhirst 2007). I offer insights into the nuances of political expressions, which are strongly influenced by class.

I am particularly interested in the representations of gender relations at the household level in the struggle for hegemonic masculinity. As suggested by Micaela di Leonardo (1987: 441) and Carla Jones (2004: 511–12), it is often at this private level—in household spaces—that men and women constantly negotiate inequalities resulting from the officially prescribed gender relations, including of labour. The cinematic representations of gender and gender relations at the household level are popular imaginings of how such negotiations are engaged with in real life.

Overturning *bapakism* by promoting the new man masculinity

This section analyses the films' narratives and situates their representations of an alternative masculine ideal—the new man—within the tradition of ideal masculinity in Indonesian cinema. I demonstrate that the filmmakers' innovation behind the films departs from the hegemonic idealisation of *bapakism* on Indonesia's silver screen. By punishing breadwinning-obsessed professionals and idealising men who are actively involved in everyday domestic and caring duties, the alternative ideal promoted by the filmmakers in these films indicates a possibility of more equal gender relations of production.

Chapter 15 Male caregiver protagonists on the silver screen 283

7/24 is a romantic comedy about a Jakarta-based young married couple, who struggle to find a balance between career and family. The couple, Tyo, a director, and Tania, a banker, have been married for five years and have a daughter. Tension builds up as their careers take off, and reorganisation of the gender relations of labour at home becomes inevitable. Due to overwork, Tyo falls ill and is admitted to hospital. Tania, who is eyeing a career promotion, must juggle the domestic and caring work at home, caring for her husband at the hospital and her own increasing work demands. Unable to physically cope, Tania becomes ill and is admitted to the same hospital suite. Tania blames Tyo for not having time to do his share of the domestic and caring duties. Tyo blames Tania for being a workaholic and obsessed with her career's progression. They are on the brink of separation because Tania feels that Tyo cannot be an equal partner at home. The conflict is finally resolved by Tyo apologising to Tania and negotiating his work demands, so that he can share the day-to-day domestic and caring responsibilities with Tania at home. Thus, he can provide room for his wife to professionally grow.

Also a comedy, *Hijab* follows four young urban-educated Muslim middle-class couples as they struggle to renegotiate gender relations when the women's careers take off, while the men's either stagnate or decline. The three married couples are Sari and Gamal, Bia and Matnur, and Tata and Ujul. Gamal, of Arab descent, Sari's husband, is a public servant at a Jakarta tax office. Matnur, Bia's husband, is a famous actor. Ujul, Tata's husband, is a successful photographer. The single woman, Anin, acts as an observer and a reminder to the others of women's premarital independent selves. Anin's boyfriend, Chucky, is a progressive independent filmmaker who often questions the conservative gender relations displayed by the other couples. Conflicts develop around the couples' inability to cope with the changing landscape of gender relations of labour. The four women build a fashion business together without their spouses knowing. As the business grows rapidly, they find it difficult to juggle double burdens. As the husbands' careers dwindle or stagnate and their wives' business flourishes, the men, except Chucky, feel threatened by the financial success of their wives. Frustrated, the husbands blame their wives for abandoning the family. Except for Sari and Gamal, the domestic conflict is finally resolved by a renegotiation of the gender relations of labour. While Ujul and Matnur recognise the significant financial contribution of their wives and become willing to share in the day-to-day domestic and caring duties, Chucky proves that he is an ideal masculine man as he always believes in equal contributions of husband and wife in breadwinning and caregiving. Gamal, however, the representation of a conservative Muslim

284   *Evi Eliyanah*

who believes that breadwinning is a man's duty, is persistent and makes his wife withdraw from the business venture.

The final film I examine is *Cinta Pertama, Kedua dan Ketiga*. Written and directed by Gina S. Noer, the film revolves around Raja and Asia, who have to take care of their ageing parents and grandparent. Their affection towards each other is complicated by the fact that their parents Dewa (Raja's father, a widower) and Linda (Asia's mother, a divorcee) fall in love and get married. Raja is the youngest of three siblings. His two older sisters have moved out of home and built their own families. Both Raja's father and grandmother suffer from different stages of Alzheimer's disease. It is Raja's quality as a caregiver that appeals to Asia despite his financial difficulties. Asia is Linda's only child. Asia must take care of her mother, who was a victim of domestic abuse and a breast cancer survivor. The conflicts sharpen as Raja struggles to find a stable job while his father's Alzheimer's progresses, and his love for Asia becomes even more complicated as their parents marry. His older sisters put a lot of caregiving pressure on him as he is the youngest and still lives with their father and grandmother. The multiple conflicts are eventually resolved with Raja's acceptance of his role as the primary caregiver and his family's acceptance of his relationship with Asia. He is no longer obsessed with finding a decent paying job and is willing to work with Asia to make ends meet. His sisters are not pressured to take the father in either.

These films, instead of pressuring women to return to their normalised gender roles, place the onus on men. These men must abandon their *bapakism* and reconfigure their masculinities in order to accommodate changes in the gender relations in their households. Drawing from discourses of gender equality, these new men negotiate their breadwinning roles and become more involved in domestic and caring duties, in some cases becoming the primary caregiver. Rather than feeling pressured, subordinated or frustrated, they take pride in not being the primary or sole breadwinners for their families. Furthermore, it makes them more desirable and worthier in the eyes of their wives and family. In short, these films render breadwinning as a less important practice in defining ideal masculinity.

Contemporaries to the cinematic new man, magazines and tabloids are also introducing more fluid gender relations of production at the household level. Men's lifestyle magazines published in Indonesia, such as *Emporium*, *FHM Indonesia* and *Playboy Indonesia*, highlight alternative ideals that encourage men to accommodate women's involvement in the public sphere (Handajani 2010). Parenting tabloids such as *Ayah Bunda* promote a 'New Father' masculinity that encourages men to be more involved in caregiving (Yulindrasari and McGregor 2011). Women's lifestyle magazine

Chapter 15 Male caregiver protagonists on the silver screen 285

Femina was no exception with its 2014 year-end edition, which explored contemporary ideal masculinity in Indonesia. The edition highlighted the different perspectives between Indonesian men and women—especially the middle classes—about ideal masculinity in contemporary Indonesia. In short, the normalised emphasis on breadwinning in defining an ideal masculinity was no longer taken for granted.

The three films also challenge the normalised idealisation of *bapakism* in Indonesian cinema. Hegemonic *bapakism* featured strongly in films produced during the New Order era. Ideal masculine men were depicted as naturally breadwinning. According to Sen (1994: 148), at least until 1991, none of the films winning the most coveted categories in Festival Film Indonesia (the biggest annual film festival, sponsored by the state) defied men's ultimate role as the family breadwinner and protector, and women's role as the procreator and homemaker. State-sponsored propaganda films, such as *Pengkhianatan G-30S/PKI* (The Treachery of the 30 September Movement, 1984, Arifin C. Noer), also glorified *bapakism* by making their male heroes ideal father figures (Paramaditha 2007). Moreover, at least until the late 1980s, the most common narrative resolution to the conflicts stemming from the changing gender relations of labour is the restoration of the breadwinning man/homemaking wife gender relations, which sustains *bapakism*. In the 1990s, for example, *Sesal* (Regret, 1994, Sophan Sophiaan), which explores the changing relations of labour between a diplomat wife and her writer husband, resorts to idealising a wife shouldering the double burden—as breadwinner and homemaker—without punishing the violent emasculated husband. So, unlike their predecessors, the films in my analysis defy the significance of breadwinning as central to defining ideal masculinity.

Around the release of the three films, there were other commercial films whose narratives were driven by men's helplessness and frustration at economic hardships. However, the other films, such as *Mengejar Matahari* (Chasing the Sun, 2004, Soedjarwo) and *Sembilan Naga* (Nine Dragons, 2006, Rudi Soedjarwo), reproduce the breadwinning men/homemaking women gender relations and valorise *bapakism* masculinity. Marshall Clark (2008, 2010) contends these films normalise the widespread violence committed by Indonesian men as a masculine response towards the 1997–1998 economic crisis. Furthermore, the flourishing of Islamisation in Indonesian consumer culture has provided religious overtones to the cinematic representation of men's responses to their emasculation during the said period. Alicia Izharuddin (2017) asserts that stoicism and spiritual devotion are central to solving Muslim men's economic problems, such as depicted in *Kun Fayakuun* (When God Wills It, So Be It, 2008, Guntur Novaris) and *Emak Ingin Naik Haji* (Mother Desires to Go on

286   *Evi Eliyanah*

a Hajj Pilgrimage, 2009, Aditya Gumay). The economically disempowered men in the films restore their masculinities by reinstating their roles as the families' breadwinners, thus reinforcing *bapakism* as the culturally exalted masculinity.

7/24, *Hijab* and *Cinta Pertama, Kedua dan Ketiga* offer an alternative solution. The films promote new man masculinity as a solution to the disempowerment of men and the increasing economic independence of women in contemporary Indonesia. The new man masculinity, which does not place primacy on male breadwinning, is depicted as liberating for men by allowing men to not be the sole or primary breadwinners, and by encouraging men to be more involved in domestic and caring duties. Male frustration, let alone violence, is considered an undesirable masculinist response.

Behind-the-scenes politics

This section discusses how the filmmakers of the selected films engaged with contemporary gender politics and the political economy of cinema behind the scenes. I argue that the filmmakers' innovation of alternative ideal masculinity is a form of political intervention aimed at steering the official gender order towards accommodating the changing roles of men in the domestic sphere and redefining ideal masculinity.

Cinematic representation of an alternative ideal like the new man was to redress the situation in which women had been bearing a disproportionate moral burden in the shifting structures of the gender relations of production in Indonesia. Various groups, such as conservative Muslims, interested in restoring the established breadwinning men/homemaking women to the gender relations of labour, and thus the hegemony of *bapakism* masculinity, worked to reinstate women's reproductive and domestic roles. These interest groups sought to limit women's involvement in the public sphere, including in the economy and politics through, for instance, curfews, dress codes and reinforcing ideas of motherhood. Thus, the portrayal of alternative ideals in the selected films was part of the filmmakers' efforts to redress this problem by inviting their audiences to reflect on the social construction of ideal masculinity.

The creative producer of *7/24* is Lukman Sardi, also a masculinity activist. Sardi has been a celebrity champion of the global fatherhood campaign MenCare+, also known as Laki-laki Peduli in Indonesia, since 2013. The campaign was founded on the belief that equal gender relations at home would prevent domestic violence (van Bemmelen 2015: 22). The campaign resonated with Sardi's personal concern that men must not

Chapter 15 Male caregiver protagonists on the silver screen   287

merely position themselves as breadwinners; instead, men should share the domestic work and child-rearing roles equally (Antara 2014). Sardi, in a parenting talk show, highlighted that men's involvement in everyday domestic and caring duties are signs of their being progressive:

> Men should not be embarrassed for doing domestic work, which is stereotypically feminine. Previously, these men were categorised as *cemen* [less masculine] by other men, but these days men should no longer care with such gender labels ... Men must be caring, more than just breadwinning. (Setiawan 2014)[1]

In so saying, Sardi recognises the changing landscape of gender relations in contemporary Indonesia, which requires shifting the ideal of masculinity from breadwinning to a caregiving focus—the central theme of 7/24. According to Affandi Abdul Rachman, the executive producer of the film, in an interview with Kania Kismadi (2014):

> (Lukman Sardi and I) would like to tell a story of relationships ... of husband–wife ... We'd also like to explore gender issues. Primarily it is because most of us [Indonesians] still think that women should not be this or that, and men should not be this or that.

Sardi and Rachman developed the film's synopsis, narrative and characterisation. The director, Fajar Nugros, in an interview with Reino Ezra of *Muvila*, mentioned that he was hired when the production was ready for filming (Ezra 2014). In short, the producers' vision of the narrative becomes more poignant in determining the narrative and character development of the film.

The filmmakers behind *Hijab* and *Cinta Pertama, Kedua dan Ketiga* also have personal concerns regarding gender ideals. They are professionally connected and have a history in making films highlighting gender and gender relations. Both directors worked together in *Ayat-ayat Cinta* (Verses of Love, 2008) and *Perempuan Berkalung Sorban* (Woman with Turban, 2009). Caregiving and non-breadwinning men are always present in their films.

In *Hijab*, Bramantyo also worked with his wife, Zaskia A. Mecca, who became the producer, costume designer, casting director and an actress playing one of the main female characters. Mecca's experience of building her Muslim fashion empire and her changing relationship to her husband, Bramantyo, were central to the development of the film's narrative. By the time *Hijab* was produced in 2014, her business had grown 100-fold (Nurdiansyah 2017). *Hijab* is a response to women's increased

---

1 *Cemen* is a colloquial adjective and abbreviation of *cetek mental*, literally meaning shallow mentality. Here, it indicates a man's inability to exhibit bravery, generally expected of his gender.

involvement in paid work. While not specifically mentioning a number, Bramantyo confirms that he earns less than his wife and consequently they must renegotiate their gender relations of production (personal interview, 21 April 2014). Indeed, in a patriarchal society, a high-income wife challenges her husband's sense of masculinity because being a breadwinner is central to a man's gender identity (Brennan et al. 2001: 171). In Indonesia, a wife's higher income is often cited as a reason for an unhappy marriage (Rachmayani and Kumala 2016) and divorce (Kusuma 2016). When questioned by a journalist for his motive in making *Hijab,* Bramantyo implied that he was concerned by masculinist responses towards the spousal income gap (cited in Subkhan 2015a). Ultimately, the film makes the hegemonic *bapakism* irrelevant and shifts the onus onto men to cope with the changes occurring within the gender relations of production.

Hijab is also a critique of the conservative Islamist approach to women's increased participation in paid work. Amid the intensified Islamisation in post–New Order Indonesia, there were persistent attempts led by certain Islamist groups and individuals to reinforce women's reproductive and domestic roles. The attempts included the curbing of women's mobility in the public domain through regional by-laws (Wieringa 2006), public protests against deliberation of the Gender Equality and Equity Bill (Fadjar 2012), and social media campaigns that criticised working women as irresponsible mothers (Hestya 2013). By reinforcing women's reproductive and domestic roles, this conservative Islamist approach liberated men from taking part in negotiating potential changes. Through the character of Gamal, a stereotypical conservative Muslim man who is persistent about making his wife a full-time homemaker due to his religious beliefs, Bramantyo demonstrates that barring women from pursuing a career is old fashioned (cited in Subkhan 2015b). To do so, Bramantyo and his team behind *Hijab* shift the onus for change onto men.

Cinta Pertama, Kedua dan Ketiga is Gina S. Noer's second film as a director. She was better known as a film writer previously. In this film, Noer intended to capture the experience of the sandwich generation who have the pressures of raising their own families and at the same time caring for their ageing parents (and grandparents). Producing the film during the COVID-19 pandemic in 2020, Gina claims that the pressure experienced by this generation has been worsened by the multidimensional crises caused by the global health disaster. She herself is the youngest among her siblings, and the film is 'a love story to her parents', who are now in her care (Indo Zone 2022). Yet, she twists the narrative by making the youngest sibling character a man. Generally, Indonesian parents are more

Chapter 15 Male caregiver protagonists on the silver screen   289

comfortable living with their daughters than their sons, if such choice is available. This is partly normalised by the stereotype of women as caregivers, while men are breadwinners in the family, and the youngest child is the last sibling to stay with the parents after the older ones leave the nest. According to Noer, in an interview with Laraswaty (2021) of *Cinemags*, she wanted to offer a fresh perspective of what constitutes a family and how gender relations among family members are supposed to be waged. Noer highlights the complexity of the shifting gender relations of labour in the family partly by making the youngest child a male and the older siblings female. In this case, the character Raja has the social pressure as a man to have a stable job to prepare him to be the breadwinner of his future family. Yet at the same time he also faces pressure in providing care for the elderly in his family, work which consumes a lot of resources, time and energy.

However, like many other cases of political engagement, not all advocacy leads to immediate change. The fact that such representations were able to be produced and circulated without attracting excessive negative reactions means that change in gender relations is not as socially confronting as it would have been in the 1970s and 1980s. Off-screen attempts to promote the same type of alternative masculinity ideals through magazines, tabloids and the men's movement have not generated any substantial direct opposition. From this we can discern that film is not the only platform where the transformation of ideal representations of masculinity for the sake of equal gender relations are presented. These political struggles continue to compete with attempts to restore *bapakism* and its supporting femininity ideal, *ibuism*. For example, in late 2014, the newly elected vice-president, Jusuf Kalla, suggested that the Ministry of Manpower should reduce women civil servants' working hours by two hours every day so that women could perform their domestic and reproductive duties (Wibisono 2014). Due to strong protests from feminist activists, the suggestion was never followed up (Gabrillin 2014). In addition, the debate on what it takes to be ideal men and women continues to be forged by Indonesians in social media around husband–wife gender relations of production. With their television re-runs, reproduction on DVDs and on-demand viewings, as well as internet pirated copies, the three films remain potent challenges to the hegemonic *bapakism* and the official structure of the gender relations of labour.

290   *Evi Eliyanah*

Middle-class biases underly the glittering scenes of the new man in 7/24 and *Hijab*

Unfortunately, the filmmakers' efforts to promote an alternative ideal masculinity through the films described here is not free from class biases. The idealised new man masculinity is cast in characters that represent middle-class Indonesians who have relatively wider options in negotiating their masculine identity, despite economic hardship and a spousal income gap. The cinematic ideal, regardless of the filmmakers' intentions, excludes the ongoing struggle of lower-class Indonesian men in negotiating their everyday reality within the official and popular construction of ideal masculinities. Moreover, the cinematic ideal is cast in the interests of middle-class men in maintaining their professional jobs as markers of both gender and class.

Clearly, the selected films cast their masculine ideal figures as middle-class professional men. They live in formal settlement complexes in an urban neighbourhood in Jakarta, instead of in a suburb or rural area. They use private vehicles as their main mode of transportation, instead of public transport. They are highly educated and work in formal occupations: as a film director, a mid-ranking bureaucrat, a photographer, an actor. Even in their financial hardship, none of these families lives below the poverty line despite their lifestyle adjustments. They do not have to entirely give up their own careers either, albeit rearrangement is inevitable. Even then, they can still comfortably maintain their middle-class lifestyle.

The struggle of lower-class men in negotiating their masculinity around the changing gender relations of production is present, although sidelined, only in *Hijab*. Here, the struggle for the male protagonists to depict alternative ideal masculinity figures is juxtaposed with that of a lower-class man, in this case a parking ranger, who is negotiating his masculinity against the culturally most-exalted form.[2] The parking ranger is a representation of a complicit and stoic man who struggles to attain the cultural ideal of masculinity amid his economic disadvantage. As the choices of the middle-class men to be more actively involved in domestic and caring duties are depicted as a sign of modernity, the parking ranger's stoicism is depicted as his lack of knowledge and exposure to alternatives.

Furthermore, the idealisation is biased towards justifying the changing roles of men in dual-income middle-class households. The involvement of men in domestic and caregiving duties is not a new phenomenon but making it a defining feature of ideal masculinity is. Before the global campaigns pioneered by White Ribbon in the early 1990s and more

---

2   A parking ranger in Indonesia is an informally structured profession.

Chapter 15 Male caregiver protagonists on the silver screen 291

recently by MenCare+ and Aliansi Laki-laki Baru (New Men's Alliance) in twenty-first-century Indonesia, many Indonesian men shared domestic and caregiving duties, albeit not discursively constructed by the state and gender activists as progressive and ideal. For example, in households where mothers migrate for work overseas, lower-class men barely have any choice but to take care of the domestic and caring duties. By 2014 more than three and a half million women had migrated overseas for work. Although data on the marital status of female migrant workers is unavailable, van Bemmelen (2015) assumes that most of them were married, and they left their husbands and children behind. Nurul Inayah (2012), Theodora Lam and Brenda Yeoh (2018) and Tyas Wulan et al. (2018) agree that while in some cases some households receive assistance from female relatives, left-behind men tend to become the primary caregivers for their children and primary caretakers of domestic work. Caregiving and giving up breadwinning are a necessary decision for men in these circumstances, rather than a sign of enlightenment. Thus, their involvement in caregiving and household chores is a marker of class—they are unable to afford the services of live-in domestic servants, a common practice among middle-class dual-income households.

Although this reality has been prevalent in many migrant worker–sending areas in Indonesia, the idealisation of men who are involved in domestic and caring duties became popular only in the twenty-first century when such images began to grace glossy magazines, tabloids, films and other pop culture products. Yulindrasari and McGregor (2011) highlight the class dimension of the representations of fathers in parenting tabloids by arguing that in catering to the need for information on parenting among the Indonesian middle classes, parenting tabloids like the popular *Ayah Bunda* promote the expansion of gender roles for fathers to also include being complementary caretakers, cognitive enhancers, children's entertainers and bravery trainers. In tabloids, representations of alternative ideals also recognise the increased participation of women in the public sphere (Handajani 2010). Men and women are depicted as sharing public-sphere roles, albeit to a certain limit. These new images of the ideal father are simultaneously a response to and recognition of women's roles outside the home.

Indonesian middle classes were faced with a pressing urgency to create alternative ideals like the new man partly because of massive economic shocks at the end of the twentieth century. Many middle-class Indonesians were among those hit hardest by the decline of real wages, inflation and soaring prices at the onset of the 1997–1998 crisis. Indeed, the economic downturn did not uniformly affect all Indonesians, including the plural middle classes (van Leeuwen 2011: 122). Yet, for many middle-class men who did not own their business, the economic crisis brought a very big income shock. Jessica Poppele et al. (1999) and James Smith et al. (2002) argued that the declining currency value significantly affected institutions that were reliant on foreign investment. These institutions apparently employed a high proportion of male labour and had been responsible for creating Indonesia's new middle classes. These included the construction sector, especially in Jakarta, where construction works were on hold, and the formal manufacturing sector, which was heavily reliant on imported materials (Cameron 2002: 145). A slightly different reality was experienced by middle-class women, who generally maintained some of their wage gains during the same period (Smith et al. 2002: 173). Consequently, middle-class men felt under the utmost pressure to perform their conventional masculine role as family breadwinners amid their decline of income.

As the economy stabilised with around 5 per cent growth annually, the COVID-19 pandemic hit hard and led to multidimensional crises. Before COVID-19 vaccines were introduced, many mobility restrictions, at both national and international levels, were implemented to prevent the further spread of the disease, which was first detected in Indonesia on 2 March 2020 (Nurita 2022). In the early period of the pandemic, Suryahadi et al. (2020) estimated that the Indonesian economic growth rate would contract between 4.2 per cent in the best-case scenario and −3.5 per cent in the worst-case scenario. While appreciating the mitigation and responses implemented by the Indonesian government, Suryahadi et al. (2021) highlighted that economic contraction inevitably led to the increase of poverty from 9.2 per cent to 10 per cent, pushing about 1.5 million people, especially those in the informal sector, into poverty. This condition also led to higher levels of anxiety, especially among the productive age group, 20–49 years, with a higher probability among those with lower levels of education (Megatsari et al. 2020). The gender dimension of the pandemic should not be overlooked. Women and children were more prone to be victims of domestic violence committed by men during the pandemic. The National Commission on Violence against Women, Komnas Perempuan, noted a 75 per cent increase in reported domestic violence against women during the pandemic, mostly committed by male partners and motivated by economic frustration (Amirullah 2021). In short, economic pressures tend to have gendered impacts. For men who adhere to the dominant construction of masculinity, the unbearable economic pressures tend to lead to frustration, which in some cases lead to victimisation of women and children.

Chapter 15 Male caregiver protagonists on the silver screen 293

The roles of women's and men's movements in advocating gender equality in post-authoritarian Indonesia should not be underestimated in motivating Indonesian middle classes, including commercial filmmakers, to reconfigure ideal masculinity. The flourishing feminist and women's movements struggles for gender equality eventually established a pathway for Indonesia's own Aliansi Laki-laki Baru. I mentioned the men's movement campaign earlier and how the partnership established by MenCare+ with Lukman Sardi had inspired the production of 7/24. These forces encouraged the middle classes to reconfigure ideal representations of masculinity around the gender relations of production (Hasyim 2009). These movements have provided a new meaning for men doing daily unpaid household chores and caregiving duties.

Interestingly, the idealisation of the new man in various parts of the world has paved the way for the idealisation of full-time stay-at-home fathers/husbands as representations of an ideal masculinity in parts of the United States and Europe. David Beckham, a former football player, has become a contemporary icon for the 'new man' father upon his retirement, while his wife continued to pursue her career in the fashion industry. Emily Sheridan (2013) portrays Beckham as supportive of his wife's career and enjoying his new role as full-time stay-at-home father. Beckham's masculinity reflects negotiation and extension of gender boundaries by 'bending the codes of masculinity' and diversifies the available options of masculinity, albeit within the context of a global consumerist society (Gee 2014). However, the idealisation of Beckham as a new man icon should not obscure the fact his financial security and social standing provide him with wider options in negotiating his masculinity.

Since the 2000s, full-time stay-at-home fathers have become an established alternative norm of masculinity in many Asian countries. In 2011, in Seoul, South Korea, there were 36,000 stay-at-home fathers, a 125 per cent increase from 2005 (Korea Times 2011). In Singapore, Theresa Tan (2015) reported that more than 10,000 men in Singapore chose to not be involved in paid work in 2014, which is triple the number in 2006. Apparently, as in Western societies, men who give up their jobs and become stay-at-home fathers/husbands are generally middle class and highly educated; they choose to care for their children, rather than being economically forced to do so (Jennings 2017).

Contrary to the abovementioned trend off-screen, the selected films in my study and almost all contemporary Indonesian commercial films do not extend the challenge of making a full-time stay-at-home father into an ideal figure of masculinity. All the male protagonists in the films continue to maintain their employment, although they had to renegotiate

294   *Evi Eliyanah*

their working arrangements, especially around timing and workload to accommodate their roles in day-to-day caring and domestic duties.

The absence of full-time stay-at-home fathers/husbands as figures representing an alternative ideal masculinity in Indonesian popular culture, including cinema, should be understood within the context of country-specific gender politics, which are rife with middle-class biases. Historically, breadwinning was not a defining feature of ideal representations of masculinity in Indonesia until the late nineteenth century. The emerging middle classes of the Netherland East Indies were prominent actors in the transformation of an ideal masculinity and a refashioning of the gender order amid modernisation and an Islamic revival at that time. Ideal middle-class households were culturally constructed in popular texts, such as magazines, as consisting of a breadwinning father who held a formal office job, and a homemaking mother who was central to the family's maintenance of a good marriage through hygiene and cleanliness (Nordholt 2011: 441). The magazine advertisements reflected the desire of the indigenous middle classes, inhabiting the centre of the late-colonial state but denied political power (ibid.: 440), to be involved with 'progress', partly by abandoning traditional gender roles. Breadwinning was thus not only a marker of gender but also of class.

Although the increasing significance of breadwinning in defining ideal masculinity never fully transformed Indonesian society at every level, clearly the reliance on male breadwinners and the idealisation of domestic-bound femininity became hegemonic during the New Order period through its gender politics. Partly through the discourse of *kodrat wanita* (women's biologically preordained roles), women are not naturally obligated to engage in paid work. When women earn an income, their financial contribution is discursively constructed as secondary to that of their husbands (Utomo 2012). The ideal discourse of femininity reinforced by the New Order eventually strengthened the idealisation of *bapakism*. Such idealisation implies the subordination and/or marginalisation of other masculinities that do not comply. Consequently, jobless men who are unable to provide for their family are often seen as somehow less masculine, or even a failure. Amid the rampant layoffs and bankruptcy experienced during the deep economic crisis in 1997–1998, middle-class men who lost their livelihood were ashamed of their incapacity to perform their conventional masculine role. In an ethnographic vignette, van Leeuwen (2011: 144) describes how an affluent middle-class man who lost his job due to the crumbling construction business would arrive at his friends' offices every morning at around nine o'clock and hang around until five o'clock in the afternoon. It was his way of coping with his job loss. Consequently, the on- and off-screen idealisation of men who can both keep their career and be actively involved in daily domestic and caring duties is biased towards justifying middle-class men's interests in keeping formal employment—a practice that simultaneously defines their gender and class identities.

Conclusion

This chapter has explained the attempts of Indonesian commercial filmmakers in undermining the hegemony of *bapakism* through their cinematic work. Their efforts to promote 'new man' masculinity as an alternative ideal depict more equal and fluid gender relations of production, albeit with biases towards Indonesian middle-class men.

A new hope is reflected in the filmmakers' rendering of breadwinning as an obsolete marker of ideal masculinity. The culturally most-exalted masculinity was depicted as putting immense psychological pressure on men who were unable to attain the ideal. This form of masculinity also constrained women in their career pursuits. The filmmakers' proposed alternative ideal new man allows men to take pride in their roles in the domestic and public sphere, instead of emasculating them. From my discussion of the film texts and behind-the-scenes politics, we can infer that the politically conscious filmmakers aimed at steering Indonesia's gender order into accommodating not only women's increased participation in the public sphere, including in paid work, but also the transformation of the cultural ideal of masculinity.

Yet, the filmmakers' works are constructed through the cultural lens of the Indonesian middle classes. The characters depicting the new man ideal are also representations of middle-class educated urban young men. These men's financial security and social standing offer them wider options in negotiating their masculine identity amid the profound changes in the gender relations of production at the household level. The old solution of hiring domestic assistants to fill in the absence of women in middle-class households (Elmhirst 2005; Jones 2004) is heavily challenged by the ethical decisions made by these educated middle-class men. The cinematic portrayals are also biased towards justifying middle-class men's interests in maintaining paid work as a marker of gender and class. The ideal middle-class masculine men do not abandon their paid jobs to embrace domestic and caring roles. Reflecting on the significance of paid work as a marker of class, encouraging middle-class men to give it up to support their spouse's career and fully participate in domestic and caring duties is still unimaginable.

Hence, politically conscious commercial filmmakers have attempted to include their perspectives on masculinity and the gender relations of labour in their films. The selected films are political vehicles through which the filmmakers expressed their engagement with contemporary gender politics and attempted to steer the gender order in a specific direction. Through the narrative and character development of the films, the filmmakers instilled their critique of the hegemonic ideal and promoted an alternative ideal masculinity despite the class biases.

To successfully stage their gender politics in commercial cinema, these filmmakers negotiated their intentions to inspire the transformation of a new hegemonic masculine ideal within the complex political-economic dimensions of commercial cinema. They may have benefited from working within a network of like-minded people. Furthermore, their own financial security that allowed them to partly finance the film, or their position within a film company, permitted the production of an alternative representation of an ideal masculinity. Yet these privileges in production were not necessarily followed by privileges in circulation. The filmmakers still had to negotiate with the state and public censorship so that their films could find an audience. Due to the absence of controversial elements, the films passed state censorship. Indeed, their takes on masculinity did not lead to substantial public debate or immediate social change. However, the absence of negative sentiments towards the alternative masculine ideal proposed in these films implies that such challenging representations were able to be produced and circulated during a time marked by profound changes in the structure of the gender relations of labour in Indonesia.

References

Amirullah. 2021. 'Kasus KDRT meningkat selama pandemi COVID-19' [Domestic violence cases increase during the COVID-19 pandemic]. *Tempo*, 20 August. https://nasional.tempo.co/read/1496559/kasus-kdrt-meningkat-selama-pandemi-covid-19

Antara. 2014. 'Lukman Sardi-Nia Dinata dukung Laki-laki Peduli' [Lukman Sardi and Nia Dinata support men care]. Antara, 19 December. www.antaralampung.com/berita/278378/lukman-sardi-nia-dinata-dukung-laki-laki-peduli

Boellstorff, Tom. 2004. 'The emergence of political homophobia in Indonesia: Masculinity and national belonging'. *Ethnos: Journal of Anthropology* 69(4): 465–86. doi.org/10.1080/0014184042000302308

Brennan, Robert T., Rosalind Chait Barnett and Karen C. Gareis. 2001. 'When she earns more than he does: A longitudinal study of dual-earner couples'. *Journal of Marriage and Family* 63(1): 168–82. www.jstor.org/stable/3599966

Chapter 15 *Male caregiver protagonists on the silver screen* 297

Cameron, Lisa. 2002. 'Women and the labour market during and after the crisis'. In *Women in Indonesia: Gender, Equity and Development*, edited by Kathryn Robinson and Sharon Bessell, 144–57. Institute of Southeast Asian Studies.

Clark, Marshall. 2008. 'Indonesian cinema: Exploring cultures of masculinity, censorship and violence'. In *Popular Culture in Indonesia: Fluid Identities in Post-authoritarian Politics*, edited by Ariel Heryanto, 37–53. Routledge.

Clark, Marshall. 2010. *Maskulinitas: Culture, Gender and Politics in Indonesia*. Monash University Press.

di Leonardo, Micaela. 1987. 'The female world of cards and holidays: Women, families, and the work of kinship'. *Signs* 12(3): 440–53. www.jstor.org/stable/3174331

Elmhirst, Rebecca. 2005. ' "Learning the ways of the Priyayi": Domestic servants and the mediation of modernity in Jakarta, Indonesia'. In *Gender, Migration and Domestic Service*, 2nd edition, edited by Janet Henshall Momsen, 237–57. Routledge.

Elmhirst, Rebecca. 2007. 'Tigers and gangsters: Masculinities and feminised migration in Indonesia'. *Population, Space and Place* 13(3): 225–38. doi.org/10.1002/psp.435

Ezra, Reino. 2014. 'Fajar Nugros tertantang bikin penonton tak bosan' [Fajar Nugros on how to not bore the audience]. *Muvila*, 28 November. [Accessed 12 May 2016; url no longer available.]

Fadjar, Evieta. 2012. 'Rancangan undang undang kesetaraan gender, masih kontroversi' [Gender equity bill is still controversial]. *Tempo*, 9 April. https://nasional.tempo.co/read/395838/rancangan-undang-undang-kesetaraan-gender-masih-kontroversi

Gabrillin, Abba. 2014. 'Komnas Perempuan: Pengurangan jam kerja perempuan akan mendiskriminasi' [National Commission on Violence against Women: Reduction of working hours for women will lead to discrimination]. *Kompas*, 3 December. https://nasional.kompas.com/read/2014/12/03/11263501/Komnas. Perempuan.Pengurangan.Jam.Kerja.Perempuan.Akan.Mendiskriminasi

Gee, Sarah. 2014. 'Bending the codes of masculinity: David Beckham and flexible masculinity in the new millennium'. *Sport in Society* 17(7): 917–36. doi.org/10.1080/17430437.2013.806034

Handajani, S. 2010. 'Selling alternative masculinities: Representations of masculinities in Indonesian men's lifestyle magazines'. PhD thesis. Perth: University of Western Australia.

Hasyim, N. 2009. 'Gerakan laki-laki pro-perempuan: Transformasi dua sisi' [Men's movement in support of women: Double-sided transformation]. *Jurnal Perempuan* 64: 53–65.

Hestya, Rindu P. 2013. 'Kicauan ustad Felix Siauw ramai di Twitter' [Felix Siauw's tweets attracted controversy in Twitter]. *Tempo*, 14 August. https://m.tempo.co/read/news/2013/08/14/219504253/kicauan-ustad-felix-siauw-ramai-di-twitter

Inayah, Nurul. 2012. 'Model pola asuh ayah dalam keluarga migran di Kabupaten Banyuwangi' [Fathers' child-rearing practices among migrant worker households in Banyuwangi Regency]. Paper presented to the Annual Conference on Islamic Studies, Surabaya, 5–8 November.

298   *Evi Eliyanah*

Indo Zone. 2022. 'Gina S Noer angkat polemik mengurus orang tua berbalut tantangan pandemi di film barunya' [Gina S. Noer dives into the problem of caregiving during the pandemic in her new film]. *Indo Zone*, 1 January. www.indozone.id/movie/BysAzyz/gina-s-noer-angkat-polemik-mengurus-orang-tua-berbalut-tantangan-pandemi-di-film-barunya/read-all

Izharuddin, Alicia. 2017. *Gender and Islam in Indonesian Cinema*. Palgrave MacMillan.

Jennings, Ralph. 2017. 'From Vietnam to Taiwan, why Asian fathers are caring more for their children'. *Forbes*, 15 June. www.forbes.com/sites/ralphjennings/2017/06/15/fathers-day-asia-why-asian-fathers-are-caring-more-for-their-children/?sh=238e44866660

Jones, Carla. 2004. 'Whose stress? Emotion work in middle-class Javanese homes'. *Ethnos: Journal of Anthropology* 69(4): 509–28. doi.org/10.1080/0014184042000302326

Kismadi, Kania. 2014. 'Wawancara eksklusif: Affandi Abdul Rachman, produser – 7 Hari 24 Jam' [An exclusive interview: Affandi Abdul Rachman, producer of 7 Days/24 Hours]. Ngobrolin Film, 20 October. https://ngobrolinfilm.blogspot.com/2014/10/wawancara-eksklusif-affandi-abdul.html

Korea Times. 2011. 'Number of Seoul's stay-at-home fathers surges 125 per cent since 2005'. *Korea Times*, 25 July. www.koreatimes.co.kr/www/nation/2023/07/113_91496.html

Kusuma, Edward Febriyatri. 2016. 'Gaji istri lebih besar dari suami juga picu ribuan perceraian di Jakarta' [Wives' bigger income led to thousands of divorces in Jakarta]. *DetikNews*, 18 November. https://news.detik.com/berita/d-3348877/gaji-istri-lebih-besar-dari-suami-juga-picu-ribuan-perceraian-di-jakarta

Lam, Theodora and Brenda S.A. Yeoh. 2018. 'Migrant mothers, left-behind fathers: The negotiation of gender subjectivities in Indonesia and the Philippines'. *Gender, Place and Culture: A Journal of Feminist Geography* 25(1): 104–17. doi.org/10.1080/0966369X.2016.1249349

Laraswaty, Nuty. 2021. 'Gina S Noer tentang film keduanya Cinta Pertama, Kedua dan Ketiga' (Gina S. Noer on her second film Cinta Pertama, Kedua dan Ketiga). *Cinemags*, 29 December. https://cinemags.org/gina-s-noer-tentang-film-keduanya-cinta-pertama-kedua-dan-ketiga/

Megatsari, Hario, Agung Dwi Laksono, Mursyidul Ibad, Yeni Tri Herwanto, Kinanty Putri Sarweni, et al. 2020. 'The community psychosocial burden during the COVID-19 pandemic in Indonesia'. *Heliyon* 6(10): e05136. doi.org/10.1016/j.heliyon.2020.e05136

Nilan, Pam. 2009. 'Contemporary masculinities and young men in Indonesia'. *Indonesia and the Malay World* 37(109): 327–44. doi.org/10.1080/13639810903269318

Nordholt, Henk Schulte. 2011. 'Modernity and cultural citizenship in the Netherlands Indies: An illustrated hypothesis'. *Journal of Southeast Asian Studies* 42(3): 435–57. www.jstor.org/stable/23020338

Nurdiansyah. 2017. '4 tahun meccanism, Zaskia Adya Mecca ungkapkan rasa syukur' [Four years of meccanism, Zaskia Adya Mecca expresses her gratitude]. *Tempo*, 14 January. https://cantik.tempo.co/read/836049/4-tahun-meccanism-zaskia-adya-mecca-ungkapkan-rasa-syukur

Nurita, Dewi. 2022. '2 tahun pandemi COVID-19, ringkasan perjalanan wabah corona di Indonesia' [2 years of the COVID-19 pandemic, a summary of the journey of the coronavirus outbreak in Indonesia]. *Tempo*, 3 March. https://nasional.tempo.co/read/1566720/2-tahun-pandemi-covid-19-ringkasan-perjalanan-wabah-corona-di-indonesia

Paramaditha, Intan. 2007. 'Contesting Indonesian nationalism and masculinity in cinema'. *Asian Cinema* 18(2): 41–61. doi.org/10.1386/ac.18.2.41_1

Poppele, Jessica, Sudarno Sumarto and Lant Pritchett. 1999. *Social Impacts of the Indonesian Crisis: New Data and Policy Implications.* SMERU Working Paper. https://mpra.ub.uni-muenchen.de/60931/

Rachmayani, F. and A. Kumala. 2016. 'Pengaruh perilaku dominan dan komitmen perkawinan terhadap kebahagiaan perkawinan pada istri bekerja yang memiliki penghasilan lebih tinggi dari suami' [The effect of dominant behaviour and marriage commitment on marital happiness in households where wives earn more than husbands]. *Jurnal Ilmiah Penelitian Psikologi: Kajian Empiris and Non-Empiris* 2(2): 1–13.

Robinson, Kathryn. 2015. 'Masculinity, sexuality and Islam: The gender politics of regime change in Indonesia'. In *Sex and Sexualities in Contemporary Indonesia: Sexual Politics, Health, Diversity and Representations*, edited by Linda Rae Bennett and Sharyn Graham Davies, 51–68. Routledge.

Sasono, E. 2012. 'The new generation (1990s and beyond)'. In *A Brief Cultural History of Indonesian Cinema*, 122–45. Ministry of Education and Culture, Republic of Indonesia.

Sen, Krishna. 1994. *Indonesian Cinema: Framing the New Order.* Zed Books.

Setiawan, Sakina Rakhma Diah. 2014. 'Lukman Sardi: Laki-laki yang enggak peduli keluarga itu "cemen"' [Lukman Sardi: Men who don't care about their families are unmanly]. *Kompas*, 30 November. http://female.kompas.com/read/2014/11/30/1548552/Lukman.Sardi.Laki-laki.yang.Enggak.Peduli.Keluarga.Itu.Cemen

Sheridan, Emily. 2013. 'Retired David Beckham settles into his new life as full-time dad and husband as he accompanies wife Victoria on shopping trip'. *Daily Mail*, 14 June. www.dailymail.co.uk/tvshowbiz/article-2341169/David-Beckham-settles-new-life-time-dad-husband-accompanies-wife-Victoria-shopping-trip.html

Smith, James P., Duncan Thomas, Elizabeth Frankenberg, Kathleen Beegle and Graciela Teruel. 2002. 'Wages, employment and economic shocks: Evidence from Indonesia'. *Journal of Population Economics* 15(1): 161–93. www.jstor.org/stable/20007804

Subkhan. 2015a. 'Film *Hijab*, komedi Muslim ala Hanung Bramantyo' [*Hijab* the movie, Hanung Bramantyo's version of a Muslim comedy]. *Tempo*, 14 January. https://m.tempo.co/read/news/2015/01/14/111634813/film-*Hijab*-komedi-muslim-ala-hanung-bramantyo

Subkhan. 2015b. 'Lewat film *Hijab*, Hanung kritik Muslim konservatif' [Through *Hijab* the movie, Hanung Bramantyo criticises conservative Muslims]. *Tempo*, 14 January. https://m.tempo.co/read/news/2015/01/14/111634810/lewat-film-*Hijab*-hanung-kritik-muslim-konservatif

Suryahadi, Asep, Ridho Al Izzati and Daniel Suryadarma. 2020. 'Estimating the impact of COVID-19 on poverty in Indonesia'. *Bulletin of Indonesian Economic Studies* 56(2): 175–92. doi.org/10.1080/00074918.2020.1779390

Suryahadi, Asep, Ridho Al Izzati and Athia Yumna. 2021. 'The impact of COVID-19 and social protection programs on poverty in Indonesia'. *Bulletin of Indonesian Economic Studies* 57(3): 267–96. doi.org/10.1080/00074918.2021.2005519

Suryakusuma, Julia I. 2011. *State Ibuism: The Social Construction of Womanhood in New Order Indonesia*. Komunitas Bambu.

Tan, Theresa. 2015. 'Mum's at work, dad's minding the kids'. *Straits Times*, 21 June. www.straitstimes.com/singapore/mums-at-work-dads-minding-the-kids

Utomo, Ariane J. 2012. 'Women as secondary earners'. *Asian Population Studies* 8(1): 65–85. doi.org/10.1080/17441730.2012.646841

van Bemmelen, Sita Thamar. 2015. *State of the World's Fathers Country Report: Indonesia*. Rutgers WPF Indonesia.

van Leeuwen, Lizzy. 2011. *Lost in Mall: An Ethnography of Middle-Class Jakarta in the 1990s*. KITLV Press.

van Wichelen, Sonja. 2009. 'Polygamy talk and the politics of feminism: Contestations over masculinity in a new Muslim Indonesia'. *Journal of International Women's Studies* 11(1): 173–87. https://vc.bridgew.edu/jiws/vol11/iss1/12

Wibisono, Gunawan. 2014. 'Wapres wacanakan kurangi jam kerja perempuan' [Vice-president calls for reduction of women's working hours]. *Okenews*, 25 November. https://news.okezone.com/read/2014/11/25/337/1070341/wapres-wacanakan-kurangi-jam-kerja-perempuan

Wieringa, Saskia Eleonora. 2006. 'Islamization in Indonesia: Women activists' discourses'. *Signs: Journal of Women in Culture and Society* 32(1): 1–8. doi.org/10.1086/505274

Wulan, T.R., D. Shodiq, S. Wijayanti, D.W.D. Lestari, A.T. Hapsari, et al. 2018. 'Ayah tangguh, keluarga utuh: Pola asuh ayah pada keluarga buruh migran perempuan di Kabupaten Banyumas' [Strong father, great family: Fathers' caring practices in Banyumas Regency]. *Jurnal Ilmu Keluarga dan Konseling* 11(2): 84–95.

Yulindrasari, Hani and Katharine McGregor. 2011. 'Contemporary discourses of motherhood and fatherhood in *Ayahbunda*, a middle-class Indonesian parenting magazine'. *Marriage and Family Review* 47(8): 605–24. doi.org/10.1080/01494929.2011.619304

Index

7/24 (film), 281, 283, 286–287
#MeToo, 269, 277

A

'Abduh, Muḥammad, 35
abortion, 24, 194, 196, 233
activism
  arts and culture, 263–277
  social media, 2, 36–37, 41–50
  visual arts, 5, 245–258
  women's rights, 9, 12, 26–27, 189, 192
Adii, Betty, 256–257
adultery, 196, 201
Afwah, Nyai, 38
Agatha, Cornelia, 267
ageing population, 28, 214–215
agriculture sector, 18, 133, 134–135
Agrivinna, Irene, 250
Ahmad, Ama, 271
AILA (Family Love Alliance Indonesia), 201, 202–203, 268
akhlak (piety), 198, 200
Aladjai, Erni, 275
ALB (New Men's Alliance), 253, 291, 293
al-Fasi, Hatoon, 26
Alfikar, Amar, 272
al-Hibri, Azizah, 47, 48
Aliansi Laki-laki Baru (New Men's Alliance), 253, 291, 293
Alimat (NGO), 40
al-Tahtāwī, Rifā'ah Rāfi', 35

Ambara, Alit, 251
ambassadors, 2–3, 70, 74, 80–83, 84
Amīn, Qāsim, 35
An-Na'im, Abdullahi Ahmed, 35
anti-communist killings, 249
Anzaldua, Gloria, 274
Arab Muslims, 18, 25
Arahmaiani, 251–252
Arivia, Gadis, 266, 267
Arkoun, Mohammad, 35
Armandhany, 273
ARTJOG 2022, 256
ARTJOG MMXXI, 248
arts sector, 5–6, 245–258, 264–277
Asian financial crisis, 9, 124, 127, 207, 280, 285, 291–292, 294
Asian parliaments, women's share, 76
aurat, 199
authoritarian rule, see New Order
Ayah Bunda (magazine), 284–285, 291
Ayat-ayat Cinta (film), 287
Ayu, Djenar Maesa, 266, 267
Ayunda, Maudy, 269
Ayuningtyas, Eka Jayani, 250–251
Azhari, Ayu, 267

B

Badan Bahasa literary awards, 270
Bakar, Siti Nurbaya, 16
Balinese art and culture, 248, 253
banci, 59
Bandung Contemporary Art Awards, 245

302 *Gender Equality and Diversity in Indonesia*

Bantuan Langsung Tunai (BLT), 207–208, 210, 218
  see also Dana Desa (Village Funds)
bapakism, 1, 6, 280, 281, 282–286, 289, 294, 295
Barlas, Asma, 44, 47, 48
Basuki, Fira, 266
Beckham, David, 293
beggars, 63–64
Beijing Platform for Action, 72
BidikMisi, 100
biological difference, 20–21
birth certificates, 236
bissu (shamen), 55–56, 56–57
Black Lives Matter, 273
BLT Dana Desa (Village Funds Direct Cash Assistance program), 214
boys, child marriage, 227
Bramantyo, Hanung, 281, 287–288
Burke, Tarana, 269
buskers, 63–64

C

cabinet ministers, *see* ministerial appointments
care work, 4, 95, 111–112, 133, 156–157, 164, 169–179, 211–212, 284, 290–291
  see also women: 'traditional roles'
cash transfer programs, 207, 209, 214, 216
  see also Bantuan Langsung Tunai (BLT); Family Hope Program (PKH)
CEDAW (Convention on the Elimination of All Forms of Discrimination against Women), 19, 72, 193
cellular networks, 147–149
cellular phone ownership, 158–159, 160
Center of Gender Studies, 44–45
child-bearing, 123, 134, 135–137, 152
childcare, 28, 134, 139–140, 211–212

child marriage
  applicant characteristics, 226–229
  child agency, 234–236, 237–238
  complexities, 5, 229–236
  court challenges, 22
  court dispensations, 225–226, 232–233, 235
  factors, 18, 24, 108–109, 224
  forced marriage, 224, 225, 230, 231
  gender-biased norms, 26, 230–233, 237
  girls, vulnerability, 226–227, 231
  government reform, 5, 28, 222
  harmful effects, 140–141
  impacts, 222–223
  policy requirements, 236–238
  prevalence, 223–224
  teenage pregnancy, 231–235, 237
children
  abandonment, 194–195
  immunisation, 99
  infant mortality, 103–104, 105
  sexual abuse of, 195–196
  stunting, 113–114
Chinese women, rapes of, 9, 22, 190, 249
Chotimah, Fanny, 265
cinema and gender politics, 6, 280–296
Cinta Pertama, Kedua dan Ketiga (film), 281, 284, 286, 287, 288–289
citizenship, *see* national identity
clothing
  manufacture, 19, 250
  religious, 40–41, 200–202
cohabitation, 196
colonial legacy of binary gender, 56
Communist Party, 191, 202, 249, 265
commuting time, 134, 138
Congress of Women Religious Scholars (KUPI), 2, 24, 26, 36, 204, 268
  see also KUPI networks
constitution
  electoral rules, 12
  human rights, 198
Constitutional Court, 10, 22
contemporary arts, 245–258

contraception, 11, 23–24, 99
Convention on Anti Torture, 198
Convention on the Elimination of All
    Forms of Discrimination against
    Women (CEDAW), 19, 72, 193
Convention on the Rights of the
    Child, 21
corruption and political
    appointments, 84
COVID-19
    arts sector impacts, 271
    care work burden, 110, 174–175
    child marriage, 109, 225, 230
    cinema, impacts on, 281
    economic impacts, 115, 175, 280
    education challenges, 108
    flexible working arrangements, 140
    health impacts, 113
    human development setbacks, 95,
        96, 107
    impact on women's lives, 110–111,
        114, 119, 156, 174–175
    labour force participation, 110–111
    social assistance programs, 213, 214
    socioeconomic impacts, 288, 292
Criminal Code
    public order, 63
    regulating gender, 54, 62, 64, 66
    regulating sexuality, 22
    revisions, 194–196
criminal justice system reform,
    185–204
customary relations, 11

D

Dana Abadi Kebudayaan arts fund,
    258
Dana Desa (Village Funds), 102, 214
    see also Bantuan Langsung Tunai
        (BLT)
Darmavati, I Gusti Ayu Bintang, 78
da'wa path, 41, 45, 49
de Beauvoir, Simone, 274
decentralisation
    health services, 23–24
    'legal disorder', 61
    political authority, 9–10, 14, 22–23

repression of minorities, 55, 62, 65
democracy, tensions, 203
deservingness, notion of, 5, 206, 208,
    213, 216–218
    see also Family Hope Program
        (PKH)
Dharma Wanita, 11, 265
digital activism, 2, 36–37, 41–50
digital economy, 3, 145–166
digital literacy, 159–164, 165
Digital Nation Roadmap 2021–2024,
    165
digital technology, 236, 263, 271
Dinata, Nia, 267
diplomats, 70, 74, 80–83, 84
Directorate of Culture, 258
Disadvantaged Villages Infrastructure
    Development Program, 102
Djuwita, Ratna, 251
domestic violence, 11, 22, 110, 114,
    177, 285, 292
domestic work, see care work
domestic worker profession, 4,
    176–178, 179
dynasties, political, 75, 77

E

e-commerce, 146, 150–151, 155
economic activity: care work, 111–112,
    171–179
economic growth, 94, 122, 127
economic policy, 114–117, 118
education
    and GDP, 94
    digital literacy, 164
    early childhood, 139
    endowment fund, 100
    gender gap, 70
    government budget, 94, 96, 100
    human capital development, 17,
        100–101, 104–106, 122, 123,
        125, 128–131
    learning indicators, 108–109
    women, 28, 101, 104, 108, 151, 169
Egypt, gender justice, 35
elderly population, 28, 214–215
electoral democracy, 12–14

304 Gender Equality and Diversity in Indonesia

electronics manufacture, 19
el-Fadl, Khaled Abou, 35, 44
El Khalieqy, Abidah, 268
el-Saadawi, Nawal, 44
Emak Ingin Naik Haji (film), 285
employment, *see* labour force
  participation
Empowering Household Economy
  program, 102
Engineer, Asghar Ali, 44
Ensler, Eve, 267
environmental waste, 250–251
ETALASE festival, 272, 275, 276
executive government, *see* ministerial
  appointments; political
  representation

F

Facebook, 146, 161, 163
Fahmina (NGO), 40, 42, 47
fakir miskin, 217, 218
Family Card (Kartu Keluarga), 209
Family Development Index, 170–171
Family Hope Program (PKH), 102,
  205, 209–213, 215, 216, 218
family ideology, 11, 25, 27, 57, 66
Family Love Alliance Indonesia
  (AILA), 201, 202–203, 268
Family Planning Program, 11, 23, 28,
  98–99, 125
Family Welfare Association (PKK), 11
Fauzi, Helmy, 80
Fauziyah, Ida, 79
female, concept of, 1, 10–11, 56
female sex workers, 60
feminism
  arts sector, 5–6, 247, 255–256,
    263–277
  decolonial thinking, 5–6, 273–277
  Java-centric, 270, 273, 274
  liberal feminism, 263, 266–270, 274
  neoliberal feminism, 269, 270, 277
  New Order era, 191, 264–266
  post-Islamist feminism, 43
  reformasi era, 266–270
  trans-archipelagic spaces, 270–277
  Western influence, 37–39, 42–43, 45,
    202

fertility rates, 23, 27–28, 99, 122, 125,
  127–128, 151, 169
Festival Film Indonesia, 285
filmmaking, 6, 280–296
fiscal policy, 114–117, 118
  social assistance programs, 216–217,
    218
fisheries sector, 214
Frankland, Emma, 248
fuel subsidies, 207
Futuwonder, 252–253

G

Gelar, Ambawani, 250
gender, binary model, 56, 57, 63
gender complementarity, 39, 40,
  42–43, 44, 48–49
gender (defined), 20
Gender Development Index, 104
gendered power, 10–11, 25
Gender Empowerment Measure, 104
gender equality
  advocacy, 293
  arts sector, 246
  care work, 4, 169–179
  constraints, 95
  digital economy, 3, 145–166
  economic indicators, 3, 122–141
  gender-just activists, 39, 40, 42–43,
    44, 46–49
  human capital development, 3,
    94–95
  policy and legislation, 185–204
  political representation, 15–17,
    70–84
  social assistance programs, 205–218
gender ideologies, 10–11, 25–27, 39,
  49, 57, 216, 218, 246, 250, 265
  cinematic representations, 6,
    281–296
Gender Inequality Index, 70
gender justice, 34–50
gender-just *ulama*, 36–50
gender mainstreaming, 17, 73, 74, 95,
  216
gender nonconformity, 2, 54, 58–61,
  63, 65

gender norms, 124–125, 206, 208, 211–212
gender order, 15, 18
gender, public, 54–55, 60–61, 64
  regulation of, 55–58, 62–64, 66
gender quotas, electoral system, 12–15
gender relations, 2
  households, 20–22, 49, 208, 212–213, 282, 288–289
gender wage gap, 20, 28, 111, 122, 125–126, 134–135
General Elections Commission (KPU), 73
Gerwani, 191, 202, 249, 265, 277
gig economy, 151, 153–155
Gini ratio, 107
girls, *see* child marriage
Global Gender Gap Index, 71
GoBiz, 157
Gojek, 151, 153
Go-Mart, 153
Gombo, Yanto, 256
governance
  public gender, 61–66
  public order, 59–60
  see also Suharto; Widodo, Joko (Jokowi)
gross domestic product (GDP), 93, 94–95, 114, 116, 117, 127, 152
Guidance for Family Welfare (PKK), 265
Gumay, Aditya, 286
Gus Dur (Abdurrahman Wahid), 36, 78, 79, 81

H

Habibie, B.J., 9–10, 14, 22, 78, 79, 81
Hadith, 42, 49
hair, cutting of, 57
Halim, Evelyn, 245
Hamid, Hildi, 80
Handoyo, Venerdi, 253
Harsono, FX, 245, 254
Hasanah, Ruhaeni Intan, 273
Hassan, Riffat, 44
Hasyim, KH Wahid, 36

health sector
  child stunting, 113–114
  government budget, 94, 96, 99
  health insurance, 99
  human capital development, 98–99, 113–114
  indicators, 103, 105
  women's health services, 23–24, 27–28, 99, 103, 114, 190
Hebi, Martha, 275–276
heterosexuality, 57, 66
Hijab (film), 281, 283–284, 286, 287–288, 290
hijrah movements, 2, 36–50, 272
history through visual arts, 247–249
Hizbut Tahrir Indonesia, 23, 45
hooks, bell, 274
housekeeping, *see* care work
human capital development, 93–119, 217, 218
human rights, 4, 185–204
Husaini, Adian, 44

I

ibu/ibuism (mother/motherism), 1, 10, 49, 216, 218, 265, 266, 272, 289
IDEAFEST, 269
IKAISYO (Association of Artist Wives), 252
Ikatan Wanita Pelukis Indonesia, 252
immunisation, 99
independence, 93
individualism, 267, 270
Indonesia Family Life Survey, 125
Indonesian Council of Islamic Scholars (MUI), 267
Indonesian Democratic Party of Struggle (PDI-P), 78
Indonesian Demographic and Health Survey, 124
Indonesian identity, *see* national identity
Indonesian Movement, 202
Indrawati, Sri Mulyani, 16, 78, 79
industrial employment, 19–20
infant mortality, 103–104, 105
inflation, 115, 116

Inkubator Inisiatif (IIN), 253–254
Instagram, 37, 41–50, 146, 269
Institute for the Study of Islamic
    Thought and Civilization, 44–45
insurance
    health, 99
    social, 213, 215
international labour migration, 17–19,
    24–25, 291
internet
    access, 148–149, 158–159
    arts sector, 271
    barriers for women, 157–164,
        165–166
    flexible working arrangements,
        156–157
    gig economy, 151, 153–155
    infrastructure, 147–149
    job creation, 150–151
    labour market opportunities,
        145–147, 165–166
    women users, 110, 145–146, 162–163
    see also social media
Inter-Parliamentary Union, 14
Inul (singer), 267
Iranian Revolution, 35
Irawan, Ria, 267
Iru, Salomi Rambu, 275, 276
Islam and Islamic community
    cinematic representation, 285
    in civil society, 280
    conservatism, 2, 25–27, 34–50, 268,
        288
    feminism, 263
    moderate, 34–50
    norms and morality, 54
    post-Islamist feminism, 43
    religious advocacy, 196, 198, 202,
        203
    Sexual Crime Law, 191
    wasatiyya Islam, 34
Islamic revival, 39

J

Jahja, Kartika, 268
Jakarta, public transport, 138
JKN (National Health Insurance), 99

jobseeking, 160
judges, women, 36

K

Kalla, Jusuf, 289
Kalyanamitra, 264
Kamila, Raisa, 273
KAPAL Perempuan, 214
Karim, Niniek L., 267
Kartini, 17, 28–29
Katmo, Els Tieneke Rieke, 272, 276,
    277
Katoppo, Marianne, 274
Khomeini, Ayatollah, 39
Kilwouw, Astuti N., 273
knowledge production, 274–277
Knowledge Sector Initiative
    Indonesia, 108
Koalisi Seni, 246, 254
Kodir, Faqihuddin Abdul, 36
kodrat, 1, 39, 49, 246, 257, 294
Koesasi, Victoria, 245, 255
Komnas Perempuan, *see* National
    Commission on Violence against
    Women (Komnas Perempuan)
Kredit Usaha Rakyat (People's
    Business Credit) program, 103
Kun Fayakuun (film), 285
KUPI networks, 39–42, 46
    see also Congress of Women
        Religious Scholars (KUPI)
KUSUKA social assistance program,
    214

L

labour force participation
    agriculture sector, 18, 133, 134–135
    automation, 146
    constraints for women, 110–112,
        133–138
    COVID-19 impacts, 110–111
    digital economy, 3, 145–166
    domestic workers, 4, 176–178, 179
    economic indicators, 122
    flexible working arrangements, 140,
        153, 156–157
    formal sector, 132, 134

Index   307

gender gap, 70, 95
high-end services sector, 133,
    134–135
industrial employment, 19–20
informal sector, 28, 125, 134,
    152–153, 155, 212, 213–215
international labour migration,
    17–19, 24–25, 291
internet use, 162–163
low-end services, 134–135
manufacturing sector, 122, 127, 133,
    134–135
mining sector, 19–20
part-time work, 140
public service, 17, 36, 70–84, 112
self-employed, 125, 132, 134
visual arts representations, 250
women, 3, 93, 123–126, 129–131,
    151–153, 165–166
    see also care work; gender wage gap;
    small businesses
Lady Fast festival, 255
Laki-laki Peduli (MenCare+), 286–287,
    291, 293
land ownership, 18
La Veggie, Syska, 250
laws, *see* legislation
Layan, Septina, 276–277
legislation
    Anti Trafficking Law (2007), 192
    discriminatory by-laws, 200–202
    Family Resilience Bill, 193
    Gender Equality and Equity Bill,
        288
    gender regulation, 61–64
    Law on Health, 194
    Law 1/1974 on Marriage, 5, 11,
        21–22, 186, 216, 224–225
    Law on Decentralisation (1999), 62
    Law on Human Rights (1999), 199
    Law 21/2000 on People Trafficking,
        188
    Law 26/2000 on the Human Rights
        Court, 186, 198
    Law 12/2003 on General Elections,
        12, 73
    Law 13/2003 on Manpower, 20

Law 23/2004 on the Elimination of
    Domestic Violence, 22, 190,
    192, 198, 246
Law 2/2008 on Political Parties, 73
Law 8/2008 on General Elections, 73
Law 10/2008 on General Elections,
    12
Law 11/2008 on Electronic
    Information and Transactions,
    188, 200
Law 40/2008 on the Elimination
    of Racial and Ethnic
    Discrimination, 199
Law 44/2008 on Pornography, 4, 63,
    188, 199–200, 202, 263, 267, 277
Law on the Protection of Women
    and Gender-Based Violence
    (2009), 246
Law 13/2011 on Handling the
    Destitute, 217
Law 8/2012 on General Elections, 73
Law on Child Protection (2014), 195
Law on Advancement of Culture
    (2017), 258
Law 12/2022 on Sexual Crime, 22,
    185–204, 225, 276, 277
Law 23/2004 on the Elimination of
    Domestic Violence, 4
Mother and Child Welfare Bill, 193
omnibus law (Cipta Kerja), 28, 119
Presidential Decree 88/2021 on
    a National Strategy for the
    Elderly, 215
Presidential Instruction 9/2000 on
    Gender Mainstreaming in
    National Development, 73, 95
Presidential Instruction on
    Disadvantaged Villages
    (1993), 102
regional currency, 23
regulating sexual violence, 197
    see also Criminal Code; Penal Code
    1946
Leksono, Karlina, 266
lesbian, gay, bisexual, transgender,
    queer and intersex (LGBTQI)
    communities, 2, 25, 53, 54, 65–66,
    248, 255–256

308 *Gender Equality and Diversity in Indonesia*

liberal feminism, 263, 266–270, 274
life expectancy, 103, 105
literary awards, 270
Lorde, Audre, 274
ludruk theatre troupes, 57
Lutfi, Muhammad, 80

M

macroeconomic policies, 114–117, 118
magazines, lifestyle, 284–285, 291, 294
Magdalene.co, 269
Maharani, Puan, 75, 78
Malay, Rully, 272
male/masculinity, concept of, 1, 10–11, 56
  cinematic representation, 280–296
manufacturing sector, 122, 127, 133, 134–135
Marcoes, Lies, 47
Mardiasih, Kalis, 269
Mardzoeki, Faiza, 265
marriage
  eligibility for social assistance, 209
  forced marriage, 186, 195
  minimum age, 21, 22, 25–26, 122, 141, 224–225
  regulation of, 20–22
  trending younger, 123, 135–137, 140–141
  see also child marriage
marriage certificates, 209, 236, 238
marriage law, *see under* legislation
Marsudi, Retno, 16
Maryana, Lena Mukti, 80
Massive Agriculture Credit Program (BIMAS/INMAS), 102
maternal mortality, 24, 28, 99, 114
maternity leave, 20
Mecca, Zaskia A., 287–288
men
  arts sector, 246, 270
  child marriage, 223, 227
  cinematic representation, 280–296
  domestic work, 164, 284, 290–291
  flexible working arrangements, 157
  household heads, 21–22, 27
  international labour migration, 18

progressive thinkers, 35–36
social assistance programs, 208, 209
stay-at-home fathers, 293–294
'traditional roles', 1, 10–11, 211, 280, 281–282, 285, 294–295
MenCare+, 286–287, 291, 293
Mengejar Matahari (film), 285
menstrual leave, 20
Merdeka Belajar program, 100
Mernissi, Fatima, 44, 47, 48
micro businesses, *see* MSMEs (micro, small and medium enterprises)
middle classes, 39, 63, 93, 127, 281–282, 290–295
migrant workers, 17–19, 24–25, 291
minimum wages, 126
mining sector, 19–20
ministerial appointments, 2–3, 16–17, 70, 73–74, 77–79, 83–84, 263–264
Ministry of Culture and Education, 258
Ministry of Women's Empowerment, 9
mobile broadband, 147–149
mobile phone ownership, 158–159, 160
Moelyono, 251
Mohanty, Chandra Talpade, 274
MokaPOS, 157
molestation, 195
morality, regulation of, 60–61
Mothahari, Mortaza, 35
movies and gender politics, 6, 280–296
MSMEs (micro, small and medium enterprises), 102, 110, 111, 146, 156–157, 162–163, 213
Mubadalah.id, 269
Muhammad, Hussein, 36
Muhammadiyah, 26, 37, 268
Mukmin, Patriot, 245
Mulia, Musdah, 47, 48, 268
Munir, Lily Zakiyah, 268
Murniasih, IGAK, 257
music and activism, 268, 276

N

Nahdlatul Ulama, 26, 37, 268
National Awakening Party (PKB), 78
National Civil Service Agency (BKN), 17
National Commission on Violence against Women (Komnas Perempuan), 4, 10, 22, 185, 190, 192, 264, 266, 292
National Democratic Party (NasDem), 78
National Economic Recovery Program (PEN), 115
National Family Planning Coordination Board (BKKBN), 23, 98
National Health Insurance (JKN), 99
national identity
    boundaries, 2, 54, 57, 66
    Islamic interpretation, 26, 54, 202, 203
    public gender focus, 55, 57, 63
    sex binary model, 56
    sexual minorities, 53
nationalists, 196, 198, 203
National Labour Force Survey (Sakernas), 123, 126
National Medium Term Development Plan 1999–2004, 73
National Medium Term Development Plan 2020–2024, 73, 95, 170, 178, 222
National Social Security System, 102
National Socioeconomic Survey (Susenas), 124, 126
National Strategy on the Prevention of Child Marriage, 22
neoliberal feminism, 269, 270, 277
New Men's Alliance (ALB), 253, 291, 293
New Order
    ambassadors, 74, 80
    anti-communism, 191, 202, 249
    arts sector, 247
    cinema, 285
    collapse of, 9, 22, 202, 280
    economic growth, 122, 127

family ideology, 11, 25, 27, 57, 66
feminism, 264–266
gender ideology, 1, 10–11, 25, 39, 49, 57, 63, 246, 265, 294
warias, recognition of, 54, 58–61, 66
see also Suharto
Noer, Arifin C., 285
Noer, Gina S., 281, 284, 288–289
Noer, Jajang C., 267
Novaris, Guntur, 285
Noviana, Wilasih, 266
Nuansa Indonesia, 252
nuclear family, 57, 66
Nugros, Fajar, 281, 287
Nurbaya, Siti, 79
nusantara, 274

O

older population, 28, 214–215
oligarchic politics, 75
omnibus law (Cipta Kerja), 28, 119
Onduko, Ruth, 252
online merchants, 155

P

Pahlavi, Muhammad Reza Shah, 35
Pangestu, Mari Elka, 78
Papua, conflict in, 256
Parawansa, Khofifah Indar, 26, 73, 79
parliamentary elections, 12–14, 75
    see also political representation
patriarchy, 39–40, 42, 49, 254, 270–271, 280
Penal Code 1946, 186, 189, 191, 194–196, 201
Penal Code 2023, 201
Pengkhianatan G-30S/PKI (film), 285
Perempuan Berkalung Sorban (film), 287
Perempuan Pengkaji Seni, 245, 250, 254–255
Peretas (Women across Borders), 253–254, 271, 272
performance art, 245, 255
Perkawanan Perempuan Menulis (Women Writers Collective), 271, 273
PISA scores, 108–109

310 *Gender Equality and Diversity in Indonesia*

PKH (Family Hope Program), 102, 205, 209–213, 215, 216, 218
pluralism movement, 273
policies/policymaking
  human rights, 203–204
  social assistance programs, 205–218
political representation, 2–3, 12–17, 27, 70–84, 112
polygamy, 199, 267
polygyny, 21–22, 25–26
population ageing, 28, 214–215
population growth rates, 99
post-Islamist feminism, 43
posyandu, 99
poverty
  child marriage, 234
  COVID-19, 292
  elderly population, 214
  social assistance programs, 102, 107, 207–213, 217
power, gendered, 10–11, 25
pregnancy, teenage, 231–235, 237
Productive Assistance (Bantuan Produktif), 213
Prosperous Justice Party (PKS), 22, 41, 43, 202
Puan Seni (Association of Women Art Workers), 271
public morality, 60–61
public order, 54, 59–64
public service representation, 17, 36, 70–84, 112
public transport, 138–139
Pudjiastuti, Susi, 16–17, 269
puskesmas, 99

Q

quotas, electoral system, 12–15, 27, 73
Qur'an, 42, 48, 49, 199

R

Rachman, Affandi Abdul, 287
Rahima (NGO), 40, 41–42, 44, 268
Rahmana, Asa, 251
Rahman, Fazlur, 35, 44
Ramadhanita, Shalihah, 250
rape, 186, 194–196, 198

Raskin (Rice for the Poor), 207, 208, 218
Ratu, Kahi Ata, 275
reformasi
  ambassadors, 80
  arts sector, 247
  economic growth, 127
  establishment, 198
  gender equality legislation, 185–204
  gender politics, 25
  gender regulation, 62–64, 66
  liberal feminism, 266–270
  ministerial appointments, 77
  religious conservatism, 36
  warias, repression of, 54, 62–63, 64, 65–66
Regional Representative Council (DPD), 13
R.F., Maria Margareth, 273
Rice for the Poor (Raskin), 207, 208, 218
ride-hailing industry, 151, 153, 156
Rifka Annisa (NGO), 268
Rizqiana, Atinna, 250
Roosvita, Karina, 253
Rotary (performance art), 245, 250
RUAS (Women's History and Archive Collective), 254
Rumkabu, Elvira, 272
rural areas
  child marriage, 223
  education, 128, 130
  employment, 18, 130–131, 134
  internet infrastructure, 147–149
  national indicators, 24

S

Sadikin, Ali, 58–59
Sadli, Saparinah, 264–265, 277
Safitri, Nabila Warda, 250
Salafi movement, 38, 45
Sardi, Lukman, 286–287, 293
Sasmita, Citra, 248, 252
sastrawangi ('fragrant literature'), 199, 263, 268
Sastrawan, Savitri, 252
School Mover Program, 108

Schools Operational Assistance (BOS), 100, 108
science and art, 251
Seeto, Aaron, 245
Sekolah Pemikiran Perempuan (School of Women's Thought), 264, 271, 272–273, 274–276
Selly, 157
Sembilan Naga (film), 285
Sesal (film), 285
sexuality
  criminalisation, 194
  plurality, 55–56
sexual minorities, *see* lesbian, gay, bisexual, transgender, queer and intersex (LGBTQI) communities
sexual relations outside marriage, 196, 201
sexual violence, 186–204, 256, 265, 271, 276
  victims' services, 189–190, 192, 193
sex workers, 60
Shabestari, Mohammad Mojtahed, 35
Shahrour, Muhammad, 35
shamen, 55–56
sharia law, 23, 25, 199
Shari'ati, Ali, 35
Siahaan, Semsar, 251
Siauw, Felix, 45
Situmorang, Lashita, 253
small businesses, 102, 110, 111, 146, 156–157, 162–163, 213
  see also labour force participation
Smart Indonesia Program (PIP), 100
Smith, Linda Tuhiwai, 274, 276, 277
social assistance, 4–5, 96, 102–103, 107, 205–218
social insurance, 213, 215
social media, 146, 161, 162–163, 236, 263, 268–269, 271
  gender activism, 36–37, 41–50
  see also internet
social protection, *see* social assistance
social reproduction, 21–22
Soedjarwo, Rudi, 285
Soemarno, Rini, 78
Solikhah, Amanatia Junda, 273

Sopariyanti, Pera, 41
Sophiaan, Sophan, 285
Soroush, Abdulkarim, 35
Sridiniari, Putu, 252
start-up companies, 150–151
'state ibuism', *see ibu*/ibuism (mother/motherism)
stunting, children, 113–114
Suara Ibu Peduli (The Voice of Concerned Mothers), 9, 266
Subianto, Prabowo, 27
Suharto
  ambassadors, 74, 80
  education policy, 17
  gender ideology, 39, 265
  protests against, 266
  public order, 60
  regime end, 9, 22, 202
  women politicians, 12
  see also New Order
Sukarnoputri, Megawati, 16, 71, 73, 78, 79, 81
Sung, Yaya, 249
Suryodarmo, Melati, 257
Sustainable Development Goals, 28, 172, 222
Swastika, Alia, 256
Syansuri, KH Bisri, 36

T

Tablighi Jama'at, 45
Tamarra, 248, 256
Tandio, Tom, 245
Tanzimat, 35
Tarbiyah, 41
Taring Padi collective, 251
tawhīd (the Oneness of God), 46–48
tax ratio, 217
teacher certification, 108
technology and art, 251
Telkomsel, 147–148
Tibet, art projects, 251–252
Tokopedia, 150–151
traffic jams, 133–134
transgender community, 2, 25, 53–67, 248
transport infrastructure, 138–139

312 *Gender Equality and Diversity in Indonesia*

transpuan community, 53
  see also waria community
Trimurti, S.K., 20
Turkey, gender justice, 35

U

Uber drivers, 153, 156
Udeido art collective, 256
Ultra Micro Credit, 102
Umar, Nasaruddin, 36
Unified Database for Social Protection
  Program, 102
United Nations, 12
United Nations Convention on the
  Rights of the Child, 222
United Nations Sustainable
  Development Goals, 28, 172, 222
unpaid care work, *see* care work
urban areas
  child marriage, 223–224
  education, 128–129
  employment, 18, 129–131, 134
  gig economy, 154
  internet infrastructure, 147–149
  transport infrastructure, 138–139
Utami, Ayu, 266, 267, 268

V

Vagina Monologues (play), 267
veil, wearing of, 200–202
Village Funds Direct Cash Assistance
  program (BLT Dana Desa), 214
Village Potential Survey (Podes), 124
Vision of Indonesia Maju 2045, 93
visual arts, 5, 245–258
Voices of Concerned Mothers Milk
  Demonstration, 9

W

wadam, 53, 59
  see also waria community
Wadud, Amina, 44, 47, 48
wage gap, 20, 28, 111, 122, 125–126,
  134–135
Wahid, Abdurrahman (Gus Dur), 36,
  78, 79, 81

Wahono, Wiyu, 245
Wanimbo, Rode, 272, 273
waria community, 53–67
wasatiyya Islam, 34
Western values, influence of, 37–39,
  42–43, 45, 202
WhatsApp, 146, 157, 163, 271
  see also internet; social media
White Ribbon, 290
Widodo, Joko (Jokowi)
  ambassadors, 80, 81, 84
  child marriage reform, 222
  digital/creative economy, 5, 269
  gender activist supporters, 27
  poverty alleviation, 102
  women ministers, 16–17, 77, 78, 79,
    84, 263–264
Wikimedia Indonesia, 253
women
  ambassadors, 2–3, 70, 74, 80–83, 84
  bodily autonomy, 268
  cabinet ministers, 70, 73–74, 77–79,
    83–84
  COVID-19 impacts, 110–111, 114,
    119, 156, 174–175
  decentralisation and repression, 55
  digital economy, 3, 153–166
  domestic worker profession, 4,
    176–178, 179
  dynastic politicians, 75, 77
  education, 28, 101, 104, 108, 151, 169
  elderly women, 28, 214–215
  executive government, 16–17,
    263–264
  family development sessions, 211,
    212
  fisherwomen, 214
  health services, 23–24, 27–28, 99,
    103, 114, 190
  human rights, 4, 185–204
  income contribution, 170
  international labour migration,
    17–19, 24–25
  internet use, 110, 145–146
  land ownership, 18
  leadership, 24
  mining sector, 19–20

political representation, 2–3, 12–17, 27, 70–84, 112
public service representation, 17, 36, 112
regulatory restrictions, 20–22, 61, 62, 66
social assistance, 4–5, 102–103, 205–218
'traditional roles', 1, 10–11, 46, 49, 111–112, 125, 133, 157, 169, 210–212, 216, 246, 250, 265, 281–282, 285, 286, 294, *see also* care work
unpaid care work, *see* care work
see also arts sector; labour force participation; small businesses
Women's March, 269, 277
Women's Studies Department, University of Indonesia, 265
women writers, 263, 266, 268, 273, 275–276
workforce participation, *see* labour force participation
World Values Survey, 124–125
writers festivals, 273
Wulia, Tintin, 257
W, You Winda Dona, 250

X

XXLab, 250–251

Y

Yayasan Jurnal Perempuan (Women's Journal), 266
Yogya Biennale, 255–256
Yok, Oei Sian, 247
YouTube, 44, 157, 271
see also internet; social media
Yudhoyono, Susilo Bambang, 16, 78, 79, 80, 81

Z

zakat, 217
Zarkasyi, Hamid Fahmy, 44, 45
Zayd, Nasr Hamid Abu, 35

INDONESIA UPDATE SERIES

1989
Indonesia Assessment 1988 (Regional Development)
Edited by Hal Hill and Jamie Mackie

1990
Indonesia Assessment 1990 (Ownership)
Edited by Hal Hill and Terry Hull

1991
Indonesia Assessment 1991 (Education)
Edited by Hal Hill

1992
Indonesia Assessment 1992: Political Perspectives on the 1990s
Edited by Harold A. Crouch and Hal Hill

1993
Indonesia Assessment 1993: Labour: Sharing in the Benefits of Growth?
Edited by Chris Manning and Joan Hardjono

1994
Indonesia Assessment 1994: Finance as a Key Sector in Indonesia's Development
Edited by Ross McLeod

1996
Indonesia Assessment 1995: Development in Eastern Indonesia
Edited by Colin Barlow and Joan Hardjono

1997
Indonesia Assessment: Population and Human Resources
Edited by Gavin W. Jones and Terence H. Hull

1998
Indonesia's Technological Challenge
Edited by Hal Hill and Thee Kian Wie

1999
Post-Soeharto Indonesia: Renewal or Chaos?
Edited by Geoff Forrester

2000
Indonesia in Transition: Social Aspects of Reformasi and Crisis
Edited by Chris Manning and Peter van Diermen

2001
Indonesia Today: Challenges of History
Edited by Grayson J. Lloyd and Shannon L. Smith

2002
Women in Indonesia: Gender, Equity and Development
Edited by Kathryn Robinson and Sharon Bessell

2003
Local Power and Politics in Indonesia: Decentralisation and Democratisation
Edited by Edward Aspinall and Greg Fealy

2004
Business in Indonesia: New Challenges, Old Problems
Edited by M. Chatib Basri and Pierre van der Eng

2005
The Politics and Economics of Indonesia's Natural Resources
Edited by Budy P. Resosudarmo

2006
Different Societies, Shared Futures: Australia, Indonesia and the Region
Edited by John Monfries

2007
Indonesia: Democracy and the Promise of Good Governance
Edited by Ross H. McLeod and Andrew MacIntyre

2008
Expressing Islam: Religious Life and Politics in Indonesia
Edited by Greg Fealy and Sally White

2009
Indonesia beyond the Water's Edge: Managing an Archipelagic State
Edited by Robert Cribb and Michele Ford

2010
Problems of Democratisation in Indonesia: Elections, Institutions and Society
Edited by Edward Aspinall and Marcus Mietzner

2011
Employment, Living Standards and Poverty in Contemporary Indonesia
Edited by Chris Manning and Sudarno Sumarto

2012
Indonesia Rising: The Repositioning of Asia's Third Giant
Edited by Anthony Reid

2013
Education in Indonesia
Edited by Daniel Suryadarma and Gavin W. Jones

2014
Regional Dynamics in a Decentralized Indonesia
Edited by Hal Hill

2015
The Yudhoyono Presidency: Indonesia's Decade of Stability and Stagnation
Edited by Edward Aspinall, Marcus Mietzner and Dirk Tomsa

2016
Land and Development in Indonesia: Searching for the People's Sovereignty
Edited by John F. McCarthy and Kathryn Robinson

2017
Digital Indonesia: Connectivity and Divergence
Edited by Edwin Jurriëns and Ross Tapsell

2018
Indonesia in the New World: Globalisation, Nationalism and Sovereignty
Edited by Arianto A. Patunru, Mari Pangestu and M. Chatib Basri

2019
Contentious Belonging: The Place of Minorities in Indonesia
Edited by Greg Fealy and Ronit Ricci

2020
Democracy in Indonesia: From Stagnation to Regression?
Edited by Thomas Power and Eve Warburton

2022
In Sickness and in Health: Diagnosing Indonesia
Edited by Firman Witoelar and Ariane Utomo

2023
Gender Equality and Diversity in Indonesia: Identifying Progress and Challenges
Edited by Angie Bexley, Sarah Xue Dong and Diahhadi Setyonaluri